The Political Dilemma
of Popular Education

An African Case

David B. Abernethy

D0930982

Stanford University Press, Stanford, California   1969

Stanford University Press
Stanford, California
© 1969 by the Board of Trustees of the
Leland Stanford Junior University
Printed in the United States of America
L.C. 69-13175
SBN 8047-0703-0

Foreword

David Abernethy's *Political Dilemma of Popular Education: An African Case* is the first full-length case study of the relationship between education and political development in a new nation. The belief that education is instrumental in creating the conditions for progress goes back to the Enlightenment and still has a powerful influence on policy making today. Leaders of the new nations have accordingly made enormous investments in education, only to find that the results are problematic or even counter-productive.

A well-executed case study, particularly in a new research area, can be of great value to scholars and policy makers. Although the problems of educational and political development faced by the new nations vary widely, Professor Abernethy's study of Southern Nigeria generates a rich set of hypotheses that may well apply to many areas of the world.

Using a conception of political development as involving greater overall capacity and productivity, greater equality, and greater socio-political integration, Professor Abernethy concludes that the rapid expansion of free primary education in Southern Nigeria during the 1950's had negative consequences for the political modernization of the country. At least in the short run, Southern Nigeria's educational policies lowered the government's capacity to achieve its goals, introduced new inequalities, and provided a basis for new social and political cleavages. In a thoughtful final chapter Professor Abernethy offers some strategies for relating educational development more closely to the needs of modernizing nations.

This book is the first in a new series, Stanford Studies in Comparative Politics, prepared under the auspices of the Comparative Politics Program of the Institute of Political Studies and published by the Stanford University Press. The members of the Editorial Board for the series are Professors Richard Fagen, John Lewis, Nobutaka Ike,

Wilbur Schramm, and Gabriel A. Almond. The series, which will include studies by the faculty and research associates of the Institute, is broadly conceived to contribute to our understanding of the problems and processes of political development. The financial support for the Comparative Politics Program comes in substantial part from the Center for Research in International Studies of Stanford University.

Gabriel A. Almond

Preface

Anyone fortunate enough to conduct research abroad has a unique opportunity to meet people with widely differing backgrounds and insights. This study has been enriched by the contributions of a diverse group of civil servants, politicians, professional educators, social scientists, and students, as well as others—met quite by chance—who through casual conversation provided me with interesting "leads." I cannot list here all who have cooperated in this research venture, but I would like to acknowledge the special assistance of Mr. Oguike Achonu, Hon. I. U. Akpabio, Mr. S. O. Awokoya, Dr. K. Onwuka Dike, Dr. Carl Eicher, Mr. E. O. Enemo, Mr. R. W. Ennis, Mr. E. E. Esua, Dr. A. Babs Fafunwa, Mr. Kola Folayan, Mr. Colin Humphrey, Mr. Alvan Ikoku, Mr. J. C. Menakaya, Father James O'Connell, Chief J. A. O. Obediyi, Chief J. F. Odunjo, Mr. Oke Osanyintolu, Dr. Richard Sklar, Dr. Dennis Storer, Mr. Robert Vassar, Dr. J. B. Webster, Dr. Babatunde Williams, Dr. Grace Awani-alele Williams, and Dr. Howard Wolpe. Grateful acknowledgment is also due the Foreign Area Fellowship Program, which supported fifteen months of research in Nigeria during 1963 and 1964; the Nigerian Institute of Social and Economic Research, which provided me with research facilities while in Ibadan; the Economic Development Institute of the University of Nigeria, Enugu Branch, which facilitated my work in the Eastern Region; the Center for Studies in Education and Development, Harvard University, and the Institute of Political Studies, Stanford University, for intellectual stimulation and invaluable secretarial assistance. Mr. Frederick Cooper did a careful and thorough job in compiling the Bibliography and checking the accuracy of citations; Mrs. Margaret Singleton gave greatly appreciated advice on the Index.

I am particularly indebted to two men who, through their personal qualities as well as their professional concerns, have greatly reinforced my own interest in African affairs. Professor Rupert Emerson's encouragement and wise counsel have benefited a host of Harvard students, and I am fortunate to be included in that roster. Dr. James Robinson, founder of Operation Crossroads-Africa, has enabled hundreds of young Americans and Canadians to test their expectations against the realities of Africa. Two Crossroads experiences, in 1958 and 1960, convinced me that it would be both fascinating and useful to study the realities.

This book is affectionately dedicated to my wife, Julie, who made the stay in Nigeria a family experience and who put in uncounted hours collating material and suggesting revisions. That she could tolerate the attention lavished for so long on her rival—this book—is a tribute to her good humor, forbearance, and fortitude.

D.B.A.

Contents

The Political Dilemma
of Popular Education

Introduction: Education, Politics, and Modernization

At first a faint stirring, the drive for modernity has now become the passionate preoccupation of societies variously described as "backward," "underdeveloped," or "emerging." The belief has spread that poverty and weakness are not tolerable facts of life but intolerable liabilities, and that through conscious effort man can realize more fully than ever before his own potentialities and those of his environment. Modernity cannot be precisely defined; it may mean different things for those who aspire to it, and it need not be incompatible with traditional practices and values. Nevertheless, certain characteristics of modernity are widely accepted in the academic literature on the subject, as well as in the writings of political leaders from the underdeveloped countries themselves. A modern economy is commonly thought to have a high and continuously rising standard of living, a largely urban-based population, and a significant industrial sector. A modern society is characterized by a high degree of vertical and horizontal mobility, mass literacy, recruitment to office on the basis of individual achievement, and the emergence of specialized and interdependent occupational roles. The modern polity is usually conceived of as an independent nation-state composed of citizens who are equal before the law and at least nominally able to participate in the selection of a ruling elite; government is relatively centralized, accepts some responsibility for the welfare of its citizens, and efficiently deploys its human and material resources in the solution of pressing policy problems. Modern man is oriented toward the future, regards change as the norm rather than the exception, is self-conscious about his own thinking processes, and places a premium on "scientific" modes of explanation.[1]

Merely to list these traits is to comprehend the enormous and complex task facing societies now starting along the road to modernity. The political leaders of these societies are fully aware of the magnitude of the task, but most of them are equally aware that the failure of their efforts to modernize virtually guarantees national humiliation, economic stagnation, and unrest among an increasingly frustrated populace. The problem for these leaders is thus not whether to modernize but how to do so, and how to devise a strategy for using their admittedly limited resources in the most productive way. How should an underdeveloped country establish its priorities? Should certain kinds of expenditure be considered indispensable for progress? Granting that traditional societies are beset by a series of often self-reinforcing obstacles to modernization, how can these obstacles be bypassed or overcome?

Clearly, no single strategy can provide the answer to these questions; but the view that education is "the key that unlocks the door to modernization"[2] has been espoused perhaps more fervently and dogmatically in the new states of Africa and Asia than anywhere else. Virtually all countries that have recently emerged from European colonial rule have with striking unanimity assigned a high, if not the highest, priority to the expansion of education. In 1958, in words that could well have been used by many other nationalist leaders, Tunisia's Habib Bourguiba stated: "When we were in the opposition, and Tunisia belonged to others, not to us, we planned and resolved that when our country was independent and the state apparatus in our hands we must treat first the problem of education."[3] After attaining self-government most Afro-Asian countries raised substantially the proportion of their budgets devoted to education, often to as much as 20 per cent, whereas in the colonial era educational expenditure commonly totaled less than 10 per cent of the budget. With increased resources at their disposal the new states quickly launched ambitious programs to expand school enrollments at all levels.[4] An extraordinary faith in education is affirmed in the report of a conference of thirty-nine African states held at Addis Ababa in 1961. The conferees proclaimed that "education is Africa's most urgent and vital need at present" and called for universal, compulsory, free primary education throughout the continent by 1980, as well as for rapid expansion at the secondary level.[5]

The leaders of new states are not alone in perceiving education as the key to the modernization of their countries. In the Western academic community educationists have sounded the theme for years, and economists increasingly regard educational expenditure as a productive investment rather than as a consumption item that only developed societies can afford.[6] The growing literature on manpower planning is based on the premise that shortages of high- and middle-level manpower constitute the major obstacle to growth in most underdeveloped countries and that an increase of school enrollments at the appropriate levels is the best way to alleviate this problem.[7] The foreign aid policies of donor nations have been affected by such considerations; in the United States, for example, attention has shifted over the years from the formation of physical capital in the new states to the improvement of their existing human resources.[8]

That an "education explosion" is necessary for the modernization of new states is a belief now accepted so uncritically that it may be useful to recount briefly the arguments supporting such a position. There is, to begin with, the view that indices of educational progress are in themselves part of the definition of modernity, quite apart from the multiple effects of knowledge on society. If access to education is seen as a fundamental right of man, as it is in the United Nations Declaration of Human Rights, then percentages of literacy or school enrollment would indicate the extent to which a government satisfies a basic obligation to its citizens. If education is regarded as an aspect of human welfare, though not necessarily a right, the view that modernity requires the provision of welfare still would obligate modernizing regimes to extend educational opportunities to the masses. In the view of one social scientist, "Literacy is indeed the basic personal skill that underlies the whole modernizing sequence."[9] A prime task of a formal educational system is to impart literacy, which broadens a person's mental horizons, increasing his capacity and willingness to change the environment. A formal educational system should provide skills as well as a broadened perspective; with the expansion of schooling, recruitment to various positions in society can be based increasingly on these qualifications rather than, as in many traditional societies, on the prestige or influence of one's kin.

EDUCATION AND ECONOMIC DEVELOPMENT

Other arguments concern the consequences of educational expansion for economic development. The obvious and ever-increasing gap in living standards between the Afro-Asian states and the more developed nations such as the United States, the Soviet Union, Great

Britain, France, and Germany helps explain the obsession of Afro-Asian leaders with rapid, self-sustained economic growth. Indeed, for most people in the underdeveloped world, modernity means the acquisition of greater wealth, new material goods, and such amenities as electricity and pipe-borne water. Education, it can be argued, contributes to economic development in several ways. Training in schools, universities, literacy centers, in-service programs, and the like imparts new skills that are lacking in an underdeveloped country or obtainable only at high cost through the use of foreign personnel. Moreover, the progress of the industrial sector depends largely on complex, highly specialized techniques of production imported from more advanced economies. The labor force cannot as in the early days of the Industrial Revolution gradually acquire new skills as new techniques themselves evolve; the African or Asian worker fresh from traditional village life now must learn rapidly to operate the latest lathe or turbine. Formal instruction in trade schools, or informal education through in-service programs, can perform a very important role in transmitting the necessary expertise quickly and efficiently.

A person's economic motivations will also presumably be affected by experiences in school: his will to achieve and to innovate may be stimulated by his studies,[10] and his aspirations will grow, if only because the educated man is aware of a whole new range of goods and services he would like to enjoy. An economy may be impelled by the wants of its educated citizens to increase total output.

Recent cross-national studies have produced data that appear to justify the high investment of the new states in education. The percentage of national income devoted to education is highly correlated with per capita income, and a minimal level of literacy apparently spurs initial growth.[11] Among countries at approximately the same level of economic or technological development, those with higher-than-average stocks of educated manpower (defined in terms of secondary enrollment during a previous generation) tend to grow faster than those that are below average.[12] Such correlations between educational indices and levels and rates of growth might easily be taken to mean that educational expansion causes such growth to occur.

EDUCATION AND POLITICAL DEVELOPMENT

Modernizing is not simply a matter of restructuring an economy: political changes are also involved. But what changes, and how should they be analyzed? Considerable academic attention has been devoted in recent years to the concept of political development, with results that are not very satisfactory. A major problem has been definitional: there is no consensus on the components of political development, even among scholars who share a Western, non-Marxist outlook.[13] An additional problem has been how to give operational meaning to terms so abstract that one hesitates to defile them by applying them to concrete situations. Political scientists who do wish to make their terms operational are hindered by the absence of a widely acceptable unit, such as money in economics, in terms of which political change may be measured. Granting all these difficulties, "political development" is used here as a convenient short-hand for describing several important kinds of change: we will view a modern or developed political system as one with a high degree of capacity, a stress on equality, and a high degree of integration.[14] This study does not propose a formula linking capacity, equality, and integration to each other. Quite apart from the improbable arithmetic of "adding up" three such qualitatively different variables, the three may in some ways conflict with each other; an excessive emphasis on equality, for example, may reduce the capacity of a political system by dispersing the scarce resources at the disposal of the government. The study's more modest task is rather to give operational meaning to capacity, equality, and integration and to show the complex links between the expansion of education and these three components of political development.

The capacity of a political system is, quite simply, the ability of a government to achieve its major goals. In the new states the goals of governments are quite ambitious and involve regulating the behavior of more people—and regulating more of the behavior of each person—than ever before. Whether a government can realize its objectives depends on the means it has for communicating with the people, the caliber of its political leaders and civil servants, the efficiency of major institutions, and the adaptability of these institutions to new problems.

Education plays a crucial role in meeting these preconditions for high capacity. The spread of mass literacy facilitates the penetration of society by government, since officials and party leaders can communicate with the populace through the written word. An expanding bureaucracy depends on the educational system to produce appropriately qualified personnel—from clerks to civil engineers, from agricultural extension agents to generalists with a knack for organizing people and making the most effective use of existing resources.

Insofar as a good education gives a politician or an administrator confidence in his own abilities, his contribution to the performance of the total political system is enhanced.[15] As in the economic sphere, schools are relevant here not simply because they impart needed skills but also because they encourage a certain frame of mind—a rational linking of means to ends, for instance, or the capacity to foresee and adapt to new problems. The establishment of new schools, training programs, and universities is also part of a wider process of institution building that must occur if capacity is to be maintained over time.[16] Experience gained, for instance, in operating a new technical school, perhaps in collaboration with foreign advisers, is bound to be useful for the indigenous administrator when he is called upon to create or strengthen other institutions.

Equality is a value to which modern man pays more than lip service, even though the very complexity of his society makes inevitable certain inequalities of power, income, and prestige. The belief in equality is expressed in many ways, among them the effort to level incomes through progressive taxation, the extension of the franchise to all adult members of a society, the notion that all citizens are entitled to a minimum of welfare, and the norm of equal protection for citizens under the law.[17] In a society stressing equality, education becomes one of the "welfare" items that all people should receive. Moreover, it becomes not simply an end in itself but a means to other equality-related ends. The larger the enrollment, the more diffused, for example, is the opportunity schooling affords for upward mobility and the more likely it is that citizens, aware of their rights and obligations, will be able to participate effectively in the political process.[18] Finally, since enrollment figures are widely used as an index of modernity, increased enrollments may be seen by underdeveloped countries as evidence that they are approaching parity with more developed nations in at least one respect.

The third characteristic of a politically developed system is a high degree of integration. An integrated polity is one that holds together, having reduced to a manageable level the differences separating groups of people from each other and the tensions that threaten to break the society apart. Underdeveloped countries tend to be poorly integrated in two respects. There is often a "vertical" gap between the small, usually Western-educated leadership and the mass of the population,[19] and there may be a number of "horizontal" gaps between groups defined in ethnic, racial, religious, or linguistic terms. Efforts at political integration must bridge the vertical gap by linking rulers and ruled in a common network of communications, so that ideas and demands can flow both "upward" and "downward" in a form comprehensible to all parties concerned. The task of closing the horizontal gaps seems especially urgent in the new states, where a sense of nationhood is not deeply engrained and where competing groups, in many instances territorially based, can view insurrection or outright secession as realistic options.[20] Leaders of these states are acutely aware of the need to create new national identities and to encourage trust and cooperation among representatives of different groups.

The expansion of education relates directly to integrative efforts on both the vertical and horizontal planes. In the colonial setting formal Western education had a vertically disintegrative effect on traditional society by producing a Western-oriented indigenous elite whose outlook was quite different from that of the masses.[21] But the best way to bridge the elite-mass gap, once it has been created, is to extend schooling to the many rather than restrict it, as in earlier years, to the few. Increased enrollments, moreover, require a larger teaching force. The primary or secondary school teacher can play an important mediating role between the elite and the people, transmitting new ideas downward and at the same time articulating local interests to a country's rulers. Interest groups formed in the course of modernization can also act as vertical integrators, because they involve their members in the country's political life and place limits on the ruling elite's freedom to act without reference to public opinion. In Africa education has contributed to the formation of many interest groups, among them the various Christian denominations, teachers' unions, and even tribal or ethnic associations.[22]

Nation builders in the new states base much of their faith in education on the belief that it will be a horizontal integrator, reducing tensions among different ethnic, racial, linguistic, or religious groups.[23] To the extent that their own education has given them a national outlook, political leaders naturally expect similar consequences to follow among the masses if schooling is provided for all. The school is one of the few institutions available to these leaders for changing popular attitudes, and it deals explicitly with young people, who are presumably more flexible in outlook than their elders and from whose ranks future national leadership will emerge. In multilingual countries a common language taught through the schools can perform an essential integrative function.[24] Whether by conscious design or not, schools can improve communication among persons of many different backgrounds by bringing them together and giving them a common set of experiences.[25] State-sponsored universal primary education can partly compensate for previous inequalities in group access to education—a politically explosive issue because these inequalities are reflected in recruitment to top civil service and private sector positions.

Apart from its role in strengthening capacity, equality, and integration, education serves a wider function, particularly in new states. Just as education can do much to remove an individual inferiority complex, so its widespread dissemination can help remove the persistent suspicion of collective inferiority, a legacy of colonialism that plagues the new states and renders the attainment of self-confident nationhood so difficult. The Nuffield Foundation study of African education describes this function well:

> The germ from which all national development grows is a deep desire among the people to be other than they are. In no way is this desire more clearly put in evidence than by the efforts a people is prepared to make to train its children to fulfill the life it desires for itself as a nation. Thus, education is inseparably linked with the deepest problems of national destiny.[26]

A number of arguments can therefore be advanced to show that the expansion of education in the new states contributes to the modernization of their economies and to political development. All of these arguments are plausible; some are even backed by empirical evidence. Is there any reason, then, to doubt that the "educational explosion" currently taking place in underdeveloped countries foretells their successful transition to modernity?

EDUCATION AND THE FAILURE TO MODERNIZE

Initial doubts must surely be caused by the failure of a number of new states, despite impressive educational achievements, to attain rapid, self-sustained economic growth or to develop politically in any sense of that term. The optimistic descriptions in the early 1960's of "developing" or "emerging" Afro-Asian states have been somewhat counterbalanced by recent writings on "political decay" and "breakdowns of modernization."[27] It is too early, of course, to tell whether the conventional signs of breakdown—a decline in gross national product, a coup, revolution, or civil war—measure anything more than passing phenomena; indeed there is no reason why a modernizing country cannot, to reverse Lenin, move one step backward and two steps forward. Still, what is meant as a caveat to pessimists should apply equally to optimists; the available evidence from such countries as Burma, Indonesia, Ceylon, the Sudan, and Nigeria hardly suggests a simple, unilinear transition to modernity. Since the performance of the new states is mixed in the short run, and impossible to predict accurately in the long run, the observer must be cautious in imputing to any one variable—in this case education—all the positive benefits of which it is theoretically capable. Education may perform a particular function, but then again it may not, and to list only the modernizing functions is to offer an incomplete and distorted analysis of the relationship between education and the processes of economic, political, and social change. Here we shall attempt a more balanced appraisal by presenting a pessimistic, or at least skeptical, point of view, and by criticizing some of the previous arguments.

Education of a certain type and in certain proportions may be a precondition for modernization, but this is not to say that the kind of education that is actually offered in a country meets the standards specified. Virtually every commentator on school curricula in developing areas has noted that the learning process restricts individual creativity by its excessive formality and reliance on rote, and that the curricula require children to digest much academic information that is totally irrelevant to them. Because a school certificate is normally considered a passport to white-collar employment, such subjects as agriculture, domestic science, and basic mechanics—when they are taught at all—are too often ignored by the pupils because the subject matter is at variance with their own ambitions. These criticisms, as Philip Foster has pointed out, are not entirely well-founded, since in the colonial setting what appears as sterile, academic education was probably the most useful, and certainly the most lucrative, form of training a young person could receive; moreover, in the early stages of economic growth there is often insufficient demand for the practical skills of the mechanic, the draftsman, or the chemist.[28] Nevertheless, it seems patently absurd that in 1963 at the Ivory Coast's new University of Abidjan, for instance, 550 Ivoiriens were majoring in law, while there were only 44 in science and 23 in medicine.[29] Leaders of new states are verbally committed to curricular reform in the direction of more science and technology, agriculture, local history, civics, and the like, but in practice their prior commitment to a rapid increase in enrollment precludes a radical revision of the syllabus. Hence many schoolchildren in the new states receive education of a type that contributes neither to rapid economic growth nor to the diffusion of national sentiments.

There is, moreover, no guarantee that in underdeveloped countries a proper balance will obtain between enrollments at different levels of education. At the one end of the spectrum is the Belgians' policy in the Congo, whereby heavy primary enrollment was encouraged and access to post-primary education severely limited; the resulting combination of widespread literacy with a dearth of high- and middle-level manpower sets the Congo's domestic problems since 1960 in an understandable light. At the other extreme is a policy of expanding university enrollment as quickly as possible, if need be by lowering entrance requirements to the universities. Such a policy has been followed in India, Indonesia, Burma, the Philippines, and Egypt. The result is not only the familiar problem of "B.A. unemployment" but low productivity among those who do obtain jobs, because they are not assisted by the right number of workers with lower academic qualifications.[30] In determining the proper educational mix one must also consider the relative importance of informal education—in-service training schemes, adult literacy and community development projects, extension services, and so forth. Many leaders of new states equate education with formal schooling and spend only nominal amounts on its informal component, which may be more immediately productive and may actually increase the productivity of the formal sector by complementing classroom teaching.[31] There is, therefore, the unfortunate possibility that, in terms of modernization, the substantial resources devoted to education may be misallocated within the educational system. Gross indices of "progress" such as literacy rates or the proportion of a budget spent on education do not tell us the nature or extent of this misallocation.

In contrast to the experience of many countries now considered modern, the rapid growth of the school system in the new states has taken place before industrialization and before the development of an effective indigenous bureaucracy. Consequently, heavy demands have been placed on the political system—for more and better schools, health clinics, and other amenities the people regard as their due—at a time when the capacity of the system to satisfy demands is relatively low. If political leaders do in fact manage to satisfy popular pressures for more educational opportunities, they risk actually increasing the gap between these pressures and government performance. Education costs relatively more in an underdeveloped area than in a developed one, since teachers' salaries are high compared to per capita income, and capital costs at the post-primary level can be exorbitant.[32] Given high unit costs and ambitious plans for expansion, educational expenditure inevitably absorbs a large proportion of total government outlay; we have seen that this is the case in many new states. But governments must also build up an infrastructure of ports, roads, and power plants, expand the communications network, increase and diversify agricultural output, and begin to industrialize. An overemphasis on education will render it difficult, if not impossible, to finance these other projects, which may be considered preconditions of modernization fully as much as the improvement of "human capital." Indeed, the economic payoff on such projects is likely to be more immediate than that of primary education, for example, whose impact on productivity may not be felt until at least a decade after the initial expenditure. There is much to be said for short-run stimulants to a backward economy, for without immediate growth not even education can be financed later.

A related factor is that the kind of education demanded by the populace may more logically be considered welfare—a consumption item—than directly productive investment. This is particularly the case where widespread support exists for the retention of an irrelevant syllabus and where the bulk of those attending school do so for only the first few years, picking up the rudiments of literacy and a taste for material benefits but not necessarily acquiring marketable skills. Financing a welfare state requires a well-developed economy. Underdeveloped countries by definition lack adequate financial resources, yet they are under pressure to provide the accoutrements of a modern welfare state largely because their educated elements know what is provided in the wealthier countries. If education is a welfare item, a high level of expenditure for it is a false index of modernity, since the economic and administrative base necessary to support a welfare state is lacking in the underdeveloped world.[33]

Another problem for those who see education as the key to modernization lies in the interpretation of correlations between educational and other variables. The fact that literacy correlates positively with per capita income, for example, does not prove that literacy rates determine income levels—a causal proposition that is implicit in arguments for stimulating economic development through mass literacy. More plausible is the reverse argument that a wealthy nation can afford to spend relatively more on education than a poor one. Bowman and Anderson's data suggest that national income levels can be used to predict primary enrollments in a subsequent generation more accurately than enrollment levels can predict subsequent income.[34] If income and education are correlated at any single point in time, it is more reasonable to infer that we are measuring the effect of income on educational expenditure than the reverse, since the economic pay-off on a given amount of education will not be apparent until several years later. We know, moreover, that educational and other indices of modernization, such as urbanization and industrialization, are often highly correlated with each other. When several variables form a cluster, it is not only difficult but misleading to single out any one of them as the only or even the principal agent of change. It may be that modernization occurs only when several interrelated variables change in certain ways, in which case changes in the educational system alone are not sufficient to set off the desired chain reaction of modernizing activities.[35]

Enthusiasts for education should further ask themselves whether policy recommendations based on the experience of developed countries are applicable in a setting of underdevelopment. If literacy rates of at least 90 per cent are a precondition for per capita incomes over $500, as Bowman and Anderson suggest, it is easy to conclude that poor countries should aim directly for total literacy. If rich countries spend a high percentage of their national income on education, a natural inference is that poor countries should follow suit. But there are serious pitfalls in this approach. It assumes that there is a single path to modernization, which is extremely doubtful given the different routes by which modern countries themselves developed.[36] It also assumes that investment priorities are similar for countries at quite different stages of development—or, more specifically, that policies suitable for remaining modern are automatically those suitable for becoming modern. This too is highly questionable, for it may in fact be argued that in order to realize its long-run objectives an underdeveloped country will have to pursue short-run policies running counter to these objectives. Thus, in order to create the conditions for high consumption a regime must initially defer consumption, productively investing high levels of savings. The ultimate goal of a modernizing leader may be the equitable distribution of income, yet the high levels of investment he needs to initiate growth may in some cases be most readily attained if income distribution is highly unequal and if resources are concentrated in certain sectors of the economy at the expense of others. In the political realm, the argument for tutelary or guided democracy is essentially that the preconditions for government by the people should be established by an elite not fully accountable to the people.

Assuming for the moment that this argument is valid, does a similar logic apply to education in the new states? Should the benefits of schooling be denied to one generation so that future generations may enjoy these benefits more fully? At the post-primary level the answer to this question may well be negative, but it is not so certain that countries in the early stages of modernization should strive for universal primary education, for example, or universal adult literacy. Even assuming on the basis of correlations that 30 per cent literacy constitutes a breakthrough for a country aiming at per capita income above $300, "rising literacy alone contributes very little to development over the range from 30 to 70 per cent literate";[37] hence the enormous effort required to push literacy up to 70 or 80 per cent may have little economic payoff. Might it not be best to postpone this effort, channeling the resources thus saved into more directly productive enterprises, the income from which could finance future literacy campaigns? The question should be openly and seriously debated in policy planning and academic circles.

The exponent of rapid educational expansion in the new states faces another complicated problem: his analysis may ignore certain unforeseen consequences of expansion. Particularly in situations of culture contact, innovations introduced with one objective in mind may have effects that outweigh and even counteract the original objective. In the view of early colonial officials, for example, the purpose of education was to strengthen their own regime by producing literates who could occupy subordinate positions and, in the case of the British and French, by creating an educated elite that would identify fully with the interests of the colonial power.[38] The British in India and in parts of West Africa, and the French for a brief period in Senegal, further hoped that this indigenous elite would be recruited from traditional high-status elements, so that the power balance within traditional society would not be unduly altered. However, those who took the greatest advantage of educational opportunities to enter a self-consciously modern elite were frequently from low-status groups, with the result that the pattern of educational recruitment had a distinctly disruptive effect on the indigenous hierarchy of power and prestige.[39] Far more serious from the colonialist standpoint, in most countries the new elite tended to regard itself not as the preserver but as the challenger of European interests, and from its ranks the nationalist leaders were drawn. There were many reasons for this unexpected development, among them the new elite's capacity to deal with Europeans on their own legal and moral grounds, its disillusionment when barriers to advancement based on race rather than on achievement were imposed, and the generalized frustration—directed against the colonial regime—of intellectuals who were "a product of modernization before modernization [had] reached or become widespread in their own country."[40] In any event the most significant consequence of colonial education was an unforeseen one: the demise of colonial rule.

The same lesson may well apply to the efforts of the new elite, once in power, to use the schools for its own objectives. Obviously schools can play an important role in the vertical and horizontal integration of a society, but this does not preclude their performing disintegrative functions at the same time. Issues of educational policy are almost always bound up with the conflicts among different ethnic, racial, religious, and linguistic groups that make the task of integration in the new states so difficult. In one respect these horizontal tensions—reflecting what Geertz has termed the pattern of primordial politics—are the consequence of insufficient modernization. Large numbers of people in the new states have been given the opportunity to participate in politics before the processes of economic change have created classes and a network of voluntary associations that cut across traditional loyalties. But in another respect the very success of modernization strengthens these loyalties and in fact creates "traditional" conflicts that never really arose in traditional society. Faced for the first time with rapidly changing circumstances, people often cling desperately to their past identity; the uneven pace of progress from region to region creates jealousies on the part of deprived peoples, and unevenness is explained in primordial terms rather than as the inevitable concomitant of economic growth; a politician seeking to weld a nation out of its component parts may nevertheless feel obliged to appeal to sectional interests as the only means of attaining power. The efforts of national leaders to accelerate economic development and to encourage mass participation in politics may bring into the open latent conflicts between groups, making political issues out of differences that formerly lay outside the political arena altogether.

In the post-Independence period the school system very often becomes the object of intense rivalry between competing groups, both because education is manifestly the key to power in the new order and because the continuity of the groups concerned may be threatened by what is taught in the schools. A language group will be fundamentally challenged if its young people are taught another tongue in the schools; similarly, a religious sect may feel itself endangered if its tenets cannot be propounded in the classroom. One of the clearest signs of horizontal cleavage in the new states may be the disputes aroused over proposals to reform or expand the educational system. In Geertz's words, "If the general strike is the classical political expression of class warfare, and the coup d'etat of the struggle between militarism and parliamentarianism, then the school crisis is perhaps becoming the classical political—or parapolitical—expression of the clash of primordial loyalties."[41] It is possible that just as the introduction of education aided the downfall of the European empire builders, so its further spread will conspire against their nation-building successors.

A final difficulty with the view that education is the key to modernization is that one all too easily assumes the educational system to be an independent variable affecting, but relatively unaffected by, its social, political, and economic environment. Educational planners often base their recommendations on this assumption, if only because their job is not to study the political pressures or economic constraints that limit the educational policy maker but rather to maximize the impact of the educational system on a society.[42] But neglect of pressures and constraints on education can lead to unrealistic policies; targets may be set whose fulfillment depends, for instance, on a degree of centralized, rational authority that simply does not exist. The good planner must realize, as does the politician almost by instinct, that "education is not the architectonic science but is subordinate to that of politics."[43] This is especially true in the new states, where the educational system is a tool for planned change in the hands of men whose careers bear witness to the primacy of politics. To understand the nature of education in a given society one must study not just its impact on that society but the mutual interaction of education and its environment. In this perspective, even if education is the key that unlocks the door to modernization, it is by no means certain that all underdeveloped societies, having as they do different income levels, social and political structures, and basic values, will be able to use the key, although they may desperately wish to unlock the door.

Thus, although it is widely and perhaps justifiably believed that the expansion of education at all levels contributes to and may even be a necessary condition for the modernization of currently underdeveloped countries, persuasive arguments can be advanced that educational expansion may contribute to the failure of these countries to modernize, or at least that the many virtues of education conceived in the abstract will not materialize in the current setting of underdevelopment. It is important to note that the two sets of arguments are not mutually exclusive but rather complementary. Taken together, they illustrate the multiple, complex, and potentially contradictory consequences of education, and the circular process by which the impact of education on the social, economic, and political environment is constantly being modified by the nature of the environment itself.

THE CASE STUDY

This book represents an effort to move beyond the stage of reasonable generalizations to an intensive exploration in a particular underdeveloped area of some of the issues just discussed. The scope of the study is more limited than the preceding discussion in order to permit analysis in depth of certain features not sufficiently discussed in the rest of the literature. First of all, we shall focus on the interaction of education and politics, treating economic and social factors as secondary. This approach may be justified on the grounds that until recently "political scientists in general have paid very little attention to the education-polity nexus,"[44] whereas the economics of education and the sociology of education are already respectable subfields within their respective disciplines. Second, the aim is to analyze the different ways in which interaction has occurred, rather than to evaluate at each stage in the narrative whether educational expansion made a positive or negative contribution to political development; speculation on the latter topic is mostly confined to the final part of the book. A third limitation is that the study concentrates on "popular education"—those forms of training introduced from Europe that have historically enrolled the largest numbers and elicited the greatest financial contribution from the people. Thus formal, academic primary and secondary education, together with teacher training, will receive the most attention. "Bush," Koranic, technical, agricultural, and commercial schools, adult education classes, in-service training programs, and universities will be discussed only in passing, even though their collective impact is considerable.

Southern Nigeria provides an interesting case study for several reasons. Formal Western schooling was first introduced over a century ago and soon won great popular approval. Indeed, it seems safe to say that by the 1930's and 1940's no people in the world placed a higher value on education or regarded its consequences more optimistically than did the inhabitants of this area. During the 1950's the two regions comprising Southern Nigeria, the West and the East, took advantage of the political autonomy granted them under British colonial rule to embark on a massive program of educational expansion, particularly at the primary school level. By 1960 each region was devoting over 40 per cent of its annual recurrent expenditure to education.* Unquestionably, Southern Nigeria has felt the impact of an "education explosion."

The two regions of Southern Nigeria lend themselves well to comparative historical analysis. The regions have much in common, for they were both molded over the years by the same administrative and educational system, yet they are dissimilar in tribal and religious patterns, wealth, and political history. Moreover, since the first experiments with limited self-government began in 1952, each region has evolved its own distinctive educational policies, quite often in a conscious effort to improve on the other's performance.

A third factor of no little importance is that Southern Nigeria has been extensively studied by British, American, and now Nigerian scholars, so the relevant historical data are not hard to obtain. Field work in the 1960–65 period was facilitated by cooperative officials, the presence of universities and research institutes, and a populace that was remarkably open in its expression of opinion. In many ways Southern Nigeria, in spite of recent events, has been an ideal location for in-depth research into education and politics.

Changes since the first military coup of January 1966 have made it difficult to speak of Southern Nigeria in the present tense, since the eastern portion of the area has seceded to form the self-proclaimed Republic of Biafra. For our purposes Southern Nigeria consists of the territory that in 1960 became the Federal Republic of Nigeria, minus its Northern Region. Appendix A provides a brief sketch of the geography, economy, and ethnic composition of the area; for more detailed accounts the reader is referred to a number of recent studies.[45] To simplify the discussion we shall assume throughout that Southern Nigeria consists of two regions, the West and the East, even though historically this has not always been the case. The term "Western Region" refers to the provinces of Lagos and Colony, Abeokuta, Benin, Ijebu, Ondo, Oyo, and Warri (later renamed Delta), which were formally designated the Western Region in 1939. Lagos and Colony ceased to be part of the Western Region when they became Federal Territory in 1954, and we are only marginally concerned

---

* The federal Nigerian government devoted a far smaller proportion to education; combined regional-federal expenditure in this field was closer to 20 per cent. Still, the regions' educational commitments constituted an enormous burden by any standard.

thereafter with developments in the Territory. In August 1963 the people of Benin and Delta provinces opted to form the new Mid-Western Region. Until events after this date are discussed, this study uses "Western Nigeria" to mean the area administered by the Western and Mid-Western regional governments from 1963 until the military reorganization of the country in 1967. The Eastern Region consists of the provinces of Calabar, Ogoja, Onitsha, Owerri, and Rivers. Provincial boundaries were altered and new provinces created in 1959, but again for simplicity all references are to the provinces as they were administered under the British.

This book attempts to treat certain topics analytically while at the same time preserving a sense of historical sequence. Part I, which covers the period from the arrival of the first Christian missionaries to the end of Britain's effective monopoly of power in Southern Nigeria (1842–1950), focuses on the dynamics of educational expansion. The initiative in opening new schools, although for quite different reasons, came from Christian missionaries and African villagers. Following a period of disinterest in educational matters and then disquiet over the destabilizing consequences of education, the colonial government began by the 1940's to increase substantially its grant-in-aid contributions to the school system, which was still dominated by the mission groups. Meanwhile, the graduates of the early schools, whose outlook had been affected by previous patterns of educational expansion, organized to press for even higher enrollments and better training at the post-primary level. Tribal unions showed what self-help might accomplish for groups wishing to catch up with their neighbors in the educational race; the Nigeria Union of Teachers and members of the well-educated elite demanded that the government take a more active and direct part in extending educational opportunities. The new groups were also instrumental in pressing for self-government at the regional and national levels, and in enabling Southern Nigerians to use the powers they did possess in the 1950's.

Changes in the political arena heralded changes in educational policy. In Part II, we examine the dramatic schemes of free, universal primary education that were introduced into the Western and Eastern regions during the mid-1950's, taking into account the impact of political factors on the decisions of both regions to launch these schemes. We then turn to the effort by politicians and administrators to translate universal primary education from paper pledge to reality. How did the regional governments, in the midst of transition from colonial to African control, find the resources necessary to raise primary enrollments from about 30 per cent of the school-age population in 1952 to about 75 per cent by the time national independence was attained in 1960? How did these governments resolve the conflicts brought about by the public control of a school system still largely in the hands of private mission bodies?

In Part III our attention shifts from the causes and the mechanics of educational expansion in Southern Nigeria to the consequences of such expansion for political development. There the conflicting arguments about education and modernization presented in the Introduction are taken up again. The impact of the educational schemes of the 1950's on the politics of Southern Nigeria is difficult to assess only a decade later, but in spite of empirical and methodological problems, some tentative conclusions are offered. We argue that mass education in Southern Nigeria, at least in the short run, has quite possibly lowered the capacity of government to realize goals, and that it has had inegalitarian and disintegrative consequences quite unforeseen by the men who launched universal primary education and related programs in the 1950's. The observation that rapid educational expansion may therefore have contributed to political decay rather than to political development in this part of the world seems neither overly extreme nor overly pessimistic. A concluding chapter suggests, however, that the tendencies toward political decay produced by educational expansion may themselves be used to further political development in the long run. The study thus ends by emphasizing the creative potential of crisis in society, and it proposes educational policies that might lead Southern Nigeria—and other developing areas like it—toward greater capacity, equality, and integration.

PART I

The Dynamics of Educational Expansion, 1842–1950

CHAPTER 1

The Mission Enterprise, 1842–1929

The praises of my tongue
I offer to the Lord
That I was taught and learnt so young
To read His holy word.
—ISAAC WATTS

Three groups took part in the expansion of education in Southern Nigeria: European missionaries, Africans, and government officials. At certain times and places one of these groups assumed a leading role, while the others responded to its initiatives; at other times their roles overlapped, for example when Africans became themselves the agents of missionary activity and missionaries became involved in the formation of official educational policy. Although new schools and rising enrollments were the product of interaction between two and occasionally all three groups, the dynamics of educational expansion in Southern Nigeria may best be understood by discussing these groups separately, for each had its own quite distinct reasons for furthering education.

The first English-speaking Christian missionary arrived in what was to become Nigeria in 1842.[1] By 1921, 130,000 Southern Nigerian children were attending mission-managed primary and secondary schools, and a decade later the figure had risen to about 200,000. In this chapter we shall consider several aspects of missionary activity that helped to account for this rapid rise in enrollment and that had important political implications as well: the missionaries' head start over the colonial regime, their heavy stress on education, the uneven geographical distribution of mission schools, the priority given to educating the rural population, and the rivalry between voluntary agencies (as the various denominational groups were termed by the government). The chapter concludes by examining the effects of mission education on Southern Nigeria's political development. The next two chapters describe the roles played by Africans and government officials in educational expansion.

THE MISSIONARY HEAD START

The most obvious characteristic of Southern Nigerian education in the nineteenth century is that it was almost entirely in the hands of Christian missionaries, who had been active for decades before the British government declared Southern Nigeria a protectorate in 1900.* The pioneer Methodist and Anglican missionaries, Rev. Thomas Birch Freeman and Rev. Henry Townsend, arrived at Badagry in 1842; the Church of Scotland Mission† under Rev. Hope Waddell was started at Calabar in 1846; and the first Southern Baptist missionary, Rev. Thomas Bowen, began his work among the Yorubas in 1850. In 1867 the first Roman Catholic station was established in Lagos, and much later, in 1893, the Primitive Methodists started their work at Archibong, near Calabar. Not content to confine themselves to the coastal areas, Townsend and Bowen traveled extensively through Yorubaland during the 1850's, and Bowen opened a station as far north as Ogbomosho in 1855. Rev. David Hinderer, another early missionary-explorer, toured the area east of Ibadan and in 1875 founded a station for the Anglican Church Missionary Society (C.M.S.) in Ondo Town. East of the Niger River, Church of Scotland missionaries gradually pushed north along the Cross River, which "for many years . . . was to remain the highway for Christian advance";[2] by 1892 a post was established at Unwana, some fifty miles upriver from Calabar. The Niger River, too, was a highway to the interior. Rev. Samuel Adjai Crowther, the famous African missionary, started an Anglican mission at the river port of Onitsha in 1857; the Roman Catholics established themselves in the same town in 1885. Thus, whereas the authority of the British government in the late nineteenth century was exercised principally along the coastal areas, the influence of the mission groups was felt inland as well.

There were several reasons why government activity in Southern

* The island and port of Lagos were ceded to the Crown in 1861, and the British exercised a shadowy control over the coastal areas through the Oil Rivers Protectorate of 1887 and the Niger Coast Protectorate of 1893. But not until 1900 were concerted efforts made to establish an administration for Southern Nigeria.

† For simplicity this mission is designated "Church of Scotland" throughout the discussion, even though in earlier periods control resided with the United Presbyterian Church (1846–1900) and the United Free Church (1900–1929). Since the 1929 merger of the United Free Church with the Church of Scotland, Nigerian operations have been directed by the latter. See Donald M. McFarlan, *Calabar: The Church of Scotland Mission, Founded 1846*, rev. ed. (London, 1957).

Nigeria was not as early or widespread as that of the missions. Generally speaking, until the 1880's little official interest was expressed in the acquisition of African territory; Great Britain's principal trading connections were elsewhere, and political control was not believed necessary for increased commerce with Africa. Moreover, the slave trade—whose abolition had provided the one reason for British intervention in tropical Africa since the transatlantic trade was "outlawed" in 1833—could be effectively reduced by patrolling the high seas and exercising control over only a few important ports, such as Lagos. The official view, in force until the 1880's, was expressed by James Stephen of the Colonial Office in 1840:

I cannot but think that even if our National resources were far more potent than they at present are, it would be very bad policy to employ in Africa that part of them which is available for colonisation....In Africa we cannot colonise at all without coming into contact with numerous warlike tribes, and involving ourselves in their disputes, wars and relations with each other. If we could acquire the Dominion of the whole of that Continent it would be but a worthless possession.[3]

The missionaries, in contrast to the government officials, had definite motives for working in Africa long before the 1880's and the scramble for European control of the continent. In fact, among the first Europeans to visit West Africa were Catholic missionaries anxious to preach to the local rulers.[4] Christians had always felt it their duty to convert the heathen, and Africa had long offered a particular challenge because its peoples were believed degraded and primitive, and because the slave trade was seen as inflicting enormous evils on the indigenous society. The theme of African degradation runs through the accounts of early missionaries as they confronted cultures whose use of violence, often to reinforce the norms or power structure of the community, was unfamiliar and therefore deemed barbaric.[5] Alleged barbarism, in fact, often attracted the missionaries; in some instances mission sites were selected precisely because an area possessed a particularly unsavory reputation.[6]

But if the early missionaries were drawn to Africa by its presumed lack of civilization, many of them were sustained in their efforts by a belief that it was entirely possible, as well as desirable, for Africa to enter the "civilized" world. This belief was shared by influential leaders of the Abolitionist movement in England. The movement's success in thwarting the transatlantic slave trade gradually directed British attention to the source of that trade in the African interior and to the need for a radical transformation of African life in order to eliminate slavery completely. Thomas Fowell Buxton's influential treatise, *The African Slave Trade and Its Remedy*, published in 1840, proposed that an alliance of Christianity and commerce could undertake such a transformation of the Dark Continent. Buxton's concept, popularly known as "the Bible and the Plough," was further developed by Henry Venn, Honorary Secretary of the Church Missionary Society from 1841 to 1872. Venn felt the Church should encourage the growth of an African middle class, thoroughly Christianized and made financially self-reliant by the production and export of cash crops. This middle class could then civilize Africa from within and do so far more effectively than European missionaries, though the latter, of course, were needed initially to preach the Christian faith and foster the spirit of entrepreneurship.[7]

There were further reasons why missionaries were specifically attracted to the area now known as Southern Nigeria. Many years after England's ban on the slave trade, a considerable traffic in slaves continued along the Nigerian coastline, where numerous creeks and inlets back of the coast made the detection of slave-running ships extremely difficult. As people in England became aware of this situation, missionaries volunteered their services to curb the illicit trade. The interest of so many early missionaries in Abeokuta, for example, is to be explained partly by that town's role as a potential counterweight to Dahomey, a neighboring kingdom noted for its slaving proclivities. In Calabar the very effectiveness of British naval pressure in reducing the profits of slave traders presented another kind of opportunity for mission work. King Eyo Honesty of Creek Town wrote to Queen Victoria in the early 1840's:

One thing I want for beg your Queen, I have too much man now, I can't sell slaves, and don't know what to do for them. But if I can get some cotton and coffee to grow, and man for teach me, and make sugar cane for we country come up proper, and sell for trade side I very glad. Mr. Blyth tell me England glad for send man to teach book and make we understand God all same white man do. If Queen do so I glad too much, and we must try do good for England always.[8]

This message spurred the Church of Scotland to send its first missionary party to Calabar.

Missionary interest in Nigeria was also stimulated by the Europeans' discovery in 1830 that the Niger River emptied into the sea at a point about midway between Lagos and Calabar. Unlike the Congo, Zambezi, and Orange rivers, the Niger is navigable for several hundred miles; hence it provided a way for Europeans anxious to reach the interior of the continent. The Church Missionary Society, fore-seeing the prospect of converting Africans in the interior, actively assisted Buxton in planning his 1841 expedition up the Niger;[9] by 1857, as we have seen, Crowther had established a permanent station at Onitsha. The existence of a major navigable river enabled the missionaries to extend their activities and to bypass African city-states along the coast that objected to European penetration of their territory.[10]

The most important cause of the early missionary interest in Southern Nigeria was a curious by-product of the slave trade. The British colony of Sierra Leone had been created in 1787 as a haven for freed slaves, and in succeeding years thousands of Africans chained in slave ships bound for the New World were rescued by British squadrons on the high seas and then landed in the aptly named port of Freetown. Once there, some of these former slaves received Christian training and an education from philanthropic groups operating in the town.* As it happened, many of the Africans taken to Sierra Leone during the early nineteenth century were Yorubas, who by the late 1830's were in a position to return to their homeland. The effect of these Sierra Leoneans, or Saros,[11] as they were called, on the missionary endeavor was profound. They had received training in religious, academic, and technical matters that was not available in the land of their birth, and they returned to Nigeria with a taste for European life that set them quite apart from Africans who had never left home. Since many of these migrants were Christian, they expressed a desire to have ministers and teachers to renew their faith and to instruct their children. In response to such a call from James Fergusson (a Saro who had returned to Badagry), the Wesleyan Methodist Missionary Society and the Church Missionary Society both began their Nigerian ministry in 1842, and a similar request led to Bowen's arrival in 1850. A leading Nigerian historian justifiably argues: "It was the emigrants who introduced the missionaries into the country, and they were an essential and integral part of the missionary movement."[12]

About three thousand Yoruba emigrants had settled in Abeokuta by 1850,[13] giving that town particular prominence in the missionaries'

---

* The Church Missionary Society owes its own establishment in 1799 to the Sierra Leone experiment. The Society's founders were members of the Sierra Leone Company, a philanthropic group formed to place freed slaves in the colony. The initial objective of the C.M.S. was to assist these persons once they had arrived.

eyes. Was this not the enlightened African middle class of which Henry Venn had spoken, sufficiently concentrated within one town to become a center of civilization? Not surprisingly, it was in Abeokuta that the printing press was first introduced and early experiments were undertaken in growing and ginning cotton.[14] Abeokuta's location, some seventy miles inland from Lagos, also gave it great strategic importance as a "hopeful centre . . . from which commerce and Christian civilization would radiate into the dark but fertile interior," in Townsend's words.[15] All the major denominations operating in what is now Western Nigeria established stations in this town and then branched out into surrounding Yoruba country. The presence of Saros in Abeokuta thus influenced the first strategies of mission advance and facilitated the drive into the interior.

Yorubaland was not the only area of Southern Nigeria to experience the impact of emigrants from Sierra Leone. Through the activities of Bishop Crowther, in many respects the outstanding Nigerian of the last century, the Christian gospel was preached along the Niger River and in the Delta from the 1850's onward.[16] Crowther was born in a small Yoruba village between 1800 and 1810, captured in one of the internecine wars that afflicted the Yorubas throughout most of the nineteenth century, rescued from a Portuguese slave ship by British warships, and then taken to Sierra Leone in 1822. He quickly showed great intelligence and industry and was one of the first to enroll in Freetown's Fourah Bay College, established in 1827 as West Africa's first post-primary institution. Crowther returned to Nigeria as a member of Buxton's Niger expedition in 1841 and was ordained three years later. He was then sent to Abeokuta, where he assisted Townsend from 1846 to 1854. While at Abeokuta, Crowther began to translate the Bible into Yoruba and to compile a Yoruba grammar and dictionary—undertakings that greatly eased the task of Europeans who subsequently worked in Yorubaland. So distinguished was Crowther's record that at Henry Venn's urging he was consecrated Missionary Bishop of the Niger in 1864; his domain covered in effect the Niger from Nupe country down to the sea and the coastal area to the east. Believing, as did Venn, that "Africa can chiefly be benefited by her own children,"[17] Bishop Crowther relied heavily on the few educated Africans whom he could find, most of them trained in Sierra Leone. This all-African missionary team introduced Christianity to the Niger and the Delta, and by 1880, despite numerous setbacks, Crowther's mission had eleven stations and over a thousand Christian adherents.[18] In view of the extremely unhealthy climate of the

Delta, it is unlikely that European missionaries would have been as effective in proselytizing there as Bishop Crowther and his assistants were, to say nothing of the advantages Africans possessed in preaching to men of their own color.

THE EMPHASIS ON EDUCATION

The missionaries from the very beginning stressed the central role of education in their work. At Calabar, for example, the Duke Town School was established in the very first year of Presbyterian endeavor there, and within a week of Rev. J. C. Taylor's arrival at Onitsha a dozen children were brought to him to be educated. "I looked upon them," wrote Taylor, "as the commencement of our missionary work. We lost no time but began to teach them the A.B.C."[19] This early emphasis on African literacy, which was sustained in the following years, was directly related to the evangelistic aims of the missionaries. Christianity is a religion of the book, particularly in its Protestant forms, which emphasize the unique role of the Bible in revealing the Word of God. It was not sufficient for a preacher or a priest merely to proclaim the Gospel; his congregation must literally see the Word as well as hear it. A man who could read the Parables did not have to rely solely on his pastor's infrequent commentary but could return to the stories and the truths they related whenever he cared to open his Bible. Eventual acceptance within a denomination, usually signified by baptism, required knowledge of the Church's tenets as well as a confession of faith; the missionaries knew that the spread of literacy within a pagan community, coupled with the provision of Bibles, prayer books, and catechisms for literates to absorb, would quicken and deepen the process of conversion. A Methodist report of 1920 doubtless represented the views of other denominations as well when it asserted: "The uneducated are always a danger to the whole church."[20]

Education also helped the missionaries solve the tactical problem of maintaining their foothold in Southern Nigeria without the aid of political authority and in the face of increasing African resistance to the European presence. After colonial rule was established in 1900, it became relatively easy for missionaries in Southern Nigeria to conduct their work: the Pax Britannica facilitated expansion into new areas, and the prestige of the European as the conqueror of the area probably made the new religion imported from Europe seem more attractive. But during the nineteenth century, when Europeans were competing with local merchants for trading profits and British consuls were arrogating to themselves increasing powers over the lives of Africans, popular dislike of Europeans and suspicion of their motives were widespread, and in many cases the mission enterprise suffered precisely because it was linked with the general extension of European influence throughout Africa.

Although it would be an oversimplification to describe them as advance agents of British (or French) imperialism, the missionaries were linked in many ways to the traders and officials who came in increasing numbers to Nigeria. Most of the leading missionaries were Europeans, of the same color and speaking the same language as those who came to Africa for profit or power. The missionaries' vision of civilization incorporated European cultural elements that were not connected with Christianity,* and the "Bible and Plough" theory gave prominence to the role that commerce, presumably involving European traders, could play in the uplifting of Africa. Then too, as James Coleman observes, "even had missionaries not identified Christianity and European culture, the African would still have considered them indivisible. His conception of religion was not unlike that of the medieval European who regarded Christianity and civilization as coterminous."[21]

Moreover, the political and economic situation in the nineteenth century hindered the advance of mission work. From 1820 to 1893 Yorubaland was racked by civil war, as the hegemony of Oyo was destroyed and new city-states, such as Ibadan and Abeokuta, fought among themselves to fill the power vacuum and to control trade routes to the coast.[22] Along the "Oil Rivers" east of the Niger lay another group of city-states (Bonny, Nembe, Kalabari, Opobo, and Calabar were the most prominent) whose inhabitants served as middlemen between European traders and the hinterland, at first in the slave and then in the palm-oil trade. These Africans knew their economic position would be undercut if the Europeans were able to gain direct access to the source of supply.[23] The general instability of Yorubaland and the often inhospitable response of the Oil Rivers trading states to Europeans convinced many missionaries that the imposition of law and order from the outside was prerequisite to the growth of

---

* Ajayi mentions a Methodist missionary who in 1844 held a tea party for his flock at Badagry, calling the occasion a token of civilization. See J. F. Ade Ajayi, *Christian Missions in Nigeria, 1841–1891: The Making of a New Elite* (Evanston, Ill., 1965), p. 14. In the Gold Coast, the Wesleyans' Cape Coast School sold copies of Beeton's *Complete Etiquette for English Gentlemen* in the bookshop. H. O. A. McWilliam, *The Development of Education in Ghana: An Outline* (London, 1959), p. 22.

Christian civilization, and some of them even became politically involved in advancing the imperial cause.

For these reasons, among others, many Africans grew increasingly suspicious of missionaries during the nineteenth century. By the 1860's and 1870's, their hostility became severe enough to provoke several incidents of general persecution of Christians in Bonny, Nembe, and even Abeokuta. To gain the Africans' confidence the missionaries needed to emphasize activities that appealed in themselves to the local people and were not explicitly connected to European imperial interests. Education was admirably suited to this tactical necessity. As will be seen, in many areas schooling quickly became popular. Literacy was for the African a tool by which he could cope with the European presence; in this sense the school became the African's self-defense against the momentous changes being imposed on him from outside. By providing, through the school, what the African desired and could use, the missionaries managed to calm somewhat the suspicions incurred by their own presence.

EARLY MISSION SCHOOLS

The first step for the missionary was to win a measure of acceptance within the community and to obtain permission to preach to at least a few of its members. Normally efforts were made to win the approval of local traditional rulers or influential elders by arguing that a mission would enhance their status and that of the community, teach their people the ways of the Europeans, and proclaim the commandments of a deity who ruled over all, black and white alike. If the argument proved persuasive, quarters were soon constructed for the missionary and his family, and the chief might attend services himself and send one of his sons to school. In many instances approval was granted even though the leading men were still dubious about the value of the mission: if pressed to send children to school, they would volunteer their slaves' children to test out the new institution before sending their own sons or daughters to it. In the very early years of the mission enterprise, the evangelist was sometimes ignored or openly suspect, in which case he had to start working with the community's rejected elements: abandoned slaves, orphans, outcasts. Whatever his audience, the missionary employed his talents to preach and teach the Gospel, heal the sick, construct buildings, operate a mechanic's tools, and cultivate available land.

As a teacher, the missionary concentrated on Africans in their adolescent or pre-adolescent years, for the young were considered more pliable and ultimately more useful to the Church than their parents. The first classes were often held in the missionary's home; some of the students' parents were paid a small amount by the missionary for allowing their children to board with him and attend his school. Pupils were provided free clothes, copy books, and slates, and liberal prizes for good performance were offered to motivate them to study diligently. At first, "standards," or classes based on age, did not exist: pupils of widely varying ages were grouped together according to their ability to absorb the materials in certain readers, written either in English or in the vernacular.* Reading aloud portions of the Book of Genesis might constitute a promotion exam from the beginning to a higher group. Subjects covered at the primary level normally included reading, writing, and arithmetic, which were taught in English, and Bible study and catechism, which were taught in the vernacular to make certain they were understood. Pupils were expected to engage in routine maintenance of the school compound, perhaps to tend a school garden, and to assist in household duties if they boarded with the missionary.

In the advanced coastal towns of Lagos and Calabar, the demand for post-primary facilities grew; by the turn of the century mission groups had established six secondary schools in the two towns, as shown in Table 1. The curriculum at this level was broader and also more controversial than at the primary level. Although it is not true that all European missionaries favored "practical" subjects and all Africans preferred a purely literary education, there were undeniably pressures in these two directions from the early years onward. Nigeria's first secondary school, the Church Missionary Society Grammar School in Lagos, was founded in 1859 by Rev. T. B. Macaulay, a Nigerian trained in Sierra Leone and England. Macaulay favored a heavy dose of classics in the curriculum, contrary to the views of the white C.M.S. missionaries, and was supported by wealthy Lagosians who wanted a prestigious education for their children. On the other hand, at Hope Waddell Training Institute, established in Calabar by the Church of Scotland Mission in 1895, highly practical pursuits were emphasized: carpentry, printing, and mechanics in addition to English literature, mathematics, and history.[24]

---

* The readers encouraged young people to persist in the drive for education. The first Ibo reader of the C.M.S., *Azu Ndu*, urged: "Friend, if there is a school in your town don't neglect it. You have teachers to teach you, so persevere to learn and learn quickly, for the time will come when education will be costly." Quoted in *Report of the Proceedings of the First Session of the Twelfth Synod of the Diocese on the Niger* (Onitsha, 1962), p. 30.

Many of the early primary schools, and all those created at the post-primary level, were boarding establishments. This was not simply because pupils lacked proper study facilities whenever they lived at home. Fundamentally, the school was an agency for imparting a new civilization; its sports, eating, and sleeping facilities, the habits it instilled of prayer in the morning and evening, and the opportunities it afforded for learning English—all were of great importance in the process of "civilizing" the students. A boarding school could recreate, as it were, the civilization of Europe, with its rigorous rules of conduct and Christian world view. The school could isolate its charges from the "corrupting" influences of pagan life and demonstrate to the whole community the advantages of European culture. But if the missionaries were to expand their work into the villages, they lacked qualified personnel and funds to set up boarding schools everywhere. The little "bush schools" that developed instead took their pupils for a few hours daily, and in many ways these schools had to adjust themselves to the community's way of life rather than the reverse.

THE UNEVEN DISTRIBUTION OF MISSION SCHOOLS

With their limited financial and human resources, the various mission groups found it impossible to disperse their schools equally throughout Southern Nigeria. Nor would such a policy have been desirable, since a certain concentration of resources was normally required before the people of a given area could be expected to respond to the missionaries' message. Some areas were favored by missionaries as sites for schools because they were easier to reach, some because they had a greater reputation for conversion than others. For these reasons, the geographical pattern of mission advance was uneven.

The first Africans encountered by missionaries were Yorubas who lived either along the coast, mostly at Badagry and Lagos, or a few miles north of it, at Abeokuta. From these centers missionaries spread into Yorubaland, concentrating first on the Ijebu area (following the conquest of Ijebu-Ode in 1892) and then on Ondo Division to the northeast. In certain areas of Yorubaland, notably the Ibadan and Oyo divisions, the powerful influence of Islam weakened the religious and educational impact of the missions. Yet in other places where Islam was strong, as in Lagos and among the Ijebu Yorubas, Christianity made great forward strides. Another early area of missionary endeavor was far to the east at Calabar, where the Efik people lived. From there missionaries moved north along the Cross River, and by the first decade of this century they had come into contact

TABLE 1. Secondary and Teacher Training Institutions Founded in
Southern Nigeria, 1859–1930

School[a]	Location	Date[b]	Agency
C.M.S. Grammar School	Lagos	1859	C.M.S.
St. Gregory's College	Lagos	1876	R.C.M.
Methodist Boys' High School	Lagos	1878	Methodist
Methodist Girls' High School	Lagos	1879	Methodist
Baptist Boys' High School	Lagos	1885	Baptist
Hope Waddell Training Institute	Calabar, E.R.	1895	C.S.M.
St. Andrew's College	Oyo, W.R.	1896	C.M.S.
Baptist Training College	Ogbomosho, W.R.	1897	Baptist
St. Paul's Training College	Awka, E.R.	1904	C.M.S.
Oron Training Institute	Oron, E.R.	1905	Prim. Meth.
Wesleyan Training Institute	Ibadan, W.R.	1905	Methodist
Abeokuta Grammar School	Abeokuta, W.R.	1908	C.M.S.
King's College	Lagos	1909	Government
Eko Boys' High School	Lagos	1913	Private
Ibadan Grammar School	Ibadan, W.R.	1913	C.M.S.
Ijebu-Ode Grammar School	Ijebu-Ode, W.R.	1913	C.M.S.
Duke Town Secondary School	Calabar, E.R.	1919	C.S.M.
Ondo Boys' High School	Ondo, W.R.	1919	C.M.S.
Ibo Boys' Institute	Uzuakoli, E.R.	1923	Prim. Meth.
Baptist Boys' High School	Abeokuta, W.R.	1923	Baptist
Dennis Memorial Grammar School	Onitsha, E.R.	1928	C.M.S.
United Missionary College	Ibadan, W.R.	1928	C.M.S.–Meth.
St. Thomas's College	Asaba, W.R.	1928	R.C.M.
St. Charles' Training College	Onitsha, E.R.	1929	R.C.M.
Government College	Umuahia, E.R.	1929	Government
Government College	Ibadan, W.R.	1929	Government

ABBREVIATIONS. C.M.S.: Church Missionary Society (Anglican). C.S.M.: Church of Scotland Mission (Presbyterian). E.R.: Eastern Region. Prim. Meth.: Primitive Methodists. R.C.M.: Roman Catholic Mission. W.R.: Western Region.

[a] Oron Training Institute is now Methodist Boys' High School, Oron. Wesleyan Training Institute is now Wesley College, Ibadan. Ibo Boys' Institute is now Methodist College, Uzuakoli. The teacher training wing of Baptist Training College was moved from Ogbomosho to Iwo in 1938 and is now Baptist College, Iwo.

[b] The founding dates given here do not necessarily mean that post-primary education was immediately offered. Many schools, moreover, did not offer a full secondary course until long after they were established. The Baptist Boys' High School in Lagos, for example, attained secondary status in 1921; St. Gregory's College attained secondary status in 1927.

with Ibo-speaking peoples. Still another center of mission activity was Onitsha and its sister port, Asaba, on the western side of the Niger River, but neither gained prominence until early in this century, when intensive efforts were made to convert the Ibo inhabitants of

TABLE 2. Enrollment as a Percentage of School-Age Population by
Province, 1921 and 1931

Province	1921	1931
Western Region:		
Lagos and Colony	28.4%	39.5%
Abeokuta	6.3	7.4
Benin	4.0	10.3
Ijebu	16.7	13.0
Ondo	4.8	7.3
Oyo	2.3	4.4
Warri	6.2	10.4
Eastern Region:		
Calabar	20.4	30.2
Ogoja	2.3	1.5
Onitsha	9.3	11.8
Owerri	5.5	13.5
British Cameroons[a]	1.8	10.4
All provinces	9.2	12.5

SOURCES: P. Amaury Talbot, *The Peoples of Southern Nigeria* (London, 1926), IV,
9–10, 131; Nigeria Census Office, *Census of Nigeria, 1931* (London, 1932), III, 19–21,
29, cited in Grace Awani-Alele, "Dynamics of Education in the Birth of a New Nation" (Ph.D. diss., Dept. of Education, Univ. of Chicago, 1963), p. 118.

[a] British Cameroons was a part of the former German Kamerun, mandated to
Great Britain after World War I.

Onitsha and Owerri provinces, and a somewhat less concentrated
drive began west of the river among the Ibos of Benin Province. The
educational importance of these three locations is illustrated by the
data in Table 1, which show that out of the twenty-six secondary or
teacher training institutions established in Southern Nigeria before
1930, seven (including the first five) were located in Lagos, two in
Calabar, and three in Onitsha-Asaba.

As a result of this pattern of expansion, the Yorubas in the area
that later became the Western Region quickly gained an educational
advantage over the non-Yoruba minority groups in Benin and Warri
provinces, whereas in the Eastern Region a non-Ibo minority group,
the Efiks, first gained an educational advantage, and the Ibo majority began to catch up only in the first and second decades of this century. Table 2 shows the disproportionately high enrollments in some
provinces of Yorubaland in the West and among the Efiks and related groups from Calabar Province in the East. It also shows the tremendous gap between the provinces that led in education—Lagos,
Ijebu, and Calabar—and other provinces, such as Oyo or Ogoja.

The uneven spread of mission schools, by creating objective differences between various ethnic groups, stimulated rivalry between them. The role that educational deprivation and the subsequent desire to compensate for it have played in the development of "tribalism" is explored in some detail in Chapter 4. Here it suffices to note that the two major ethnic groups of Southern Nigeria—the Yorubas and the Ibos—were initially very unevenly matched in terms of primary and post-primary facilities. The 1921 census recorded 14,000 Yorubas and only 4,900 Ibos in the "educated" category.* Moreover, of the twenty-six post-primary institutions listed in Table 1, seventeen were located in Yoruba country and only six among the Ibos. These disparities acted as an incentive for the Ibo people to catch up to the Yorubas, and thus began an educational race that was to have highly significant political consequences. As for the minority groups in the Western and Eastern regions, the uneven spread of schools influenced their demand for separate states within the Federation of Nigeria during the 1950's. The claim by non-Yorubas of Benin and Delta (formerly Warri) provinces that they had been educationally deprived figured prominently in their campaign for a Mid-West state; their argument was usually directed against the Yorubas rather than against the early missionaries who had chosen to work in Yorubaland.[25] In the Eastern Region, the movement for a non-Ibo Calabar-Ogoja-Rivers state has not stressed educational deprivation, because Calabar and Rivers provinces (though not Ogoja) received early and favorable treatment from the missions. In Calabar the Efik-speaking elite has complained of losing its former influence, not of never having tasted power.†

EDUCATION AND CONVERSION

Although the missionaries were unable to spread educational facilities equally among the peoples of Southern Nigeria, they did try to reach all the people in areas where stations were established. Unlike the early Christian missions of Freetown and Cape Coast, which

* All schoolteachers, and any person who had completed Standard Six, were classified as "educated." Among the "imperfectly educated"—those who were attending primary school or who had attended it without completing Standard Six—Ibos held the lead with 130,000 to the Yorubas' 76,000. P. Amaury Talbot, *The Peoples of Southern Nigeria* (London, 1926), IV, 127.

† The Eastern Region's cabinet crisis of 1953, resulting in the overthrow of Eyo Ita by the supporters of Nnamdi Azikiwe, was widely interpreted in Calabar as an Ibo power move to displace an Efik from the government. See Richard L. Sklar, *Nigerian Political Parties: Power in an Emergent African Nation* (Princeton, N.J., 1963), pp. 122–23.

taught in English and purposefully created an urban elite, the primary goal of the Southern Nigerian missions was to convert as many persons as possible.[26] This objective took them back into the rural, or "bush," areas where the vast majority of Africans lived, and it led some groups—notably the Church Missionary Society—to teach in the vernacular. A striking feature of missionary activity was the heavy reliance on the "bush schools" as the key to mass conversion. One advantage of the school was that its pupils could be organized to make an impression on the surrounding community by participating in public processions, displays of drilling, and the like.[27] These events, usually timed to coincide with market days when a particular town was bustling with activity, brought the school's activities to the attention of parents and of children not yet in school.

Since education soon became popular, the best way for a mission to gain support among the people was to provide what they wanted by starting a school. With the passage of time, in fact, the missionaries began to emphasize their role as educators, giving secondary consideration to strictly evangelistic work. Father M. Wauters, a pioneer in Catholic activity among the Ondo and Ekiti Yorubas, wrote: "We knew the best way to make conversions in pagan countries was to open schools. Practically all pagan boys ask to be baptized. So, when the district of Ekiti-Ondo was opened [in 1916] we started schools even before there was any church or Mission house."[28] Of the 186 Catholic churches standing in Ondo Diocese in 1962, not one had been erected before the Catholic school adjacent to it was built.[29]

All the mission groups in Southern Nigeria were interested in educating the common people, but none served this cause more energetically than the Roman Catholics of the Eastern Region. The history of Catholic education in the East can best be told through the words and actions of a remarkable man, Bishop Joseph Shanahan, who from 1905 until his retirement in 1932 was Prefect Apostolic for Southern—in effect, Eastern—Nigeria. Bishop Shanahan's work, which we shall describe in some detail, had a profound effect on the subsequent political history of the Eastern Region, and his career gives an insight into the motives and behavior of missionaries from other denominations as well.

As we have already noted, the Catholics began their work in the East in 1885, when Father Lutz of the Holy Ghost Fathers acquired a mission site at Onitsha. For the first few years the missionaries made little progress; many of them spoke only French, sickness decimated their ranks, and the Ibos' unwillingness to cooperate forced the Fa-

thers to concentrate their efforts on slaves, orphans, and social outcasts. Father Shanahan arrived from Ireland in 1902, and soon after
began reappraising Catholic tactics. There were, as he saw it, a number of alternatives. The mission might continue as a haven for the
castoffs of Ibo society, but the Ibos would then associate the mission
with people from their own culture whom they despised, and the
more important task of penetrating Ibo society itself would thus be
thwarted. Another tactic might be to construct enclosed communities
of Christians on the pattern of the Paraguayan Fathers,* but this
would not be feasible on a large scale owing to lack of funds and
trained personnel. The missionaries might devote their energies to
converting the village chief, hoping that when he turned to Christianity the village would follow suit. But such a technique, though it
might work well in Yorubaland, with its hierarchical social structure,
would not necessarily be as successful among the highly egalitarian
Ibos.

There remained the method, already used by the Protestant missionaries, of converting the children in the villages, and through
them, the elders. Bishop Shanahan observed:

If a Nigerian chief has no desire to go to heaven because he is pretty sure
all his boon companions are going to hell, what will he not do to avoid per-
dition if all his own grandchildren and sons and daughters are going to
eternal happiness? Will they not persuade him that they want him up there
as their family head?[30]

The establishment of a school would not only affect the generation
in power indirectly by changing the orientation of the young; it
would also give the missionary a direct entree to the entire community.

The school keeps the missionary in contact with the people, because the
children give him free entry into every house. He is no longer a stranger,
but a member of the family. This fact alone makes what he can effect, and
what he can prevent, really incalculable. He is known everywhere, and he
alone [among Europeans] can go through the country without danger.[31]

---

* A community along these lines was started by the Société des Missions Africaines at Topo, near Badagry, in 1876. Under rigidly disciplined conditions orphans, redeemed slaves, and local families learned new argicultural techniques.
The scheme was not popular with the Africans and was not repeated elsewhere.
See M. L. Walsh, "The Catholic Contribution to Education in Western Nigeria"
(M.A. thesis, Univ. of London, 1951), chap. 5; J. F. Ade Ajayi, *Christian Missions
in Nigeria, 1841–1891: The Making of a New Elite* (Evanston, Ill., 1965), pp. 114–
16.

Most important, the school's effect on the village would eventually be reflected in society at large, for "those who hold the school, hold the country, hold its religion, hold its future."[32]

By about 1906, having decided that the village school was the key to Catholic expansion, Bishop Shanahan embarked on a series of expeditions deep into Ibo country, using Onitsha as his base. Traveling on foot, by bicycle, or by canoe, he went first to villages and towns to the south and east. By the second decade of the century, the Bishop and his assistants were visiting places never before reached by Europeans in Owerri Province to the south and Ogoja Province to the east. In 1918 the Bishop even undertook a strenuous thousand-mile trip into the virtually uncharted hinterland of the British Cameroons. His aim in all of these ventures was to establish certain major centers of Catholic activity,* each with a central or Standard Six school. Smaller stations surrounding the center would contain schools that taught up to Standard Two or Four, after which the students could attend the central school.

Bishop Shanahan's choice of mission sites and his approach to the people revealed a shrewd understanding of the local society and its values. During his tours he would find out whether neighboring villages were friendly with each other, in which case they might be persuaded to sponsor a school jointly, or were rivals, in which case each village's pride could be appealed to when the siting of a school was being discussed. A town with indigenous religious significance, such as Nri, would be chosen as a mission site both to undercut paganism at its source and to endow the new religion with an aura of traditional eminence. Once a mission was established, great care was taken to set up a local church committee that was responsible for raising money to construct a church, pay the teachers, and carry out other local projects. Every effort was made to place influential men from all quarters of the village on this committee so that its decisions would be universally accepted. The consultation procedure within the church committees was long and involved, as is the African fashion, but once decisions were made, the Bishop could be fairly certain they would be adhered to, because they were self-imposed.

The Bishop employed a number of arguments to convince suspicious villagers of the value of education. He pointed out that the growth of European business and of Native Courts had given rise to

---

* By 1918 these included Ozubulu, Emekuku, Anwa, Ogboli, Calabar, and Nteje. The work in Calabar Province was later entrusted to the Fathers of St. Patrick's Society.

new roles for Africans as interpreters and court scribes, and that such
men held enormous power by virtue of their command of English.
Shanahan would then ask the elders whether they thought it better
to send their own children to school to become interpreters than to
be at the mercy of unscrupulous people from other villages. Since the
common man stood in justifiable fear of the dishonest literate, the
Bishop's argument was well received. When government jobs became
available in large numbers for primary school leavers,* the Bishop
would flourish before the villagers telegrams from Lagos to the mission headquarters at Onitsha requesting qualified clerks. The high
cash value of education was thus made unmistakably clear to people
whose income from agriculture barely enabled them to pay local
court fines. Bishop Shanahan always emphasized to each community
that it would be expected to pay for its own school. In this way, he
believed, the inhabitants would regard education as a privilege and
not as something to be taken for granted.

The effect of the Catholics' extensive efforts in the Eastern Region,
and the close relationship between education and conversion, are
shown by the statistics in Table 3. From 1915 to 1924 the number of
children attending Catholic schools leaped ahead of the number of
Catholics, whereas after 1924 the reverse was the case. The most logical explanation for this is that the initial surge into the schools was
soon reflected in church membership figures, which continued to
soar because the intake of young people was not being offset by deaths
among an older Catholic population. The effectiveness of the school
as a gateway to the church is also indicated by the fact that even as
early as 1920, only one-fourth of the twenty thousand baptized Catholics had been baptized outside the school.[33]

Bishop Shanahan was one of many missionaries who were concerned with educating the people where the great majority of them
lived, not simply in the Europeanized towns of the coast. One result
of this approach to education was a relatively high degree of social
mobility: the children of rural peasants were given the opportunity,
and the desire, to make good in the modern world.[34]

Given the interest of all the Christian missionaries in education
and their desire to reach large numbers of people, it quickly became
apparent that a few persons sent to Nigeria from Europe or the
United States could not do the job alone; Africans themselves were

* As used in this study, the term "school leaver" refers both to a person who has
completed a certain stage of education—normally the primary school course—and
to one who drops out before completing the stage.

TABLE 3. The Catholics in Eastern Nigeria, 1906–32

Year	Catholics	Students	Teachers	Schools and churches
1906	1,488	2,057	33	24
1909	2,894	2,591	58	43
1912	5,563	5,368	124	86
1915	7,924	13,158	256	159
1918	13,042	22,838	552	355
1921	25,000	41,455	927	721
1924	40,768	41,050	1,178	1,026
1929	81,285	37,275	1,947	1,403
1932	110,049	30,390	1,773	1,386

SOURCE: John P. Jordan, *Bishop Shanahan of Southern Nigeria* (Dublin, 1949), p. 140.

needed. Most missionaries realized that the future of the Church depended on the development of a class of indigenous teacher-catechists, men who could establish a village station, teach the children to read and write, instruct them in the catechism, and preach to the entire community on Sunday. These men, as the purveyors of civilization, were to occupy the important intermediate position between the African villagers, who presumably lacked refinement altogether, and the European missionaries, who being overly "civilized" might have difficulty communicating with the Africans and might make too abrasive an impact on their society. Henry Venn, in his instructions to three leading C.M.S. missionaries in 1844, wrote that the native teacher "should not be too highly raised above his countrymen in his habits and mode of living ... [but] he must always be a little ahead of the civilisation of the people around him and by his example and influence lead that civilisation forward."[35]

With so much depending on the production of teacher-catechists, the missions soon confronted the problem of teacher training. They had to balance their desire to train large numbers against their insistence on certain minimum standards—recognizable English and a fund of religious knowledge that bore some resemblance to Christian doctrine. At the start, the missions had to institute a monitorial system of pupil-teachers within the school and use the school's graduates, with only six or eight years of education and no pedagogical experience, to teach elsewhere. As the number of educated Africans increased, teacher training classes were set up, either in separate institutions or in conjunction with secondary school courses.[36] Two teacher training colleges quickly gained renown for their contribution to Nigerian education: Saint Andrew's College in Oyo and Hope Waddell Training Institute in Calabar. The former has been the mainstay of the Anglican secondary school effort in the West, and the graduates of the latter have contributed considerably to education not only in the Calabar area but also in Lagos, Ibadan, Onitsha, and other major towns of Southern Nigeria.

The missions' need for teachers to effect mass conversion, together with the economic and psychological rewards teaching offered, rapidly swelled the number of Nigerians engaged in this calling. There were 3,860 teachers in Southern Nigeria in 1921; a decade later the number had more than doubled to 8,640.[37]

INTERDENOMINATIONAL RELATIONS

Interdenominational relations played an important part in the dynamics of educational expansion in Southern Nigeria, for competition from other Christian groups pressured each denomination to start more schools.* For example, in petitioning the Wesleyan Methodist Missionary Society to open a secondary school in Lagos, leading Methodist citizens of the town wrote in 1874:

> The majority of the community of this town have directly or indirectly been brought under the influence of the teaching of Methodism, but on account of the facilities which are generally afforded by the Church Missionary Society as regards the higher standard of education, many of our people, who have passed under its teaching, have become Churchmen ... [because of] the necessity of their being sent to the Church Missionary Society Grammar School. . . . The result is, after their training, it always becomes very difficult with them to shake off the prejudice which they have imperceptibly imbibed against that Church with which their parents had the honour and privilege to be connected.[38]

The activity of the most education-minded denominations usually spurred the others to follow suit.† For this reason school enrollment grew at a faster rate in Southern Nigeria with several missions operating than it might have with only one, though all too frequently an

---

*Although Roman Catholics do not regard themselves as a denomination, the term "interdenominational" is used in passages concerning Protestant-Catholic relations in preference to such awkward alternatives as "intra-Christian."

† For example, J. K. Coker, a leader in the breakaway African Church Movement, wrote in 1913: "The plan of the Anglican Church of sending so many young men to college to qualify in Arts will surely place us at a disadvantage if these young men cannot be connected to the African Church or if the African Church does not pay great attention to education." "The African Church" (unpublished manuscript, 1913), courtesy J. B. Webster.

unfortunate consequence of inderdenominational rivalry was an unnecessary duplication of school facilities.

Rivalry did exist among the various Protestant denominations, but far more important were the concerted efforts made by Protestant mission leaders to minimize friction among themselves. The comity arrangements or agreements reached by these leaders differed somewhat, however, in Western Nigeria from those in Eastern Nigeria. In the West, the major Yoruba towns were too large for a single mission to minister to the spiritual or scholastic needs of their inhabitants; consequently, two or more Protestant groups were at work in Lagos, Abeokuta, Ibadan, Ijebu-Ode, and Oyo. In the rural areas different missions acquired tacit rights to expand in particular areas—the Baptists around Ogbomosho, the Methodists in Ijebu-Remo, the Church Missionary Society in Ondo and Ekiti, for example—and although no mission could exclude others from its special domain, it was given priority if it wished to expand its activities there. In Eastern Nigeria, comity arrangements between the major Protestant missions were more formal. In a series of conferences in 1909, 1911, 1922, 1925, and 1927, the region was divided into three north-to-south spheres of influence.[39] Broadly speaking, Anglicans were to concentrate on the western third of the region, running parallel to the Niger River. To the Methodists was assigned the middle portion, running north along what became the Port Harcourt–Enugu railway. The eastern third was reserved for the Church of Scotland, which could work the Cross River area to the north of Calabar. In large towns such as Aba and Port Harcourt, all missions were to be allowed a foothold, for friendly competition was not deemed harmful there and each mission could be kept busy with the migrants from its assigned zone.

By the 1920's inter-Protestant cooperation in both regions assumed institutional form with the creation of the Christian Council of Nigeria, composed of the Church Missionary Society (Niger and Yoruba missions), the Niger Delta Pastorate, the Church of Scotland Mission, the Wesleyan Methodist Missionary Society, the Nigerian Baptist Convention, and smaller agencies such as the Salvation Army, the Basel Mission, and the Qua Iboe Mission.* The Council tried to

---

* It is worth noting that although the Southern Baptist Convention in the United States has not favored institutional cooperation with other denominations, as in the World Council of Churches, the Nigerian Baptist Convention, which includes Nigerians, has been more willing to join with other Protestant groups. The pagan environment of Nigeria apparently had the effect of encouraging Protestant solidarity, whereas in the predominantly Protestant United States the Southern Baptists could afford the luxury of insularity.

avoid duplication of effort by the various missions and to present a united Protestant position to the government on education and other matters.

Between Protestants and Catholics, of course, there were no comity arrangements; the rivalry that developed between these two groups was to be of great significance in the political as well as the educational history of Southern Nigeria. To historical and theological differences was added a nationality factor: the bulk of the Protestant missionaries were English or Scottish, whereas the Catholic missionaries came either from Britain's rival for empire during the late nineteenth century, France, or from her obstreperous colony, Ireland. This factor was perhaps most important in relations between the Church Missionary Society, which represented the official Church of England, and the Irish Fathers, whose confreres at home were championing the cause of Catholic Eire. Within the general context of the Protestant-Catholic rivalry, however, there was a significant difference in tone and intensity between the Western and Eastern regions; by all accounts relations were consistently more strained in the East.

Intense rivalry began in the East during the early years of this century. As both Catholics and Anglicans spread out from their common headquarters, Onitsha, into Ibo country, they quickly became engaged in a leapfrogging operation. In the villages of Onitsha Province, where C.M.S. agents had established stations first, the Catholics would enter by taking advantage of rivalries within a village. For example, a quarter that felt it had been slighted in the siting of the Anglican church or school would be persuaded to adopt the Catholic faith so that it could enjoy similar facilities. Traditional rivalries constituting the structural basis of village life were thus reinforced by denominational rivalries, and the reinforcement often had the effect of weakening or even destroying the village's sense of identity. The rivalry in Owerri Province, where in many areas Catholics had arrived first, followed a somewhat different pattern. A village with a Roman Catholic Mission (R.C.M.) school or church would be "presumed lost" by the Church Missionary Society, which would then press on to the next community. The Catholics in their turn would bypass the C.M.S. village and open a station in some neighboring area. Thus Orlu and Emekuku soon became known as Catholic towns, whereas Nkwerre was generally considered an Anglican stronghold.[40] When an influential chief was converted to one faith or the other, he sometimes discouraged other Christian groups from entering his territory. The favored group naturally did not question the chief's exercise of "traditional" authority in such instances. Rivalry was less acute further to the east, in the Methodist and Presbyterian spheres of influence. Still, dislike of the Catholic presence was sufficient to send Mary Slessor, a well-known Presbyterian missionary, on a quick reconnoitering trip to Bende when she heard the Fathers were arriving there. The Church of Scotland had its own unpleasant memories of the papacy in the time of Mary Queen of Scots and did not want Africa to be won for the Holy See.

Several explanations could be advanced for the more intense rivalry east of the Niger than west of it. Probably the most important factor was the unquestioned numerical superiority of the Protestants in the West (as shown in Table 4), whereas in the East the rapid advances in Catholic strength challenged this superiority. Protestant missionaries in the West arrived earlier than the Catholics in almost every area; they had a lead of eleven years (1892, 1903) in Ijebu territory, twenty-one years (1896, 1917), in Ado-Ekiti, and forty years (1875, 1915) in Ondo. Catholic educational activity in the West was also hampered by the fact that many of the early Fathers sent out by the sponsoring body in that region, the Société des Missions Africaines, spoke French rather than English, and some of its members felt that education should not be stressed. In contrast, many areas of Eastern Nigeria were first visited by Catholic missionaries, particularly in Owerri and Ogoja provinces, and the Holy Ghost Fathers under Bishop Shanahan relied heavily, as we have seen, on their schools as the key to mass conversion. In 1921 the Roman Catholic Mission accounted for one-sixth of school enrollment in the West and one-third of enrollment in the East. To illustrate the intensive Catholic activity in the East further, 29 per cent of the Nigerian Protestants in 1921 were Ibo and 30 per cent were Yoruba, whereas 66 per cent of the Catholics were Ibo and only 10 per cent were Yoruba.[41] Eastern Region Protestant missionaries accordingly felt they should accelerate their educational programs to counteract Catholic influence, just as Bishop Shanahan had been influenced in his own choice of tactics by the early success of Protestant schools. Religious rivalry in the East thus fed on itself, and it served as both cause and effect of educational expansion.

Another explanation for the greater rivalry in Eastern Nigeria concerns the number of different religious groups operating in a given area. In the West the religious situation was very complex. There was a large and growing Muslim community advancing, as Table 4 sug-

TABLE 4. Adherents of Religions by Province, 1921
(Number per thousand of population)

Province	Protestant	Catholic	Total Christian	Muslim	Pagan
Western Region:					
Lagos and Colony	191	40	231	401	367
Abeokuta	74	7	81	209	709
Benin	9	8	17	27	955
Ijebu	213	21	234	294	471
Ondo	113	4	118	43	841
Oyo	42	2	44	125	831
Warri	92	10	102	4	894
Eastern Region:					
Calabar	145	24	169	1	830
Ogoja	5	1	6	2	991
Onitsha	34	32	66	2	933
Owerri	90	27	117	2	880
British Cameroons	33	22	55	4	940
All provinces	74	19	93	46	861

SOURCE: P. Amaury Talbot, *The Peoples of Southern Nigeria* (London, 1926), IV, 105.

gests, in the very places where the missionaries had concentrated their efforts: Lagos, Abeokuta, Ijebu-Ode, Ibadan, Oyo, Ogbomosho.[42] Independent African churches were also influential, especially in Lagos and its immediate vicinity. Because comity arrangements in the West tended to avoid setting strict boundaries, each of the various Protestant missions operated in virtually every major Yoruba city. Rivalry between Protestants and Catholics was thus submerged in the struggle for adherents among a large number of religious persuasions. In the East, in contrast, only 2 per cent of the population were Muslims, and those independent religious movements that did exist were more fragmented and less ably led than the ones in Yorubaland. Comity arrangements among the Protestants, moreover, gave the three major denominations their own spheres of influence, and there was far less overlapping of Protestant churches and schools in the East than in the West. As a result, a given area of Eastern Nigeria was usually presented with a choice between the Roman Catholics and one large Protestant denomination, and religious rivalry was polarized rather than diffused.

The pattern of mission advance into the Yoruba and Ibo heartlands may also help to account for the difference between the two regions in Protestant-Catholic relations. In the West, Lagos and Abeokuta served as points of entry into Yorubaland for each of the missions as it arrived, but since some of these missions established centers of operations elsewhere, the two cities did not become focal points for intense interdenominational rivalry. Onitsha, on the other hand, was used as the entry into Iboland for the two major Eastern Region missions, and it remained the headquarters for both. In the nineteenth century, relations between the Church Missionary Society and the Roman Catholic Mission were fairly cordial; in fact, the Catholics' first mission site was on land donated by the Obi of Onitsha to Bishop Crowther, who in turn gave it to the Holy Ghost Fathers. Cooperation deteriorated, however, in the era of Bishop Shanahan, and Onitsha became a focus of bitter competition. Today, on the bluffs overlooking the Niger and within half a mile of each other, two cathedrals—the Anglican and the Catholic—stand as if vying for control of the river and the routes inland.

MISSION EDUCATION AND POLITICAL DEVELOPMENT

We have argued in this chapter that in order to understand the dynamics of educational expansion in Southern Nigeria one must understand the dynamics of the missionary movement that first introduced Western-type schooling: the motives of the missionaries, the timing and geographical direction of their advance, the techniques they employed, and their relationships with each other. The mission impact has not been confined to Southern Nigeria's educational system, however, for through their educational activities the voluntary agencies also affected the area's political development. The fact that the missions had opened schools long before the British established a colonial regime increased the capacity of the new government, for literate Southern Nigerians were available to assume subaltern positions within the government from its earliest years, enabling the British more easily to assume effective control over Southern Nigeria and to engage fairly rapidly in developing its economy. The colonial government did not have to pay for the training of these literate Nigerians. Nor did the government need to convince the populace of the advantages of Western-style progress; the missionaries, after all, spread an interest in the plough as well as in the Bible.

At the same time the early educational activities of the missionaries increased the capacity of Southern Nigerians to resist colonial rule, for the beginnings of their nationalist movement were grounded in the very same values and organizational techniques that had been imported by the Europeans. Within the Christian Church itself, for example, many Nigerians during the late nineteenth and early twentieth centuries left European-controlled denominations to form their own independent religious movements. There were a number of causes of these breakaway movements, but the main one is that the early missionaries' optimistic beliefs about the Africans' potential for religious leadership—symbolized in Bishop Crowther's appointment to the Niger Diocese—were replaced during the 1880's and 1890's by a far more negative view of Africans, in keeping with the racialist and jingoist sentiments that accompanied, and helped to rationalize, European imperialist expansion.[43] Nigerians who had been treated as equal to the white man in ecclesiastical matters now confronted a new type of missionary who was convinced of the inherent inferiority of those he had come to save. When an Englishman was chosen to succeed Bishop Crowther, who died in 1891, Crowther's son and a few others broke with the C.M.S. and established the Niger Delta Pastorate. Other schisms divided the Anglicans in the Lagos area, and the Methodists and Baptists were similarly affected.[44] If we employ Thomas Hodgkin's definition of the term "nationalist" to describe "any organization or group that explicitly asserts the rights, claims and aspirations of a given African society (from the level of the language-group to that of 'Pan-Africa') in opposition to European authority, whatever its institutional forms and objectives,"[45] then the formation of these separatist churches must be regarded as an aspect of early African nationalism.

Mission-educated Nigerians were capable of opposing European authority in the political as well as the religious realm. The existence of several secondary schools in Lagos by the end of the nineteenth century helps to explain the emergence of the Lagos elite that was to give Sir Frederick Lugard such a difficult time during his Governor-Generalship. Enough educated Africans lived in Lagos to support a nationalist press from the 1890's onward—the *Lagos Weekly Record* of John Payne Jackson and then the *Lagos Daily News* of Herbert Macaulay—and it was here that the country's first political party was formed in 1923. In Abeokuta, another early educational center, a remarkable and in many respects very modern experiment in self-government was begun in order to stave off imperial rule over the Egba branch of the Yorubas. From 1898 to 1914, Abeokuta was ruled by the Egba United Government, an effort by the educated and Sierra Leonean elements in the town to form a bureaucracy patterned on the British model that by its very effectiveness would leave the British no excuse to assume control themselves. Had Abeokuta not been a center of mission-sponsored educational activity for fifty years prior to the formation of the Egba government, it is improbable that this imaginative effort would have been conceived, let alone able to postpone the declaration of British sovereignty over the Egbas until the First World War. J. F. A. Ajayi's assessment seems amply justified:

The Christian missionaries introduced into Nigeria the ideas of nation-building of contemporary Europe. They also trained a group of Nigerians who accepted those ideas and hoped to see them carried out, and later began to use those ideas as a standard by which to judge the actions of the British administration. In doing this, the Christian movement sowed the seeds of Nigerian nationalism.[46]

In later years the mission-run secondary schools and teacher training colleges produced the great bulk of Southern Nigeria's political leaders—men who by the 1950's were able to assume the tasks of self-government. As Table 1 shows, twenty-two of the twenty-six post-primary institutions established in Southern Nigeria before 1930 were managed by the missions, three were government schools (two of which were founded in 1929), and one was private. It is therefore quite likely, from a purely statistical point of view, that the secondary education received by most leaders was strongly oriented toward Christianity. Whether this kind of education, in addition to providing skills that men could employ in becoming political leaders, also instilled the ideal and the practice of leadership is difficult to ascertain. It has been said of the mission and Koranic schools during the colonial period that "although both types provided some elementary —one might say, primitive—social skills, neither dared nor cared to approach subjects directly relevant to the training of good citizens in a self-governing Nigeria."[47] This may be true in the sense that modern civics courses were not taught in those days, but there is evidence that in at least some secondary schools a conception of responsible self-government was instilled by the very manner in which the institution was run. A particularly interesting case is that of Methodist College in Uzuakoli, which under the principalship of Rev. H. L. O. Williams from 1924 to 1939 developed a student government that combined traditional and English patterns of government. The pupils lived in a large rectangular compound divided into four houses, each headed by a "Captain," and the equivalent of the Senior Prefect was known as "Chief." The Chief, the Captains, and a few boys elected by the students themselves formed a "Cabinet," which held court fortnightly to try those charged with offenses. Trustworthy students called "Police Constables" served as prosecutors in these cases.[48] It may well be that the practice of self-government within the school partly accounts for the active part later played by Uzuakoli's Old Boys, or alumni, in political life—that they did so is unquestionable. Uzuakoli produced ten Eastern House of Assembly members elected during the 1951–61 period, including a regional Premier and a Minister of Education, and four members of the Federal House of Assembly, elected in 1954 and 1959.

Intentionally or not, mission schools thus increased the capacity of both the British colonial regime and the small group of Southern Nigerians who were eventually to challenge that regime successfully. As for the realization of equality, we have seen how the uneven geographical distribution of mission schools left the Ibo people at an educational disadvantage compared to the Yorubas and Efiks during the early years of this century. Still, the missionaries' commitment to convert the entire populace meant that educational opportunity was not confined to the city but was extended to rural areas as well. And the Biblical message itself, stressing the equality of all men before God and His concern for the salvation of each person, provided Southern Nigerians with an intellectual weapon against the inegalitarian aspects of European colonialism.

The missionary impact on integration in Southern Nigeria may be discussed in terms of its horizontal aspects, which concern cleavages along ethnic and religious lines, and its vertical aspects, which concern communication between the European political and religious elite and the African populace. Insofar as mission patterns of advance gave certain ethnic groups an educational head start over others, the missionaries unintentionally contributed to the ethnic rivalries that serve as a topic of discussion later in this study. At the same time, however, the early secondary schools or training colleges, being few in number, necessarily recruited their students from a large area and thus brought together young men from very different tribal and cultural backgrounds. St. Andrew's College in Oyo, for example, trained a number of teacher-catechists from as far away as the Niger Delta before the training college at Awka, Onitsha Province, was opened in 1904.[49] Hope Waddell Training Institute, the East's only secondary school for thirty years, enrolled students during the early years of the century from Yorubaland, Ghana, and Sierra Leone.* By bringing together young people from different ethnic groups the mission schools helped to broaden the perspectives of potential leaders and fostered friendships across ethnic lines.

* Data concerning the composition of Hope Waddell's enrollment from 1902 to 1963 are given in Table 13, p. 258.

Another important consequence of missionary activity was the introduction of cleavages along religious lines. One division was, of course, that between Christians and Muslims. Another, even more politically important, was the division between Catholics and Protestants. During the late nineteenth century and the early years of the twentieth, rivalry was keenest among the European missionaries, for they brought to their work a knowledge of the schism that had split the Christian Church in the sixteenth century as well as the religious prejudices inherited by European society since that time. But in the process of converting and educating Nigerians, the missionaries conveyed their sentiments to those around them, and many Nigerians adopted as their own the religious fears and stereotypes of their mentors.* Of course, not all Nigerians did so; particularly in the Western Region there has been a remarkably pragmatic attitude toward Christianity and a willingness to shift denominational loyalties if this would further the course of one's education. But in the Eastern Region, at least, sufficient numbers of Africans became personally engaged in the struggle between Protestants and Catholics for religious considerations to interfere with political life. In the Eastern Region's elections of 1957 and 1961, bloc voting along religious lines figured in the election or defeat of certain candidates for the House of Assembly. Perhaps more significant, issues of public policy involving the voluntary agencies have invariably become infused with denominational rivalry, and decisions made on these issues are widely thought to be motivated primarily by religious considerations. The account given in Chapter 7 of universal primary education in the Eastern Region spells out the effect of "religious politics" on the formulation and execution of educational policy.

One difference between Protestant and Catholic missionaries in educational approach has had important political consequences in the East. Table 1 shows that in the period prior to 1930, Protestants dominated post-primary education in both regions: of the twenty-six institutions listed, nineteen were Protestant and only three were Catholic. This fact was of little consequence in the West, for the Protestants also dominated the primary school sector, but in the East, where the Roman Catholic Mission was the largest single denomination at the primary school level, it did have repercussions. Because Bishop Shanahan was convinced that the village primary school could most effectively convert large numbers of people, he neglected secondary education altogether. The result was that none of

---

* For example, a young boy in Onitsha told the author in all seriousness that "Protestants have no morals."

the sixty thousand children attending over one thousand Catholic primary schools in 1927 could receive post-primary training without entering a non-Catholic institution.[50] The Catholic missionaries in the East tried belatedly to rectify this situation with the establishment in Onitsha of St. Charles' Training College in 1929 and Christ the King College four years later. But despite their academic excellence, these institutions obviously could not match the output of Hope Waddell, Uzuakoli, Dennis Memorial, and a few other Protestant or Protestant-oriented schools that had been opened by the early 1930's. As a result the Nigerians who emerged as political leaders in both the East and the West had almost all been educated in Protestant secondary schools or training colleges and consequently viewed events from a Protestant, or at least a non-Catholic, perspective. The legacy of Bishop Shanahan's educational work was that political leadership in the East fell into Protestant hands, whereas the mass base of any political organization would have to be very largely Catholic. Hence public issues that divided the two religious groups were also likely to divide the region's leaders from a substantial segment of their supporters, causing problems of vertical as well as horizontal integration. This phenomenon is discussed further in Chapter 7.

The predominant role of mission groups in education—a role they still play—has had two direct consequences for vertical integration. First, the missions firmly entrenched themselves in the administrative and political system of Southern Nigeria. As the colonial administration began to assume responsibility for education—and it did so increasingly over the years—officials found they had to negotiate with mission leaders in order to achieve any significant change in the kind of schooling provided the masses. The missionaries for their part had to negotiate with African villagers in order to open stations and fill newly built schoolrooms, and if the missions were to expand, they needed to fill at least their lower ranks with trained Africans. The missions thus came to occupy an intermediate position with regard to education, helping the government on the one hand with the formulation and execution of policy and helping the African on the other hand to satisfy his craving for more schooling. Because communication between the rulers and the ruled on educational matters passed through the medium of the missions, they became highly important interest groups whose views could not be disregarded with impunity. The replacement of British by Nigerian rulers did not drastically alter this situation, for virtually all of the new rulers were themselves products of mission schools. As we will point out in Part II, even though the politicians of the 1950's wanted to secularize the school system to some extent, they did not call for the take-over of schools directly under voluntary agency control. Consequently the missions have continued to act as intermediaries in the era of Nigerian self-government.

The teacher-catechists produced by the missions in the drive for mass conversion have been an indispensable link in the communication of ideas between Europeans, whether missionaries or colonial officials, and the people of Southern Nigeria. Indeed, these mission teachers may be said to be the most important indigenous agents of modernization, at least in the rural areas. Bishop Shanahan once paid tribute to their religious contribution in a melodramatic fashion:

They were the real apostles of the people. There would be no Church in the country today if they had not done their work so well.... Who transformed the dying hours of old men whose long lives had been passed in the darkness of paganism? The teacher. Who brought the life of God to dying babies? The teacher. Who controlled the Church services on Sundays and taught the people their knowledge of God? The teacher. Who kept the idea of God and Church before the minds of the people during the long months of the Father's absence? The teacher.[51]

At the same time, mission teachers were in a unique position to understand and to articulate the desires of the people. Teachers assigned to the rural areas were in direct contact with the mass of the population engaged in subsistence agriculture, and they were sometimes the only persons in a large area with sufficient English at their command to communicate popular grievances and demands to Europeans. That they were employed by the missions gave them far more freedom to express themselves and to engage in organizational activities than they would have had as employees of the colonial regime. For these reasons, among others, an unusually large number of Southern Nigeria's political leaders during the 1950's and early 1960's were drawn from the ranks of the mission teachers, who in a previous period had mediated between the European elite and the illiterate masses.

By the 1950's political rather than religious factors were the paramount influence on Southern Nigeria's educational system. But the constraints on political leaders, as well as their desire to expand and change the system, were affected to a large degree by the mission legacy. Thus, not only were the missionaries directly responsible for educational expansion in the short run by opening schools and training teachers; they also had a substantial indirect effect on expansion by influencing the Southern Nigerian political process.

CHAPTER 2

The African Response, 1842–1929

The primary school system of the South is almost entirely the result of popular demand and the response of
voluntary effort to that demand. It is . . . largely the creation of the people themselves, guided by the disinter-
ested devotion of the Christian missions.
—SIR SIDNEY PHILLIPSON

To understand the growth of Southern Nigeria's educational system,
we must assess not only the efforts of the European missionaries but
also the response of the indigenous culture they came to change. One
cannot, in fact, comprehend the educational strategies of the missionaries themselves without taking the African factor into account, for
the different response rates of local groups to missionary work
strongly influenced decisions about the location of mission schools,
normally in favor of those groups that seemed most receptive to Christianity and education. Bishop Shanahan's emphasis on Iboland, for
example, must have been influenced by his intuition that, as a current saying goes, "Ibos make good Catholics." On the other hand,
several of the early missionaries in Western Nigeria planned to concentrate their efforts among the Muslim states north of Yorubaland,
but they abandoned this strategy when it became clear that the organized hostility encountered there would make their efforts almost
useless. Attainment of the missionaries' goals depended, from the very
beginning of their efforts, on their sensitive response to the variety of
African responses to them. The African factor thus strongly influenced the density and distribution of enrollment in mission schools.

It is not sufficient, however, to know who went to school; one would
also like to know what meaning this act had for Southern Nigerians.
Culture contact never results in the uncritical and wholesale adoption by one group of the customs and beliefs of another. Invariably
the less dominant group is selective in its absorption of foreign cultural elements,[1] and the reasons its members have for adopting a pat-

tern of behavior may differ sharply from the reasons for that pattern's evolution within the dominant culture or for its export to the recipient culture. The social and psychological functions of education are not necessarily the same in England and Southern Nigeria; certainly the motives of the missionaries in setting up schools were different from the motives of local parents in sending their children to those schools. A study of the African factor is necessary if we are to understand this subjective dimension of educational expansion.

This chapter attempts to answer several questions concerning the popular response to education: Are there stages or patterns of response, and if so, how may they be described? What were some of the reasons for the acceptance or rejection of education? Who were the most important indigenous agents in stimulating a widespread demand for new schools? What factors may have been responsible for the variety of responses to education by different tribes or subtribes? What effects has the African response had on the nature of Nigeria's educational system?

STAGES OF RESPONSE

A British social anthropologist, Margaret Read, has suggested that the African response to British education went through several stages over time.[2] Africans initially rejected the schools and what was taught there because they clearly perceived education to be a threat to their traditional way of life. Then certain skills and habits learned in school—reading and writing, handling money, wearing a uniform—gained acceptance by the African community. The third stage was marked by the rejection of certain traditional patterns, such as tribal rites connected with puberty. In the fourth stage, British education was enthusiastically accepted in its entirety, as Africans strove to prove themselves on the colonial ruler's own ground by passing European-oriented public examinations. Then began a reevaluation of African culture by those who "had gone furthest in the studies in the dominant culture, . . . had proved their ability to benefit by them, and . . . were therefore free from the fear of being held back if they looked back to their own past and their own traditional culture."[3] In a final stage the school curriculum is suitably Africanized to reflect a new cultural self-awareness and to help produce a feeling of national identity. The first four of these stages describe the situation in Southern Nigeria during the period up to 1930.* Generally, the Ni-

* There were signs of the fifth stage in the late 1940's. It is doubtful whether the sixth has been reached in Nigeria even in the 1960's.

gerian response to education shifted from rejection to partial acceptance to wholesale adoption of the British system of education,
although within this pattern there were several variations that will
be noted.

There were a number of instances of outright rejection of or public
apathy toward mission schools, particularly before the First World
War, when the financial advantages of literacy were not so widely
appreciated as they were later. For example, an attempt by Bishop
Crowther in 1875 to start a mission and school in the Benin River
area failed because of strong opposition from the local chiefs.[4] No
Christian missionaries were allowed to enter Opobo during the reign
of Jaja or to establish stations in Ijebu-Ode until the British occupied
the town in 1892. Some groups, such as the Isokos of Delta Province
or the inhabitants of Abakaliki Division in the East, remained resis-
tant to schooling well into the twentieth century.

In many places where schools were opened they proved virtually
ineffective. An official report on the Aba District in 1911 observed:
"The Aba School is not a success and never was. The Aba people do
not want this school and do not make use of it. Practically all the
pupils come from places not in the Aba jurisdiction. This school is
merely a waste of money and would be better abolished."[5] In other
places schools were accepted, but in a manner that indicated misgivings about the consequences. In 1911, Rev. F. W. Dodds of the Primitive Methodist Mission journeyed to Uzuakoli, a town in Bende Division that had been prominent as a slave market during the late
nineteenth century and where government officials suspected continued slaving activities. Dodds encountered great hostility from the
Uzuakoli elders, who charged that the coming of the white man interfered with their customs, their trading patterns, and their way of
dispensing justice. Only after he had talked at length about the benefits of education did they allow him to open a school, on the condition
that it was not to be located near the market. The elders recognized
the advantages a school would provide within the framework of a
new economic order, but at the same time they shrewdly foresaw and
tried halfheartedly to delay its destructive impact on the old order.*
Another example of a mixed reaction to education was the chiefs'
practice of sending young slaves instead of their own sons to school
to test the effects of European learning.

* In recounting this incident, Dodds added that the son of the chief who led
the opposition to him was sent to the school and later became a certificated Methodist teacher. See A. J. Fox, *Uzuakoli* (London, 1964), pp. 93–102.

To the young people themselves, attendance at school meant an interruption of more enjoyable pursuits, and for this reason it was often difficult at first to attract large numbers to class. Writing to Henry Venn just after the opening of the first school in Onitsha, Bishop Crowther described the local boys:

[They] love to rove about in the plantations with their bows and bamboo pointed arrows in their hands to hunt for birds, rats and lizards all day long without success; but now and then half a dozen or more of them would rush into the [school] house and proudly gaze at the alphabet board and with an air of disdain mimick the names of the letters as pronounced by the schoolmasters and repeated by the girls, as if it were a thing fit only for females and too much confining to them as free rovers of the fields. But upon a second thought, a few of them would return to the house and try to learn a letter or two.[6]

In other places Western education quickly won acceptance, particularly where influential men in the community favored cooperation with the missionaries. Bonny, under its kings William Dappa Pepple and George Pepple, quickly took advantage of the schooling offered by Crowther, and the missionary efforts in Abeokuta were well received from the first moment of mission contact with the town. Surprisingly, however, Africans in the areas where education was initially accepted were the most likely to develop a suspicious attitude toward it later, as the persecution of Christians in Bonny and Abeokuta during the late 1860's suggests. Although this reaction was caused by the Christians' suspected role in undermining the autonomy of these towns, Christianity and education were so integrally related that school enrollments suffered during such episodes. A twentieth-century reaction against education took place on an even larger scale in parts of Yorubaland during the 1930–31 Babalola movement.* The initial effect of this movement was a great increase in school attendance by pagans and Muslims, but when Babalola's followers later turned against all organized religion, attendance dropped for a time to 10 per cent of the normal figure.[7] Such reversions to hostility or rejection expressed the ambivalence felt by many Africans toward schooling and its effects on their way of life.

In Nigeria, as we have seen, the school was an agency for transmitting far more than basic education and the catechism. It was, as Read has written, "a culture deliberately set up within another culture,"[8] and certain elements of European culture that the school relayed to

---

* The movement was named after Joseph Babalola, a young engine driver employed by the Public Works Department who experienced a sudden conversion and began to preach a faith-healing message.

its African surroundings were accepted more rapidly than the school itself. For example, the information dispensed in arithmetic classes on the value of different types of currency was quickly utilized by pupils and their parents, for money was becoming increasingly important, whether it was used to pay court fines and taxes or to purchase imported consumer goods.

The rejection of traditional practices described in Read's third stage is represented in Southern Nigeria by the decline of the indigenous bush school, the means by which African cultural values and practices were passed on to the younger generation. Among many African peoples, children were taken away from their families at the start of puberty and sequestered in the bush, the boys being separated from the girls. There knowledgeable elders trained them intensively in folklore, agricultural skills, group cooperation, and self-discipline; at the completion of the training, rites were held to initiate the young people into an adolescent age-grade, signifying the end of childhood.[9] Initial resistance to Western schooling was based in part on a desire to preserve this traditional form of education. Once children began to attend the new schools, bush schools died out, and many cultural values were no longer transmitted. The new schools also weakened the age-grade system because children in class obviously could not perform the tasks normally assigned to them, such as sweeping the village streets and clearing bush paths. Teacher-catechists did not need to inveigh against the bush school or the age-grade system; their very presence as agents of another civilization was sufficient to weaken the hold of these traditional institutions.*

The fourth stage—enthusiastic acceptance of education—is the primary concern of this book. Within the general pattern of acceptance in Southern Nigeria, however, there were significant variations. In some places, the value of education became apparent at first to only one person, who pursued his training in spite of the hostility or apathy of those around him. Mazi Mbonu Ojike, a prominent Eastern Region politician during the mid-1950's, states in his autobiography that he and his brothers began attending school in spite of their father's opposition.[10] When it was seen that education helped these persons to become successful, the schools gained a wider base of support. Sometimes a particular family emphasized academic excellence,

_____

* Where Islam was strong, as in northern and western Yorubaland, Koranic schools offered a viable alternative to Christian ones. But the indigenous bush schools were not linked to an expansionist world religion, and this was doubtless a major reason for their failure to survive.

either because the head of the family had received training himself
or because he wished for his children the benefits denied him by his
own lack of schooling.[11] In many families two or more brothers
achieved prominence, owing largely to their father's insistence on the
value of education.

Far more significant in numerical terms than the favorable response
of individuals and families were the responses of groups of people,
from villages and clans up to the tribal level. At certain times the enthusiasm for education swept through entire communities, often accompanied by mass conversion to Christianity. An epidemic response
of this sort apparently affected Ijebu territory after 1892, for by 1921
Ijebu Province was 23 per cent Christian—a higher percentage than
any other Southern Nigerian province, including Lagos Colony—
and its ratio of schoolchildren to total population was about one to
thirty, whereas in Abeokuta the ratio was about one to seventy-five,
and in Oyo Province, about one to two hundred.[12] Ijebu enthusiasm
thus more than compensated for the lead that had been acquired by
the Egbas during the nineteenth century and far surpassed the response to education of the Yorubas in Ibadan and Oyo divisions, who
had been visited by missionaries during the 1850's. About 1911 rapid
conversion began in Ondo Province, eventually to become the most
thoroughly Christianized of the Yoruba provinces. Such responses
were not only the result of European mission work: the rapid conversion rate east of the railway line between Lagos and Ogbomosho
during the period from 1890 to 1921 was caused by a series of spiritual
movements led in many instances by Africans who had broken with
the conventional denominations.[13]

In Eastern Nigeria similar rapid conversions took place. The Ohaffias, an Ibo subtribe living near the Cross River, were notorious in the
nineteenth century as headhunters and slave-gatherers for the Aros,
a people who exercised extensive religious and judicial authority
throughout the East because they controlled an oracle (known to Europeans as the Long Juju). The Ohaffia attitude toward the Church
of Scotland missionaries was initially one of intense hostility, but
with the opening of a school at Elu in 1911, suddenly "the desire for
education swept the Ohaffia towns like a bush fire. . . . Chiefs came in
with their retainers to lay donations of money before the eyes of the
missionary as proof of their intentions to support the new learning."[14] Support for the new learning has been intense ever since, and
by the mid-1960's no less than five Ohaffias had received doctoral degrees. The reception of education among the Aros was similar:

Although [the Long Juju] had been the centre of their wealth and power, their high intelligence quickly adapted them to the new ways the white man was bringing.... Among the people of such a virile tribe the missionaries found opportunities for the spread of the Gospel greater than they could have dreamed a few years before. The growth of the work was as rapid as it had been slow in the early days.[15]

Ibos living closer to the Niger showed a greatly increased interest in education at almost exactly the same time as the Ohaffias. Bishop Shanahan noted a very friendly response in the villages he visited during 1911, and by 1912 the Catholics began to fall behind in meeting requests for teachers.[16] The intensity of the drive for education among the Onitsha and Owerri Ibos is evidenced by the fact that in 1921, when Southern Nigerian schools that were not receiving government assistance enrolled 111,000 pupils, 47,000 came from these two provinces alone.[17]

FACTORS IN THE ACCEPTANCE OR REJECTION OF EDUCATION

Many diverse factors were involved in the acceptance or rejection of education in Southern Nigeria. Sometimes education was rejected because it challenged traditional ways of life, or because it was closely associated with other aspects of European culture—most notably Christianity—that were regarded with suspicion. Economic factors played a role on occasion; chiefs, for example, feared the loss of income and prestige that might result if educated young men forsook local trading positions for government employment in the cities or elsewhere.[18]

The reasons for accepting education were even more varied, and when an African parent decided to send his child to school, his motives were probably complex. Most important, schooling opened up a host of hitherto undreamt-of possibilities for its recipient. A perceptive English observer wrote in the 1920's:

[Education] is to the present generation of adults what a gun was to the previous generation—something which will put them on a level with the European who has come into their midst. For reading and writing are to the "raw" Native not merely a new thing, but a new *kind* of thing. In the same way to our own forefathers the steam engine was not only a new method of locomotion but something which involved altogether a new principle.[19]

Once the European had clearly gained control over the Africans, and the latter saw that revolt was useless because of the colonial ruler's military and technical superiority, many felt compelled to discover the source of the white man's power and to participate in it.* Education offered a clue to that power, and it now reaped the reward of being associated in the public mind with the new rulers and their religion. The close connection between the school and Europeanization can be seen in the attitude of illiterates toward educated Africans, who are often referred to in Yoruba today as "Oyinbo alawo dudu," or dark-skinned Europeans; in earlier decades the "right" to wear European clothing was virtually confined to literate Africans.

If education was for some the entree to European civilization in its fullness, for others the school provided certain quite specific and limited "civilizing" benefits. A letter from the people of Abeokuta to Queen Victoria in 1848 requested: "We want all those who will teach our children mechanical arts, agriculture, and how things are prepared as Tobacco, Rum and Sugar."[20] The letter from the Calabar chiefs quoted in Chapter 1 requested instruction in the most productive use of the labor surplus created by the abolition of the slave trade. The people of Itu initially wanted a mission and school because they feared an attack from nearby Calabar and thought that the presence of Mary Slessor, a missionary, would forestall the attack.[21] In this instance the missionaries represented the Pax Britannica; as the weaker party in the dispute with Calabar, Itu knew that a guarantee of peace would protect it.

In Southern Nigeria, as in Ghana,[22] it was not until the British administration consolidated its authority and began to stimulate basic changes in the economy that the African demand for schooling became widespread. It is significant that mass "conversions" to education among groups as diverse as the Ondo Yorubas and the Ohaffia and Owerri Ibos occurred almost simultaneously between 1910 and 1912, a decade after Southern Nigeria was formally declared a protectorate and a time when Great Britain's impact was first being seriously felt back of the coast. The African acceptance of education was clearly linked to employment opportunities created by the colonial presence. The British administration needed literate young men to fill minor positions; the missions needed teachers; businesses (such as the United Africa Company and John Holt's, Ltd.) needed accountants, produce buyers, and salesmen. Very soon funds spent to educate the young came to be regarded quite explicitly as an invest-

---

* Following the conquest of Ijebu-Ode in 1892, the Ijebu rulers reversed their previous stand of cultural isolation from Europe and specifically requested the religion of their conquerors. This helps to account for the strength of the Anglicans in Ijebu country. Interview with J. B. Webster, March 4, 1964.

ment in future employment that would yield high and steadily increasing returns. Each year of additional schooling was believed to raise a young person's job income to a level that rapidly compensated for the school fees incurred and income foregone during that year. The popular association of education with salaried employment is well known, and even today, when the enormous increase in school enrollments has destroyed the efficacy of the First School-Leaving Certificate as a sufficient condition for employment, the belief that certificate and job *should* be linked is tenaciously held by millions of Nigerian parents and schoolchildren.

Mistrust of literates was, ironically enough, an extremely important factor in the early popular enthusiasm for literacy. Education provided a man with the tools to exploit as well as to serve others, and the first literates, employed by government and by European business firms, often took advantage of their unique position as intermediaries between the white man and the African to exploit their own countrymen. An interpreter might threaten to distort an illiterate's story unless offered a bribe; a commercial agent might undervalue a farmer's produce, knowing that the farmer could not check the offered price against the list price in the agent's notebook. Even if these linguistic middlemen were not personally unscrupulous, they were the bearers of bad tidings from the new rulers—of head and hut taxes, orders for arrest, higher quality controls for cash crops. The only way to protect oneself against dishonest literates or to check on the validity of the directives relayed by an employee of the government was to learn to read and write oneself, or to have a younger member of the family taught these vital skills.*

Traditional rivalries between quarters, villages, and clans led Africans to use the missionaries and their schools to gain advantages over each other. The presence of a school in one community would rouse fears in other communities that they were falling behind in the race for progress, and they would hasten to have schools of their own built. The establishment of a school in Bonny by Bishop Crowther provoked an early instance of rivalry between towns. Referring to the example of Bonny, the King of Brass in 1867 begged Crowther to establish a school in his own town; the same Bonny school "was the only inducement of the New Calabar Chiefs in requesting the Bishop to establish his mission in their country."† The chiefs were

---

* As we have seen, Bishop Shanahan used this argument quite effectively to convince Ibos of the usefulness of education.

† E. M. T. Epelle, *The Church in the Niger Delta* (Port Harcourt, 1955), pp. 21, 28. New Calabar was located in the creek area northwest of Bonny and is not to be confused with Calabar.

so eager to have a school established that they paid virtually all the fees for a boarding institution, which became the nucleus of the Bishop Crowther Memorial School in Abonnema. Within a town or village, rivalry was sometimes expressed by the establishment of a number of schools, one for each quarter or important segment of the community. In the early years the paucity of teachers limited the number of schools within a village, but by the 1940's the proliferation of small and therefore uneconomic schools was a problem viewed with great seriousness in the Department of Education. The contest for prestige and power within African society resulted in a pressure for more education from those who, justifiably or not, believed themselves to be falling behind some other group. And the size of the relevant group seemed to expand over time; educational competition, which at first was confined to small communities, began to occur in the late 1920's at the subtribal level or higher, as expressed in the educational activities of tribal or progress unions.[23]

AGENTS OF EDUCATIONAL EXPANSION

For Africans, education provided access to the power and wealth of the European ruler; it also enhanced individual dignity and group prestige. Not all Africans, however, were equally aware of the benefits of schooling, and it usually fell to certain persons and groups to act as the agents of educational expansion, either by publicizing these benefits or by actually arranging to open new schools. The catalytic agent might be a traditional ruler, like Sodeke of Abeokuta, who welcomed Freeman and Townsend, or the Oba of Ilesha, himself a Christian, who upon his installation in 1891 invited the Methodists into his kingdom. In the East, shortly after a British expedition in 1902 destroyed the Long Juju, the head chief of the Aros took the lead in requesting missionaries and offered to build a house for any who came.[24] The key figure might be an influental herbalist, like Agwu Otisi of the Abiriba Ibos, who early in the century "realized that the old gods were doomed ... destroyed his jujus in front of the townspeople and renounced the influence he had claimed as a witch doctor.... Before his death he called his relatives young and old about him, and strictly charged them that the young members of his family must be given education."[25] A native son who had been highly educated sometimes provided the needed initiative for education in his community. After attending Fourah Bay College in Sierra Leone, Rev. M. C. Adeyemi of Ondo returned to his home and with the assistance of the traditional rulers established Ondo Boys' High School in 1919.

Two occupational groups, traders and migrant farm workers, were also instrumental in the establishment of schools. The growth of schools in Ilesha during the early 1900's, for example, was encouraged by the African traders, who needed literate young men to assist them in working out the most favorable arrangements with the European traders who were then penetrating the area.[26] During the same period farm laborers began to migrate from many parts of Yorubaland to work on the cocoa plantations being established by wealthy African merchants near Lagos. There they came into contact with Christianity and acquired a taste for education; on returning to their homes they transmitted the desire for new ways to those around them. The first Catholic initiatives in Ondo began with a request for priests by migrant farm workers who had learned of Catholicism while on the plantations.[27] The spread of the independent African Church movement was particularly aided by the farm laborers, since many of the plantation owners were active in the movement.*

The role of the independent religious movements in the expansion of education, at least in Yorubaland, has been of some importance, for through these movements many Africans who otherwise would have turned to Islam adopted Christianity. At a time when traditional local religions failed to halt the coming of new ways, and foreign missionary efforts virtually required literacy for acceptance into the Church, many Africans were attracted by the methods of the independent African religious movements, which demanded only a simple confession of faith before baptism. The African churches emphasized emotion and faith rather than the intellectual component of religion and were thus able to convert to Christianity thousands of persons whose spiritual needs were not adequately met by the more cerebral approach of the European missionaries.[28] Had the same Africans become Muslims, they would have been less disposed to send their children to Anglican or Catholic schools, for example, than they were as Christians. The independent churches freed, as it were, a large number of young people for recruitment into the schools of the denominations that did emphasize education. Moreover, the school was

---

* "[Their] purpose was to send the labourers home with a Yoruba Bible which they could read and from which they might draw spiritual and moral sustenance. Thus while evening classes [in the vernacular] were optional, Sunday church services were virtually compulsory. By 1920, more than 10,000 Yorubas were carrying the Bible and the plough, or more specifically Christianity and cocoa throughout the length and breadth of their homeland." See James Bertin Webster, "The Bible and the Plough," *Journal of the Historical Society of Nigeria*, II, 4 (Dec. 1963), 432.

still an element in the African churches' plans for expansion, and since these churches had no intention of seeking comity arrangements with the conventional denominations, they often set up their own schools directly opposite the ones founded by their rivals. The resulting competition among the schools for pupils led the African churches to assign more importance to education than they had before.*

Leaders of the independent church movement who were prominent planters—J. K. Coker, F. E. Williams, A. A. Obadina, Rev. J. A. Lakeru, T. B. Dawodu, and S. S. Jibowu, among others—helped introduce vocational training to Nigeria. At Ifako, near Lagos, they established in 1917 the African Normal and Industrial Institute, where mechanics, domestic science, and agriculture were taught. The Institute did not outlast the economic crash of 1921, but a teacher training college for the African Church was built on the same site and is still in operation. Mojola Agbebe, the African Church leader, preached "the gospel of coffee, cocoa, cotton and work as well as the scriptures," and with the help of a West Indian established Agbowa Industrial Mission, which operated from 1895 to 1908.[29] The approach of these men to industrial education was similar to that of Booker T. Washington in the United States, although they were more vigorous than Washington in protesting the black man's subservient status.

THE DIFFERENTIAL GROUP RESPONSE TO EDUCATION

For a variety of reasons certain Southern Nigerian groups responded more rapidly and enthusiastically to schooling than others; no single-factor theory can possibly do justice to this differential response. Here we shall touch on some factors that appear to have been important: location, residential patterns, traditional values and patterns of authority, attitudes toward religion, and wealth.

A group of people living along the Nigerian coast, or along an important trade route, was naturally more likely to come into contact with Europeans than a group living in the hinterland or in an eco-

* The merger of the Salem and Bethel branches of the African Church in 1922 was marked by a resolution of the General Committee making baptism conditional on knowledge of the catechism and literacy as well as a confession of faith. See James Bertin Webster, *The African Churches among the Yoruba, 1888–1922* (Oxford, 1964), p. 129. J. K. Coker, the African Church leader, particularly insisted on education and financed the studies of no less than thirty young people, including four in England. See James Bertin Webster, "The Bible and the Plough," *Journal of the Historical Society of Nigeria*, II, 4 (Dec 1963).

nomically backward area. Coastal or riverine ports such as Lagos, Brass, Bonny, Onitsha, and Calabar gained educational as well as economic advantages from their long-standing relations with Europeans, and educated Africans from these towns were the first Nigerian teachers to enter the interior. In contrast, tribes in the Ogoja and Abakaliki areas of Eastern Nigeria had almost no contact with Europeans, much less with educators, until the second decade of the twentieth century. The Egbado Yorubas, although they lived close to Lagos, were bypassed by the railroad to the north and did not emerge from cultural stagnation until the 1940's. The Anang Ibibios lived close to the sea but were blocked from early contact with the West by Jaja of Opobo's policy of denying Europeans access to his hinterland. In addition, the Church of Scotland's interest in establishing missions in the Cross River area left them educationally neglected for years.[30] Geographical factors also contributed to the relative educational decline of the Niger Delta's inhabitants. Because of the difficulties of staffing and managing schools in the swampy creek areas, the Ijaws had by 1930 retrogressed from an educationally advanced to a backward state, at least in comparison with the major inland tribes.

Although it might be expected that urban populations would accept education more readily than others,* the Yorubas, who are urbanized to a degree unique in Africa, did not respond as quickly and positively to education as the Ibos, who live in densely populated but much less urbanized areas. The large Yoruba towns showed the effects of early missionary influence and hence had respectable enrollment figures, but their very size may have militated against their experiencing the sudden, intense, and virtually total conversion to education that occurred in the more compact Ibo villages. The latter were large enough to support a school yet sufficiently small for their inhabitants to know what other villagers were thinking, and village loyalty was usually strong enough to create a sense of competition between neighboring communities.[31]

The receptivity of traditional societies to change is another important factor in differential group responses to education. Several au-

---

* Daniel Lerner has suggested that "the more people there are in a given area ... the harder it is to get a rising proportion of literates among them—until they begin to be redeployed in cities. ... In populous societies urbanization ... is critical for the take-off toward increasing literacy. Only when dense populations show a significant rate of urbanization do literacy rates being to rise." See Lerner, *The Passing of Traditional Society: Modernizing the Middle East* (New York, 1958), p. 66.

thors have noted that the Ibos have a high capacity for change; even before the imposition of British rule they displayed a quite modern willingness to migrate, to adopt useful customs from other tribes, and to reward personal achievement.[32] The current stereotype of the Ibo as "pushy" and aggressive is the grudging tribute paid by other ethnic groups to the Ibos' orientation toward progress. The school may be viewed as an imported, modern institution through which the Ibos have been able to channel their traditional behavioral dispositions. They not only caught up with the Yorubas, who had a head start in education, but also eventually surpassed them in many respects.*

Why are some traditional societies more receptive to change than others? One explanation, advanced by David Apter, is based on a distinction between two types of value systems: some societies judge an action by its immediate, tangible results, whereas in others an action is meaningful only in association with transcendental values. Apter has called the first type of value "instrumental" and the second "consummatory." Societies with instrumental values are seen as more receptive to change because they are able to judge an innovation on its own merits without reference to an entire system of interrelated social, economic, and religious values. In contrast, societies with consummatory values may view a single innovation as a threat to their fundamental social institutions. Thus one would expect modernization to take place more readily in instrumental systems than in consummatory ones.[33] The distinction between instrumental and consummatory value systems is not very helpful, however, in explaining the differential response of Nigerian ethnic groups to education. Although according to Apter the Ibos and the Hausa-Fulani of Northern Nigeria both have instrumental value systems, the Hausa-Fulani have resisted education almost as heartily as the Ibos have accepted it. Instrumentalism is also presumably characteristic of the Yorubas, who as a whole have not caught on as rapidly to education as the Ibos.

Another factor in the receptivity of a traditional society to change is the structure of authority within it. In accounting for the more rapid acceptance of education by the Baganda of Uganda than by the Ashanti of Ghana, Apter suggests that because authority among

---

* By 1921, 130,000 Ibos were attending or had attended primary school without completing Standard Six, as compared to only 76,000 Yorubas. The Yorubas held a considerable lead at the post-primary level, but by the early 1940's this gap had been virtually closed as well. See P. Amaury Talbot, *The Peoples of Southern Nigeria* (London, 1926), IV, 127; James S. Coleman, *Nigeria: Background to Nationalism* (Berkeley, Calif., 1958), p. 333.

the Baganda was "hierarchical," or highly centralized, education and other aspects of modernity could be rapidly spread among the populace once the king, or Kabaka, and the other influential members of the society approved of them. Among the Ashanti, however, authority was "pyramidal," or more decentralized; the Asantehene was a ritual but not a political leader, so that even had he favored education he could not have affected popular attitudes as directly as the Kabaka.[34] But the inference from these two cases should not be that hierarchical societies are more easily modernized than pyramidal ones; rather it is that hierarchical societies are likely to respond more uniformly to outside influences than pyramidal ones, whether in a progressive or a conservative direction. In a pyramidal society, where power is held by individuals at the local level, the response is likely to vary from place to place depending on the attitude of the local elite. In a "segmental" society, where power is highly diffused, one might again expect a uniform response, depending for its direction on the general response of the people. Thus, taking the Southern Nigerian case, wide variations in response to education may be noted among the "pyramidal" Yorubas, reflecting the fact that in such areas as Ilesha, Ife, and Ondo the traditional rulers initially welcomed missionaries and schools, whereas their counterparts in Ibadan and Oyo did not. Similarly, the more even pattern of Ibo response may be accounted for by the absence of local Ibo rulers whose differing views on education might have affected large numbers of people.

The influence on educational expansion of the egalitarian social values common to most African societies can be much more clearly seen than the influence of instrumental and consummatory values or of structures of authority. Philip Foster's observations about Ghana in this regard apply equally well to Nigeria and, for that matter, to most African territories. After pointing out that social class distinctions have retarded the popular demand for secondary education in parts of the Western world, Foster contrasts the situation in Ghana, where "class correlated values which limit the educational aspirations of subgroups do not appear to have emerged.... There has been a fundamental cultural egalitarianism in the education field reflected in a rapid diffusion of educational demand at all levels of society."[35] Within a given ethnic group there was no significant category of persons who believed that Western education was suitable for others but was "not for the likes of us." Consequently, when the leaders of a particular group decided to send their own children to school, their example was widely emulated among the populace.

Differences in the impact of Islam and in traditional attitudes toward religion may help to account for the different evolution of education among the Yorubas and the Ibos. By the mid-nineteenth century the influence of Islam in Yorubaland was already significant, owing largely to the establishment of trade routes connecting the Muslim emirates in the north with the major Yoruba towns, and to the famous *jihad* or holy war of Othman dan Fodio, whose followers had overrun the northern portions of Yorubaland by the 1830's. The existence of a sizeable Yoruba Muslim population kept many young people from receiving a Western education, since their parents justifiably feared that a child with mission schooling would convert to Christianity. As Table 4, p. 48, shows, the Muslim population in 1921 was almost double that of the Christians in Lagos Colony and almost three times as large in Abeokuta Province; Muslims even outnumbered Christians in Ijebu Province. The Yorubas in these areas responded well to education, but they could not do so as wholeheartedly as the Ibos, among whom Muslims accounted for only 2 per cent of the population. Muslim unwillingness to attend Christian mission schools was not confined to Southern Nigeria; it has been noted in many other places where the two religions have confronted each other, such as Northern Nigeria and India.[36]

Given the theological differences between Christianity and Islam, one would expect to find considerable tension between Yorubas of opposing faiths, manifesting itself ultimately in politics. In fact this has not happened, because the Yorubas have adopted a highly pragmatic approach to religion: "Both Islam and Christianity have gained large numbers of adherents, especially Islam, yet neither of these religions holds together the social edifice; they are simply the religious departments of life. Thus the act of joining one or the other does not undermine the social structure, and the family remains the real cement of Yoruba Society."[37] Among the Ibos, on the other hand, the rivalry between Protestants and Catholics seriously undermined the social structure of many villages. The reasons for the more doctrinaire Ibo approach to religion are unclear. Whatever they may be, the deep social cleavages that were created within Ibo society in the process of conversion to one Christian persuasion or another help to account for the intensity of Catholic-Protestant rivalry in Iboland and for the intrusion of religious matters into political life.

The relationship between wealth and differential response to education is not at all clear. In general the Yorubas benefited economically from the introduction of cocoa late in the nineteenth century;

concentrated at first around Lagos, Abeokuta, and Ijebu-Remo, cocoa farming had spread to Ondo Province by the early 1920's. Only in southern Yorubaland did there develop a well-to-do landed African middle class (similar to that in the southern Gold Coast) that could afford to educate its children in Great Britain. But the income from cocoa was not responsible for the popular reaction to schooling, since in many areas this reaction occurred before the cocoa trees began to yield their maximum dividends.[38] Moreover, there was no guarantee that high income, earned from whatever source, would be spent on education. The ease with which an uneducated Ibadan man, for example, could acquire wealth, either by tilling the rich soil or by trading in that great commercial center, might have disposed him against wasting money on schooling for his children. Often it was in the poorest areas, where there was no alternative to education as a means of becoming wealthy, that enthusiasm for it was greatest. A poor, densely populated division such as Owerri tended to export its manpower to the cities for employment, and these migrants returned with their appetite for education whetted by experiences in the urban areas. Both wealth and poverty thus in their own ways stimulated an interest in education among different groups of Nigerians.

The fact that Southern Nigeria's economy was based on peasant agriculture did, however, increase the effective demand for schooling. Unlike many other colonial territories, Southern Nigeria did not have a "dual economy," with highly developed mines or plantations operated by Europeans in the midst of, yet scarcely affecting, the mass of subsistence farmers. What prosperity Southern Nigeria enjoyed depended on the export of cocoa, rubber, and palm oil produced by hundreds of thousands of peasant families, each with its own small plot of land.[39] Cash income was therefore spread fairly widely throughout the rural areas, enabling villages to construct school buildings and pay their own teachers.

CONSEQUENCES OF THE AFRICAN RESPONSE

This study is more concerned with the quantitative than with the qualitative aspects of educational development. Questions about quality are obviously important, however, and we may conclude this chapter by asking how the African response affected the kind and quality of instruction offered in Southern Nigerian schools. In general, both the pupils and their parents favored a curriculum with a strong literary, nonmanual emphasis. This was only natural, for the European rulers, who served in many ways as a reference group for ambitious young Africans, had themselves received a predominantly literary training, and the prestige of the generalist in the colonial hierarchy was higher than that of the specialist or technician. Moreover, government, business, and mission alike made literacy a prerequisite for any well-paying job. Africans, valuing education primarily as a means to salaried employment, consequently preferred training that stressed linguistic rather than manual skills. White-collar salaries were so much higher than the earnings of the subsistence sector that it was perfectly rational for the individual African to try to escape from the "dignity" of laboring on the land or fashioning bricks and pottery. As the educational system developed, those who wanted technical training might seek it through the traditional apprenticeship system or within the Public Works or Railroad departments, which had their own training schemes; the ordinary primary or secondary school was not expected to provide this sort of instruction. In any case, one of the striking features about education in Southern Nigeria has been the long-standing unwillingness of young people to enter vocational and trade schools, despite the encouragement of Europeans and a few leaders of the African Church movement. A similar phenomenon has been amply demonstrated for Ghana.[40] The current tendency of many educated Nigerians to blame the British for an overly bookish and nonpractical curriculum completely misreads the temper of earlier generations of Nigerians and underestimates the role of public opinion in the success of the grammar school and the failure of the vocational school.[41]

The prestige of a literary education resulted in a heavy reliance on rote memorization as a technique of learning. In their efforts to pass English examinations, African children necessarily had to learn a great deal that was utterly foreign to their past experience and irrelevant for their future careers; under these circumstances much information was simply memorized, for there was little intellectual or emotional incentive to digest it. Moreover, the pressures for the expansion of school facilities created continual shortages of trained teachers, and a young pupil-teacher was likely to mask his own ignorance of subject matter by repeating to his pupils exactly, and only, what the textbook contained. These observations do not imply that the pupils learned nothing of importance; just to be a pupil was to partake of what Edward Shils has termed "the mystique of modernity."[42] What mattered was not so much the specific content of the lessons—though the skills of literacy and mathematical calculation that were acquired in the classroom were clearly valuable—as the insight that the total experience of attending school provided into the workings of the dominant European culture.

The effects of the school on the surrounding community were limited by the Nigerians' view that the major purpose of education was to gain salaried employment. African parents often felt they were too old to change jobs, and learning to read and write therefore did not seem necessary for them; the children, on the other hand, were in a position to make full use of schooling, and their income could sustain the parents in later years. Because the school came to be regarded as a place for children, adults often felt it was beneath their dignity to attend literacy classes. Education thus became in the public mind something for the younger segment of the community, not for the community as a whole. The irrelevance of much of the curriculum further restricted the impact of the new teachings. Yet these limitations on the effects of education did not render the adult population any less enthusiastic for it. On the contrary, the school could be so readily accepted as a symbol of community status precisely because, although it prepared the young to adapt to new ways of life, it was not seen as frontally challenging the traditional ways of the older generation.

CHAPTER 3

The Role of Government, 1882–1929

The early history of education in Southern Nigeria is primarily the story of missionary activities and of African responses to them. But no account would be complete without reference to the colonial regime, whose impact on the educational system increased over the years. This impact was largely indirect; in order to rule effectively the British needed literate Africans to fill subaltern bureaucratic positions, and the official demand for graduates of primary, and later secondary, schools undoubtedly stimulated the popular demand for education. The colonial regime also affected education directly when policies were formulated concerning such matters as the establishment of government schools, the desirable rate of expansion in voluntary agency schools, the content and quality of curricula, and the public funding of voluntary agency activities through the grant-in-aid system. This chapter deals first with the indirect role played by the colonial government in the expansion of enrollment, and then with the evolution of educational policy as it affected the number of children in school and the kinds of subjects they were taught. For comparative purposes we will refer to official policy and practice in areas adjacent to Southern Nigeria, such as Northern Nigeria and Dahomey.

THE COLONIAL BUREAUCRACY AND THE SCHOOLS

In Southern Nigeria the flag followed the Cross: not until 1900 was the Protectorate of Southern Nigeria established and a serious effort made to enforce the Pax Britannica inland as well as along the coast.

Militarily this did not prove difficult. The punitive expedition against the Aro Ibos during 1901–2 was the last significant British show of force in Southern Nigeria during the early colonization period,[1] whereas the British faced more intense and protracted armed resistance in what became, as of 1900, the Protectorate of Northern Nigeria. The ease with which the British established their authority in the South permitted them to turn their attention fairly quickly to the economic development of the area. Since the peasant farmers readily adopted a pattern of producing cash crops for export and purchasing imported goods, Southern Nigeria's government was able to pay its own way almost from the start, and to do so through customs duties rather than through the politically risky policy of direct taxation. Rapid economic growth, in part a consequence of effective British rule, itself contributed to financing the expansion of the colonial bureaucracy.

The nature of this bureaucracy varied, in different parts of Nigeria, according to the complexity of the traditional political structures the British encountered and the values of leading colonial administrators. The existence of an already sophisticated administrative apparatus among the Muslim emirates of Northern Nigeria, combined with a severe shortage there of British officials, led the North's first governor, Sir Frederick Lugard, to inaugurate a policy of indirect rule whereby many governmental functions were performed through traditional, or native authority, structures. Policy on this matter was less coherently expressed in Southern Nigeria, at least prior to its amalgamation with the North in 1914. If anything, however, there was an early tendency toward direct rule, particularly east of the Niger, where traditional authority structures were decentralized and often quite weak. Native councils and native courts were established, but the appointment of Africans to key positions in them was based not so much on traditional qualifications as on competence and loyalty to the British. As the colonial government assumed responsibilities beyond the maintenance of law and order, the native authority system of the North was strengthened by being assigned many new tasks, whereas in the South a bureaucracy emerged that was directly accountable to British officials and that clearly excelled, in power and prestige, such native authority institutions as were officially recognized.

One consequence of the system of indirect rule in Northern Nigeria was that the recruitment of Africans to administrative positions was only indirectly linked to their knowledge of English. Hausa-Fulani officials who determined entry into key native authority positions were highly concerned with the ascriptive status of applicants—a status that personal achievement in a European-oriented school could do nothing to change. Hausa was the language of administration in many areas of the North, moreover, and British officials were expected to use it in dealing with Africans. The colonial rulers made some effort to provide education in English for the scions of leading Hausa-Fulani families, but the success of indirect rule did not hinge on the acquisition by large numbers of people of skills taught through the imported school system—particularly when the Koranic schools had their own means of training students for participation in the political and administrative life of the Northern emirates.

In Southern Nigeria, on the other hand, the link between bureaucratic power and Western education was stronger and far more explicit. There it was the British who set standards for recruitment into a bureaucracy they directly controlled. And since the new jobs open to Africans were often as nontraditional as the bureaucracy that generated them, it made little sense to consider the traditional status of an African applying, for example, to become an interpreter, accountant, court clerk, sanitation inspector, surveyor, or stationmaster. What mattered was not a person's ascriptive status but his potential for effective performance in institutions employing English as the official medium of communication. Educational achievement thus became the most important criterion in selecting and advancing African employees, for in school the young person learned the skills of English literacy that were directly relevant to the clerical duties he was expected to perform. As a modern Western institution, moreover, a school was in many ways similar to the colonial bureaucracy. Both consciously stressed the careful gathering of data, the importance of logical analysis, the application of information to the solution of specific problems, and obedience to authority. The British rulers of Southern Nigeria could see fairly quickly that the success of their efforts to build an effective bureaucracy depended heavily on the capacity of the schools to produce substantial numbers of literate, disciplined, and cooperative Africans. The absence of such a pool of manpower was, in fact, a constant complaint of early administrators.[2] Lugard, reviewing the scene at the end of his tenure as Governor-General of Nigeria (1914–19), declared that there were an estimated 5,500 posts in government and business requiring Africans with a good command of English; yet, he complained, few could pass the easy entrance tests, and less than three hundred Nigerians per year completed secondary school.[3]

The fact that recruitment into the ruling bureaucracy was more closely linked in Southern than in Northern Nigeria to performance in European-oriented schools, coupled with the far greater difficulties encountered by the Christian missionaries who wished to open schools in the North, resulted in an enormous education gap between the two parts of Nigeria.* The consequences of this gap for national integration are explored in Chapter 11. Of more immediate consequence for the South was the impetus that a burgeoning colonial bureaucracy gave to African educational aspirations. Employment in a government office provided at one and the same time high income, high security, high social status, and an opportunity to escape from tiresome and tedious agricultural work. Clearly, the way to gain such employment was to enter schools that emphasized literary skills over manual skills. "In practice," as Philip Foster has noted, "academic education has been the most vocational type of education in West Africa."[4]

EDUCATIONAL POLICY PRIOR TO AMALGAMATION

As the British consolidated their position within Southern Nigeria, the government began to evolve an educational policy. A small group of officials took charge of such matters as the inspection of voluntary agency schools, the administration of grants-in-aid to these schools, the formulation of an approved syllabus, and the establishment of government schools. An education ordinance was passed in 1882 authorizing the appointment of an Inspector of Education for all the British West African settlements, including Lagos; an ordinance of 1887, applying only to Lagos Colony, created a Board of Education headed by the Governor. In 1892 the prominent Nigerian educator Henry Carr was named Inspector of Schools for Lagos, a post he filled with distinction for many years. In 1903 a Department of Education for the Southern Provinces was created, which was merged with that of Lagos when the Colony and the Protectorate were administratively joined in 1906. An ordinance of 1908 made provision for education boards in what were then the Western, Central, and Eastern provinces of Southern Nigeria; these boards were allowed to vary certain regulations according to local circumstances. Thus an administrative apparatus gradually emerged with at least nominal responsibility for Southern Nigerian education.[5]

* Primary school attendance figures for 1912 and 1926 were, for the North, 950 and 5,200 respectively, whereas in the same years the slightly less populous South had 35,700 and 138,250. These figures are rounded off from Table 14 in James Coleman, *Nigeria: Background to Nationalism* (Berkeley, Calif., 1958), p. 134.

Generally speaking, government schools were established in areas that the missionaries had not reached or that, because of a heavy concentration of Muslims, were likely to be unreceptive to Christian education. Between 1900 and 1910 officially sponsored schools were established in such coastal sites as Bonny and Sapele; another was founded in Ahoada District, following a report by the District Commissioner in 1909 stating that "the Ekpaffia tribe is a numerous one and its customs are in need of some refinement."[6] These schools enlisted, where possible, the financial assistance of local chiefs and British traders; staff and equipment were provided by the government. In Lagos, where there was a large Muslim population, the government began in 1896 to assist the leading Koranic school and to introduce basic education into its curriculum.[7] By 1908 over fifty government primary schools were operating in Southern Nigeria, and the following year King's College, soon to become the country's most prestigious secondary school, was opened in Lagos.

What is striking about these early years, however, is not how extensive but how limited and indirect was the role played by the government in education. After 1908 the number of government schools actually declined, since British officials preferred to encourage education by giving financial assistance to voluntary agency schools that met certain academic standards. The grant-in-aid system, which originated in 1872 with an allocation of thirty pounds distributed equally among the Church Missionary Society, Methodist, and Roman Catholic missions,[8] expanded greatly in scope and complexity over the years. By 1912 every mission school that attained certain standards was assisted on the basis of its examination results, the unit of average attendance, and "organization and efficiency."[9] The grants were allocated directly to the mission or to its education secretary and were used primarily to supplement teachers' salaries; sometimes building and maintenance grants were also awarded. The grant-in-aid system enabled the government to maintain a kind of indirect rule over the educational process by applying financial pressure to the best voluntary agency schools. But the vast majority of mission schools did not meet government standards and consequently were not even subject to indirect rule by colonial officials.[10]

Several factors contributed to the colonial government's willingness to let the missionaries undertake the major task of educating the populace. British administrators had no particular reason arising out of their own background to oppose missionaries or organized religion as such, for anti-clericalism had never made much headway in

England, and Church-State conflict was not intense there at the turn
of the century. Because Southern Nigeria was for the most part pagan, the administrators did not worry that the people would actively
rebel against intensive Christian missionary work, as they might in
the predominantly Muslim provinces of the North. In any case, the
missionaries had the advantage of a head start in educational work,
and considerable effort would have been required to control their
activities with care; certainly it would have been difficult to replace
them.* The grant-in-aid system represented, moreover, a considerable saving of scarce administrative talent and of government money,
for if the government had assumed control of the mission schools
it would have incurred the expenses of the whole apparatus of inspection, administration, and teacher training that each mission was
financing with its own resources. A further saving was in teachers'
salaries. Whereas teachers directly employed by the government were
paid civil service salaries according to the amount of training they
had received, the government insisted that it was not responsible for
ensuring equivalent salaries for voluntary agency teachers, although
it might subsidize them through grants-in-aid. As a result, mission
teachers invariably received less than government teachers, and the
government benefited from the former's services at little cost to itself.

In contrast to the British government's reliance on the mission
education system in Southern Nigeria was the policy in French West
Africa, where the government became much more directly involved
in education. Many French administrators were strongly anti-clerical
because of the bitter struggle taking place within France itself, at
the turn of the century, over the role of the Catholic Church in education. These administrators tended to regard religion as a threat to
constituted authority rather than a buttress of it. Even had they been
disposed to encourage the expansion of education under Christian
auspices, the French would have risked arousing the anger of the
African populace, most of whom were Muslim. French officials were
consequently suspicious of missionaries and were anxious to keep
missionary influence from spreading too widely. In most areas of
French West Africa, moreover, the Tricolor arrived prior to the Cross,

* There was one occasion in the 1890's when the Governor of Lagos, Sir Henry
McCallum, proposed placing mission primary schools under direct government
supervision. But the proposal was soon dropped, under heavy pressure from the
Church Missionary Society in London, and was never officially revived. See Grace
Awani-Alele, "Dynamics of Education in the Birth of a New Nation: Case Study
of Nigeria" (Ph.D. dissertation, University of Chicago, Department of Education,
March 1963).

and in such areas there was no educational system already operated by the missions to accommodate. An exception was Dahomey, a colony in which a substantial majority of the children enrolled in school attended Roman Catholic institutions. But precisely because of Catholic influence in Dahomey, Church-State conflict there was pronounced from the early days of the consolidation of French rule. The missions were denied government grants after 1902, and subsequently the government made a concerted effort to limit the influence of the existing mission schools and to prevent their expansion by strengthening its own school system.[11] French officials had to take the leading role in education themselves, because they wanted their educational system to be secular; the British, who were willing to work through religious organizations, left many of the basic questions about the purpose of education in a colonial society to be answered by the missionaries. In a sense, the British grant-in-aid policy in Southern Nigeria represented an abdication of policy-making responsibility.

Aside from the difference in their attitudes toward missionaries, there were other reasons why the British did not become as directly and actively involved in the educational life of Southern Nigeria as did the French in French West Africa. Since Napoleonic days the French educational system had been under the control of the state to a far greater degree than was the British, and colonial rulers often measured their own responsibility for education in terms of the pattern prevailing in the mother country. Moreover, the purposes of the British in colonizing Africa were not as closely related to the task of educating the African as was the French *mission civilisatrice*. A principal aim of French imperialism was to spread French culture; instruction in the French language was a major justification for the whole colonial enterprise.* The British tended to be less explicit about their objectives, but in general they were more interested in the export of their political institutions than of their culture, and although they needed English-speaking Africans to aid them in administering their colonies, they did not regard the spread of the English language as a *raison d'être* for the colonial effort itself. The French also depended more than the British on education as a means of maintaining their position as colonial rulers. Through a long pro-

---

* The French had a saying that when the Portuguese colonized they built churches; when the English colonized they built trading stations; when the French colonized they built schools. William Bryant Mumford and G. St. J. Orde-Brown, *Africans Learn to Be French* (London, 1937), p. 50; see also Georges Hardy, *Une Conquête Morale: L'Enseignement en Afrique Occidentale Française* (Paris, 1917).

cess of schooling at a high academic level, the French hoped to create a thoroughly acculturated or "assimilated" indigenous elite whose interests would be identical with those of the rulers and who would assist in the task of spreading the civilization and buttressing the power of France.[12] The British were not so sure that well-educated Africans would be their most dependable allies. From the beginning, in fact, the British attitude toward the Southern Nigerian intelligentsia was ambivalent; under Lugard and his successor, Sir Hugh Clifford, official hostility toward this group became quite explicit. Because the creation of a highly educated elite was not considered a principal method for sustaining British control over the colonies, the British government did not pay as careful attention as did the French to controlling enrollment and curriculum at the post-primary level.

The willingness of the British administrators to leave education in the hands of the missionaries, and the relative indifference of the colonial government to the role of education in justifying colonial rule, produced a laissez-faire educational policy in Southern Nigeria during the period before 1914. Some effort was made through the grant-in-aid system to improve the quality of voluntary agency schools, but in general the educational system was permitted to expand in accordance with the wishes of the missionaries and of the African populace.

LUGARD'S REASSESSMENT OF EDUCATIONAL POLICY

Educational policy changed noticeably under Sir Frederick Lugard, who became Governor of Southern as well as Northern Nigeria in 1912, and who in 1914 engineered the amalgamation of the two areas under one administration.* Amalgamation may be seen as Lugard's effort to provide the North with some of the revenues enjoyed by the South and to provide the South with the system of local government he had devised for the North. Appalled at the haphazard way the Southern administration had developed, Lugard resolved to build up a strong native authority system such as the one he had found, and strengthened, in the North; doing this involved recognizing the "natural" rulers of each tribal group, investing important rulers with considerable administrative and judicial power as "sole native authorities," and financing the native authorities through di-

---

* Not all individual departments were merged in 1914, however. It was not until 1929 that a single Education Department for both Southern and Northern Nigeria was formed.

rect taxation of the populace. Thus to the east of the Niger began the ludicrous game of "finding the chief" among people who had none; the result was the appointment of so-called Warrant Chiefs who frequently lacked popular support for their authority, and the growing influence of semiliterate native court clerks, who took advantage of the virtual vacuum of authority in Iboland.* The major Yoruba Obas, who were traditionally checked by advisory councils, became in 1917 sole native authorities whose power was more difficult to limit from below. Meanwhile, the imposition of the direct tax on people who had previously enjoyed government services without it naturally caused deep-seated unrest, even though one of the professed objectives of taxation was to compensate native authorities for their loss of revenue from traditional tribute. The Iseyin Rebellion of 1916 and the Abeokuta Revolt of 1918 were reactions against the imposition of a direct tax on the Yorubas. Riots and demonstrations occurred in Sapele and Warri when the direct tax was introduced there in 1927. The most famous disturbances were the so-called Aba Women's Riots, which occurred in many areas of Owerri and Calabar provinces in 1929, a year after the imposition of taxes in the Eastern Region. Here the women were protesting not only the possibility that they would be taxed as well as their husbands, but also the excesses of Warrant Chiefs.[13] Lugard's political reforms, carried out in the name of "traditional" Africa and for the sake of greater political stability, clearly had the very opposite effect from that intended. A set of policies that was politically realistic for Northern Nigeria proved strikingly unrealistic in its application to the South.

In seeking to consolidate British power in Southern Nigeria, Lugard had to deal directly with educational matters. The Governor-General was committed to increasing the scope and effectiveness of central administrative services, yet he was trying at the same time to strengthen, if not create from the beginning, a native authority system that in some respects paralleled the central administration in structure and function. In order for this kind of dyarchy to perform effectively, the schools would have to educate the right number of persons with the skills and attitudes needed for employment in each bureaucracy. Specifically, this meant that the graduates of the schools

---

* Margery Perham, *Native Administration in Nigeria* (London, 1937), p. 202. The decentralized authority system of the Ibos may help to explain why they expressed greater public concern than the Yorubas at the unscrupulous practices of literate Africans during the early part of this century.

should not be so poorly trained that they could not meet the educational standards set for employment in either the modern British or the "traditional" African bureaucracy, nor should they be so highly trained that they threatened to take over the responsibilities of British officials or native authorities. Educational output should be neither too small nor too large for the manpower demands of the government and the major European firms, and education should inculcate respect for the authority of both the British and the native authorities. The government, Lugard believed, should intervene in the educational system to see that the voluntary agencies met these requirements. Lugard viewed education, in short, as an instrument to be used explicitly for political ends. In this respect he was similar to the French, even though his philosophy of indirect rule ran counter to the direct-rule theories of French colonialism.

Sir Frederick soon found, however, that Southern Nigeria's educational system was not serving his objectives. The schools were producing large numbers of people with skills either too limited or too great for use within the existing political and administrative structure and with attitudes that directly threatened its continued effectiveness. "With some notable exceptions," Lugard wrote, "education seems to have produced discontent, impatience of any control, and an unjustifiable assumption of self-importance in the individual."[14] Consequently, of all the problems posed by amalgamation, he felt, "there was none comparable in importance and in urgency with that of education."[15]

Well-educated Africans, the polished graduates of grammar schools and perhaps even of universities, were difficult to accommodate within the colonial system. The British could not realistically expect a highly trained African to work contentedly under the native authorities when so many of the traditional rulers were illiterate and unprogressive; the educated elite would probably either usurp the traditional rulers' rights or sabotage the native authority system itself.* Nor could the British envisage employing a substantial number of well-trained Africans in the central administration. Such a practice would threaten the job security of British administrators and under-

---

* The only instance in the South where an intelligentsia did work within a nominally traditional structure was the Egba United Government, and since the educated Africans there really managed their rulers rather than the reverse, this government was the very antithesis of what Lugard desired. It is thus only superficially ironical that the philosopher of indirect rule made it one of his first objectives to dissolve this experiment in semiautonomy by the Egba. (I am indebted to Grace Awani-Alele for this observation.)

mine the prestige of the white man in general. It might also create serious problems of morale and communication within the bureaucracy, since many of the British found it difficult to get along personally with educated Africans.* Another problem was presented by the political awareness of well-educated Africans and by the inclination of many of them openly to oppose British policies. Lugard and the educated elite of Lagos were in continual disagreement over such matters as the status of the local traditional dynasty, the imposition of a water rate, and British efforts to curb the indigenous press;[16] at times the issue was not so much the wisdom of specific government measures as the legitimacy of British rule itself. The administration also tended to feel that because an African with an education was unlike his countrymen in this respect, he was therefore unqualified to represent them in any discussions having political overtones. Lugard, and Sir Hugh Clifford after him, firmly rejected the claim of such nationalists as Herbert Macaulay to speak on behalf of the African masses: "It is a cardinal principle of British Colonial Policy that the interests of a large native population shall not be subject to the will either of a small European class or of a small minority of educated and Europeanized natives who have nothing in common with them, and whose interests are often opposed to theirs."[17] There was almost nothing an educated African could do, in short, that did not represent a threat to the established order. This fact was not lost on the educated elite; indeed, it was a major reason for the elite's dissatisfaction with British rule, a sentiment that eventually led to the replacement of British rulers by educated Africans.

A far greater number of Africans were too poorly educated. By 1913 there were about twenty or thirty thousand Southern Nigerians attending unassisted village schools; these pupils represented for Lugard a large pool of insufficiently trained manpower, and a political liability as well. In Lugard's view, low academic standards seemed to produce men of poor character, and this moral weakness would in turn threaten political stability. Lugard thus deplored the enormous number of private schools "conducted for profit by half-educated boys and others who cannot read or write properly themselves. They are lacking in discipline and in loyalty to any constituted authority

---

* Lugard's comments are fairly typical: "I am somewhat baffled as to how to get in touch with the Educated Native....I am not in sympathy with him. His loud and arrogant conceit are distasteful to me, his lack of natural dignity and courtesy antagonize me." Quoted in Margery Perham, *Lugard: The Years of Authority, 1898–1945* (London, 1960), p. 586.

whatever, and the local chiefs find it very difficult to exercise any control over them."[18] Sir Hugh Clifford expressed similar concern in 1920 about the products of the unassisted schools, who, he said, "prefer to pick up a precarious and demoralizing living by writing more or less unintelligible letters for persons whose ignorance is even deeper than their own."[19] The fact that most schools were controlled by the voluntary agencies aggravated the problem. Although Lugard favored Christian education in pagan areas as a means of teaching Africans to be properly deferent,[20] the interests of Church and State conflicted on the recurring issue of quantity versus quality in education. The missionaries wanted to extend the benefits of literacy to as many Southern Nigerians as possible; in this effort they relied heavily on small village schools staffed by poorly trained, though hopefully pious, teacher-catechists. But the colonial officials grew alarmed at the political dangers resulting from the high enrollment and low academic quality of such village schools. They concluded that the central aim of their educational policy should be to limit the expansion of enrollment and improve the quality of the curriculum. In order to realize this aim, the government clearly had to take a more active role than before in overseeing the work of the voluntary agencies and in outlining its own philosophy of education.

THE EDUCATION CODES

To achieve greater control over the Nigerian educational system, the colonial government set forth two education codes, one in 1916 and the other in 1926. The code of 1916, promulgated under Lugard, attempted to improve "the formation of character and habits of discipline" among African students by revising the criteria for grants-in-aid to the schools: thereafter the decision to assist a school was to be based 30 per cent on "tone, discipline, organization, and moral instruction." Lugard pressed for the inclusion of moral instruction as a separate subject in the curriculum apart from religious studies. In order to gain greater control over the operation of the voluntary agency schools, the code provided for more of them to receive government assistance.*

The education code of 1926, promulgated under Clifford, was more far-reaching: it required the registration of all teachers, gave

---

* As a result of this provision, the number of assisted schools more than doubled from 82 in 1915 to 167 in 1917. M. L. Walsh, "The Catholic Contribution to Education in Western Nigeria" (M.A. thesis, Institute of Education, University of London, 1951).

the Governor power to close or refuse to open schools considered inefficient or not beneficial to the community, and increased grants-in-aid again in order to bring even more schools under government influence. The missions were provided with additional grants for the purpose of employing education supervisors to oversee more closely the work of unassisted mission schools; each voluntary agency was also encouraged to consolidate its own school system by gradually closing small two- or three-year schools and replacing them with "central" schools offering the full eight-year primary course. Finally, greater coordination of effort and more constant communication between the government and the voluntary agencies were to be ensured through an enlarged Board of Education, with at least ten members representing the voluntary agencies.

To what extent could such provisions be enforced? To what extent could they achieve the aims of government officials? Formal mechanisms of control were easy to establish, but limitations on the colonial regime made the implementation of the education codes at the local level almost impossible. The only truly effective ways to lower enrollments and improve the quality of education were to construct a bureaucracy capable of closing inadequate schools, and keeping them closed, or to alter radically the education-employment nexus. A bureaucracy that prevented schools from operating would have been highly unpopular and quite expensive to maintain; it would also have required the recruitment of many more educated Nigerians into the lower ranks of the civil service, thus actually reinforcing the link between education and employment. To destroy this link, on the other hand, would undermine the effectiveness of the colonial bureaucracy itself, which depended on literate Nigerians to fill subaltern positions. The implementation of the codes was thus left primarily to the voluntary agencies, which cooperated with the government at least to the extent that the number of Southern Nigerian unassisted schools declined from 3,578 in 1926 to 2,519 the following year.[21] But cooperation was limited, for the missionaries continued to pursue their original aims and were wary of the government's attempts to regulate their activities in greater detail. And even if the voluntary agencies had themselves wished to limit primary school enrollments, they would have been hard pressed to do so because of the intense enthusiasm of the people for education. Popular enthusiasm was undoubtedly the most important factor in defeating the objectives of the two education codes. The unassisted schools, even with their untrained teachers and apparently irrelevant curricula, provided an outlet for the powerful and almost desperate aspirations of Southern Nigerians for modernity. By the time the education codes were formulated, the drive for education had become too powerful to stop.

In any case, the formulators of the codes miscalculated in their attempts to check the popular response to education. They assumed that by expanding the grant-in-aid system the government could exercise a restraining influence on enrollment and encourage the maintenance of high educational standards: the assisted schools could be controlled by the threat that government funds would be withdrawn if their standards were lowered. With these schools serving as models of proper education, the standards in all schools were expected to rise. Once Africans were acquainted with superior education, it was thought, they would demand it from every school. But these assumptions turned out to be incorrect. The average villager could not realistically insist on high educational standards; his choice was not between the best schools and the mediocre, but between the mediocre and nothing. Moreover, by increasing the funds available for education, the government further stimulated popular enthusiasm for it. Each village school hoped one day to receive government assistance— an honor for the community as well as a financial windfall. Consolidation with other schools was therefore to be avoided unless the new central school was to be located in one's own village or the consolidated school was assured of an immediate grant-in-aid. Thus the increased government grants accelerated the very trends they were designed to discourage. It is not surprising that the number of unassisted schools, following a momentary decline in 1927, rose steadily thereafter.*

It is doubtful whether the efforts of the colonial regime to instill certain desired moral qualities through school curricula could ever be more than partially successful. The purpose of schooling was, in the eyes of many Nigerian pupils and their parents, to liberate a young person from the confinements of his way of life, and this purpose inevitably outweighed the substance of what was taught in school through a curriculum designed to make the child willingly accept these confinements. Often, too, texts in moral instruction were dull and unconvincing.[22]

---

* Attendance at unassisted primary schools rose from between 20,000 and 30,000 in 1913 to 81,000 in 1929 and 164,000 a decade later—about two-thirds of the total primary school enrollment of Southern Nigeria in each case. See Nigeria, *Annual Report of the Education Department, 1949* (Lagos, 1949), p. 7.

THE THEORY OF ADAPTION

The education codes of 1916 and 1926 may best be understood in the context of a broader philosophy of "adaptionist" education that attained the status of canon law during the 1920's, not just in Southern Nigeria but in British Africa as a whole. Derived from the efforts of Samuel Chapman Armstrong, Booker T. Washington, and others to improve the lives of Negroes in rural areas of the southern United States, the theory of adaption was applied to Africa by the influential Phelps-Stokes reports of 1922 and 1925.[23] Official recognition was given the theory in a 1925 memorandum, *Education Policy in British Tropical Africa*: "Education should be adapted to the mentality, aptitudes, occupations, and traditions of the various peoples, conserving as far as possible all sound and healthy elements in the fabric of their social life, adapting them where necessary to changed circumstances and progressive ideas, as an agent of natural growth and evolution."[24] Since the vast majority of Africans were engaged in agriculture, adaption meant in practice that the school curriculum should be geared to rural life. Since almost all Africans worked with their hands, the theory held that education should "instil into pupils the view that vocational (especially the industrial and manual) careers are no less honourable than the clerical," and that the government ought "to make [vocational careers] at least as attractive—and thus to counteract the tendency to look down on manual labour."[25] Because most Africans still lived within a tribal framework, "education should strengthen the feeling of responsibility to the tribal community." And because of the importance of religion in African life, "what is good in the old beliefs and sanctions should be strengthened and what is defective should be replaced,"[26] presumably by regulated doses of Christianity. The impracticality of curricula was deemed responsible for the "detribalizing" consequences of education; the solution was therefore to adjust the curricula to the practical needs of Africans through instruction in such courses as gardening, handicrafts, health education, domestic science, local history, and morality.

The British faced many difficulties in trying to put the adaptionist theory into practice in their African colonies. Pilot projects were started in various places,[27] but large-scale implementation required funds and trained personnel far beyond the capacity of Great Britain, even had the Depression of the 1930's not followed close upon the Phelps-Stokes reports and the 1925 memorandum. More serious than these practical problems, however, were the conceptual difficulties inherent in the theory of adaption. The assumption that selected elements of African and European culture could be taken out of their respective cultural contexts and harmoniously fitted together, and further, that institutions and values performing certain functions in one culture would have similar effects in another culture—such were the ingredients of bad anthropology, to say the least. One would have thought that the very problem the adaption theory was meant to solve—the destabilizing effects in Africa of a type of education that in Europe generally served to reinforce the existing power structure —might have called these assumptions into question.[28] The theory placed far too much faith in curriculum change as the basis for attitude change; it underestimated the aspirations for academic success that impelled local communities to build schools and parents to enroll their children in them. Perhaps most serious, the theory analyzed African society in relatively static terms, failing to appreciate the revolutionary impact of British rule: the creation of new high-paying jobs within the colonial bureaucracy, the demonstration effect of the British presence on African aspirations, the increased importance of cities, the rise of new economic interests, the recruitment through education of a new stratum of potential political leaders. The only thing the British left out of their model was themselves, and this omission made all the difference between a helpful and a misleading model. In an environment changing more rapidly than the colonial rulers themselves realized, the effect of their educational reforms would have been to train the child to make his way in a society that was becoming outmoded rather than to prepare him for a future society that was bound to be even less traditional than the Nigeria of the 1920's. And where a colonial regime was in power, educating the African "along his own lines" meant in practice keeping him "in his place." A contemporary critic, A. Victor Murray, acutely observed: "The Phelps-Stokes reports emphasize differentiation [along racial lines] before there has been attained equality. Differentiation without equality means the permanent inferiority of the black man."[29] Small wonder that many educated Africans criticized the new idealization of traditional Africa by the British as a device to keep Africans from coveting the goods and services and pursuing the ideals of modern life.[30]

The principal contribution of the colonial rulers to Southern Nigeria's educational expansion was an indirect one: by providing high-paying, high-status jobs for the educated, the government gave young

Nigerians an incentive to go to school. During the years before the Depression—particularly in the laissez-faire period before Lugard's tenure as Governor-General—the impact of the government's educational policy was small; later, when colonial officials took a firmer hand in educational matters, they were unable to effect the enrollment and curricular changes deemed necessary for a stable and effective Pax Britannica. This limited capacity was due in part to constraints of finance and personnel that were inherent in an essentially self-financing colonial operation. But the limitations were also of intellect and vision: a failure to understand the rational basis of African enthusiasm for education, to perceive colonialism as a dynamic phenomenon, to appreciate that indirect rule could not be buttressed through moral and religious instruction in the schools. As a consequence, measures taken by the British proved either irrelevant or self-defeating. Although the British correctly recognized the spread of education as a threat to their own authority, they could not act forcefully and effectively against that threat.

CHAPTER 4

Pressures for Expansion, 1930–50: Old Groups and New

During the 1930–50 period a high degree of interdependence developed among the missionaries, the Africans, and the colonial government based on their common involvement in education. In addition new groups emerged, themselves the products of earlier patterns of educational expansion, and pressed for even more widespread educational opportunities. A circular process thus developed by which the educational system created interests conducive to its own maintenance and enlargement. The new groups also provided the organizational basis for the relatively rapid assumption of regional power by Southern Nigerians during the 1950's—a phenomenon whose effects on primary and secondary education are described in Part II.

The years 1930 and 1950 represent important watersheds in Southern Nigerian political history. From 1900 to 1929, the British faced relatively minor difficulties in gradually consolidating their rule: a growing economy financed a growing bureaucracy, and the African populace was still so inert and unorganized that it posed no serious threat to British hegemony. The 1930–50 period, marked by the worldwide Depression, the Second World War, and the emergence of a Nigerian nationalist movement ready to challenge the authority of the British, may be considered the era of "troubled colonialism." The Depression severely limited the funds available to the government for all purposes, and a concomitant drastic decline in terms of trade caused widespread suffering among the people precisely because so many Southern Nigerians had successfully supplemented subsistence production with cash crops for export and had acquired, in the

process, a taste for imported consumer goods.* The war also placed
constraints on the capacity of the British to finance and staff projects
to which they were committed; at the same time it stimulated anti-
colonial sentiment among an ever-increasing number of educated
Southern Nigerians.[1] The postwar period was one of unprecedented
prosperity and of ambitious government projects for which funds
were available. But changes in British colonial policy, coupled with
powerful pressures for self-government from Southern Nigerians,
brought to the fore the question of how rapidly the British exit from
political power could be arranged. Nigerians of many political persuasions were represented at the official conference held in 1950 to
review the 1946 constitution, and their views strongly influenced the
1951 constitution, which launched the Southern Nigerian regions on
the road to self-government. Educational changes between 1930 and
1950, then, occurred during the crucial transition from a self-confident, secure colonialism to a colonialism that was beginning to prepare for its own demise.

RESTRICTIONIST AND EXPANSIONIST PHASES
IN GOVERNMENT POLICY

Up to the late 1920's the initiatives in education generally came
from the missionaries and the African populace, but from the 1930's
onward the government began to play the central role. Not only did
colonial officials take new initiatives in educational matters; there
was also a greater tendency for the voluntary agencies and at least the
educated Africans to look to the government for solutions to pressing
educational problems. As a result of government policies, educational
opportunities were restricted during the 1930's. By the 1940's, however, the trend was very much toward the expansion of enrollments
at all levels, from adult literacy classes to higher education.

Some important aspects of the restrictionist phase were outlined
by E. R. J. Hussey, Director of Education from 1929 to 1936, who in
1930 suggested changes that would in effect limit the type and quality
of education available to Nigerians.[2] In Hussey's proposal, the primary course would be shortened from eight years to six, and instruction would be given in the vernacular. The curriculum would
strongly emphasize agriculture, handicrafts, hygiene, and "the arousing of an intelligent interest in the pupils' environment."[3] Secondary

---

* Per capita real incomes for Nigeria as a whole were probably lower in 1945
than in 1929. See Gerald K. Helleiner, *Peasant Agriculture, Government, and Economic Growth in Nigeria* (Homewood, Ill., 1966), p. 18.

schools were to teach the final two years of the primary sequence in addition to four years of so-called middle school. This meant that the coveted Oxford or Cambridge School Certificate, which required study beyond Form Four, would to all intents and purposes be unavailable. Instead, a new West African School Certificate, its standard uncertain but probably inferior to the English certificates, was to be awarded. The top level of education was to be a "higher college," located at Yaba, which would offer graduates of the middle schools a three- to five-year course in such subjects as medicine, agriculture, engineering, and pedagogy.

Hussey's innovations were not necessarily intended to reduce enrollment at any level; indeed, the students at Yaba Higher College received advanced training in certain fields that had previously been unavailable in Nigeria. But his curriculum changes, particularly at the primary and secondary levels, were aimed to limit the employment opportunities of educated Southern Nigerians. In accordance with the adaptionist notions of the 1920's, Hussey hoped that "a large number of pupils would automatically return to work on their father's farms" after completing the shorter and more practical primary course.[4] The new curriculum would thus prevent detribalization among the great majority of pupils who would not continue past the primary stage. (As one education officer revealingly wrote in 1937, "Our educational problem is largely to protect the native against himself."[5]) To those who did continue their education, certificates were to be awarded whose value was confined to British West Africa. Nigerians who had earned these certificates still could not compete with the medical and technical personnel imported from Great Britain for key positions. Educated Southern Nigerians soon realized that the new certificates were designed essentially to consolidate the British position within Nigeria, for although in some ways they facilitated African entry into middle-level bureaucratic and teaching positions, they imposed definite limits on further upward mobility within the colonial framework.

Educational opportunities were further restricted when the financial crisis precipitated by the Depression forced the government to curtail its programs. Expenditure by the Education Department for the country as a whole decreased during the 1930's;[6] although the 1926 education code had envisaged substantial grant-in-aid increases in the near future, the grant levels instead had to be stabilized and the money allocated in a fashion that actually reduced the amount given to each assisted school. In another economy measure, the government between 1930 and 1938 turned over twenty of its fifty-one primary schools to voluntary agencies and native administrations; the grants paid for these schools amounted to about a fourth of their previous cost to the administration.* The voluntary agencies, which had come to rely heavily on government assistance, found it difficult under the stringent new conditions to expand operations, or even to maintain existing ones.

By the 1940's colonial officials had begun to question the static bias of adaptionist thinking, and rapid economic development, coupled with aid from Great Britain, enabled the government significantly to increase its expenditure on education. Official outlays for Nigerian education more than doubled between 1941 and 1942, doubled again by 1947–48, and doubled once again by 1950–51. This startling development reflected not only a rapid rise in overall government expenditure but also a new set of priorities: a greater portion of government funds was being spent for education than ever before.[7] Large amounts of financial assistance to education were also provided through Colonial Development and Welfare funds, first voted by the British Parliament in the dark days of 1940 and then greatly increased in 1945.[8] The allocation of these funds depended less on the financial resources of a particular colony than on its ability to plan for sensible long-run development. Enticed by the prospect of aid from Britain, the Nigerian government began to draw up educational plans with fairly detailed cost estimates attached.[9] Nigerian planners were encouraged by the Colonial Office to make generous estimates of expansion. Indeed, the Ten-Year Educational Plan, written in 1942, which called for a rise from 12 per cent to about 17 per cent in the proportion of the 7–14 age group attending school, was rejected by the Advisory Committee on Education in the Colonies because it "hardly touches the fringe of the educational problem.... The present trend of events demands a more radical treatment on a far wider front."[10] The British were willing to export the notion of ambitious long-range planning to their colonies before they tried it seriously at home.[11]

Of equal if not greater significance than the increased amounts spent on education in Nigeria was the shift in the avowed purpose of the educational system itself. As is well known, the destructive impact on Europe of the Second World War, the promises of self-determination contained in the Atlantic Charter, the rise of two os-

---

* It was rumored that all government schools would be handed over to the missionaries, but this did not prove to be the case.

tensibly anti-colonial superpowers following the war, and the attainment of independence by several Asian countries combined to create a climate of world opinion that was distinctly hostile to the continued rule of Europeans over Africans and Asians.[12] Colonialism was to be atoned for, if at all, by a rapid transfer of power from European bureaucrats to indigenous political leaders. Unlike the other major colonial powers, the British had long declared it their aim to prepare their colonies for self-government, but in the prewar years this commitment had been little more than rhetorical. After 1945 the rhetoric had to be translated into action, particularly since the Labour Party, itself the repository of anti-colonial sentiment, had gained control of the British government. Rapid economic, social, and political change thus became a primary object of British policy rather than a by-product of the colonial presence. Because of this shift in its overall aims, the government had to assume more direct responsibility for education; the success of its experiment in decolonization depended on the number and ability of the educated people to whom power would be transferred. What was involved was not simply an expansion of enrollments at existing educational levels but the creation of new levels as well. A cadre of university graduates was needed to perform important political and bureaucratic functions, and a large body of literate adults was needed to form what would soon be the voting populace. At all levels training for active, democratic citizenship was to be given. These ideas found their way into a number of official documents emanating from London during the 1940's.[13]

The Nigerian government, prodded by the Colonial Office—and by Nigerian nationalists—moved to prepare the country through education for political autonomy. The government assumed increased responsibility for subsidizing voluntary agency work in primary and secondary education; in fact, the phenomenal increase in total government expenditure for education can be accounted for largely by the rise in grants-in-aid, from 28 per cent of the total education expenditure in 1930–31, to 38 per cent ten years later, and then 74 per cent by 1950–51. Between 1941 and 1947 a series of *ad hoc* concessions was made granting government payments to large numbers of voluntary agency teachers. The government was gradually coming to accept in fact, if not yet in theory, that it should pay all teachers even if it did not directly employ them.[14] Higher salary scales for teachers, arranged in 1947 under the threat of a teachers' strike, further raised the official subsidy of the voluntary agencies. In 1948 the government, worried about the financial effects of these rapidly rising costs, appointed Sidney Phillipson to review the grant-in-aid system. His carefully reasoned and influential report set out a formula by which the costs of schooling could be borne more fully than in the past by local communities.[15] At the same time Phillipson envisaged a substantial increase in primary school enrollments, particularly in the first four years of primary instruction, which had reverted to an eight-year sequence. The effect of his report, which spoke of universal, free, and compulsory primary education as a long-range goal for Nigeria, was less to stabilize government expenditures at current levels than it was to prepare both the government and the populace for even heavier burdens in the future.

In addition to increasing subsidies for private groups engaged in primary and secondary education, the government directly sponsored new projects at other levels. University College, Ibadan, was opened in 1948; it superseded Yaba Higher College as the country's premier institution and offered regular London University degrees.[16] The number of highly educated Nigerians was further increased by the expansion of the government's scholarship program for higher studies abroad, which had finally been started in 1938 in response to strong demands from the nationalists.[17] New technical and trade schools were also opened with extensive support from Colonial Development and Welfare funds.

To promote mass education, a number of literacy campaigns were launched in Southern Nigeria after the war, with ex-servicemen and uncertificated teachers serving quite successfully as adult education organizers. These campaigns were most successful in the East, where there was great popular enthusiasm for progress through community self-help. For example, largely as a result of the pioneering work of E. R. Chadwick, a District Officer, Udi Division in Onitsha Province experienced a surge of interest in basic education that in turn stimulated community development work.* Chadwick found that adults who learned to read gained confidence in themselves along with the ability to perform new kinds of tasks: "A village asks to be allowed to start literacy classes, and when the people see that it is easy to learn

---

* Under Chadwick's direction, shingles made from rejected railway ties were distributed free of charge to the villagers for use as blackboards. Local teachers held literacy classes on market days, when farmers from miles around traveled to the villages to sell their produce. Each village had its own wall newspaper, presenting items of local interest, and a "chart of development," where the village's progress in literacy and community development was recorded as well as the progress of neighboring villages; inter-village competition was thus used to spur greater communal activity.

to read and write they begin to realise that there is nothing to stop them from developing in other directions if they like to make the effort."[18] Mass education projects in Udi—and lesser-known ventures in Ilaro, Ijebu, Bende, and Afikpo divisions—clearly depended for their success on a latent, if not already manifest, sense of community pride. But government officials performed an important catalytic role by providing the administrative facilities necessary to channel popular enthusiasm into a set of ongoing programs.

Another important development of the late 1940's was the decentralization of educational administration and finance, which must be understood as part of a wider trend in postwar Nigerian politics. In the 1946 Richards constitution the British moved toward a federal form of government by establishing an advisory House of Assembly in each of the country's three regions. This constitution was severely criticized by Nigerian nationalists because of the arbitrary way in which it had been imposed and its rather obvious divide-and-rule implications,[19] but as Nigerians became more actively involved in discussions of their future political system it became fairly clear that some kind of federal structure was needed for a country as enormously diverse as theirs to remain politically viable. The trend toward decentralization was reflected in the 1948 education code, which provided for a deputy director and a chief inspector of education in each region and instituted regional boards of education, some of whose members were to be selected by the relevant House of Assembly. In another change, which at first affected only bookkeeping procedures but which had many consequences for the 1950's, the bulk of educational expenditure from 1949 onward was considered a charge against the regional, rather than the central, budget.[20] The regionalization of education occurred in effect before the regionalization of political power enunciated in the 1951 constitution.

Government efforts toward decentralization extended below the regional to the local level. Although by 1945 the prewar idea of basing Nigerian self-rule on a federation of native authorities had been discarded,[21] the belief that the native authority structure should be reformed and strengthened remained stronger than ever in government circles. For some, reforming local government was a means of absorbing the attention of the African intelligentsia in practical matters, thus deflecting pressures from Lagos and reducing the momentum of Nigerian nationalism. For other officials, a revitalized native authority system was the logical concomitant of increased Nigerian participation in regional and central affairs. These persons cited as the precedent for strong local government England herself, where efficient local councils were considered an important element in the success of the British political system. In any event, as greater reliance was placed on local Nigerian communities, they were assigned increased responsibility for education. Native authorities were encouraged to establish more of their own schools, particularly in the large towns where pressure on existing facilities was rapidly increasing. Local education committees were formed to apprise education officers of popular sentiment, to survey future needs, and to give advice regarding the siting and proprietorship of new schools. These committees usually consisted of representatives from the voluntary agencies, district officers, chiefs, teachers, and leaders of progress unions. In planning for expansion they encouraged consideration of the needs of the community as a whole rather than just the desires of the mission groups serving the community.[22] Colonial officials hoped that local education authorities on the British model, closely linked to partially elected local councils, would eventually be established.

The most important new contribution of local communities to education was financial. Colonial officials argued with increasing urgency that unless the people helped to pay for a greater portion of the educational expansion they were so insistent on, the combined resources of the regional and central governments would prove inadequate to meet future demands. In trying to formalize the relationship between the grant-in-aid system and local finance, Phillipson proposed in 1948 that each community make a contribution, called the Assumed Local Contribution, toward the "recognized expenses" of its own schools; the amount of this outlay would vary somewhat according to the poverty and literacy levels of the community. Grants-in-aid would then make up the difference between recognized expenses and the local contribution. Phillipson wanted to stabilize local contributions for the first three years at about the amount contributed by sources outside of the government in 1947–48, but there was little to prevent officials from subsequently reducing the grant-in-aid burden by simply raising Assumed Local Contribution requirements.* Charging school fees was, of course, the most common way for a community to raise money, although in 1950 the Native Authority Ordinance was amended to grant native authorities the power to impose

* This was done in the East in 1950, and in 1952 the Council of Ministers in Lagos moved that in the future 45 per cent of the total cost of primary education should be borne locally (rather than the estimated 30 to 35 per cent financed locally at the time).

education rates, or taxes. This amendment removed one of the most serious handicaps to the growth of local government in Nigeria.

LIMITS ON GOVERNMENT ACTION

Granting that the Nigerian government made serious efforts to expand and decentralize its role in education during the 1940's, there still remained definite limits to what the colonial regime could do. Any crash program in education would doubtless necessitate curtailing other projects or raising taxes. British officials rightly believed that the former course would be unpopular, and from their experience of the riots in Abeokuta, Aba, and elsewhere they knew that tax increases would stir popular sentiment against "colonial exploitation" and heighten nationalistic feelings. The British, who tended to view any project in terms of its cost, did not see how an extensive educational program such as universal primary education could be financed. In any case, their estimates of the cost of universal primary education were much higher than those of the Nigerians who in the 1940's were proposing such a scheme,[23] and the question Lugard had posed was still frequently asked in official circles: would not a mass of "semi-educated" young Nigerians lead to future political instability? Thus although the British were quite willing to quicken the pace of educational expansion, their concern with the possible dislocative effects of their efforts led them to think in evolutionary rather than revolutionary terms.

Educational expansion was also limited as a result of the way in which power is exercised in colonial regimes. Because in the final analysis colonial bureaucracies are uncontrolled by the popular will, the professional educators in Nigeria had considerable power to formulate educational policy without having to subject their plans to the scrutiny of politicians. Professional educators tend to be conservatives in their own field: they are usually more concerned with the maintenance of standards and the improvement of the existing system than with a radical expansion or new orientation of the system. The Nigerian Department of Education viewed as one of its major tasks the maintenance of academic standards in the face of the overwhelming demand, at least in the South, for more education. An official report observed almost despairingly: "Numbers are the dominant factor in Nigerian schooling today. Floods of children pour into the lower strata of our primary schools. Hordes of boys clamor for admission at the doors of high sounding academies. Hundreds from every vocation in the land beset Government with demands for oversea scholarships."[24] For the department, and for Sidney Phillipson himself, "the main task . . . for some years should be the consolidation and strengthening of an educational system already established"[25] rather than a headlong rush to construct new facilities. Thus, enrollments could be increased by reducing the enormous dropout rate in Southern primary schools.[26] The Chief Inspector of Education for the Western Region wrote in 1947: "Until action is taken to combat this wastage planned expansion on any extensive scale is unrealistic and inadvisable."[27] There was as yet no Nigerian politician's voice above the Department of Education to counter the professional's view that consolidation should be the primary goal of educational policy.

MISSIONARY ACTIVITIES

Because the missionaries had come increasingly to depend on the Nigerian government for financial assistance to support their educational work, the grant-in-aid restrictions imposed during the 1930's limited their endeavors; conversely, the grant-in-aid explosion of the 1940's and Phillipson's virtual assurance that large grants would be regularly forthcoming enabled the voluntary agencies greatly to expand operations. Links with the government, already close thanks to regular meetings of the influential Nigerian Board of Education, were further tightened by the wartime appointment of two education advisers—one Catholic and one Protestant—who were able to channel large sums of Colonial Development and Welfare money into voluntary agency school-building programs.

But greater financial dependence on the government did not render the missionaries any less autonomous in pursuing their own aims; the drives that had impelled earlier mission educational activity were strongly in evidence throughout the 1930's and 1940's. If the voluntary agencies, by establishing closer ties to the government, became a part of the colonial system, they also deepened and broadened their contacts with the African populace; in this way they played an important vertical integrative role. Missionaries founded schools in neglected areas such as Ogoja Province and often charged no fees at first in order to attract pupils. Usually, however, each village paid its own way, if only because the Depression and the war virtually eliminated mission contributions from abroad. School fees, which usually accounted for about half of the salary bill, ranged in 1949 from nothing to £1/5 a year in the first four years of primary school (junior primary) and from £1 to £2/10 at the senior primary level.[28] The remainder of the salary bill was usually raised through monthly assessments on church members or by the establishment of an education or building fund to which the entire community contributed. Villagers also volunteered their labor to reduce school construction costs. The link between the mission and the community was the school committee, which included the most influential traditional as well as educated African leaders and was charged with responsibility for supplying labor, helping to raise funds, and selecting new school sites. This strategy of working through rather than imposing on the local power structures was very successful in increasing enrollment in voluntary agency schools during the 1940's.*

The rivalry between Protestants and Catholics, particularly in the Eastern Region, increased markedly in extent and intensity during the 1940's, mainly because the Roman Catholic Mission was able to expand its activities faster than the Protestant missions. The progress of both groups was hindered by the war, which halted the flow of European missionaries to Nigeria and drew many already there into service as army chaplains. After 1945, however, the Catholics enjoyed an advantage in personnel, for a strong missionary movement in Ireland during the 1930's resulted in an increased postwar flow of Irish priests to underdeveloped countries, whereas many English Protestants who might have gone abroad as missionaries stayed in their own country to meet the heavy demand for teachers brought on by the 1944 Education Act. Because the Catholic priests were not supporting families and were willing to contribute a sizeable proportion of their grant-in-aid salaries to mission work, the Catholic Mission could devote a higher proportion of its total budget to education than its Protestant counterparts.[29] In addition, the very fact that the Catholics were behind the Western Region Protestants in every respect and behind Eastern Region Protestants at the post-primary level spurred them to make a greater effort. This sense of rivalry was not confined to the missionaries. The Federal Association of Catholic Teachers, a

---

* Between 1941 and 1947 enrollment in assisted voluntary agency primary schools rose from 89,000 to 154,000; enrollment in unassisted primary schools rose from 220,000 to 359,000. In the latter year, 96 per cent of the primary, 93 per cent of the teacher training, and about 85 per cent of the secondary institutions were under voluntary agency control. The major European missions managed an overwhelming majority of voluntary agency schools. See Nigeria, Education Department, *Annual Report, 1942* (Lagos, 1942), p. 2; Nuffield Foundation and the Colonial Office, *African Education: A Study of Educational Policy and Practice in British Tropical Africa* (London, 1953), pp. 47–48.

Nigerian organization, argued in a 1945 memorandum to the Church hierarchy:

> In a young country like Nigeria, there are so many tendencies that we feel Catholic influence can go a long way to shape the course of development. This cannot happen unless Catholic men and women can take their places in the forefront of all other people and can lead the country in morals and social life. This will not be possible if their young people are largely products of Protestant schools. We feel that this is a strong reason for providing much wider facilities for our Catholic community.[30]

The Catholic mission advanced on several fronts, particularly in the East, where Bishop Shanahan's legacy and the highly receptive Ibo populace promised the greatest success. At the primary school level the mission moved into previously neglected areas as well as into Protestant strongholds such as the Cross River area. By 1948 the Catholics managed half of the East's primary schools—and almost twice the number managed by the next largest denomination, the Church Missionary Society.[31] At the same time unprecedented efforts were made to provide more teacher training and secondary education, which had been left to the Protestants almost by default.[32] Eastern Region Protestants thus felt threatened both by the Catholic invasion of formerly Protestant territory and by the breakdown of the old Protestant monopoly in post-primary education. In response the Protestants intensified their own efforts at conversion through the schools.

AFRICAN ACTIVITIES: THE POPULAR RESPONSE

The period between 1930 and 1950 witnessed an extraordinary outpouring of enthusiasm for education on the part of Southern Nigerians themselves. But this enthusiasm was manifested in quite different ways by various groups of people, depending on their degree of contact with European education and other accoutrements of modern life. Four such groups, with partially overlapping membership, were the traditional villagers, the tribal or progress unions, the Nigeria Union of Teachers, and the well-educated Southern Nigerian elite. In at least the latter three cases, previous patterns of educational expansion influenced the formation and later activities of new organizations with a considerable capacity for effective action. The remainder of this chapter considers how Southern Nigerians employed their increased organizational capacities to press for more and better education, as well as for changes in the political system.

For the average Southern Nigerian adult, education was still valued primarily as a way for his children to achieve upward mobility;

a related but probably secondary consideration was the honor and wealth literate young people would bring to the traditional social unit—the extended family, lineage, clan, village quarter, or village. The Depression, far from dimming popular enthusiasm for schooling, actually reinforced it by demonstrating in the starkest possible fashion the risks of relying on cash-crop farming—not to mention subsistence agriculture—for economic security.* One Nigerian wrote of the 1930's: "Those who had savings spent them to send their children to schools and colleges, because they saw that only salaried people were secure even in spite of salary cuts and stabilization. . . . It was then that I began to look at education as a commodity that does not fall in price."[33] The Depression and the war also changed the methods used by villagers to educate their children. If the government was unable to provide grants-in-aid for new schools because of overall budgetary limitations, the people did not send protests to the Education Department; instead they proceeded on their own, using whatever resources they possessed. After unsuccessfully petitioning the government for money so that "at least three fourths of the burghers of this town [could] know the three R's," one chief stated: "In view of these disappointments I often made deductions that our salvation lies not without but within."[34] Another reason for self-reliance, at least during the 1930's, was that the popular interest in academically oriented education conflicted with the official commitment to adaptionist theories. In practice the villagers ignored Hussey's proposals for a six-year, strongly vocational primary school syllabus, and insisted wherever possible that the voluntary agencies retain the old eight-year scheme. Rather than announce their disapproval of the government's directives, the villagers quietly disregarded them.

The 1930–50 period was the great age of voluntarism in Southern Nigerian education. Had not the desire for individual and communal improvement been unusually strong, it is most unlikely that the government-sponsored programs in mass education or the missionaries' continued efforts would have been at all successful.† Moreover, Nigerians began increasingly to organize quite independently of European agencies. The community development movement of the 1940's, which spread to villages and clans throughout the South, did not, of

---

* During the depths of the Depression palm oil sold for only fourpence a tin, and at least in Ibibio country the people thought it hardly worthwhile even to climb the trees to collect their fruit. Interview with W. T. Smith, July 28, 1964.

† If it is true that colonial officials and missionaries used Southern Nigerians for their own ends in erecting schools, it is equally true that Southern Nigerians, in choosing to attend schools, used the officials and missionaries for African ends.

course, confine itself to school construction. But as a British commentator observed, "its successes have been greatest in the 'welfare' fields of medicine and education. In education the success has been embarrassingly large, and the demand for quantity is endangering the standards of quality."[35] In some instances community development projects were organized by the traditional age-grades. More frequently the projects were started by village or clan unions—organizations usually formed by young men who had migrated to the cities in search of paid employment but who still had "the feeling of obligation toward the homeland, which has been a striking characteristic of African social organization."[36] In the cities these men joined others from their village or clan for mutual aid and protection and for cultural activities. The city organizations then encouraged the formation of branches in the home area, and in time unions emerged that were federations of urban and rural branches. These organizations, also known as patriotic, progress, or improvement unions, were quite successful in raising funds for local primary and, on occasion, secondary schools. Their education levies, graduated according to the members' incomes, tapped the considerable resources of local sons working in the cities; anyone who did not pay his share, whether he lived in a rural area or in the city, was subject to unpleasant social sanctions.[37] The unions were indispensable in organizing the manpower of the community for school construction or payment of the Assumed Local Contribution.[38] And with increasing frequency they assumed direct responsibility for staffing and managing community schools without turning to the missions for assistance. This tendency was particularly marked in the East, where in the absence of centralized political systems kinship and parochial loyalties were extremely strong, and where disputes over which mission—Protestant or Catholic—to invite could threaten the very sense of community that prompted the drive for schooling. In many ways, then, illiterate villagers were starting effectively to organize themselves for progress.

THE ROLE OF TRIBAL UNIONS

Southern Nigerians who had migrated from rural homes to the city remained interested in the improvement of traditional social units such as the village, lineage, or clan. But a sign that loyalties were shifting outward was the formation during the 1930's and 1940's of organizations purporting to speak for entire tribal groups or even a "nationality" of several million people, such as the Yorubas or Ibos. The spread of education affected the formation of these tribal unions in several ways, and the unions in turn had an important impact on educational expansion. A rather general outline of the factors at work in this complex process will be followed by illustrations from the early history of several tribal unions.

The primary schools located in rural areas gave their young students skills that could best be utilized in an urban environment and ambitions that could be realized only in the city. Migration to large Southern Nigerian cities was not, of course, confined to literates, but a young person who had been to school was far more likely to leave his home than an illiterate whose skills and outlook fitted him more nearly for rural life. The young African who arrived in the city soon discovered that the whole basis of social relations was different from that to which he was accustomed. Traditional society in Africa, as elsewhere, is built on kinship or descent ties and on face-to-face relationships within a quite limited geographical area. The typical city, on the other hand, brings together persons who are culturally as well as biologically unrelated, who are too numerous to establish face-to-face relationships with all whom they see, and who by their very presence in the city bear witness to new possibilities of geographical mobility. A parochial frame of reference, although sufficient for coping with village life, proved quite inadequate for the newcomer to urban life, who inevitably faced a kind of identity crisis. The kinsmen and other acquaintances who may have joined him in the city were too few in number to be politically effective, and in some cases too few to form a social circle of their own. It became necessary for the migrant to establish a broader social identity by seeking others who were culturally similar to him; in the process he formed liaisons with migrants from villages that he would formerly have regarded as rivals or even outright enemies of his own village. As the boundaries of the new in-group were extended, so the nature of the out-group changed; the outsiders were no longer a neighboring village or clan but a group of culturally distinct people with whom the migrant may have had no contact whatsoever before coming to the city. Tribalism became an issue for the urban migrant when it probably had no meaning to his more traditional parents.

Education and urbanization, as well as other components of "social mobilization," are usually associated, quite correctly, with the rise of nationalism.[89] In Nigeria, however, nationalism has not been the only result of social mobilization, for the literate resident of the city, in transcending his traditional frame of reference, may become aware of several new identities, of which the national is only one. Which of these identities the socially mobilized person finds most congenial depends largely on the particular social and political situation in which he finds himself. Thus the liberation from parochialism may produce nationalistic sentiments in the highly educated person, who can visualize the potentialities for himself and for all his countrymen of an independent, unified nation-state. But the less educated are not apt to take such a broad view, and what has been variously termed "ethnicity" or "super-tribalism" is, in Africa, the likely result.[40] The ethnic group features a certain amount of cultural uniformity rooted in African experience—usually a common language and similar social stratification patterns at the local level. Urban migrants not yet attuned to the imported practices that characterized political and administrative life at the national level thus found it easier to view the world through ethnic than through national lenses. But ethnicity is not just a relic of the past; rather it is, like nationalism, a creative response to the forces of change. In both ethnicity and nationalism the principle of kinship and traditional man's almost total reliance on face-to-face relationships have been abandoned. In some instances ethnicity and nationalism are complementary; in other instances they may follow a collision course.[41] But whatever their relationship, the two phenomena have much in common in terms of their origins and basic dynamics.

Ethnicity may thus be viewed as the product of a modernization process that, far from detribalizing the African, in a sense actually tribalized him. As already suggested, education played its part by stimulating migration to the cities, which then became the real crucibles of ethnic identity. In Southern Nigeria, the desire of missionaries and colonial officials to educate people in the rural areas unintentionally stimulated this trend by drawing away from these areas the ablest and most energetic young people once they had completed their schooling. In addition, the widespread provision of limited amounts of schooling, although it enabled large numbers of Nigerians to read the new nationalistic journalism of Nnamdi Azikiwe,[42] also heightened ethnic consciousness, for those who went to the cities were too poorly educated to compete directly against the British for jobs and found themselves competing instead against other Africans. The struggle for employment was bound to produce frustration, and those not chosen for the best jobs found it easy to blame their plight on the advantages possessed by members of other groups. Of course, different groups clearly did have differential access to education, which in turn was the key to job mobility. Educational achievement became a "modern" criterion for distinguishing between groups that were different from each other in various traditional ways as well. And the new criterion was the one that really counted, given the values and aspirations of the urban migrants. Once a particular group gained access to the best jobs, moreover, its members could use their positions to find jobs for their friends, or at least to pass on news of job opportunities to other members of their tribal unions. In this way group inequalities based initially on education alone could easily become cumulative; their repercussions were felt in unequal levels of employment and income and in different degrees of social status. As Aristide Zolberg has observed, an informal ranking of ethnic groups emerged during the colonial period in West Africa; it was widely believed, by Africans and Europeans alike, that certain tribes were more progressive, intelligent, or generally worthy of respect than others.[43] Differential group access to education was of critical importance in this stratification process.

What was the best course of action open to the urban migrant who was acutely concerned lest his ethnic group fall behind others in the struggle for wealth, power, and status? Certainly the rural masses had to be informed of the problem. If the masses were not aware of their ethnicity, then they would have to learn who they really were through the efforts of "ethnic missionaries" returning to the homeland. These "missionaries" would also have to outline a strategy by which the ethnic group, once fully conscious of its unity and its potential, could compete with its rivals. Clearly the competition required enrolling more children in school, particularly at the secondary level, for the graduates of a good local secondary school would be assured rapid individual mobility within modern society while at the same time enhancing the power and status of the group as a whole. If scholarships could be raised to send "sons of the soil" abroad for university studies, so much the better. The gospel of ethnicity and the gospel of education were thus mutually reinforcing. Educational schemes sponsored by the tribal unions fostered ethnic consciousness in the rural areas; a heightened sense of ethnicity, in turn, facilitated the spread of education.

The dynamic relationship between ethnicity and education can best be understood by tracing the history of some of the tribal unions active during the 1930–50 period. The examples given here include "tribes" that are not exactly comparable in size or in cultural differentiation from neighboring groups—the Urhobos, Ibibios, Egbados, and Ibos. The Urhobos and Ibibios are linguistic minorities within their respective regions; the Egbados are a subgroup of the Yorubas; the Ibos are not a tribe so much as a pan-tribal or national entity, with several million members.* Despite these differences, there are remarkable similarities in the way changes in ethnic identity were engineered and in the emphasis urban ethnic missionaries placed on post-primary education.

The first three of these groups have in common a history of oppression at the hands of their neighbors during the pre-colonial period. The Urhobos were subjected to raids by nineteenth-century Ijaw pirates, who often sold their captives into slavery; the coastal people still tend to regard the Urhobos, who live inland from the Niger Delta, as primitive and "bush." The Ibibios were raided by Ibos and sold to Europeans by Efiks, who have generally considered the Ibibios their inferiors.[44] The lands inhabited by the Egbados to the west of Abeokuta were often ravaged in battles between the Dahomeans and the Egba Yorubas of Abeokuta for the control of slave and trade routes.[45] Victims of oppression and scorn from other Africans in the nineteenth century, these groups were neglected by Europeans in the twentieth. The missionary thrust into the Western Region through Lagos and Abeokuta—and the railroad that followed the same route—bypassed non-Yoruba minorities to the east, like the Urhobos, and Yoruba subgroups to the west, like the Egbados. The Ibibios were generally ignored by the missionaries, who concentrated on Calabar and other areas along the Cross River. It is difficult to generalize about the Ibos, but they received missionary education later, and were less prosperous, than the other major nationality with which they could be compared, the Yorubas.

By the 1920's and 1930's young men from all four groups were migrating to urban areas in search of suitable employment. Each group soon discovered, however, that some other group was ahead of it in

---

* As recent studies of nationalism have pointed out, it is fruitless to search for a set of objective characteristics that are both common and unique to the average nation. See Rupert Emerson, *From Empire to Nation* (Boston, 1960), pp. 89–209; Dankwart Rustow, *A World of Nations* (Washington, D.C., 1967), pp. 38–62. The same caveat applies to any effort to find the distinct defining characteristics of African ethnic groups. In many instances ethnic missionaries are themselves quite unclear about these matters. In other instances the characteristics may be fairly well defined but reflect classification schemes devised by Europeans for administrative or religious purposes rather than traditional characteristics. The Bangala of the Congo are perhaps the classic example of an artificial ethnic group; see Crawford Young, *Politics in the Congo* (Princeton, N.J., 1965), pp. 242–46. Then too, the fact that ethnicity is a response to the forces of change implies that ethnic boundaries can be quite fluid. The ultimate test of a man's tribal affiliation, as of his nationality, is subjective: he is who he says he is.

education and hence monopolized the best jobs. Urhobos, Egbados, or Ibos in Lagos were at a disadvantage compared to Lagos or Egba Yorubas; Ibo or Ibibio migrants to Calabar had to compete with Efiks, Urhobos in Warri with Itsekiris, Ibibios in Port Harcourt or Aba with Onitsha Ibos. Faced with these handicaps, and with the contempt frequently shown them by members of economically or socially dominant groups, the migrants began to meet together in an effort to improve their lot. Eventually tribal unions were formed in the cities: the Ibibio Welfare Union (later Ibibio State Union) in Ikot Ekpene (1928), the Urhobo Brotherly Society (later Urhobo Progress Union) in Warri (1931), the Egbado Union in Lagos (1935), and the Ibo Union (later Ibo Federal Union and Ibo State Union) in Lagos (1936). The men who took the lead in founding these organizations often had only modest educational attainments and held jobs as clerks, minor functionaries, traders, teachers, and the like.[46] They used their contacts with urban migrants elsewhere to set up branches of the union in other cities, and they established rural branches through their own villages. In visits to the rural areas these men tried to convince people to forget old feuds between or within villages and, as the Urhobo Progress Union said, to "foster the spirit of love, mutual understanding and brotherhood."[47] But brotherhood was difficult to practice when people did not yet know that they were brothers. As the General Secretary of the Ibo Federal (State) Union, B. O. N. Eluwa, found during his tours of Iboland from 1947 to 1951, the villagers "couldn't even imagine all Ibos."* Similar problems of parochialism plagued other union leaders as well—men like T. J. Adewale, a teacher and adult education organizer actively involved in the Egbado Union, or I. U. Akpabio, who returned in 1943 from university studies in the United States to spend the next three years traveling from village to village on behalf of the Ibibio State Union.

The tribal unions were active on many fronts. The Egbado Union, for example, pressed successfully to consolidate the native authorities operating in its area and to change the division's name from Ilaro to Egbado; the Urhobo Progress Union raised funds to pay the court costs of a protracted land dispute with the Itsekiris of Warri. But in no field were these organizations more active than in education. Each

---

* Interview with B. O. N. Eluwa, Aug. 22, 1964. In the 1930's many Aro and Onitsha Ibos consciously rejected identification as Ibos, preferring to think of themselves as separate, superior groups. The very term "Yoruba" was popularized by Church Missionary Society leaders during the nineteenth century who were anxious to produce a Bible in a uniform language for several city-states that were warring against each other at the time.

of the four unions mounted a drive to establish a new secondary school, and each finally achieved this aim, after years of painstaking efforts to collect small sums from union members.[48] These funds were used for both the capital costs of the school and for university scholarships; the first principals of Ibibio State College and Urhobo College were in fact recipients of tribal union scholarships who knew they were being groomed abroad for these posts.[49] Even aside from financial matters, the establishment of these schools was not easy, for the issues of where to site the school, what to name it, and whom to appoint as administrators brought to the fore the very internecine conflicts that the tribal unions were attempting to resolve. It was therefore a major triumph for ethnic unity, as well as for educational progress, when the doors were opened to Ibibio State College (Ikot Ekpene, 1946), Urhobo College (Effurun, 1949), Egbado College (Ilaro, 1950) and Ibo State College (Aba, 1952). In each case about two-thirds of the places were reserved fairly explicitly for students from the sponsoring ethnic group. Once these institutions were in operation, many communities, particularly those that had been unsuccessful in the competition over siting and administrative leadership, set up their own secondary schools. In this indirect way the tribal unions had a quite significant effect on the expansion of secondary school enrollments during the 1940's.[50]

THE NIGERIA UNION OF TEACHERS

As enrollments rose during the early years of the twentieth century, increasing numbers of young Southern Nigerians entered teaching as a full- or part-time career. The growth of the teaching force—from under 9,000 in 1931 to over 40,000 in 1950—in turn made possible an almost sixfold jump in primary school enrollment, from 174,000 in 1930 to 971,000 two decades later.[51] One of the more important functions of the schools, in fact, was to train and recruit people to staff new schools a few years later, thus assuring the continued expansion of enrollment. But a teacher's educational influence is not confined to his work as an individual in the classroom; as a member of an organized group of teachers he may affect the formulation of policy concerning the educational system as a whole. How did the relationship between Southern Nigeria's teachers and the educational system predispose the teachers to think and act as an organized interest group? What changes in educational policy did the leaders of the group envisage, and were they successful in influencing the formulation and execution of policy?

As the largest category of regularly paid employees in Southern Nigeria, primary and secondary school teachers have long enjoyed at least the potential strength of numbers. But this potential could not be realized until problems arose that required coordinated action. The underlying problem for the typical Southern Nigerian teacher, and one that became more acute over time, was his uncertain and highly ambiguous status in society. European missionaries regarded the African teacher as the ideal intermediary between the white, Christian culture and the black, pagan one; insofar as the European culture was dominant, the teacher was to be a vertical integrator between the rulers and the ruled. In many ways the teacher performed this role admirably. Along with a new religion and literacy he also brought to the villages new habits of dress, health standards, and the example of self-help through study.[52] On the other hand, he was ideally placed to express the views of the local community to European missionaries and government officials. This position midway between the colonial elite and the masses enabled many teachers eventually to gain political power during the early 1950's as local representatives to regional and national legislatures. But what was subsequently a political asset was a source of some frustration during the period when power was still effectively monopolized by the British. Teachers were clearly not a part of the masses they had come to educate, but neither were they necessarily members of the emerging Southern Nigerian elite; they were too numerous, and most of them were too poorly educated, to gain acceptance at the highest level of Nigerian society.

The fact that the vast majority of Southern Nigerian teachers were employed by European mission groups further contributed to the ambiguity of the teacher's status. During the early years of missionary activity, teaching and preaching were inseparable: the teacher was expected to preach to the local community on Sundays, and in certain voluntary agencies like the Church Missionary Society, teaching was considered a stepping-stone to the ministry. As the educational system expanded, teaching became a more specialized vocation, and the development of teacher training institutions as distinct from seminaries encouraged the view that teaching could at least theoretically be separated from preaching and might even lead to other occupations in which literacy was valued. With specialization came secularization: many young Nigerians began to regard teaching not as a calling but as a job, and the European missionaries not as fellow evangelists but as employers. This trend in the outlook of the teaching force disturbed many missionaries, who felt that they had given up the comforts of their homeland to convert the African and who therefore expected their converts to show a similar spirit of self-sacrifice. But African teachers viewed the missionaries' objections to materialism as hypocritical, because the living standards of the missionaries were far superior to those of the Africans. In addition, during the Depression the salaries of Africans were sometimes cut by a higher percentage than the salaries of Europeans. The resulting tensions between teachers and the major voluntary agencies over financial matters blurred the old image of the teacher as a humble laborer in the vineyard of the Lord.

The growing role of the government in financing and supervising educational institutions further complicated the issue of the teacher's place in society. If a voluntary agency was his employer but the government was his paymaster, which of the two was actually responsible for his welfare? Teachers naturally began to look to the paymaster for assistance and to compare their own salaries with those of government teachers, who were paid more even when their training was similar.[53] The government's new interest in education probably also strengthened the tendency of voluntary agency teachers to define their occupation as a secular one. But if the government began to replace the missions as a reference group for teachers, British officials were either unaware of this development or unprepared to admit that the Department of Education bore anything more than minimal responsibility for the salaries and service conditions of voluntary agency employees. The voluntary agencies and the government each claimed that the other was responsible for the teachers' welfare. These evasive tactics became a serious matter in the Depression, when the missions and the government assigned each other the blame for laying teachers off or reducing their salaries. Failure to clarify the extent to which a teacher could claim status as a civil servant was a major source of frustration prior to and during the period from 1930 to 1950.

Teachers, then, were in an ambiguous position in at least three respects: they were neither elite nor mass, their occupation was secular as well as religious, and they were both private and public employees. As early as the 1920's many teachers were voicing a desire for an improvement, as well as a clarification, of their position. But the changes in government policy initiated by Director of Education Hussey in 1930 only added to the teachers' grievances. Along with his adaptionist proposals, Hussey introduced a new set of teaching categories that in effect demoted teachers with long experience and made it difficult for them to qualify for higher pay. This action, and the grant-in-aid cuts that followed in 1931, had a catalytic effect in bringing teachers together for appropriate organized action. On July 8, 1931, representatives of informal teachers' groups from five Southern Nigerian cities met in Lagos to form the country's first union, the Nigeria Union of Teachers (N.U.T.).[54] The organization grew slowly during its first decade, but after the General Secretary, E. E. Esua, began working on a full-time basis in 1942, membership grew quite rapidly, from 2,000 in 1944 (50 branches), to 17,000 in 1947 (90 branches), to 22,000 in 1950 (176 branches).[55]

It was difficult for Nigeria's teachers to act as one body because the teaching force was scattered throughout a very large country, comprised many different ethnic groups, was employed by competing religious agencies, and was highly differentiated in terms of educational attainments and formal training in pedagogy. But the union's leadership made a concerted and generally quite successful effort to overcome these internal differences. Although the N.U.T.'s initial base of operations and leadership reflected the educational lead of Yorubaland and Calabar over the rest of the country,* active recruitment campaigns were undertaken in Ibo areas during the late 1930's and in the Northern Region during the 1940's. Contacts between the North and the South were severely limited, and organizational work in the North was difficult, but the fact that the union attempted to recruit members in the North is evidence of its effort to think along truly national lines.[56] Esua urged teachers to form local branches on territorial or "professional rather than on denominational lines,"[57] so that they might be united professionally even if divided confessionally. The problem of Protestant-Catholic competition was, of course, very serious, particularly since the union's leadership was almost exclusively Protestant and included a number of Anglicans who were preachers as well as teachers. But special efforts were made to involve Catholics in the union's affairs. The Catholic Bishop of Lagos was made a patron of the union, and in 1942 the presidents of the two important Onitsha and Lagos branches were Catholic teachers. The Federal Association of Catholic Teachers, formed in 1937 by J. F. Odunjo to negotiate directly with the mission for better terms of ser-

---

* Prominent early Yoruba leaders, mostly from Lagos and Abeokuta, were Rev. I. O. Ransome-Kuti, President of the union from 1932 to 1955; Rev. J. O. Lucas; Rev. Seth Kale; and Rev. A. A. Efunkoya. Esua and Eyo Ita, one-time editor of the union's magazine, are from Calabar. Alvan Ikoku is an Aro Ibo with a Calabar mother. Esua, Ita, and Ikoku all attended the Hope Waddell Training Institute, Calabar.

vice, was closely associated with the N.U.T. in negotiations between teachers and the government. Odunjo, who encouraged Catholic teachers to join the Nigeria Union of Teachers as well, was made Acting General Secretary of the union during Esua's visit to the United States in 1944. By cutting across ethnic, regional, and denominational lines, the union performed a unique role as a horizontal integrator of this influential group of Nigerians. Similarly, the union served as a vertical integrator by including all grades and classes of teachers in its membership.

The goals of the Nigeria Union of Teachers may be described as responses to the Nigerian teacher's ambiguous status. Clearly, if teachers were considered professionals, with high standards of training and performance, they would have a better chance of becoming part of the Southern Nigerian elite; more teacher training facilities, opportunities for upgrading on the job, curricular improvements, and so on would serve this end. If only for reasons of self-interest, the teachers' union was a pressure group demanding quality in education at a time when popular pressures were overwhelmingly for quantitative expansion of the system. The N.U.T. also drew a clear distinction between teaching and preaching, in spite of the fact that many of the union's leaders combined the two in their own lives. This emphasis on secularity was intensified by the leadership's concern with specific problems of material welfare—low salaries, uncertain opportunities for advancement, inadequate pension schemes, salary cuts, and termination of employment without adequate explanation. Better salaries and conditions of service were advocated as ways to improve the quality of the profession by attracting talented Nigerians into teaching and holding them there.[58] The N.U.T. tried to resolve the dilemma of responsibility for the teachers' welfare by insisting, in Reverend Ransome-Kuti's words: "It is the duty of the government to foster education and to look after the welfare of teachers, and no amount of whatever the missions can say or do can exonerate the government from final responsibility."[59] The union did not want voluntary agency schools to be taken over entirely by the Department of Education, for voluntary agency teachers enjoyed a freedom to organize and to express opinions on current issues that they would forfeit if they were to become full-fledged civil servants. Yet the union did want the government to supervise the voluntary agencies more carefully in order to stop such abuses as cutting African salaries more heavily than those of European missionaries or imposing salary cuts prior to the effective date of grant-in-aid reductions.

More important was the argument that the government should extend grants-in-aid to cover virtually all voluntary agency teachers. Personal qualifications rather than the presumed efficiency of each school should be the basis for determining salaries, which should be brought up to the level of government teacher scales.[60]

The objectives of the Nigeria Union of Teachers strongly influenced its tactics. Because the government was its main target, the union needed a centralized structure capable of dealing with officials in Lagos; negotiations with the voluntary agencies were secondary. To demonstrate their professional respectability, teachers had to work within the established system as much as possible, making constructive suggestions for educational reform rather than launching a frontal assault on the system itself. This approach did not preclude pressuring the government publicly through newspaper releases, letters to political groups, and letters to Nigerian members of the Legislative Council—tactics that were all regularly employed. Nor were strikes necessarily precluded; a 1947 strike by the N.U.T. National Executive was instrumental in securing substantial pay raises for teachers and, incidentally, in raising union membership figures. But in general union leaders preferred to work with key British officials rather than against them, and to do so by "silent actions, not just empty words," as one leader phrased it. That they had opportunities to work in this fashion is clear. Shortly after its formation the N.U.T. was accorded representation on the central Board of Education, an important precedent because it marked the first time that Nigerians were permitted to join a government body to offer advice on specific problems.[61] Particularly close communication was maintained with Hussey despite disagreement on many issues. Later, in 1943, Reverend Ransome-Kuti was appointed a member of the Elliot Commission, which examined the possibilities of university education in British West Africa, and in 1946 Alvan Ikoku, another union leader, was appointed to the Legislative Council as a special representative for educational interests. The willingness of the British to consider union requests was doubtless influenced by the fact that the union's leaders, with only a few exceptions, were political moderates.*

How effective was the Nigeria Union of Teachers in achieving its

---

* Ikoku once made explicit the connection between his vocation and his preference for gradualism: "I am a school-master, and if I did not adopt such a policy I should be a very bad teacher. We must regulate the tempo of our advance—not too slow, not too fast. I have carried my school methods into my politics." Alvan Ikoku, in Nigeria, *Proceedings of the General Conference on Review of the Constitution, January, 1950* (Lagos, 1950), p. 55.

objectives? The union's decision to work within the established colonial system makes it extremely difficult to answer this question, because one cannot determine the extent to which N.U.T. leaders
reduced their demands in order to be heard at all, or the extent to
which the decisions of various directors of education were altered by
union arguments and protests. But the union seems to have been a
relatively successful pressure group during the 1930–50 period. It was
able to call the government's attention to voluntary agency abuses,
most notably in the 1936 Calabar teachers' strike against the Church
of Scotland Mission, when in response to union protests the Director
of Education intervened on behalf of teachers protesting unwar-
ranted salary cuts.[62] The extension of grant-in-aid coverage during
the 1940's was in some measure a result of sustained union pressure;
certainly the threat of a teacher strike in 1947 pushed salary scales
significantly higher. The N.U.T. proposed more than forty amend-
ments to the first draft of the 1948 education code; according to Alvan
Ikoku all but one of these were subsequently accepted by the Director
of Education.[63] The government could not, of course, afford to pay
voluntary agency teachers civil-service salary rates. But the pay raises
that were granted probably kept many teachers from leaving their
jobs; their departure would have posed serious staffing problems for
the new schools being opened throughout Southern Nigeria.

Some political analysts have noted how few effective, bargaining
interest groups there are in non-Western countries.[64] The Nigeria
Union of Teachers is clearly one of these select few, perhaps because
its members were the products and the employees of an educational
system imported from Europe. But, as we have seen, teachers were
not content just to perpetuate the system. They organized in order
to shift the burden of responsibility for both the quality and the
quantity of education from several private religious institutions to
one public secular one. In so doing they encouraged a tendency,
which was developing somewhat independently within British colonial and Nigerian nationalist circles as well, to look to the government for any major educational changes that might occur in the future.

THE EDUCATED ELITE

As secondary school enrollment expanded, and as a few Southern
Nigerians began to return after completing university studies in
Great Britain and the United States, an indigenous elite emerged
with educational qualifications close to those of the colonial rulers.

The new elite was not an organized group, but a category of people defined by their educational achievements and generally active in the politics of transitional colonial rule. Some were politically moderate and were willing to serve on various advisory committees appointed by the government. Others, deeply frustrated by the slow pace at which the British were transferring power to Nigerians, took a stand of political opposition to the government and went to the people for support.*

With striking unanimity, however, all members of the elite, whether moderate or radical, considered education the key to progress, happiness, and successful self-rule in Nigeria and in Africa as a whole. J. E. Casely-Hayford, the prominent Gold Coast lawyer, spoke for all educated Africans in his 1929 address to the National Congress of British West Africa:

History tells us how other peoples have risen to nationhood, to economic security and power. We must tread the same path if we would see salvation as a people; and that path is primarily educational.... There must be an educational awakening throughout West Africa greater than at any time in African history, and when this pentecost breaks in upon us, we shall begin to tread the sure path to national emancipation.[65]

The same faith in education's unlimited potentialities for good may be seen in a letter written by Nnamdi Azikiwe while he was still a student in the United States: "I pray that the Lord may help me so that I may return to Africa with the golden fleece, and propagate from the Zambezi to the Nile, yea! from the Nile to the Congo, the new learning, the recent philosophy of education, that education itself is life and not necessarily a preparation for life."[66] The new elite stood as one in insisting that post-primary standards be kept high, and not "adapted" to the point where Nigerians could not obtain the best education available in England or elsewhere. More than perhaps any other issue, the question of educational standards could rouse the elite not just to protest, but to organize its protest. Thus, dissatisfaction with the quality of Yaba Higher College diplomas precipitated the formation in 1934 of the Lagos Youth Movement,

---

* Sir Adeyemo Alakija, Francis Ibiam, Alvan Ikoku, and Rev. O. Effiong were some of the more moderate members of the new elite. The more radical included Herbert Macaulay, Nnamdi Azikiwe, Eyo Ita, H. O. Davies, Obafemi Awolowo, Mbonu Ojike, K. O. Mbadiwe, and other members of the Nigerian Youth Movement (active nationally by 1938), the National Council of Nigeria and the Cameroons (founded in 1944), the Zikist Movement (1946), and the London-based West African Students' Union (1925). The role of these organizations in the Nigerian nationalist movement is described in detail in James Coleman's study *Nigeria: Background to Nationalism* (Berkeley, Calif., 1958).

which "became the nucleus of Nigeria's first genuine nationalist organization," the Nigerian Youth Movement;[67] dissatisfaction with the government's handling of a 1944 student strike at King's College, Lagos, led the Nigerian Union of Students to call a public meeting, out of which came the impulse to establish the National Council of Nigeria and the Cameroons (NCNC) to further the nationalist cause.[68] Many educated Southern Nigerians used their organizational skills in another way by establishing new secondary schools.[69] The elite also pressed for the rapid expansion of post-primary scholarship programs. For example, Nnamdi Azikiwe, who quickly gained repute as a journalist and nationalist upon his return home from the United States in 1937, proposed in his 1943 *Political Blueprint of Nigeria* that the British send two hundred Nigerians abroad annually to study for the next five years. These persons could then take over the posts held by the British, ensuring self-rule for Nigeria within fifteen years.

Elite concern that secondary and higher education be improved and expanded reflected the coincidence of personal ambitions and nationalist leanings. By limiting access to university education or instituting reforms that might lower academic standards, the British not only restricted the educated Nigerian's opportunity for upward mobility but also secured the hold of colonialism on the country. For the educated Nigerian upward mobility meant the opportunity not only to gain personal power (largely through his academic accomplishments) but also to demonstrate that Nigerians, or Africans generally, were as intelligent and as capable of self-government as any other group of people.*

The emerging Southern Nigerian elite did not by any means confine its attention to secondary and higher education; demands for free, universal, and compulsory primary education were sounded with increasing frequency by Nigerian politicians and elite organizations. The three successful Lagos candidates for the Legislative Council in 1923 pledged to work for compulsory primary education throughout the country, and the 1938 Youth Charter of the Nigerian Youth Movement urged that "mass education ought to be the true

* Consciousness of the stereotype of African mental inferiority weighed heavily on many well-educated Nigerians. Azikiwe wrote in 1934: "The African is human, and is intellectually alert just as the average European, Asiatic, or American. What he needs is an opportunity to demonstrate his capabilities.... African 'backwardness' is judged on his failure to measure up to the standards of Western education which has been purposely denied him." B. N. Azikiwe, "How Shall We Educate the African?" *Journal of the African Society,* XXXIII (April 1934), 143, 150.

pivot of the educational policy of our Government. We will therefore urge on the Government to make elementary education progressively free and compulsory."[70] Similar demands were voiced in the
West African Students' Union conference resolutions of 1941 and
the 1943 memoranda of the West African Press Delegation and the
Nigerian Youth Movement. By 1943 the Lagos Town Council had
even established a committee to consider the feasibility of free primary education for children of the city's permanent residents.[71] In
1946 and again in 1949, Francis Ibiam tabled a motion in the Legislative Council calling for free and compulsory primary education,
and an amended motion, passed in 1949, urged native authorities to
levy education rates in order to realize this objective in certain local
areas.[72] This emphasis on primary education for the masses, like the
elite's emphasis on post-primary education, reflected both personal
ambitions—the desire to gain popularity by demanding more of an
already popular commodity—and the belief that self-government and
economic development for Nigeria as a whole would be hampered unless the benefits of education were extended to all. That the individual and collective aims of elite members were so complementary in
these matters only increased the elite's tendency to regard education
as an infallible cure for the ills of Africa. A few years later, as we
shall see, the elite's efforts to fulfill pledges made during this period
led them to institute universal primary education schemes in the
Western and Eastern regions.

THE POLITICAL ROLE OF THE NEW GROUPS

The new groups formed as a direct or indirect result of previous
patterns of educational expansion—tribal unions, the Nigeria Union
of Teachers, and the educated elite—differed from each other in
their reasons for valuing education, in the levels of schooling they
considered most important, and in their tactics vis-à-vis the government. But the cumulative effect of their separate efforts was to reinforce the expansionist tendencies already present in the work of missionaries, villagers and colonial officials.

The contribution of the new groups to education extended beyond
their specific educational activities during this period. In different
ways these groups enabled the people greatly to increase their organizational capacities, so that by the early 1950's Southern Nigerians
were able to assume, and then take advantage of, a considerable
amount of political power. Experience gained in administering organizations like the Egbado Union, the Lagos branch of the Nigeria
Union of Teachers, or the Nigerian Youth Movement could be em-

ployed later in forming political parties or ensuring an effective chain of command within a government ministry. Such experience was spread among men with widely different educational levels, from the "ethnic missionary" or village schoolteacher with only a few years of primary education to the sophisticated Lagos lawyer. And organizational experience was widely diffused geographically, benefiting the rural teacher, the urban intelligentsia, and the tribal union leader, whose task was to maintain links between rural and urban areas.

The activities of the three groups, moreover, reached different but complementary clienteles. The tribal unions constituted the building blocks, as it were, of Southern Nigeria's political parties: from its inception until 1951 the National Council of Nigeria and the Cameroons was really a federation of other organizations, many of them tribal or progress unions, and a pan-Yoruba organization, the Egbe Omo Oduduwa (founded in 1945 and reorganized in 1948) was the nucleus of Southern Nigeria's second major party, the Action Group (founded in 1951). The tribal unions not only provided these two parties with a mass base in both urban and rural areas but also affected the public image of the parties; the NCNC was popularly linked with Ibo nationalism, and the Action Group with Yoruba nationalism. Teachers played a critical part in the emerging party system because they comprised the largest occupational bloc in the regional and central Houses of Assembly. These men, many of them active in the Nigeria Union of Teachers, were particularly prominent as representatives of rural areas, and once in the legislatures they became local leaders for one party or the other.* From the educated, predominantly urban elite emerged the key organizers and ideologues of the parties. To put the point somewhat too simply, tribal unions provided the votes, teachers the local leadership, and the educated elite the regional and national leadership for the two political parties. Because of these organizational factors, and because of the intense competition for power between the parties themselves, Southern Nigerian life assumed by the early 1950's a highly political character. The new political realities, in part the result of educational expansion, were to have a profound impact on the educational policies of subsequent years.

* In cases where a teacher was associated with the activities of a tribal union, his chances of gaining political prominence were quite high. The first principals of the four tribal union secondary schools described earlier were all elected to regional or federal legislatures. Two of these men, I. U. Akpabio of Ibibio State College and J. A. O. Odebiyi of Egbado College, later became ministers of education in their respective regions.

PART II

The Era of Universal Primary Education

CHAPTER 5

The Political Setting

For Nigeria, the decade of the 1950's was marked by the crucial transition from colonial to independent status. Once the British government had accepted the inadequacy of the 1946 constitution as a vehicle for African self-expression, the devolution of power to Africans proceeded far more swiftly than in all the previous fifty years; because of this greatly increased pace of change, Nigeria had a new constitution every three years from 1951 to 1960, whereas only two constitutions (1923 and 1946) had been promulgated in the preceding decades. The transitional phase was begun in earnest by the Macpherson constitution of 1951. Through its provisions the regional Houses of Assembly, which had been impotent advisory bodies since their formation in 1946, were given power to raise and appropriate funds and to pass laws in specified fields such as education, health, agriculture, and local government. The method of selecting regional legislators was democratized: the great majority were to be elected through a multi-stage electoral college system with taxpayer suffrage at the primary level, and Nigerians were to constitute a majority in the Executive Council (or cabinet) of each House of Assembly. At the same time the Macpherson constitution tried to maintain the influence of the central government by establishing a Federal House of Representatives, most of whose members were selected from among those who were already members of the regional Houses. This central legislature had power to pass laws in all fields, including those that were also in the regional legislatures' domain. The civil service remained unified, even though within each department a certain amount of decentralization was brought about by the granting of new powers to the regions.[1]

Most Nigerian nationalists were dissatisfied with the 1951 constitution, which they felt was ambiguous in many important respects and did not grant Nigerians any more than "semi-responsible" government. But even those who opposed the constitution were attracted by the prospect that a political party might implement its programs by gaining control of the regional, if not national, legislature. Southerners in particular might profit from the decentralization of power, for they would not have to wait for the approval of the less advanced North in order to carry out their own reforms. The Macpherson constitution therefore set off a flurry of activity among Southern Nigerian politicians to gain control of the Western and Eastern Houses of Assembly, and it led to the creation of a new political party to rival the National Council of Nigeria and the Cameroons (NCNC). Although the NCNC was national rather than regional or tribal in orientation, the activities of its President, Nnamdi Azikiwe, and the mass support Azikiwe enjoyed among the Ibo people gave certain prominent Yorubas cause to fear that the party was a vehicle for Ibo rather than Nigerian nationalism. The possibility of an NCNC victory in the Western as well as the Eastern Region spurred these men to consider forming another party, and in March 1951, after a year of behind-the-scenes negotiations among prominent Western Region lawyers, teachers, publishers, businessmen, and traditional rulers, the Action Group was launched as a political party under the leadership of Obafemi Awolowo.[2]

In the regional elections that followed, the NCNC emerged as the decisive winner in the East, with sixty-five seats compared to four seats won by the small United National Party. In the West, however, the Action Group scored a narrow victory over the NCNC, winning some forty-five seats to about thirty-five for the NCNC.[3] In each House of Assembly the ruling party selected the members of the Executive Council, and a certain number of legislators was chosen to represent the region when the House of Representatives convened. Awolowo became Western Region Minister for Local Government and acted as unofficial Leader of Government Business; Eyo Ita, a vice-president of the NCNC, served as Minister for Natural Resources and unofficial Leader in the East. Azikiwe, who had been elected to the Western House of Assembly from Lagos, was blocked in his efforts to enter the Federal House of Representatives and became instead Leader of the Opposition in the Western legislature.

EDUCATIONAL POLICIES OF THE NEW LEGISLATORS

Although the new legislators in both the Eastern and Western regions were prepared to consider a variety of matters, it soon became apparent that they planned to assign high priority to a massive expansion of educational facilities, particularly at the primary level. In the West the theme was clearly sounded by Awolowo. Only two days after the House had assembled for its first budget session, he spelled out one of the principles by which his party was guided: "As far as possible expenditure on services which tend to the welfare, and health and education of the people should be increased at the expense of any expenditure that does not answer to the same test."[4]

In July 1952 the new Minister of Education for the Western Region, S. O. Awokoya, presented a detailed set of proposals calling for an "all-out expansion of all types of educational institutions."[5] The major proposal was that a program of free, universal, and compulsory education (popularly known as U.P.E.)* be introduced in the region not later than January 1955. To make such a program possible without lowering standards drastically, teacher training facilities were to be rapidly increased. In addition, secondary modern schools on the British model were to be built as an outlet for some of the primary school leavers, and ten new secondary schools were to open soon "in areas that are underserved."[6] In Awokoya's view, these proposals deserved top priority: "Educational development is imperative and urgent. It must be treated as a national emergency, second only to war. It must move with the momentum of a revolution."[7]

In 1953, when the Eastern Region Minister of Education, R. I. Uzoma, presented two carefully reasoned white papers outlining his government's educational policy,[8] the emphasis was again on universal primary education. Uzoma hoped that if local government bodies contributed 45 per cent of the cost, a free junior primary (or four-year) program could go into effect throughout the region by the end of 1956. To prepare for this program the output of trained teachers would be increased from about 1,300 to 2,500 annually "in the next few years," and a secondary school would be provided in every division that lacked one.[9] As might be expected, the proposals of Awokoya and Uzoma generated great interest among the populace.

As Awokoya had urged, universal primary education was intro-

---

* "U.P.E." stands for "universal primary education." The programs in both the Western and Eastern regions, although different in several respects, were widely known by these initials.

duced to the Western Region by January 1955. The registration of
schoolchildren was celebrated in Ibadan with a parade and speeches
by Awolowo and Awokoya; January 17, 1955, when the new school
year began, was officially named Education Day. A commemorative
brochure published by the government for the occasion pronounced
it "the beginning in this country of a social revolution" and quoted
Awokoya's earlier description of universal primary education as "a
gilt-edged security against the hazards and difficulties of the coming
years."[10]

The language of politicians is not noted for understatement, yet in
a sense January 17, 1955, did mark the beginning of a social revolution, at least in the Western Region, and there is considerable justification for Awokoya's description of the bill that provided for universal primary education as "the greatest piece of social legislation
that has ever been made in this country."[11] In one year, between 1954
and 1955, primary school enrollment rose from 457,000 to 811,000 (or
from 35 per cent to 61 per cent of the 5–14 age group), the number
of primary school teachers increased from 17,000 to 27,000, and the
number of primary schools rose about 30 per cent, to 6,270.[12] The
regional government's outlay for education leaped from £2.2 million
(34 per cent of total expenditure) to £5.4 million (47 per cent of the
total); almost 90 per cent of the increase was spent on primary school
grants-in-aid.[13] In the 1955 school year alone, £2.4 million was spent
on the construction of primary school buildings, and between 1954
and 1958 about £5 million was spent for this purpose.[14] These few
statistics indicate the dramatic and rapid expansion of school facilities that occurred once Nigerians came into "semi-responsible" positions of power. Unquestionably, an enormous effort was required to
implement a scheme of this magnitude.

But the Western Region was not alone in introducing universal
primary education. Two years later, in January 1957, the Eastern Region abolished all primary school fees and began what an official publication described as "without dispute, the most momentous scheme
ever to be undertaken to date by this or any other Government of the
Eastern Region."[15] As in the West, the politicians made much of the
event; said one member of the House of Assembly:

On the question of Universal Primary Education, we should be grateful to
this Government for their tremendous efforts. Nobody, Sir, . . . can challenge
that in quality or in quantity any Government in the Federation can beat
our Free Primary Education scheme. . . . We are hoping, Sir, that the day
will not be far distant when it will be possible for the people of the Western
Region to enjoy the quality and quantity of education we have given to our
people.[16]

Again there was good reason for the legislators to congratulate themselves for the impressive dimensions of the accomplishment. Between 1956 and 1957 primary school enrollment rose from 775,000 to 1,-209,000 (or from 48 per cent to 73 per cent of the age group), the number of primary school teachers from 30,000 to 41,000, and the number of primary schools from 5,060 to 6,986.[17] Expenditure for education rose from £3.6 million in the 1956 calendar year to £6 million in 1957; recurrent primary school expenditure alone rose from £2.1 million to £4.5 million—about a third of the region's total budget.[18]

For both the Western and Eastern regions, universal primary education was the most widely publicized, most expensive, and most administratively demanding scheme launched during the 1950's. Clearly, the accession to power of Southern Nigerians was closely related to the dramatic expansion of their educational system; the impetus for expansion, which before the 1950's had come from the missionaries, the populace, and the colonial regime, now came from a new group of party politicians. But how precisely did changes in the political arena account for the high priority given in both regions to universal primary education? This chapter examines the following causal factors: popular pressures for educational expansion, convictions of party leaders, the "legitimacy crisis" faced by these leaders, the important role of teachers in politics, and competition between the two Southern Nigerian regions. Chapters 6 and 7 will examine the universal primary education schemes in detail, showing some of the administrative and financial problems that arose in translating paper priorities into concrete actions.

POPULAR PRESSURES

It is extremely difficult to gauge public opinion or to assess its importance even in well-developed societies—to say nothing of developing ones in Africa. But the period up to the 1950's had at least demonstrated that the average Southern Nigerian was enthusiastic about education. The very success of the educated in attaining power doubtless reinforced the popular view that education was the key to power, wealth, and prestige; it also gave the people an unprecedented opportunity to present their demands directly to the government. An article printed in the Lagos *Daily Service* clearly pointed out the pressures to which education ministers would soon be subject: "What we therefore say is this. We want to appoint an African Minister of Education, give him £294,980, the vote of the Department for the financial year 1950–51, and see whether he cannot open more Government elementary schools in five years. If he cannot, we vote him out and put another man in his place."[19]

Once the regional ministers of education did assume office, they were besieged with requests from legislators for more schools or scholarships for particular groups of constituents. Of the 111 oral and written questions posed by Western Region legislators during the first two days of the July 1952 session, the largest number, 35, were directed at the Minister of Education.[20] It is little wonder that Awokoya felt his proposals for full-scale expansion were "the embodiment of public desires with regard to the educational development of the country."[21] Popular pressures seem to have been particularly effective in focusing his attention on primary education. Presumably the most effective way to educate the masses was through an extensive adult education program, but Southern Nigerian adults were generally far more enthusiastic about their children's education than about their own. Consequently, educational efforts centered on the younger generation, and adult education was virtually ignored.*

CONVICTIONS OF PARTY LEADERS

Pressures from the populace for educational expansion were complemented by the convictions of Southern Nigerian leaders. Study and travel abroad made such men as Nnamdi Azikiwe, Obafemi Awolowo, Eyo Ita, S. O. Awokoya, Mbonu Ojike, and K. O. Mbadiwe painfully aware of the great economic, cultural, and psychological gap between the modern world and Africa. They tended to judge Nigeria's progress not in relation to its own past but in relation to changes in more advanced countries, which were steadily increasing their economic and technological lead over the less developed areas of the world. Caught in a revolution of rising expectations, Nigerian leaders were not content with the progress of recent decades; Awokoya, for example, complained bitterly: "We are not living here in

---

* In this respect Southern and Northern Nigeria offer an interesting contrast: "Up to the middle of the 1950's, the Southern Governments were so committed to the introduction and the organization of universal primary education of children that adult education was virtually relegated to the background. The North, on the other hand, has taken its time about the primary education of children and has not slackened its activities in adult education." Pius Mbonu Igboko, "Adult Education in Nigeria" (M.Ed. thesis, University of Birmingham, 1964), p. 149. The existence of a competitive party system in the South and the overwhelming dominance in the North of a single political party that was not quite so concerned with popularity may help to explain this difference in emphasis. Other historical and cultural factors, such as the tradition of Islamic education in the far North, were, of course, operative as well.

Nigeria; we are only existing."[22] The facts that adult literacy in Southern Nigeria, exclusive of Lagos, was 15 per cent in 1952–53 and that a third of the school-age population attended primary school in 1952 were seen not as cause for rejoicing but as *prima facie* evidence that the British had been unable or unwilling to break the vicious circle of African ignorance, poverty, and impotence. The new political leaders were impelled by a sense of urgency, by a drive for rapid action on a wide front—in short, by the ideology of speed. As Awokoya wrote: "We are gradually coming into the world heritage of knowledge. It is a legacy which we have missed for ever so long. We must therefore acquire our rightful portion of this heritage with great avidity."[23]

Although they did not consider their efforts in these terms, the men who launched the universal primary education programs were motivated by considerations involving capacity, equality, and integration—elements of political development. Widespread schooling would hopefully strengthen the capacity of Southern Nigerians for self-government by increasing their self-confidence and encouraging active citizenship.[24] An informed citizenry would make a democratic system of government more feasible; Awolowo remarked in his autobiography: "To educate the children and enlighten the illiterate adults is to lay a solid foundation not only for future social and economic progress but also for political stability. A truly educated citizenry is, in my view, one of the most powerful deterrents to dictatorship, oligarchy, and feudal autocracy."[25] It was hoped that popular education would enable the people to control and develop their own economy. Out of a literate younger generation would come more efficient low-level workers as well as the African replacements for expatriates holding high-level positions in industry and commerce. If the curriculum were revised to include more technical and vocational training—and almost all politicians paid lip service to this reform— young people would learn skills directly relevant to their future occupations, including modern agricultural techniques. A self-governing Nigeria required not only informed and productive citizens but also skilled administrators—men who could implement the programs to which the leaders had committed themselves. Expanded facilities for secondary and higher education were of particular importance in this respect, but a program of universal primary education was useful as well because it would discover talent that could then be recruited into the post-primary sector.

In addition to their preoccupation with increasing Nigeria's capacity for self-government, the new political leaders were concerned with the realization of equality. Perhaps because their outlook was different in many respects from that of the illiterate masses, the leaders took great pains to identify themselves with the interests of the masses and to justify their authority as emanating from the people.[26] Universal primary education was perfectly adapted to the populist goals of Southern Nigerian leaders, for it benefited large numbers of people and enabled previously disadvantaged groups—the poor, females, Muslims, inhabitants of areas neglected by the voluntary agencies, and others—to reach the level of more privileged groups. Because primary schools were inexpensive to construct and relatively easy to staff, they could be more widely distributed throughout a given region than any other amenity demanded by the people. The international viewpoint of those who had been educated abroad reinforced this commitment to equality. If Great Britain and other advanced countries were becoming welfare states, with certain benefits provided all their citizens, should not Nigeria move in the same direction?

Concern with political integration was another reason for the leaders' commitment to universal primary education. The more literate the population, the easier the vertical communication between elite and mass and the more readily could the people be involved in formulating and executing government programs. The expansion of school facilities could aid horizontal integration by benefiting educationally deprived areas, thus removing a potent source of ethnic discord. The Eastern Region government made this point quite explicitly in a 1957 statement: "The policy of the Ministry [of Education] is to disperse opportunities for education extensively, in order to destroy once and for all the notion that certain areas are earmarked and favoured for the purpose of educational development and advancement at the expense of so-called 'neglected' areas."[27] Through civics courses and the common experience of schooling, moreover, young people might come to think of themselves as Nigerians regardless of the diversity of their ethnic and religious backgrounds.

The high priority given to universal primary education reflected not only the goals of the political leaders but also their assessment of the resources at hand. As the history of education in Southern Nigeria had clearly shown, the area's greatest resource was the energy and enthusiasm of its people, who could perform remarkable feats of self-help if inspired by a vision of future progress. The British had failed to tap this enthusiasm, if only because they feared the political and financial implications of mobilizing an entire population for development. The career of the Southern Nigerian politician, on the other hand, depended on his ability to popularize a vision of a far better future, to mobilize the population, and to channel newly aroused energies into specific projects with quickly realized and visible benefits. In order to rouse public enthusiasm the politician needed a dramatic program whose very magnitude, far from discouraging people, would call forth the resources necessary to implement it. The British bureaucrat, focusing on existing human resources and assuming them to be more or less fixed, reasoned his way to gradualism. The African politician, focusing on potential human resources and assuming that serious challenges could encourage the realization of potential, reasoned his way to a crash program—a program whose very economic and administrative impracticality recommended it as being highly practical from a political point of view. A commission that subsequently reviewed the educational situation in the Western Region pointed out: "If the government had waited for ideal conditions to arise before taking action, they would have waited too long. The finicky planning and over-cautious attitude of the old Colonial Government in launching programmes of development could not be imitated by a nation wishing to telescope historical events enacted elsewhere in a thousand years into a few decades."[28]

THE CRISIS OF LEGITIMACY

The politicians who launched the universal primary education programs acted to benefit their regions and their country. But they also acted to protect their own political careers. The most pressing problem faced by Action Group and NCNC leaders during the early 1950's was that of consolidating their power at the regional, if not the national, level. In those early years the political resources available to party leaders were quite limited. The Macpherson constitution permitted the regions to pass legislation pertaining only to certain matters, and it did not clearly specify how much power African members of regional executive councils would have compared to European members, particularly the Governor. Because of the slow pace of Africanization within the civil service, the politicians found themselves working through an administrative apparatus directed almost entirely by the British; if policy conflicts arose, the administrators would be in a position to undermine the effectiveness of programs approved by the politicians. Nigerian leaders were similarly circumscribed by their dependence on influential party members at the local level. Electoral reform took place so rapidly in Southern Nigeria that the political parties competing in the 1951 elections were very loosely organized and lacked a widespread following; indeed, most candidates ran in 1951 on an independent ticket and were asked to join the Action Group or NCNC after they had already been elected to the House of Assembly. Party leaders therefore relied on local notables for popular support, rather than the reverse. Later in the 1950's, as funds became available and opportunities to exercise patronage increased, party organization became tighter and more centralized. But in the formative early years of "semi-responsible" government this was not so.[29]

The limited power available to the new leaders might not have posed a serious problem for them had they received widespread, unequivocal support from the populace. But colonial rule in Southern Nigeria had created a three-way struggle for legitimate authority among the British (who as the distant, powerful rulers of the country possessed enormous prestige, especially among illiterates), the chiefs (whose authority was rooted in traditional life), and the educated elite. Initially, this elite lacked the prestige that comes from having substantial political or administrative power, and with some exceptions its members could not appeal to the people on the basis of traditional status. The source of the new elite's power was its ability to master Western education, and although this conferred considerable prestige, it was not in itself a sufficient basis for legitimacy. Writing in the late 1940's, Obafemi Awolowo candidly admitted that there was an enormous gulf between well-educated men like himself and the average peasant farmer; thus a great deal of mistrust had to be overcome before the new leaders could gain a widespread rural following: "Given a choice from among white officials, Chiefs, and educated Nigerians, as the principal rulers of the country, the illiterate man, today, would exercise his preference for the three in the order in which they are named. He is convinced, and has good reason to be, that he can always get better treatment from the white man than he could hope to get from the Chiefs and the educated elements."[30]

The political leaders of the early 1950's could expect to gain popular support only by promising certain benefits that neither the British nor the chiefs were likely to provide. This was a risky enterprise, for failure to deliver promises could produce a hostile public reaction, and the regional leaders possessed admittedly limited resources. Nevertheless, the risk was worth taking, for otherwise the leaders would continue to be isolated from the masses and the British would be confirmed in their charge that educated Nigerians were too different from the masses to represent the country's interests.

Universal primary education was an admirable aid in resolving the "legitimacy crisis." British officials, who were generally suspicious of dramatic innovations and tended to be more concerned with the quality than with the quantity of education, would almost certainly express grave doubts about the scheme; traditional rulers lacked the ability and in some cases the will to extend primary education to all young people under their jurisdiction. If the Southern Nigerian politicians could alone provide something that obviously satisfied already existing public demands, they would be able to build up the reserve of popular support they badly needed to consolidate their rather tenuous hold on power. As an additional benefit, universal primary education would hopefully produce a younger generation that would be more skeptical of British or traditional claims for loyalty and more likely to value an indigenous leadership that was determined to modernize.

In order to appreciate the function performed by universal primary education in linking political leaders with the masses, one must view the program as a classic instance of welfare politics, and welfare politics as a central feature of Nigerian life. Because the British administration was relatively progressive in Nigeria, yielding gradually to nationalist demands for autonomy, and because there were no conflicts with white settlers (in contrast to Kenya, for example), Nigerian political parties found in the 1950's that militant anti-colonialism gained them little popular support. The Action Group's first badge was a mosquito, to symbolize the ejection of Europeans from the country, and its first motto was "Freedom from the British Rule." But party leaders soon discovered that this approach held little attraction; consequently, they changed their badge to a palm tree, a symbol of prosperity, and their motto became "Freedom for All and Life More Abundant."[31] Freedom, in other words, meant not so much ousting the British as increasing the Nigerian standard of living. Significantly, the Yoruba name for the Action Group denotes not action but welfare: Egbe Afenifere, "the society of the lovers of good things."[32] Moreover, party politics in Southern Nigeria has not generally been ideological in character: insofar as Action Group or NCNC members have called themselves socialists, the term has referred more frequently to equality of opportunity than to nationalization of industry or even careful state planning of the economy. In the absence of anti-imperial or ideological issues, political parties have discovered that they can win votes most readily by promising to provide amenities for the people.[33]

The communal nature of African politics has also contributed to the emphasis on welfare in party politics. The loyalty of men and women to their ethnic group, clan, or village cannot be challenged with impunity by the politicians, since it frequently provides the mass basis of their support. There is thus "very little in the way of fundamentals that a political party can seek to change with any hope of support; parties tend rather to vie with one another in promising the same things—hospitals, educational facilities, roads, and the like."[34] Moreover, group loyalties are reinforced and the politician's local base is strengthened when amenities are provided that benefit the community as a whole, without favoring some persons more than others and without appearing to disrupt established social patterns. A primary school admirably satisfies all of these requirements.

TEACHERS IN POLITICS

The emphasis placed on education by party leaders and legislators may have stemmed partly from the fact that many of these men were teachers or former teachers. In the new Houses of Assembly, twenty-one out of eighty-seven members in the West were teachers, and twenty-nine out of eighty-eight in the East.[35] The political prominence of teachers was due to several factors, not all of them immediately obvious. Given the organizational weakness of both parties in 1951 and the fact that party candidates had not previously been elected to a regional legislature, most communities chose as their representatives prominent local men. The first criterion used by the local electors was whether a candidate had actively helped the community; in this respect politically ambitious teachers or men active in educational affairs usually qualified. Whereas lawyers, doctors, and other professional workers tended to confine their activities to the larger towns, many teachers worked in villages and small towns, where their contribution to rural well-being was obvious to all. Teachers were engaged in the altruistic task of conveying skills to others, whereas local traders, for example, were in business to make money for themselves. In their spare time, many teachers benefited the areas where they worked by serving as officers of local progress unions, literary and debating societies, or Boy Scout troops.

Another criterion applied by local electors was the candidate's ability to represent his constituents effectively in the House of Assembly. Once again, the teacher held distinct advantages over rival candidates. His command of English was almost always superior to that of others in the community—an important qualification, since English was the language of debate in the legislature. During the school holidays the teacher would presumably have time to attend to the needs of those who had elected him. Of course, involvement in political affairs might reduce his effectiveness as a teacher, but even here there was a counter argument, for it could be presumed that a secondary school teacher or principal would benefit the community educationally by obtaining special grant-in-aid favors from the government for his school.*

It is difficult to evaluate with any precision the impact of teachers —or of former teachers, another large category of legislators—on the political process, and the statement that education was given high priority because so many politicians were educators should not stand without certain modifications. Given the variety of educational qualifications of teachers and the differences among the constituencies they represented, one cannot say that teacher-politicians were distinguished from other legislators by any "political style" or ideology. Members of other professions or trades were often as eager for educational expansion as professional educators. Moreover, many teachers felt impelled to enter politics precisely because their profession offered them an unpromising future; once in power, they were reluctant to devote their energies to raising the status of other teachers.[36]

Nevertheless, it must be said that teacher-politicians did help to give legislative priority to their own field of professional competence. To begin with, teachers were particularly conscious of popular pressure for more education in the backward rural areas. For example, both I. U. Akpabio in the East and J. A. O. Odebiyi in the West, as principals of secondary schools in educationally deprived areas, were able to argue persuasively, on the basis of their own experience, the advantages of a universal primary education program and of in-

---

* A striking illustration of this phenomenon occurred in 1954 when I. U. Akpabio became Eastern Region Minister of Education. One of his first acts was to tour the unapproved secondary schools in the region, as well as a few schools already approved, with a view to granting them financial assistance. Grants were given to seventeen institutions, most of whose principals or proprietors were politically active. Recipients included Africa College, Onitsha (P. R. Chukwurah), New Bethel College, Onitsha (M. C. Awgu), Merchant of Light, Oba (E. I. Oli), West African People's Institute, Calabar (Eyo Ita), Aggrey Memorial College, Arochuku (Alvan Ikoku), and Ibibio State College, Ikot Ekpene (I. U. Akpabio). Interview with I. U. Akpabio, June 30, 1964; for a list of aided schools, see Eastern Region, *Education in the Eastern Region with Special Reference to Universal Primary Education* (Enugu, 1957), pp. 8–9.

creased secondary school facilities. Similarly, because of their special training teacher-politicians frequently asserted their competence in matters of educational policy.* This meant that parliamentary debates on this topic were generally longer, livelier, and more informed than debates on other matters. More important, it meant that Nigerians were able to plan quite specifically for educational expansion themselves, whereas they had to rely heavily on the advice of expatriate civil servants regarding noneducational matters. During the late 1940's, for example, an informal study group of teachers met regularly at Ibadan to discuss "what a Nigerian educational policy should be if the British called our bluff and left the country."† From this group emerged the Action Group's 1951 policy paper on education and the 1952 Awokoya proposals.

The self-confidence of teachers in educational matters was of greatest significance in the performances of Awokoya (1952–56) and Akpabio (1954–57) as ministers of education in the West and East, respectively. Since both men had studied education abroad and had served as principals of secondary schools, they tended to assert themselves more readily and self-confidently than other Nigerian ministers when confronted with the objections of British civil servants. Moreover, before they entered politics both Awokoya and Akpabio had come into direct contact with members of the Education Department; thus when they became ministers they already had some idea of whom among the expatriates they could and could not trust.‡ These factors help explain the capacity of the Ministry of Education to expand its operations rapidly when other ministries continued to operate essentially as they had before the constitutional changes of 1951.

* In the debate on the 1956 Western Region Appropriation Bill, F. H. Utomi remarked that he was able to comment on the education vote because "we are teachers and experts in the field. I am a teacher in charge of a school for over twenty-four years." A. O. Ogedengbe began his contribution by saying, "I rise to state on the floor of this House that I left St. Andrew's College in 1928. I therefore know what I am saying." Western Region, House of Assembly, *Debates*, March 8, 1956, p. 338.

† Interview with Chief T. T. Solaru, Dec. 3, 1963. In addition to Solaru, the group included Canon E. O. Alayande, M. A. Ajasin, Canon S. A. Adeyefa, and S. O. Awokoya. These men, all of whom became prominent in the Action Group, may be considered the principal architects of the West's educational policy in the early 1950's.

‡ Both Molusi College, Ijebu-Igbo, of which Awokoya was Principal, and Ibibio State College were community schools sponsored by Africans, and neither received grants-in-aid during the 1940's. Awokoya and Akpabio felt that a number of Education Department officials, particularly in the Inspectorate, practiced discrimination against African-managed secondary schools.

REGIONAL COMPETITION

Competition between the Eastern and Western regions also encouraged educational expansion. Although each of the regions interacted with the North and with the central government, these relationships did not have much influence in the 1950's on primary or secondary educational policy. The North was far behind the South educationally (the North's 1953 primary school enrollment was only about one-eighth that of the South), and Southerners, though disturbed by the North's numerical superiority, expressed little concern that Northerners would overtake them in the important educational race. As for the central government, it was in a weak position to affect educational developments in the regions, even though technically speaking it disbursed grants-in-aid to them under the Macpherson constitution. The House of Representatives was designed as the principal law-making body, but since its Council of Ministers was inevitably an uneasy coalition of representatives from regionally based parties, its potential for decisive action was never realized, and the regions with their dominant political parties assumed responsibility for passing significant legislation.[37] The 1954 constitution further entrenched regional predominance by assigning the regions exclusive control of primary and secondary education and by regionalizing the civil service, including expatriate employees in the Department of Education. The West and the East were thus relatively autonomous agents in formulating educational policy during the 1950's.

Politically, there was a high degree of interaction between the two regions. The rivalry between Yorubas and Ibos that had become so evident by the late 1940's was reflected in the relationship between the Action Group and the NCNC, since each party thought the other represented ethnic interests. Moreover, each party was predominant in one region and aspired to power in the other. The NCNC sought support among the non-Yoruba population of the West and capitalized on communal rivalries among the Yorubas; by 1954 the Action Group was contesting the election in the East, seeking support among the region's non-Ibo elements. In this sense, Southern Nigeria's political life during the period of transition to independence was characterized by a competitive two-party system.

Political competition affected educational expansion in both regions, but first in the West. During the early 1950's the Western Region was educationally behind the East; an estimated 33 per cent of the 5–13 age group in the West, compared to 37 per cent in the

East, were enrolled in primary school as of 1952, and secondary school enrollment was slightly higher in the East.[38] This education gap spurred Action Group leaders to introduce universal primary education and to take measures toward increasing post-primary enrollments. More important, the Western leaders believed their region was much further behind the East than it actually was.* Chief Awolowo's concern about the East's educational lead was apparent when in 1953 he introduced a proposal to raise an education and health levy primarily to finance universal primary education. As reported in the Action Group paper, the *Daily Service*, Awolowo referred in his speech to education rates of up to thirty-seven shillings per capita imposed by Eastern communities, and then "challenged anyone to say whether the Easterners were more in need of education than the West, 'or are we poorer than Northern or Eastern tax payers?' Since the Easterners had resolutely set their feet on education they had never looked back. 'We will do injury to our generation if we look back now,' asserted the Minister."[39] When Azikiwe, speaking for the Opposition, alleged that the average Westerner could not afford the levy of ten shillings and sixpence, J. F. Odunjo, the Minister of Works, replied that the NCNC was "desirous to lull the West into a sense of security so that the East where they are in power may go on forging further ahead in the race for education than the West."[40] One reason why universal primary education received such high priority, in other words, was that the leaders of the West felt they could not lose this race.

The West may have lagged behind the East in education, but in some respects it was quite favorably placed to take the lead. The political advantages of the Action Group leaders in the West over their NCNC rivals in the East were substantial. The Action Group was oriented toward regionalism, and it regarded the ambiguities of the 1951 constitution not as a trap but as a challenge for regional ministers to exercise their limited powers to the full, whereas the NCNC during the early 1950's was committed to a more unitary form of government than the Macpherson constitution envisaged[41] and could not decide whether to obstruct the constitution or to work within it.

---

* Chief Awolowo claims in his autobiography that primary school attendance rates were 65 per cent in the East and 35 per cent in the West. He further claims that there were 105 grammar schools in the East compared to only 25 in the West. See Obafemi Awolowo, *Awo: The Autobiography of Chief Obafemi Awolowo* (Cambridge, Eng., 1960), p. 262. The source of his figures is a mystery. In fact, the West plus Lagos actually exceeded the East in number of grammar schools and in grammar school enrollment when the Action Group took office.

The Action Group appeared to have few leadership problems: Awolowo was on his way to becoming Premier of the Western Region, and whatever conflicts may have existed within the party hierarchy were not publicized. Azikiwe, on the other hand, found himself blocked from power in both Lagos and Enugu, and his efforts to direct the affairs of the NCNC in the East accentuated an already serious leadership crisis in Eyo Ita's government. The result was the so-called "sit-tight" crisis of January and February 1953, when six Eastern ministers refused to resign their portfolios under pressure from the younger, more militant supporters of Azikiwe.[42] This crisis brought government business to a complete halt and forced the dissolution of the Eastern House of Assembly at the very time when the Western House was pressing to carry out the Action Group program. Finally, in the West, as Richard Sklar has pointed out, "planning was the keynote of the Action Group's inception and has remained a first article of Action Group belief."[43] Since the party was new, it could gain electoral support only by promises of things to come. In this respect the party was fortunate, for the intellectuals in the West who had been intimately involved in planning for educational reform during the late 1940's were also involved in the formation of the Action Group and applied their talents to outlining party policies. The NCNC, on the other hand, relied more on Azikiwe's personal magnetism and on its reputation as a nationalist party than on specific policy proposals. And many of the East's intellectuals remained aloof from politics or opposed the NCNC because they were to a large extent non-Ibos and believed the NCNC to be an instrument of Ibo domination. The alienation of these intellectuals in the East deprived the government of many capable planners and administrators.

The Western Region's advantages were economic as well as political. Prior to 1954 the West, as the wealthiest region in the country, in effect subsidized development of the East and North because the British fiscal commissioners maintained that central government revenues should be allocated to the regions on the basis of need (in effect, population) rather than derivation (each region's proportion of the country's exports and imports).[44] At the London Constitutional Conference of 1953, Action Group leaders pressed vigorously for a reallocation of federal revenues on the basis of derivation. A new formula that took these demands into account shifted significantly the economic position of Nigeria's political units: on balance, the federal government lost £9 million, the East lost £200,000, the North gained £1.2 million, and the West gained £3.8 million.[45] The West won an-

other significant financial victory when the commodity marketing
boards were regionalized in early 1954. These boards, established following the Second World War ostensibly to stabilize the prices of
Nigeria's major exports, in fact accumulated vast sterling reserves,
estimated at £92 million by the end of 1953.[46] When Nigerians came
into power, they wanted to use these funds for development purposes.
As part of the trend toward federalism, it was decided that the assets of the marketing boards would be distributed to each region
according to its share of the commodities exported; the West thereupon received £34.4 million, the North £24.8 million, and the East
£15.1 million.[47] In view of the enormous sums involved in this distribution of funds, "possibly no single decision in the decade prior to
independence has been more fateful for the development of the political economy of Nigeria."[48] The Western government was thus in a
unique financial position to implement a crash program like universal primary education.

Once the Western Region had introduced free primary education
for all, the Eastern government was under considerable political pressure to follow suit. That Azikiwe, as a member of the Western House
from 1951 to 1953, had seen the potential benefits of such a program
may help account for his eagerness to introduce it in the East when
he assumed the Premiership there in 1954. In 1955 the Minister of
Education, Akpabio, tacitly admitted in replying to criticism of his
primary education policy that the example of the West and of the
Federal Territory of Lagos left his own government no choice: "We
have heard that in the Federal Government [Lagos], universal primary education will be introduced in 1957. The West has already introduced this. I would just ask the Honourable Member: Where do
you want us to go?"[49]

The East's major problem in implementing the program was financial. Funds allocated from the federal government were being shifted
from the East to the West, and by 1956 it became clear that local education rating, the expedient on which Uzoma had relied in his initial
proposals, was "in a state of collapse."[50] Widespread poverty, corrupt
practices by local councillors, and inadequate tax collection machinery all severely limited the amount that could be collected from local
resources, and popular resistance to paying education rates intensified
with each increase in the rates. Thus, just when political pressures on
the regional government to provide eight years of free primary education were growing, the financial assistance coming from Lagos and
from local communities was proving increasingly inadequate. The

East attempted to deal with this almost impossible situation by passing a finance law in 1956 that substituted a regional income tax for local rates in the hope that regional revenue, collected more efficiently than local revenue, would then be passed back to the local councils in the form of grants. Unfortunately, in its first year of operation the new method of tax collection yielded less than half the revenue that had been anticipated, and the regional income tax was popularly interpreted not as a substitute for local rates but as a means of paying for the complete cost of a region-wide free education program.[51] This misinterpretation, it must be added, was fostered by Azikiwe himself. NCNC leaders had decided in January 1957 to call for new regional elections to reaffirm public confidence in the Premier, who had been charged by a British tribunal with misconduct in personal financial matters. The introduction of free primary education just prior to the election promised to win support for the party; stressing the full cost of the program would only antagonize voters and might strengthen candidates currently or potentially allied with the Action Group. Regional competition thus virtually forced the Eastern government to take certain steps that were irresponsible from a financial point of view. The political factors behind educational expansion were decisive in this case; the economics of educational expansion were temporarily ignored.

CHAPTER 6

The Program in the Western Region

So far, in tracing the development of Southern Nigeria's educational system during the 1950's, we have been concerned primarily with the political factors that contributed to an unprecedented increase in enrollment by 1960.* We shall now describe the process of expansion itself by looking at the actions of regional politicians and administrators as they tried to translate universal primary education from an exciting slogan into the reality of teachers, school facilities, and free admission for all eligible young people. In both regions the effort to provide universal primary education was a classic test of the government's capacity to realize the ambitious goals set for it by the populace on the one hand and the new Nigerian political leaders on the other. Since the two regional governments followed rather different courses in pursuing their goals, the programs of each region are considered separately in this and the next chapter. The following topics will be discussed: the educational goals of politicians and planners during the early 1950's and the ways political pressures altered these goals; major changes in educational administration; patterns of consultation and cooperation between the government and private groups; and the evolution of government policy to deal with certain critical problems of expansion—managing new schools, accommodating large numbers of pupils, and financing education from limited resources.

---

* In 1950 some 971,000 children were enrolled in primary school and 12,000 in secondary grammar school; by 1960 enrollment at the two levels was 2.5 million and 48,000, respectively. See Figure 1, p. 263, and Figure 2, p. 265, for enrollment trends.

THE MODIFICATION OF ROLES

The goals for the Western Region's universal primary education program were first set forth in May 1951 by the Action Group's policy paper on education, which called for free and compulsory education for all eight years of the existing primary course.[1] There was some discussion within the party of whether school fees should be abolished simultaneously for all primary classes or phased out as the Primary One class entering school in 1955 moved through the system. The former view prevailed, if only because a phased abolition of fees was thought politically risky.[2] But political and economic considerations forced a revision of other aspects of the 1951 proposal. Six free years would obviously be easier for the region to finance than eight, and many of the teachers and educational planners in the party felt that a child might, with an improved syllabus, acquire basic literacy skills in six years. The government accordingly reduced the primary school course by two years—an unintentional reversion to the Hussey proposals that had been so strongly resisted by Africans two decades earlier.

The issue of compulsory attendance proved quite controversial. In his 1952 *Proposals for an Education Policy*, Awokoya, the Minister of Education, suggested that compulsory attendance be introduced gradually, beginning with the 1955 Primary One class; thus attendance by the entire school-age population would not be required until 1960. But the notion of requiring attendance at all was questioned by Awolowo and some other Action Group leaders. Many poor families still depended on their children's labor for farm work, rubber tapping, and the like; Awolowo believed that the government should not require these families to send their children to school, even though the families would probably profit eventually from their children's education.[3] Compulsory attendance appeared financially unwise as well, for by increasing enrollment it would force grants-in-aid to "unnatural" levels; it would also incur heavy administrative expenses for enforcement. In any case, if children were forced to attend school against their parents' wishes, or if parents were fined for noncompliance with statutes requiring attendance, a program designed to increase the Action Group's popularity might have precisely the opposite effect.

Awolowo's position on compulsory attendance was not initially accepted by the party executive, and in deference to its views he publicly defended a policy that in private he had opposed.[4] But by 1954, when the parties named their candidates for direct election to the federal legislature, it became apparent that the NCNC was making the question of compulsory attendance a political issue. NCNC candidates charged that under the Action Group's policy children would be forcibly removed from their parents' farms, and a grim picture was painted of the punishment awaiting anyone who did not send all his eligible children to school. In view of this exploitation of the issue by the Opposition, the Action Group executive abandoned compulsory attendance late in 1954. Awokoya, bitter about the reversal of policy, charged before the House: "The misrepresentations of certain politicians have of late assumed such proportions that it will be foolhardy at the present stage of our political development to make universal education compulsory."[5] The Minister was clearly referring to the NCNC, but it is conceivable that the leader of his own party was included in the denunciation.

As a result of these modifications, made between 1951 and 1954, the Western Region's plan for primary education began to look increasingly feasible, both administratively and financially. The adoption of more modest goals eased the burden on Ministry of Education officials, who were already busy trying to provide six years of free education on a voluntary basis, as well as expanding teacher training and secondary grammar school facilities. These policy changes did, however, pose problems for the Ministry's planners, whose enrollment and cost projections became obsolete whenever basic policy guidelines were altered.

CONTROLLING AND STRENGTHENING
THE EDUCATIONAL BUREAUCRACY

Once the Action Group leaders had determined their educational goals, would the British officials who controlled the bureaucracy cooperate in trying to achieve them? The answer to this question was by no means obvious, at least in the early 1950's, and Awokoya soon began to suspect that some of the high-level civil servants in the Department of Education were undermining his position. Part of the problem lay in the very nature of transitional government. The ministerial system was an innovation for both the African ministers and their civil servants, and the shift from European control to African autonomy was bound to create situations of overlapping authority. The Macpherson constitution provided little guidance, for it was deliberately vague in describing the powers of a minister and recommended simply that civil servants work "in collaboration" with him. The quasi-federal structure established by the constitution was a further source of confusion, for regional ministers were expected to work through civil servants who were ultimately responsible to their superiors in the central government. Awokoya, for example, had to rely on the Department of Education, composed of professional educators and headed by a Director of Education who was accountable to an Inspector-General in Lagos.

As might be expected in this ambiguous situation, a struggle for power developed between the Minister and the Director of Education. One interesting and subtle form this struggle took concerned the provision of an office for Awokoya. When the ministers were installed in 1952 there were no offices or living quarters for them in Ibadan; for several months they lived in the Government Rest House and shared small rooms in the Secretariat building. The Director of Education already had his own office and felt that he and the Minister could best do business there. But this arrangement meant that the Minister would have to come to see the Director; instead Awokoya wanted the Director to come to see him at the Rest House, where he did most of his work. The Director disliked having to drive to the Rest House and promised to get Awokoya a suitable office near his own. But then an argument erupted over whose room should be larger! Behind the apparently petty matter of office space lay the fundamental question: who was really in charge?

Compounding the conflict over roles was a conflict over policy. The leading members of the Nigerian Department of Education were chiefly interested in maintaining standards and consolidating the existing school system. They also tended, as officials in a colonial regime, to be very concerned about the possible economic and political consequences of changes in government policy. Because the universal primary education program as it was presented to them virtually guaranteed a decline in the quality of instruction, seemed so prohibitively expensive, and promised to increase significantly the number of "semi-educated," unemployable young Nigerians, many Education Department officials throughout the country were opposed to it in principle. Even those who felt the program was desirable in the long run argued that it could not be realized unless the highest priority were given to training primary school teachers by expanding enrollments in the teacher training colleges and secondary grammar schools.[6] Nigerian politicians, on the other hand, believing in the necessity of a dramatic crash program in education, were less disturbed over the lowering of standards, relatively unconcerned about the financial implications of their proposals, and certain that a massive expansion of enrollments would increase prosperity and usher in an era of stable self-rule. The Nigerian politicians' interests thus conflicted with the more cautious attitude of the British civil servants.

Yet another problem in the relationship between the Minister and some of his high-level civil servants was the barrier of age and temperament. Awokoya was in his early forties and extraordinarily energetic; the leading men in the Department were older and tended to be more relaxed in their approach to life. Although recruitment to the Colonial Service following World War II brought to Nigeria a substantial number of young, active British civil servants who were basically sympathetic to the Nigerian point of view, by the early 1950's these men were still "in the field" and did not have much influence in policy matters.

These differences between Awokoya and some of his leading civil servants eventually produced a deadlock.* Awokoya's relationship with the Director of Education was particularly strained. In the judgment of Awokoya, the Director stalled in releasing the Department's files to him, opposed his plans to expand the Department by creating new sections, did not cooperate in preparing answers to parliamentary questions, and opposed the upgrading of African education officers. Within a few months of taking office, Awokoya had grown so suspicious of the Director that he insisted on having the Director's views transmitted in writing rather than orally. Matters came to a head in early 1953, when the Director apparently circulated an unfounded rumor that all voluntary agency primary schools were to be turned over to local councils. Awokoya protested so vigorously to the Lieutenant-Governor that the Director was moved to a post in Lagos and another Englishman appointed in his stead. Ministerial authority was further consolidated in July 1953, when the Department of Education was incorporated into a new Ministry of Education, and an administrator rather than a professional educator was brought in as the Ministry's Permanent Secretary. At this point relationships between the Minister and his civil servants improved markedly. The civil servants became more willing to accept the Minister's authority and were generally more sympathetic to the objectives of the universal primary education program; the Minister, for his part, came to trust the new men. An informal planning committee consisting of

* The man who first served Awokoya as Chief Inspector had on a previous occasion—before the regional election—given a highly unfavorable report on Awokoya's school, Molusi College, after the most cursory of inspections. The Minister was not inclined to trust this man's judgment when he believed that on at least one occasion it had seriously erred. Interview with S. O. Awokoya, May 11, 1964.

Awokoya, the Director of Education, the Permanent Secretary, and the Inspector for Teacher Training met regularly to deal with administrative matters.

The magnitude of the universal primary education program demanded a rapid expansion of the Ibadan-based educational bureaucracy: the number of sections dealing with education rose from nine in 1952 to about twenty by early 1954, and all the sections enlarged their staff as the work load increased. Of particular importance were the planning and statistics sections, which were charged with gathering and projecting data on enrollment, teacher requirements, and costs. These sections confronted the recurring problem of planners in developing countries that the data needed for successful planning were either unavailable or unreliable;[7] one of the greatest imponderables, of course, was the extent to which the people would respond to the educational opportunities the government was providing. Simultaneous with the expansion at headquarters there was a considerable devolution of authority to the provincial and divisional levels. Provincial education officers assumed greater responsibility for gathering data and making on-the-spot decisions. They were aided by administrative assistants for planning—all Nigerians—who distributed questionnaires to schools regarding their present and future enrollment capacity and conducted surveys to determine where new schools should be sited, gaining invaluable administrative experience in the process. Thus although the basic administrative decisions were made by expatriates in consultation with the Minister, Nigerians played a vital role in implementing universal primary education.*

A program of such magnitude required more, however, than an expanded Ministry of Education: it required the assistance of other government agencies and of sympathetic parliamentarians. The Western Nigeria Information Service of the Ministry of Home Affairs helped greatly to publicize it, particularly during the registration period. Not only were modern techniques—leaflets, loudspeaker vans, public notices, posters on lorries—employed, but bell ringers and drummers, the traditional purveyors of information, were engaged to spread the news of registration for "free, universal," as it was sometimes called. Individual ministers and other members of the House were helpful in a number of specific ways. The allocation of

---

* Africanization occurred more rapidly in the Ministry of Education than elsewhere, since more Nigerians were already employed by the Ministry—as visiting teachers, education officers, principals of grammar schools and teacher training colleges, for example—than in any other government service. By 1954 two of the provincial education officers were Nigerians.

funds for teacher training colleges was decided on the basis of a report by J. F. Odunjo, Minister of Lands, E. A. Babalola, Minister of
Works, and T. T. Solaru; Odunjo, Solaru, and Canon Alayande
formed a troubleshooting committee to settle local disputes over the
siting of schools and to ensure that wherever possible sites were donated rather than sold. This committee worked largely through the
local Action Group apparatus to make its influence felt. All the ministers toured the region frequently during their early years in office,
and in many of their speeches they stressed the significance of universal primary education, the necessity of financing it adequately
through the education and health levy, and the importance of local
cooperation with the representatives of the Ministry of Education.

PATTERNS OF CONSULTATION

In undertaking programs of universal primary education, the two
regional governments assumed increased responsibility for an educational system that had been largely in private hands. Of course, the
government's capacity to realize its educational goals would be increased if the skill and experience of those in the private sector could
be utilized in carrying out official policies. A striking feature in the
Western Region was the government's close and continuous consultation with the voluntary agencies, the Nigeria Union of Teachers,
and the general public. The voluntary agencies were strongly represented on the Board of Education and helped to formulate the
Board's recommendations on such subjects as the new six-year syllabus, the First School-Leaving Certificate Examination, the secondary
modern school syllabus, and grant-in-aid regulations. In addition,
the Education Advisory Committee of the Christian Council of Nigeria considered the draft of a new education bill, and many of the
council's suggestions were incorporated into the bill before it became
law in 1954.[8] The Nigeria Union of Teachers was also consulted at
various times and made its views known on syllabus revision and on
the automatic promotion of pupils, which it opposed. The union
pressed successfully for an advisory Terms of Service Committee for
teachers, half of whose members were to be chosen by the N.U.T.,
and for a Teachers' Council to advise the Director of Education in
matters involving possible disciplinary action.

More significant than these formal channels of communication
were the informal relationships between Action Group leaders and
spokesmen for the voluntary agencies and the teachers' union. The
major mission bodies in the West—notably the Church Missionary

Society and the Methodists—had pursued a relatively liberal Africanization policy over the years, so that by the 1950's there were a number of Nigerian clergymen who could present the case for the voluntary agencies. Often in politics it matters less what is said than who says it. The fact that men like Canon E. O. Alayande, Rev. S. A. Banjo, and Rev. T. T. Solaru could speak for voluntary agency interests blunted the argument that the Christian missions were foreign, white-controlled institutions not to be relied on in the future. In this respect the Africanization policy of some of the Protestant denominations was their surest guarantee of survival in an age of African self-determination. Moreover, because the early missionaries had concentrated on the Yoruba areas of the West, the graduates of their schools who rose to prominence as clergymen or as spokesmen for the N.U.T. were almost without exception Yorubas—men, in other words, who had strong ethnic reasons for affiliating with the Action Group. The opinions of Alayande, Banjo, and Solaru were respected in government circles because the three were members in good standing of the ruling party and had helped to formulate its educational policy. Canon Alayande, in fact, in addition to being an Anglican cleric, was a leader of the N.U.T. and a party activist.

To solicit cooperation among the people themselves, *ad hoc* district planning committees were established in late 1953 by the local education committees of district councils; ministry officials were active behind the scenes in selecting their membership and explaining their functions. The district planning committees were composed of a variety of local people, including chiefs, local councillors, teachers, pastors, and traders. In choosing them an attempt was made to include representatives of different occupations, religions, and social strata so that the decisions reached by the committees would be based on consensus and thus would be more acceptable to the people. The district planning committees performed extremely important work, and did so quite efficiently. Initially charged with estimating the number of classrooms locally required and advising on the siting and proprietorship of new schools, the committees later supervised, in July 1954, the registration of children for Primary One.[9]

Because the Western Region government did not feel threatened by the private sector and, as we shall see, was not intent on undermining vested private interests, it was able to profit by advice and cooperation from nongovernment agencies experienced in educational matters. In this regard the situation in the West was markedly different from that in the East.

CONTROL OF THE SCHOOLS

The prospect of unprecedented expansion of the primary school system raised, as a matter for immediate decision, a fundamental question that the government had managed to avoid during the previous half-century: should the voluntary agencies, and in particular the Christian missions, continue to own, manage, and staff virtually all of the schools? It was administratively and financially impossible for the regional government to assume direct control of the new schools being built, but local government might take on this task. Whether local councils or voluntary agencies should supervise the expanded school system became the subject of a rather lengthy and involved discussion among Action Group leaders.

Some Western Region leaders argued that in the missionaries' home countries education was managed predominantly by local government, and that any step toward secularization was a move toward modernity.[10] Action Group leaders were unquestionably committed to strengthening and democratizing local government; one of the first bills submitted to the House of Assembly had established a three-level system of divisional, district, and local councils. The populace would more readily accept the authority of these new institutions, it was argued, if the councils were given responsibility for constructing and managing their own primary and secondary modern schools— tasks that would visibly benefit their communities and yet were not beyond the technical competence of council staffs to perform. This line of argument was buttressed by the fact that one-third of the West's population (and over 40 per cent of its Yorubas) were Muslims. As we have seen, fear that their children would be converted to Christianity dissuaded many Muslim parents from sending them to any school managed by Europeans. Since one objective of universal primary education was to reach groups that had previously received little education, it was argued that the views of Muslim parents should be taken seriously into consideration. The Action Group leaders, virtually all of whom were Christian, were also aware that the Muslims might organize on their own if the government continued to subsidize the Christian missions as heavily as in the past. This matter had already caused some discontent in 1952 and 1953,[11] and it was argued that the best way to prevent the discontent from assuming a more explicitly political form would be to establish more nondenominational schools run by local authorities.

But there were many arguments to support the contrary view that educational expansion should occur primarily through the voluntary agencies. It was pointed out that these groups had acquired expertise in running schools and more often than not had gained the confidence of the populace through their efficiency, integrity, and high standards. To deprive the voluntary agencies of the capacity to expand would in effect deprive the region of its capacity to catch up to the East, for the West would be rejecting a system that had proved successful for one that was yet to be tested. The region would probably have difficulty enlarging its educational system if it attempted at the same time to alter the system's basic structure. The economic advantages of continuing to rely on the voluntary agencies were also pointed out. The voluntary agencies paid for their schools partly through local contributions, the proceeds of harvest festivals, bazaars, and so forth, whereas local authorities would have to impose compulsory rates or taxes. And the greater the educational role of the local councils, the higher education rates were likely to be. Many politicians thought it better to work through agencies that operated their own informal tax system than to increase to unpopular levels the taxes owed directly by the people to their government. Muslim charges of discrimination could be countered by granting concessions to Muslim educational agencies rather than penalizing all voluntary agencies because the most prominent ones were Christian.

Actual government policy, spelled out in the directives of the Ministry of Education, the Education Law of 1954, and subsequent legislation, represented an artful compromise between these two sets of arguments. Voluntary agencies were not asked to turn over their existing schools to local authorities, and voluntary agency schools previously unassisted by the government were to receive grants-in-aid. Of the new primary schools to be constructed, 60 per cent were to be under local authorities and 40 per cent under the voluntary agencies, allocated in each district according to the relative strength of the different missions there. Whenever a dispute arose between religious groups over the proprietorship of a new school, the local authority would assume control of it. In addition to their portions of the 40 per cent granted to the voluntary agencies, Muslim educational agencies might claim 10 per cent of the new schools, to be subtracted from the percentage assigned to the local authority; in this way the government recognized the Muslims' claim to special treatment as an educationally deprived group. Religious worship and instruction in a voluntary agency school would be in accord with the wishes of the proprietor, but if parents requested other forms of religious instruction these were to be provided as well, and a child who did not want instruction in this subject might be excused from religion classes. The voluntary agencies were free to expand their activities at the post-primary level, including secondary modern schools, which were built in substantial numbers beginning in 1955. Local education authorities—in practice, district or divisional councils advised by local education committees—were to be established to estimate future needs, manage the schools not under voluntary agency supervision, sponsor teacher training colleges, and disburse grants-in-aid to the voluntary agency schools in the area. To help finance universal primary education, the councils were expected to contribute 15 per cent of the teachers' salaries in their area and to provide a grant to all schools for paper, chalk, and similar supplies.

These policy decisions aroused virtually no controversy because they contained provisions to satisfy all the parties concerned. The voluntary agencies welcomed the grant of 40 per cent of the new schools because it enabled them to expand their own operations at little cost, with the government paying for teachers' salaries as well as for classroom construction. The voluntary agencies did not on the whole oppose the establishment of local education authorities because they believed, quite correctly, that they would be adequately represented on the education committees that made the fundamental decisions. Nor were the provisions for religious liberty opposed, partly because the regulations appeared just, but probably also because neither parental insistence on alternative religious instruction nor strict official enforcement of the regulations appeared likely. The Muslims were placated by special concessions, and the government was careful to approve and financially assist their secondary schools and training colleges. Thus the religious agencies, having been consulted as policy was formed, obtained many of the measures they had requested and were willing, in turn, to cooperate with the government in planning and implementing universal primary education.

The local authorities could hardly complain that the Ibadan government had given them too little to do. Indeed, they were in danger of being overwhelmed by their educational responsibilities at a time when their legitimacy was still not recognized among the people and their own employees lacked administrative experience. The regional government planned to cope with this problem by assigning some of its education officers and clerical staff to assist the district and divisional councils in their work and to train future local education officers, who would then be employed directly by the councils. But since the Ministry of Education was itself seriously understaffed, little assistance of this sort could in fact be offered. The disparity between the educational tasks of local government and its administrative and financial resources posed serious difficulties once universal primary education was instituted, but before the program began there was little consideration, public or private, of this problem.

UNIVERSAL PRIMARY EDUCATION
IN PROJECTIONS AND IN PRACTICE

Planning for universal primary education had been based on the assumption that enrollment would increase slowly in 1953 and 1954 over the 1952 figure of 381,000, that in 1955 it would rise to 492,000, and that it would then grow by about 100,000 annually until by 1959 a plateau would be reached at 900,000. But these figures turned out to be grossly understated. Because of unreliable data, the initial estimates of the school-age population were about 15 per cent too low. Even more serious, the early projections failed to take into account the people's response to extensive party and government publicity for a crash program in education. By 1954 enrollment had already reached 457,000, and in July of that year 380,000 children registered for Primary One, over twice the figure of 170,000 six- to seven-year-olds that had been expected. When the time came for registration, children ranging in age from four to about ten crowded into waiting lines, their parents solemnly declared that each of them would soon be six, and the beleaguered registrars issued admission cards to almost all who claimed to be eligible. Ministry officials were aware that this was going on, but they did not try to enforce the regulations strictly because they knew the difficulties in determining the precise ages of the children* and the practical and political problems of trying to head off the stampede they themselves had helped to start. Many officials thought it unjust, moreover, to deprive children over six of an opportunity to begin primary school. The Ministry, the district planning committees, the local education authorities, and the contractors in charge of building classrooms did not anticipate this sudden rise in enrollment. And when a plateau was finally reached in 1959, as predicted, it was closer to 1.1 million than to 900,000.

As a former teacher, Awokoya realized that the success of the pro-

---

* The usual method of estimating age was to ask a child to reach over his head and touch the opposite ear. If he could not do this he was considered underage; if he could barely do it he was considered six.

gram ultimately depended on the availability of qualified teachers. He noted in 1952: "Unless . . . this problem is solved urgently and in a big way, all our talks about expansion will be mere wishful thinking incapable of realization."[12] In that year about 37 per cent of the region's 11,000 primary school teachers were trained. Awokoya anticipated a net annual increase of 600 trained teachers in 1953 and 1954, of 950 annually in the succeeding four years, and of 2,450 in 1959 and 1960. In view of his original enrollment projections, this meant that the trained proportion of the teaching force would remain fairly constant through 1958 and would then rise to 50 per cent by 1960. In fact, however, the net increase in the critical years of 1955 and 1956 was only 75 per cent of Awokoya's initial estimate. This fact, coupled with the unexpectedly rapid enrollment rise in 1955, meant that thousands of Nigerians with only six or eight years of primary schooling behind them had to be recruited as teachers for the first year of the program. The teaching force reached 27,000 in 1955, just under the figure it was supposed to reach in 1960. And the proportion of trained teachers fell drastically with the onset of universal primary education—to 31 per cent in 1954 and 22 per cent in 1955. Not until 1963 was the 50 per cent mark reached.[13]

As the start of the 1955 school year approached, many people began to realize that the rapid expansion of the primary school system promised by Action Group politicians could not be achieved without a temporary deterioration of educational standards. NCNC politicians were naturally quickest to articulate popular uneasiness over this aspect of universal primary education. A full-scale attack on the program was launched in August 1954 by Sanya Onabamiro, who had earlier left the Action Group because he disagreed with its educational policies. Onabamiro charged that a six-year course lowered the standards for graduation from primary school and that policy makers favored automatic promotion of pupils, which would lower the quality of education and produce disciplinary problems.* In Ibadan a communal party called the Mabolaje that was allied with the NCNC opposed the program on more ingenuous grounds: "When we paid for [education] the children did not learn much; now that it is free they will learn nothing."[14] In the House of Assembly debate over the education bill in December 1954, several NCNC members

---

* Onabamiro also challenged three Action Group ministers to remove their children from the special Staff School at University College, Ibadan, and to enroll them in schools operated under the universal primary education program. See the *Daily Times*, Aug. 14, 1954.

singled out the region's insufficiently trained teaching force as a grave weakness. The following exchange took place during the speech of Opposition Leader Dennis Osadebay:

My party welcomes the Bill wholeheartedly, but my Party goes a step further and says, "If you are going to bring such a momentous, such a gigantic scheme, then you must be ready"; and my Party is asking the question, "Have you got sufficient teachers for this scheme?"

Government: "Yes!"
Opposition: "No!"[15]

Privately, many Action Group members were not so sure that the answer to the question was yes.

FINANCING UNIVERSAL PRIMARY EDUCATION

The abolition of school fees, of course, did not really make education "free"; it merely shifted the financial burden from individual citizens to various levels of the government. The government in turn had to pay for education by extracting funds from the people. The political appeal of universal primary education—that parents no longer needed to pay £2 or £3 a year to send a child to school—was offset by the politically unattractive necessity of raising taxes. As we have seen, the greater wealth of the Western Region enabled it to implement universal primary education earlier than the East, but the West was certainly not affluent by welfare state standards, and the financial windfalls of 1954 came too late to help the region in the initial stages of planning for educational expansion. Accordingly, the Ibadan government announced at the end of 1952 that an education and health levy of a little over ten shillings per taxpayer would be collected by local authorities and then forwarded to Ibadan until the local authorities needed it to pay their share of the region's welfare plans. The government hoped that this levy would bring in £1.5 million by 1955 for use in primary education and health programs. Party officials recognized that the people would not welcome the levy, but they saw no alternative to imposing it. Awokoya stated: "Anyone who seriously wants to serve his people . . . must be prepared to face also the odium of unpopularity. It is only temporary unpopularity. We must tell our people the unpalatable truth that these services must be paid for."[16]

The truth was indeed unpalatable to many in the Western Region who could not understand why a program described as free required any local financial support at all. Public uncertainty over the functions of elected representatives compounded the difficulty; many people believed that their legislators had power to obtain services from Ibadan but that only their chiefs had authority to levy taxes.[17] Widespread resentment against the levy was exploited by the NCNC, which claimed that only two shillings and sixpence was needed, rather than ten shillings and sixpence, and charged that the money was enriching Action Group ministers at the expense of the people. The most serious instance of political manipulation of anti-tax sentiment was at Oyo, where a communal party opposed to the Action Group used the issue to draw support for the town's traditional ruler, who was embroiled at the time in a dispute with the government. The ruler was eventually deposed after riots in which several people were killed.[18]

The extent of the unrest deeply disturbed the Action Group leaders, who spent much of their time during 1953 and 1954 touring the region to explain the need for the levy. But it was difficult to convince the people when no results could be shown; the new tax, after all, was designed to collect funds before children flooded into primary schools in 1955. The Action Group consequently suffered badly in the November 1954 elections to the Federal House of Representatives. The party received only 35 per cent of the vote and eighteen seats, the NCNC received 53 per cent of the vote and twenty-three seats, and anti-tax parties and independents received 12 per cent of the vote and one seat. Awolowo frankly blamed the defeat on the education and health levy.[19] The NCNC's victory entitled it to the three Western Region seats in the Central Council of Ministers and excluded the Action Group from a share of power in the federal government. The political consequences of a seemingly innocuous tax measure were thus quite harmful to the Action Group. But the economic consequences were beneficial, for more than £500,000 was collected annually. This amount was used in 1955 to reimburse local councils for their educational expenditures, which almost quadrupled in one year to £2.8 million.[20]

The public dispute between the two parties over educational finance was paralleled by an unpublicized controversy among Action Group leaders over the same issue. Initial estimates of the capital and recurrent cost of the government's education program—£52 million over the 1955–62 period[21]—seemed high enough; with the enrollment bulge coming sooner than expected it was likely that costs would rise still further. Moreover, party leaders and educational planners had not sufficiently realized when they assumed office that expenditure at the post-primary level would also have to rise rapidly, if only to train qualified primary school teachers and to provide further education for the greatly increased number of primary school leavers. These factors prompted a growing resistance within the Executive Council to Awokoya's requests for more money. Despite the Minister of Education's careful marshaling of statistics to substantiate these requests, his case was weakened by what several other ministers regarded as too cavalier an attitude toward spending money,* and naturally they had their own special projects to finance. Because of the government's commitment to universal primary education, Awokoya's requests were inevitably granted, but by 1954 approval was given so begrudgingly that at one point the Minister threatened to resign if he did not receive greater support from his colleagues.

Behind the dispute over the costs of education was a personality conflict of growing intensity between Awolowo and Awokoya. There were several grounds for this conflict. Awolowo was distressed that Awokoya was allegedly running a private bus service and using government garages to house the buses; he was even more disturbed to hear that Awokoya had made a bid for party power on one occasion when Awolowo was away from Ibadan. For his part, Awokoya felt that the party leader was acting as a dictator despite the public appearance of collegial leadership. The Minister of Education also suspected that Awolowo was jealous of him because of his administrative and public-speaking abilities and because of the great publicity he was receiving in connection with the universal primary education program. Some people in the region were terming the new primary schools "Awokoya schools"; the Minister suspected that Awolowo wanted them to be known as "Awolowo schools." Their growing estrangement, which may have been related to the fact that both were Ijebu Yorubas and hence had roughly the same political base, reached a crisis in April 1956, when it became clear that Awokoya was not going to be renominated by his constituency for the new House of Assembly. He then resigned his post and left the Action Group, charging that "unless some public declaration is made before it is too late, this Region will be ruled by a totalitarian government dominated by the personality of Chief Awolowo, and thereby doomed for at least one generation to a dictatorship that may drag us to the most dreadful depths of human degradation."[22]

* Awokoya had once stated in a public speech: "If we want compulsory education, we would not mind even running into debt to get it." Quoted in *Daily Service*, June 28, 1952.

The Action Group fared much better in the regional election of 1956 than in the federal election of 1954, winning almost half of the popular vote and forty-eight of the seventy House of Assembly seats; Awokoya, despite his personal prominence, was badly defeated when he ran against the regular party machine.* No single issue was dominant in this election, but public satisfaction with the Action Group's welfare policies was doubtless an important factor in that party's victory. After all, in 1954 the populace was being asked to pay for a program that had not yet materialized, whereas in 1956 they were enjoying government-financed primary education, thanks in part to their earlier contribution to the regional exchequer. During the 1953 debate over the education and health levy, the Minister of Health, S. O. Ighodaro, had stated: "I am sure that though some people, when they listen to the rhetoric of the Opposition, may be inclined to curse us now, yet when the people begin to reap the advantages adumbrated in Policy Papers on education and health, then they will bless us and not the Opposition."[23] By 1956, despite all the controversy over compulsory attendance, standards, costs, and other issues, it looked as if Ighodaro's prediction was being fulfilled.

* One consequence of this resolution of the power struggle is that school children in the West today tell the visitor that they are attending "Awolowo schools."

CHAPTER 7

The Program in the Eastern Region

The history of universal primary education is more dramatic in the Eastern than in the Western Region, for the Eastern government had a much shorter period of time in which to make the basic decisions, pursued a more radical policy with regard to the voluntary agencies, and confronted a more serious financial situation than did the government in Ibadan. Educational policy in the Eastern Region during the 1954–58 period was formulated in an atmosphere of crisis, caused both by the complexity of the factors—political, administrative, religious, and financial—that decision makers had to consider and by the severe time constraints under which these men labored. The decisions that were made in turn sparked a series of controversies within the region that were by no means fully resolved when Nigeria attained independence in 1960.

THE ESCALATION OF GOALS

The goals set forth by the Eastern Region's first Minister of Education, R. I. Uzoma, in his 1953 policy paper on education were in many respects quite modest. The primary course was to remain at eight years until improvements in the standard of teaching warranted a reduction to six; in the meantime, however, the government would commit itself to universal education for the first four years only. The term "free education" was avoided because, as the paper was careful to point out, "There is no such thing"; Uzoma spoke instead of "education without payment of fees."[1] Given the region's financial limitations, the abolition of fees depended on the action of local councils, which were to raise 45 per cent of the costs of primary education. This meant that wide variations might be expected in the timing of the introduction of universal primary education by different communities, depending on their resources and enthusiasm for schooling. The hope was expressed that fees would be abolished "over the greater part of the region" by the end of 1956,[2] but the realization of this hope depended primarily on the local authorities, and it was not explicitly stated that the regional government would assume more than 55 per cent of the cost if at the end of 1956 the various local authorities had not met their obligations. According to Uzoma's plan, compulsory attendance was a matter to be introduced by the local people when they felt they were ready to enforce it.

The accession to the premiership of Nnamdi Azikiwe in 1954 and the breakdown of the local rating system in 1955 and 1956 radically altered the major assumptions on which the early planning for universal primary education in the East had been based. Azikiwe's decision to seek power at the regional level reflected a new willingness on his part to push significant legislative measures through the Eastern House of Assembly. He could see that the Action Group's accomplishments in the West were bearing fruit politically and that if the NCNC were to retain its populist image it would have to sponsor progressive measures in the region where it held power. The pressures for the rapid introduction of universal primary education on a larger scale than previously envisaged grew quickly once the new regional government assumed office and I. U. Akpabio took over as Minister of Education in 1954. The collapse of local rating meant, of course, that the financial assumptions of the 1953 white papers were no longer tenable.

As a result of these changes, by early 1956 a new set of plans for universal primary education was being developed. Proposals for a six-year primary course were abandoned, since the NCNC in the West had sharply criticized the Action Group for lowering the standards of primary education with a six-year syllabus. And instead of four years the assumption was that all eight years would be included in what was now proudly proclaimed the "free education" scheme. Instead of permitting local variations in educational opportunity, the regional government decided that by the beginning of 1957 fees would be abolished throughout the region; instead of requiring local authorities to bear 45 per cent of the costs, the Finance Law virtually abolished local rating for educational and other purposes. Government policy remained the same with regard to only one issue—compulsory attendance—perhaps because the NCNC feared that the propaganda it had spread in the West might be used with equal effectiveness by the Action Group in the East if school-age children were required to attend classes.

Thus by early 1956 the education program proposed in the East had grown from major to monumental proportions; the closer the January 1957 deadline approached, the more the region committed itself to accomplish. Under these conditions, the kind of preliminary planning that had occurred in the West simply did not take place in the East. If it was difficult in 1952 for the Action Group leadership to prepare properly for 1955, it was almost impossible for the NCNC government to plan in 1956 for the huge influx of children scheduled for 1957.

THE EDUCATIONAL BUREAUCRACY

Like Awokoya, Akpabio had to work through a Department of Education all of whose leading officials were British—a situation that hindered the effective formulation and execution of educational policy. The NCNC had never been particularly friendly toward expatriate civil servants, because party members suspected the British of sympathizing with the moderates who had comprised Eyo Ita's government or with leaders of the opposition United National Independence Party. The fact that several NCNC leaders, including Azikiwe, Akpabio, and Finance Minister Mbonu Ojike, had been trained in the United States caused further discord, since it was common knowledge that the British considered the American educational system quite inferior to their own and disliked the independent outlook that schooling in the United States tended to produce. In 1955 the House of Assembly went so far as to express unwillingness to vote expatriate allowances for several permanent secretaries.[3] Akpabio felt particularly aggrieved against certain members of the Education Department whose unfavorable reports on Ibibio State College had kept the school from receiving grants-in-aid, and he felt that his first Director of Education was not sufficiently willing to approve African-managed schools for financial assistance.

This underlying current of suspicion seriously hampered the discussions between Nigerian and British officials when it became necessary to consider the financial implications of universal primary education. All but one British adviser in the ministries of Education and Finance warned that the region would be unable to pay for such a program; one prediction was that the East's expanding commitments in primary education would cost at least £2.5 million more than the already inflated education estimates approved for 1956–57. Officials also pointed out the danger of embarking on an expensive crash program at the very time that a new and untried method of tax collection was being introduced. But party leaders suspected either that these arguments were based on faulty calculations or that they represented a convenient excuse for inaction on the part of expatriates who were basically unsympathetic toward African self-government. The politicians perceived the bureaucrats' figures not as a set of financial constraints on policy but as symbols of other issues quite unrelated to economics. When one expatriate in the Ministry of Finance offered the unorthodox view that the 1956 finance law would pay for the education program by netting £5 million, the Executive Council was only too eager to believe him.

The educational bureaucracy expanded rapidly to cope with its vastly increased work load, but officials at all levels faced severe problems of understaffing. The Ministry of Education's annual report for 1956 pointed out: "The planning and implementation of Universal Primary Education found the Region with a senior provincial staff almost identical to that of 1939."[4] This personnel constraint meant that the government's commitment to expansion at the primary school level directly interfered with its post-primary responsibilities: teachers in government secondary or trade schools were frequently called away from their work to help register children for primary school or to supervise the construction of local council schools. Most of the actual field work was performed by Nigerians, who thus gained valuable administrative experience. But it proved more difficult in the East than in the West to find Nigerians qualified by training or length of service for the upper ranks of the educational hierarchy, largely because Easterners had not enjoyed as many opportunities as Westerners for secondary and post-secondary education before 1950.

The role of government agencies, other than the Ministry and Department of Education, and of the NCNC apparatus in introducing universal primary education does not appear to have been as extensive in the East as in the West, although the Eastern Nigeria Information Service gave wide publicity to registration and party leaders spoke of the scheme during the 1957 election campaign. Informal troubleshooting committees composed of ministers and other NCNC leaders were not formed, nor was the party at the local level active in settling disputes over the siting and proprietorship of schools. One reason for the apparently insufficient use of government and party resources may have been that Azikiwe was a more dominant figure within the NCNC than Awolowo was in the Action Group, so that the major decisions were often made by the Premier rather than by a circle of teacher-politicians as in the West. Another reason was that the controversy precipitated in mid-1956 by the government's stand on voluntary agency schools split the NCNC rank and file along religious lines; the party, far from being an agent of reconciliation in this delicate issue, was itself a victim of the religious warfare being waged throughout the region. Efforts to involve the NCNC in the enforcement of controversial government policies might have served only to weaken the already fragmented ruling party.

PATTERNS OF CONSULTATION

Because of the pressure to accomplish a great deal in a short time, and because "the Ibos and Ibibios of Eastern Nigeria were and still are great believers in a government by discussion,"[5] it might be supposed that extensive consultation would have taken place between the policy makers and nongovernment groups. But one of the remarkable aspects of the Eastern Region's universal primary education program was the absence of such consultation, either with the voluntary agencies or with the Nigeria Union of Teachers. The regional Board of Education did not even meet in 1956 or 1957, and the voluntary agencies were not involved in the framing of the Education Law of 1956, which specified the procedures to be followed in making future educational policy. The breakdown in communication between the government and the voluntary agencies was perhaps best illustrated in January 1955, when the Presbyterian, Methodist, and Catholic education secretaries called on Akpabio to ascertain their status with the government.[6] Not only was consultation with the Nigeria Union of Teachers minimal, but friction between the government and the union provoked the N.U.T. to call a strike in June 1956. Thus the regional government most in need of extensive discussion and advice to cope with its formidable educational problems relied hardly at all on consultative procedures.

The lack of consultation can be largely explained by differences in the personal backgrounds of NCNC leaders, on the one hand, and of voluntary agency and N.U.T. leaders, on the other. The party was, of course, composed of and directed by Africans, whereas the voluntary agency hierarchy, with the partial exception of the Church Missionary Society, was almost entirely foreign. Africanization of the largest agency, the Roman Catholic Mission, had been particularly slow for a number of reasons: the belatedness of Catholic efforts to open secondary schools, the amount of training required for the priesthood, the unwillingness of young Africans to take celibacy vows, and a general unwillingness on the part of the Irish priests to accept the fact that the colonial era was ending. Negotiations over the educational role of religious groups were therefore likely to be negotiations between the races as well—a situation in which conflicts could easily arise. And there were few prominent men within the party who could forcefully articulate the interests of the voluntary agencies. The East did not have the equivalent of Saint Andrew's College, whose teacher-preacher-politicians played such an important part in formulating the West's educational policy. The Catholic mission limited its own role within the NCNC by initially discouraging its few well-trained Nigerian laymen from entering politics, though this policy was abandoned by the mid-1950's.

Relations between party leaders and the Catholics were further strained by a legacy from the region's early educational history. As noted in Part I, the earliest secondary schools in the East were all Protestant, and not until the 1940's did the Roman Catholic Mission seriously begin to challenge the Protestant lead. Because educational accomplishment was closely linked to political prominence, the early leadership of the NCNC was overwhelmingly Protestant and tended to view religious and educational issues from a Protestant—or at least a non-Catholic—perspective.* Catholic spokesmen therefore had to surmount a religious as well as a racial barrier in their dealings with policy makers.† The best strategy for the Catholics in the event of conflict was, in fact, to bypass the party leadership and go directly to the people for support. Thanks to Bishop Shanahan's emphasis on primary education, perhaps half of the NCNC rank and file was Catholic; by mobilizing popular support the mission could remind NCNC leaders of their dependence on a large bloc of votes that might, on occasion, be withheld. Thus, early patterns of educational expansion made consultation during the 1950's less likely by reducing the opportunity for meaningful communication between the government and the Roman Catholic leaders and at the same

* Only one member of Ita's cabinet was a Catholic; the same applies to Azikiwe's cabinet in 1954.

† The religious barrier operated even where the racial barrier did not, for most of the expatriates in the Department of Education were English Protestants. One high official who was an Ulsterman was suspected by many Irish priests of having nationalistic reasons for opposing the Roman Catholic Mission.

time tempting the Catholics to engage in public controversy with the government.

The legacy of early missionary activity also affected the relations between party leaders and the Nigeria Union of Teachers. The union drew its national leadership from the areas where the first intensive missionary effort had taken place—Calabar in the East and the southern Yoruba areas in the West. Union leaders from the West, as Yorubas, had the proper ethnic background for influence within the Western Region government, whereas the leaders from the East, President Alvan Ikoku and General Secretary E. E. Esua, were not from the same ethnic group as most members of the NCNC.* Ideological differences compounded the ethnic one: NCNC leaders, who saw themselves as the vanguard of the anti-colonial struggle, criticized the long-standing willingness of Ikoku and Esua to work with the British administration. The very source of the N.U.T.'s strength during the colonial era thus became, at least in the East, a liability when Africans took over the reins of power. The political relevance of these differences was reinforced by Ikoku's constant opposition to the NCNC in the Eastern House of Assembly; he formed the United National Party (later the United National Independence Party) in 1952 and was its leading spokesman from 1953 to 1957. NCNC leaders feared that Ikoku would use the teachers' union as an instrument to embarrass the Eastern government; Ikoku felt that the government was unwilling to negotiate in good faith with the N.U.T. because the union's leadership was not under NCNC control.

Relations between the government and the Nigeria Union of Teachers reached a low point in 1956 when the government, having promised a year earlier to bring voluntary agency teachers' salaries in line with those of government teachers, failed to keep its promise and then refused to negotiate with union leaders over new salary scales and conditions for promotion. After making several verbal protests, the N.U.T. Executive called for a sit-down strike on June 8. The strike call was not widely heeded, however, and after about a week the union asked its members to return to work. Government leaders naturally viewed the strike as a thinly disguised attempt by the Opposition to embarrass the government during the critical stages of planning for universal primary education; Akpabio charged that the union's "principal leader was wearing the robes of a politician rather than those of a trade unionist."[7] The lack of government

* Ikoku is an Aro Ibo with an Efik mother; Esua is an Efik.

confidence in the N.U.T. was reflected in the 1956 Education Law, which provided for four members on the Board of Education to represent the interests of teachers but did not specify, as in the West, that the union be consulted prior to their appointment. The law also established a Teachers' Disciplinary Council without indicating how its members were to be selected.[8] The first chairman of this council was J. K. Nzerem, an NCNC stalwart whose appointment was opposed by union leaders.

Because the Eastern Region's government did not seek the advice of private groups experienced in education, its capacity to provide universal primary education was lowered in certain respects, and policies were formulated that were "little more than a series of improvisations."[9] Moreover, the private sector's uncertainty over educational policy left it unprepared to carry out the various directives that issued from Enugu between 1956 and 1958. But the lack of consultation had a positive aspect as well, for it enabled the government to carry out certain measures that might have been impossible had the interests of key private groups been considered. As we shall see, one of the aims of the NCNC leaders was to reduce the influence of the voluntary agencies both among the populace and at the policy-making level; insofar as consultation with the mission groups would further entrench their position in the machinery of government and necessitate concessions to their point of view, it would defeat this objective. The NCNC leaders were apparently willing to forgo the benefits of communication with the voluntary agencies in return for greater freedom of maneuver in policy making.

By way of contrast, the government did make a serious effort to involve local people in the planning process through district planning committees. These committees were usually composed of seven members—two from the district council, four from the voluntary agencies in proportion to each denomination's strength in the area, and one from the Education Department. In several areas care was taken to include outspoken opponents of universal primary education on the district planning committees, in the hope that when they became responsible for the success of the program, they would become committed to it. One influential Aba chief who had expressed fears that the program would create confusion and cost too much was later seen after his appointment to the committee stripped to the waist directing the clearance of a local council school site.[10] As in the West, the principal functions of the district planning committees were recommending school sites, estimating enrollment needs, supervising the registration of children, and assigning those on the supplementary register, or waiting list, to classrooms. Without this contribution at the grass-roots level, it is clear that universal primary education could not have been implemented at all.

CONTROL OF THE SCHOOLS

The issue of who would control the new primary schools aroused much greater controversy in the East than in the West. Three factors were central to the evolution of government policy on school super-vision: the pattern of denominational rivalry in the East, the per-spective from which the NCNC leadership viewed this rivalry, and the attitude of many Easterners toward the role of government. As we have seen, the intense competition between Protestants and Cath-olics in the Eastern Region may be traced to a number of causes, among them the virtual absence of Islam, the comity arrangements negotiated among the major Protestant bodies, the Catholic drive for educational predominance under Bishop Shanahan, a marked Ibo receptivity to Catholicism, and the divisive effect of religious differ-ences on the social life of such politically decentralized ethnic groups as the Ibos and Ibibios. The Catholics expanded their activities more rapidly than the various Protestant denominations in the 1940's, a trend that was even more pronounced in the 1950's. Between 1950 and 1955, for example, the number of Catholics claimed by the Onit-sha and Owerri Archdiocese increased 64 per cent, to 640,000, and enrollment in Catholic schools rose 85 per cent, to 287,000.[11] By the mid-1950's the Catholics were proprietors of about half the region's primary schools, and they were expanding rapidly in the secondary and teacher training fields, where they had previously been weak.[12] There was even talk of establishing a Catholic university separate from the university being planned by the Eastern Region govern-ment. The Protestant groups, fearful that in a few years the region would "go Catholic," expanded their own educational activities ac-cordingly—just as Bishop Shanahan in an earlier period had favored mass education to prevent the East from "going Protestant."

The government's commitment to educational expansion doubt-less contributed to religious rivalry, since it led to further competi-tion among voluntary agencies for liberally dispensed grants-in-aid and acted as an incentive to immediate expansion while the grants were still available. During 1956 more voluntary agency primary schools were constructed than in any previous year, for parents and church members "knew that the Church that had the greatest num-ber of children also had the surest hope of survival."[13]

NCNC leaders viewed interdenominational rivalry with increasing alarm; they were aware that it disrupted community life and resulted in an unnecessary and expensive duplication of school facilities. If the educational system could be secularized to some extent, it was believed, communal harmony might be restored and the cost of education simultaneously reduced, whereas if the voluntary agencies controlled the new schools constructed for universal primary education, religious animosity would be even more deeply entrenched among the people. More than a hint of such a future danger was provided in May 1956 during the registration of children for Primary One. Despite the government's warning that children could not be guaranteed admission to the school at which they registered, each voluntary agency strongly urged its adherents to register children in its own schools. The Roman Catholic Mission was particularly insistent: the May 19 headline in its newspaper, *The Leader*, told parents, "Do not on any account register in a non-Catholic school," and the editorial said plainly, "If you want your child to go to heaven, to see God, register him in a Catholic School."[14] This mentality would be encouraged, it was felt, if the voluntary agencies were allowed free rein to construct and manage new schools. A few influential party members went so far as to oppose mission education of any sort because they believed it turned the African against his own culture and perpetuated a subservient attitude toward the colonial rulers and white men in general.

The Protestant or non-Catholic perspective of most of the NCNC leaders also influenced their view of the role secular agencies might play in education. Protestants have generally been less opposed in principle to an expanded government role than have Catholics, and as a practical matter Eastern Nigeria's Protestants realized that a halt to all voluntary agency expansion, although it would hurt them, would hurt the Catholic mission more because of the strength and tempo of the Catholics' educational advance. As it turned out, the Protestants were more afraid of Catholic domination than of a secular school system, so to some extent they welcomed a policy that restricted the power of the voluntary agencies.[15]

There was also a more positive argument for greater secular control of education. Many Easterners idealized the State and believed, as one Minister said in an interview, that "Government should act like God." The view that a well-organized State could do almost anything was more prevalent in the East than the West, perhaps because of the unfamiliarity of Ibos and Ibibios in their traditional life with the constraints under which even highly centralized regimes must operate. Azikiwe's extraordinary magnetism probably contributed to the idealization of the State, for his followers in the East were convinced that once the Premier had decided on a course of action he would be able to carry it out. This mode of thinking legitimized increased activity by the regional government in education as well as other fields, although it did not have the same effect on local government. Indeed, during the 1950–56 period an effort to increase the responsibilities of the local authorities failed; in 1955 a restrictive Local Government Law was passed, superseding the liberal ordinance of 1950, and by 1956 the experiment in local education rating had collapsed. Still, policy makers envisaged a time when local education authorities might be established (Uzoma had explicitly favored this measure as early as 1953)[16] and when elected councils might control a large proportion of the region's primary schools. The position of the Azikiwe government on the question of local control of the schools was not clearly stated by early 1956, but the Catholics feared that Uzoma's program of "nationalization," as they termed it, still formed the basis of primary education policy.[17]

After informing the voluntary agencies in late May 1956 that all construction of classrooms for first-year pupils should cease, except in certain specified cases, the government issued a detailed statement on August 17 outlining its educational policy. The proprietorship of existing voluntary agency schools was to remain unchanged, and previously unassisted mission primary schools acccepting children under the new program would receive grants-in-aid. At the primary level, voluntary agency schools might expand their first-year intake to three streams (120 children per school); no restrictions were placed on voluntary agency activities at the post-primary level. Unopened voluntary agency schools whose construction had begun before May 31 could be managed by the sponsoring agency if application had been made for them to open by August 23, but proprietorship would be assumed by the local authority, usually a district council. In the future all new primary schools were to be under the control of the local authorities, and only local authority schools would receive building grants from the government. In cases where a local authority did not wish to manage its schools, the rights of management might be assumed for a specified length of time by a voluntary agency, to be selected by a government education officer in consultation with the agencies in the area. Religious instruction in local authority schools was to be in accord with the wishes of parents, and a student's freedom to absent himself from such instruction would

be recognized in all of the region's primary schools. Children unable
to gain admission to the school of their choice would be assigned to
other schools by education officers in consultation with the local district planning committees. The policy statement concluded by expressing the hope that local education authorities would be established "in the near future" and that teachers might be bonded directly to the government rather than to the voluntary agencies.[18]

In a related statement, the government announced that trained
teachers were to be posted only to schools that earned grants in 1956;
until a certain proportion of trained staff had been attained in these
schools, the new local authority schools were not to be staffed with
trained teachers. In light of the government's commitment to expansion through schools controlled by local authorities, such a policy
seemed self-defeating, and indeed it was one of the principal reasons
why the local government schools did not win public confidence when
they were opened. But some distinction between school categories
was deemed necessary to "avoid an unchecked dilution and a general
lowering of standards all over the Region."[19]

THE REACTION OF THE VOLUNTARY AGENCIES

The Protestant denominations did not react enthusiastically to the
government's program: some of their education secretaries complained about the building grant provisions; others expressed doubts
about the honesty and competence of the district councils. But criticism was muted by an appreciation of the government's purpose and
a recognition that Christian missions could no longer monopolize
Nigerian education. In a press release of October 1956 the Niger Diocese of the Church Missionary Society made its position clear:

> We, in the past, in common with other churches have used our schools as
> one of the means of spreading that Christian Faith which we believe to be
> the true way of life for all. We shall naturally be sorry to see those particular
> opportunities restricted in future, but we recognize that when education is
> provided universally at public expense the churches cannot claim to con-
> tinue to control nearly all the schools. . . . We do not feel it right to claim
> that all parents who registered their children at a Church School were con-
> scientiously insisting that there alone must their children be educated. In
> many places they had no option but to register at one denominational
> school or another.[20]

The statement asked that unnecessary controversy over educational
policy be avoided by all.

The Catholic hierarchy, although careful to point out that it favored universal primary education in the abstract, strongly objected

to certain aspects of the government's policy. The ceiling on voluntary agency expansion and the power given district planning committees to assign children who could not be accommodated in one school to other schools were regarded as violations of a parent's right to choose where his children would be educated. The bishops of the Eastern Region stated:

This right is entirely fundamental. Children belong to their parents by natural law, and the parents are responsible before God for their proper upbringing and education. They cannot fulfill this responsibility unless they are free to choose the agency (or Mission) to which they give their children. Freedom to choose a school for one's children is an essential freedom. It should not be removed by any Government.[21]

This position implied that the government should never limit the expansion of mission schools; whenever Catholic parents, for example, wished a Catholic school, they should have it by right, and the government should presumably subsidize it. The Church was further disturbed by references to local education authorities and government bonding of teachers, since both suggested eventual state control of the educational system and a slackening of religious emphasis. An editorial in *The Leader* warned: "If we accept this first step [the establishment of local education authorities] without protest, the second and third steps will provide a 'full education service' which will exclude our Catholic religion from all grant-aided schools. The loss of Catholic education will be followed inevitably by the loss of faith."[22]

Certain practical considerations influenced the Catholic position. The mission was investing a great deal in its building program—one Catholic member of the House later estimated the expenditure at £500,000[23]—and it expected that it would be reimbursed by the government, as in the West. When this did not occur, the mission was not only hurt financially, but also lost the respect of its own adherents, who had been promised government aid. The Catholics were also interested in education as a political issue. The mission hierarchy had by the mid-1950's come to regret its previous disinterest in politics and its lack of influence within the NCNC;* the education issue offered the Catholics a chance to demonstrate their political power to

---

* Ejike Chidolue, a Protestant politician, is said to have taunted the Catholics during the 1961 regional election by saying that Catholics were like the leaves of the oil-bean tree—numerous but without much importance. Chidolue, the NCNC candidate for a constituency near Onitsha, was defeated by the President of the Eastern Nigeria Catholic Council, J. M. Nwosu, who ran as an independent and stressed Catholic solidarity. Interview with E. O. Enemo, July 25, 1964.

the party leaders within the region by mobilizing mass opposition to what they suspected was a deliberately anti-Catholic policy.

A wide variety of tactics was employed by the Catholics in their battle with the government. Catholic views were publicized in *The Leader*, a weekly with a circulation of more than twenty thousand, and in the widely distributed *Catholic Case in Eastern Education*. Priests frequently used their pulpits to attack government educational policy, and as the election approached they sometimes openly intervened on behalf of anti-NCNC candidates.[24] Mass protest meetings were held, as in Port Harcourt on September 30, 1956, when five thousand Catholics passed a resolution calling on the government to withdraw its restrictions on voluntary agency expansion. Messages urging a revision of policy were sent to Enugu by many villages, some of which based their case on explicitly political considerations. An example is the letter sent to Azikiwe through the Minister of Education from the chiefs and elders of Ndielo Nkporo, Bende Division:

> The people of Nkporo as a whole have been supporters of NCNC (your party) and its leadership, because it is the party which caters for the welfare and development of every town and Division in Nigeria. In view of the above facts and our implicit confidence in the party, we have all hope that the Government which it leads will not give a deaf ear to our humble and immediate demand, i.e. the approval of the Catholic School in our town before December, 1956.[25]

A great deal of the agitation was organized behind the scenes by the Eastern Nigeria Catholic Council, a group of lay Nigerian Catholics whose interpretation of their religious rights was even more far-reaching than that of the Irish Fathers. The council viewed government policy as a conspiracy against the Catholics; it charged that in the past the government had discriminated against Catholics in allocating grants-in-aid and spread the rumor that a handful of European freemasons in the Department of Education were really responsible for the government's educational policy.[26] This was an interesting rebuttal of the charge of "Irish imperialism" frequently leveled against the Roman Catholic Mission, for it shows that politicians in both religious camps tended to see their Nigerian opponents as the unwitting pawns of clever, malicious Europeans.

The intensity of religious conflict varied from area to area, depending on the number of Catholic adherents, the tradition of rivalry, and the relationships between Education Department officials and mission leaders. The scene of greatest conflict was Onitsha—the springboard into Iboland for Anglicans and Catholics, and the regional headquarters of both. Prior to 1956 the major issue in Onitsha politics was a struggle for power between the indigenous inhabitants and a growing number of Ibos from elsewhere who had settled in the town. But with the education issue, "a spectacular realignment of political groups occurred; overnight the formerly intense ethnic conflict between the Onitsha indigenes and the non-Onitsha Ibo settlers was eclipsed by an inter-denominational row between Catholics and Protestants that persisted well beyond the 1957 election."[27] The Eastern Nigeria Catholic Council was strongest in Onitsha; to counter it a group of the town's Protestants, accusing the Roman Catholic Mission of trying to overthrow the government, formed the Convention of Protestant Citizens in February 1957. The charge was indignantly denied by Archbishop Charles Heerey, but that it was ever made suggests the temper of the times.

The response of the local authorities to government policy was significant, for they, after all, were responsible for educational expansion under the universal primary education program. Many district councils accepted this responsibility and resolved to manage their own schools,[28] but a disturbingly large number opposed official policy in one respect or another. In part their opposition was caused by financial considerations, for many councillors doubted their ability to run new schools when education rating had just failed. More serious was the fact that local government organizations, far from operating as a unified, active pressure group to defend their interests against those of the voluntary agencies, reflected within themselves the very religious rivalries that government policy, by increasing local educational responsibilities, had attempted to reduce. Thus the Awgu, Orlu, and Oguta rural district councils, among others, petitioned the government to allow voluntary agencies to expand, and ten of the twelve councils in Onitsha Province (excluding those for Onitsha and Enugu townships) opted for voluntary agency management of their schools. Even in cases where overt opposition to government policy was not expressed, the construction of local authority schools lagged far behind schedule because of the inexperience and inefficiency of the councils and their staffs. And where local government schools were actually ready by January 1957, it soon became clear that they were unpopular, for with their almost totally untrained teaching force they were no match academically for the voluntary agency schools.[29]

By late 1956 the Eastern government was in a quandary. Its commitment to expand the local authority school system had already been made, and its dislike of religious interference in political matters and underlying fear of Catholic aggressiveness remained as strong as ever. Yet a regional election was in the offing, and universal primary education had obviously become not the monumental political asset it was designed to be but quite possibly a serious liability. NCNC leaders were being shown convincing evidence that the Catholic Church commanded a sizeable popular following, and the possibility that Catholics might run against the NCNC as independents was disquieting, particularly to Azikiwe, whose home town of Onitsha was the focal point of the struggle. Catholics who were active in the party, including the Government Chief Whip, B. C. Okwu, were publicly decrying the government's stand. And local authority schools were not being constructed rapidly enough to accommodate the thousands of pupils assigned to them.

The government tried to resolve the dilemma by defending its position and at the same time offering a series of substantial concessions to the voluntary agencies. Various official statements insisted that the government, far from opposing the Catholic Church, had in the past greatly assisted it through grants-in-aid, and that the government had a right to decide how schools sustained by public funds should be controlled.[30] At the same time, the voluntary agencies—in effect, the Catholics—were placated by revisions in educational policy. Through concessions made shortly after the August 17 pronouncement, teachers in local authority schools managed by voluntary agencies were to be bonded to the missions, and primary schools started by the voluntary agencies before May 31, 1956, whose application to open had been received by late August were to be allowed to open in 1957 as local authority schools managed by the agencies that constructed them. The second concession spurred the missions to continue constructing schools beyond the May 31 deadline in the hope that government policy would change again. This hope proved realistic, for on December 28 the government announced that all voluntary agency schools completed by December 31 for which a request to open had been received by January 1, 1957, could operate under voluntary agency management. In February 1957, after children had crowded into mission schools, it was announced that these schools could expand by an additional stream and that the streams themselves could be temporarily enlarged. Thus before the universal primary education program began, virtually all barriers to voluntary agency expansion were removed, rendering about a hundred new local authority schools superfluous, because so few children were attending them. In making its concessions, the government emphasized that a ceiling on voluntary agency expansion would be established for the 1958 school year. This "hard line" statement meant little, however, because 1956 was the crucial year during which a marked change in the ownership and management of the primary school system might have been effected.

Thus appeased, the Catholics somewhat modified their protest campaign. But its effects were still felt in the election of March 15. As *The Leader* pointed out in an election-day editorial:

> It is an incontestable fact that the main issue at stake in the election is that of education. The natural rights of Catholics have been violated, their protestations ignored. They and their Church have been the object of a lie-and-smear campaign. On March the 15th the religious future of their children is in their own hands. After March the 15th it is in somebody else's![31]

The election was an NCNC sweep, and only one Catholic independent won a seat. But NCNC candidates who were also Catholics did particularly well in Onitsha, and in general "organized Catholic action appears to have made an impression on the NCNC leadership."[32] Six of the fourteen ministers appointed to the post-election cabinet were Catholic; one of them, G. E. Okeke, became Minister of Education following Akpabio's transfer to another ministry later in 1957, and during Okeke's illness in early 1958, Okwu, who had earlier been one of the most vocal Catholic opponents of government policy, was made Acting Minister of Education. These men were not able to change the basic policy of halting the growth of voluntary agency primary schools, but they did represent the Catholic viewpoint in the government and may have modified its stand on some issues. It is noteworthy, for example, that the 1956 proposals regarding local education authorities and bonding of teachers were never pressed thereafter by the government.

After the election a truce of sorts was reached over the religious issue, partly through the efforts of the Premier, who used his personal influence with the Anglican and Catholic archbishops in Onitsha to reduce tempers on both sides. But the conflict continued to simmer beneath the surface, making it more difficult for the local councils and district planning committees to function effectively. The legacy of interdenominational bitterness was revealed occasionally in House debates. On April 1, 1957, P. N. Okeke, an Onitsha Catholic, delivered a frontal attack on government policy, saying that it contradicted an NCNC campaign statement guaranteeing parents the right to choose where their children would be sent to school. In reply, Rev.

M. D. Opara said: "I must warn the Government that it must be cautious against some of our people who try to assist these foreign people to keep us under bondage forever. We must be free not only from British rule but also from the church rule too."[33] This exchange was by no means the last of its kind in the annals of the House.

PROBLEMS IN HANDLING ENROLLMENT

So intense was the religious controversy over universal primary education, and so widespread its ramifications, that it overshadowed other more purely administrative issues raised by the program. These issues were present, however, though they were not the same as the ones that concerned the Western Region government. The Eastern Region's major administrative problem was how to construct and staff new local authority schools in a limited amount of time so that all registered children could be accommodated by February 1957. The task was formidable. Of the 482,000 children who registered in May, 300,000 were allocated to existing classrooms; a high proportion of the remainder had to be allocated in September to local authority schools.[34]

Because time was short bureaucratic efficiency was of paramount importance, yet the pressure of events produced delay and confusion. Two thousand building plans were ordered from Lagos for distribution to the district councils, but as of late August they had not arrived, and the councils were clamoring for them. Also in late August, the Chief Executive Officer requested that the Ministry of Finance advance certain councils at least £100 per new school for construction costs, but he was informed that no funds would be available for this purpose until mid-September. A source of considerable misunderstanding was the government's promise that it would provide education officers to councils requesting them; when the requests began to come in, the Ministry realized that its personnel were overworked on other vital assignments and could not be spared after all. Then there was confusion over the recruitment of teachers for local government schools. In early October the Permanent Secretary requested certain councils to postpone their recruitment drive because the Ministry had not yet decided on the proper grading of the staff. This request was made at a time when the vast majority of council teachers would inevitably have to be persons whose education had stopped at Standard Six.

The administrative problems involved in establishing new primary schools were compounded by the series of concessions made to the voluntary agencies. Each concession required a re-estimate of the number of local authority schools that were needed, and since the precise enrollment effects of each new ruling could not be determined in advance, the estimates could be based only on informed intuition. The government's uncertainty strained relations between Enugu and the local councils. Matters became worse when the Ministry of Education requested the councils in February and March 1957 to terminate the contracts of hundreds of probationary teachers who had just been hired but were no longer needed in the poorly attended council schools.* In coming to terms with the objections of the voluntary agencies, the government alienated itself to some extent from the local government bodies it was firmly committed to strengthening.

FINANCING UNIVERSAL PRIMARY EDUCATION:
THE MODIFICATION CRISIS

Such was the furor over religious aspects of the government's educational policy, and so frantic were the efforts of public officials and private citizens to prepare for the influx of first-year pupils in early 1957, that the public paid almost no attention to the program's financial aspects. This was most unfortunate, because perhaps the fundamental question raised by the East's commitment to universal primary education was whether a region with a per capita income of less than £25 could finance eight years of free primary education. NCNC leaders knew in a rather general way that the program would be expensive, but they did not trust the specific revenue and expenditure estimates prepared by expatriate civil servants. The politicians assumed that the 1956 Finance Law would bring in much more money than the previous local rating system, that first-year enrollment in 1957 would not be so heavy as to raise capital and recurrent costs above anticipated levels, and that reforms in the pattern of school ownership would reduce costs by preventing duplication of school fa-

---

* In Port Harcourt, for example, fifteen of thirty-four teachers newly hired by the Municipal Council were fired in late March 1957 on the grounds that insufficient numbers of students were attending council schools. A council committee dealing with this matter blamed the Provincial Education Officer for interfering with local government affairs; the officer replied that appointments and terminations were really the concern of the Ministry. After extensive publicity the Municipal Council was able to increase enrollment sufficiently to justify rehiring three of the teachers, but the officer refused to give his approval. Minutes of Meeting of Education, Library, and Welfare Committee, April 25, 1957 (Port Harcourt Municipal Council, U.P.E. File 953/A, May 27, 1957); letter from Town Clerk to Permanent Secretary, Ministry of Education (Port Harcourt Municipal Council, U.P.E. File 953/A).

cilities by rival voluntary agencies. By the beginning of 1957, moreover, the leaders had strong political reasons for remaining committed to these economic assumptions. The universal primary education program had already stirred controversy on religious grounds;
to raise the prospect of insufficient revenue for the program might
turn the people against the NCNC at a time when the party needed
all the support it could muster for the upcoming regional election.
So while civil servants grumbled to themselves about the financial
disaster that lay ahead, politicians said little about this matter among
themselves and even less to the public.

Once the NCNC had carried the election, however, government
leaders could no longer ignore financial realities. On the revenue
side, taxes collected under the Finance Law for fiscal year 1956–57
amounted to only £2.4 million rather than £5 million. On the expenditure side, the payment of salary arrears to teachers, the volume
of popular response to free education, the concessions to voluntary
agencies, and the cost of constructing local authority schools, some of
which were initially poorly attended, guaranteed that the actual cost
of the program would be higher than anticipated. By mid-1957 it was
learned that the Ministry of Education had spent about £2 million
more than the £2.9 million allocated to it for fiscal year 1956–57. By
autumn the cost of education was again seriously exceeding the
greatly increased 1957–58 estimates; in a subsequent House debate
the Acting Minister of Education calculated that if primary education continued to be free and post-primary expansion continued at
current rates, the education bill would be £6.6 million in 1958 and
£14.8 million in 1964.[35] Since these amounts would constitute about
half of the region's total expenditure for 1958 and virtually all of its
revenue by 1964, emergency measures to reduce government outlays
on education were clearly in order.

The first hint of things to come was given in November 1957, when
the Ministry informed the voluntary agencies that they could expect
no increase in grants to cover their administrative expenses. Then on
December 18 the Ministry wrote to all district council secretaries that
building grants for the construction or expansion of facilities would
no longer be available for local authority schools. These schools, still
struggling for public acceptance, thus lost the one advantage they had
possessed over voluntary agency schools, and since most councils were
unable to finance expansion for the 1958 intake at such short notice,
if at all, they were forced to crowd their new classes into existing
schoolrooms.

But the most basic change in the government's fiscal policy remained to be announced. On January 8, 1958, the Ministry informed school proprietors and managers that the Assumed Local Contribution—which in almost all instances meant school fees—would be reintroduced at the rate of £6 per pupil for Standard Five and £8 for Standard Six. In addition, an "enrollment fee" of ten shillings per pupil in Infant One and Two and of £1 from Standard One to Standard Four was to be paid at the start of the 1958 school year.[36] "Free" education was free no longer.

To the people of the Eastern Region this announcement came as a great shock. They were unaware that the government was in financial difficulties and had received no prior warning that school fees might be reintroduced; even administrative officers in the provinces heard the news for the first time from the radio and newspapers. The initial surprise was soon replaced by anger as the populace reflected that the revered "Zik" had broken his promise. One of the legacies of colonial rule, which the NCNC had in fact done little to dispel, was the popular belief that the government always had large sums of money at its disposal.[37] Most Nigerians did not realize that a government must work with limited resources and keep its expenditures roughly in line with its revenues; they therefore could not understand why educational policy was being modified after the NCNC leaders had fully committed themselves to the abolition of primary school fees. The level at which the Assumed Local Contribution had been set for standards Five and Six also angered the people, for it was about three times higher than the fees usually charged for that level before universal primary education had been introduced.

To explain the government's case to the people and to prevent popular unrest, Okeke set out on January 10 for a tour of the region. But so severe were the pressures on him that he became ill and was flown off to London; earlier, the Permanent Secretary, an Englishman, had collapsed under the strain and also been flown to London, where he died. The public relations efforts of the Ministry of Education were thus crippled at the time they were most needed. The astute Azikiwe then appointed B. C. Okwu as Acting Minister. The man who had earlier opposed universal primary education on religious grounds was charged with defending the modification of the program on economic grounds.

But it was too late to avoid violence. In late January crowds of women surged through Owerri town protesting the reimposition of fees. The demonstrations spread to other parts of Owerri Province and to Onitsha Province, and in several instances school buildings were burned and the homes of politicians looted or threatened with destruction.* In a few cases the demonstrators shouted "Down with black man rule"—a slogan widely reported in the foreign press and used, no doubt, by those who questioned the African's capacity for self-government. The unrest was most serious in the backward rural areas, which had the most to gain from free education and which were inadequately staffed with law-enforcement officers. The great majority of the demonstrators were women, and their general behavior was remarkably reminiscent of the Aba Women's Riots of 1929.†

In an effort to stem the rioting the government announced on January 31 that parents would be given two extra weeks to pay the newly imposed fees. But this had little effect, and on February 3 an official warning was issued against violence. The next day it was announced that the House of Assembly would soon be convened in emergency session to discuss modification, and on February 5 the Governor-General declared a state of emergency in nine Eastern divisions and sent five hundred Federal police to the region to reimpose law and order. Four days later, in a radio address to the region, Azikiwe said that the government had shown great patience with the demonstrators but that there could be no surrender to mob violence. He assured

---

* No distinction was drawn between regional and federal NCNC representatives. The home of Chief Jackson Mpi, a member of the House of Representatives from Ahoada, was demolished. Another member of the federal House, A. E. Ukatah, was besieged in his home by angry women, who replied in answer to his plea that he was in the federal legislature: "The federal government should have told the regional government what to do." Police with tear gas were sent to Ukatah's house to conduct him to safety. Interview with Senator A. E. Ukatah, July 22, 1964.

† Margery Perham's description of the 1929 disturbances applies almost exactly to the outbreak in 1958: "When the character of the riots themselves is reviewed, the overwhelming impression is of the vigour and solidarity of the women. Men occasionally make a flickering appearance in the background, but they seem, with a few exceptions, to have stood completely on one side, passive, if consenting parties, to the extraordinary behavior of their wives. . . . [The women's] organization into societies and age groups, . . . their concentration in markets and wide dispersal along the trade routes, are factors which may help to account for their rapid mobilization over two Provinces." Margery Perham, *Native Administration in Nigeria* (London, 1937), p. 211. I. C. Jackson noted in 1956: "Women's organizations possess an extraordinary cohesion, largely because of the custom of exogamy. . . . Exogamy results in all the married women being newcomers, while their husbands are natives of the quarter, and the women must therefore achieve unity to counterbalance the ties of blood which unite their menfolk. The women's 'meetings' possess a strength usually absent from similar organizations of the men." I. C. Jackson, *Advance in Africa: A Study of Community Development in Eastern Nigeria* (London, 1956), p. 42.

the people that when the House of Assembly met on February 13, its opinions would be seriously considered by the government.

Meanwhile, several delegations of irate women were preparing to descend on Enugu to present their views in person to the Premier or to Okwu, the Acting Minister of Education.* One group arriving from Awka, some forty miles away, demanded to see Okwu; included in the group was Okwu's mother, unaware that she was marching on her own son! The Acting Minister invited the delegation into his office and arranged seats for the women but kept his British Permanent Secretary standing. Speaking to the women in Ibo, he explained that the government, like a household, had to pay for what it consumed. "I could resign and turn the government back to the white man," he said. "Would you want that?" The women, looking at the foreign civil servant standing uncomfortably in the background, emphatically rejected that suggestion. Having made their objections they returned home to reflect on the financial problems of Azikiwe's "household."

Another delegation of women, this one chanting war songs, boarded the train for Enugu at Aba and Umuahia and refused to pay for their tickets. The Premier felt it was dangerous for Okwu to go out to meet them, but Okwu drove to Agbani, a point about ten miles south of the capital where the train was temporarily stopped, ordered the police away, and went alone to confer with the women. Picking out the four who seemed to be leading the march, he invited them to talk with him in his car. After giving bottles of palm wine and snuff to each of them and telling them good-naturedly that he enjoyed their war songs, Okwu explained in simple terms that the government had a limited amount of money, that the education program had cost far more than had been anticipated, and that for these reasons modification was necessary. He added, in accordance with his personal views as a Catholic, that the program was a trick devised by white civil servants to embarrass the NCNC. The women's principal grievance was that no warning of a change had been given: "Tell the Big Man he must *tell* us before something happens." After Okwu assured them their views would be taken into account, they agreed to return to their homes. They reboarded the train the wiser for their lesson in elementary economics, and a potential siege of Enugu was averted.

The House of Assembly met in emergency session February 13 to debate a motion approving "in principle" the need to modify the

* The discussion that follows is based on an interview with Hon. B. C. Okwu, Aug. 29, 1964.

universal primary education program. Okwu began the session by outlining the extent of the financial burden imposed by the program,
arguing: "No Government in the world could contemplate maintaining from its ordinary revenue a system of education which absorbs
such a proportion of that revenue."[38] The Premier admitted: "We
have explored all sources of revenue and we have almost reached the
end of the road."[39] S. E. Imoke, the Finance Minister, attributed the
government's difficulties to its acceptance of a British adviser's optimistic financial estimates, although he said the man meant well, and
offered to resign himself. Imoke poignantly described the dilemma of
"a comparatively young Government passing frequently through various constitutional phases and emerging from each, never financially
placed but worse, and never having any chance of controlling her
fate but finding herself always controlled by events yet extremely
zealous in building up a welfare state for her people."[40] The debate
also included, for the first time, open expressions of doubt concerning
the wisdom of expanding school facilities so rapidly. Azikiwe referred
to primary education as "this unproductive social service," and another minister, E. Emole, pointed out that the United Kingdom had
followed "the pattern of industry and increased productivity first,
free education second. Never free education first, as there must be
jobs for the newly educated to take up, and only industry, trade and
commerce can provide such jobs in bulk. . . . *We must hesitate to
create political problems of unemployment in the future.*"[41]

Opposition leaders charged that the government had practiced de-
ception and could not blame the people for objecting. The demonstrations, they pointed out, were concentrated in Ibo areas usually
regarded as NCNC strongholds and hence could not be attributed to
the Action Group or the United National Independence Party. Like
the NCNC politicians in the West during the debate over the education and health levy, Opposition spokesmen alleged that the government's difficulties were largely the result of extravagant spending by
regional ministers and urged that the ministers reduce their own standard of living before imposing austere measures on the people. One
Action Group member referred to an underlying cause of the trouble
when he said: "We are very much in sympathy with the Government
for undertaking a scheme without any planning."[42] The Opposition
agreed that additional funds were needed under the circumstances
but argued that the money might be obtained by means other than
school fees.

Following a thorough debate, the House voted on February 17 by sixty-two to eleven to modify the universal primary education program. The charges announced the previous month were somewhat altered, however, to preserve a semblance of "free" education and to reduce the exorbitant school fee for Standard Six. Enrollment fees were to be abolished, no charge was to be made for the two Infant classes, and fees for the remaining six classes were reduced to £2 for each of the first two classes, £4 for the next two, and £6 for the last two. By mid-February the people's wrath had subsided, and the riots, which had cost four lives and resulted in the conviction of more than 270 people, finally came to an end. The very poverty of the masses, which was one reason for the intensity of their reaction on being told by rich politicians that they would have to pay school fees again, also helped to quell the outburst, for a population living on the margin of subsistence can ill afford to engage in destructive and anomic behavior for extended periods of time. An estimated 260,000 children were withdrawn from primary school because their parents could not afford to pay the fees,[43] but neither the children nor their parents made politically significant protests once the new school year was well under way.

CONCLUSION: THE TWO REGIONS COMPARED

In both of the Southern Nigerian regions, the effort to provide free, universal primary education was the most administratively complex, financially burdensome, and politically controversial task undertaken by government during the pre-Independence decade. We have seen that the leaders of the two regions had quite similar reasons for expanding their educational systems, particularly at the primary school level. And they faced many of the same problems in implementing their plans: the absence of reliable data, uncertainty over the magnitude and timing of popular response, tension between Nigerian ministers and British civil servants, and insufficient numbers of trained teachers, to name a few.

It is equally clear, however, that the problems faced by the two regional governments and the methods they employed to resolve these problems differed in several important respects. The Western Region held an overall advantage—even though a lower proportion of the West's children were enrolled in primary school by the early 1950's— for it profited from continuous political leadership under the rule of a party that accepted the ambiguity of the Macpherson constitution as a challenge rather than a trap, was committed to planning, and enjoyed the support of the region's leading intellectuals. The East underwent a leadership crisis in 1952–53, and its most popular leader did not assume the premiership and concentrate on regional advancement until 1954. Its ruling party, the NCNC, did not emphasize planning as much as the Action Group, and many of the region's intellectuals were unwilling to cooperate with the Azikiwe government in devising and carrying out its programs.* Educational planners in the West had three years in which to prepare for universal primary education, and their goals became somewhat more modest over time; Eastern officials had only months to prepare for their program, which became increasingly ambitious as the deadline for implementation approached. Western leaders were sufficiently sympathetic to the goals of private agencies involved in education to benefit from their advice without compromising basic principles in order to obtain their cooperation. Eastern leaders, by contrast, had religious and racial reasons for opposing the spread of voluntary agency schools, and ethnic and ideological reasons for not cooperating with the Nigeria Union of Teachers. The East therefore did not benefit from outside consultation, though the very absence of consultation freed the government to make a serious if only partly successful assault on the influence of the voluntary agencies. The West had more Africans ready to move into the educational bureaucracy, and it had more funds to work with than the East, particularly after the 1954 changes in the financial structure of the Nigerian federation. These differences, taken cumulatively, account for the relative ease with which the West carried out its plans and for the series of crises that plagued the Eastern government's efforts at educational expansion.

Whereas in the West the people were asked to pay for universal primary education in advance, in the East the people were not informed of the costs involved until it was too late to continue government-financed education. The short-run consequence of fiscal responsibility in the West was the Action Group's defeat at the polls in 1954, but once universal primary education was introduced the party was rewarded in the 1956 election. The short-run consequence of fiscal irresponsibility in the East was an electoral victory for the NCNC in 1957, but when the economic realities could no longer be ignored the party lost stature in the riots of early 1958. The East's modification crisis had a beneficial effect, however, for out of it came a new awareness on the part of the people and their leaders of the

* It is only a slight exaggeration to claim that St. Andrew's College produced the intellectuals who held power in the West, whereas Hope Waddell Training Institute produced the intellectuals who led the Opposition in the East.

nature of self-government. Prior to 1958 it could be said that Easterners regarded their government as a Leviathan capable of performing whatever it wished—a mentality stemming both from the colonial era and from the charismatic leadership of Azikiwe. With the modification of the education program, the Eastern government appeared as a more human institution, limited in resources and led by fallible men. The leaders for their part were made painfully aware of the limits placed by democracy on their mandate to rule, and they learned the necessity of explaining their actions to the people, even if this meant admitting past errors of judgment. In a sense, the battle for responsible self-government was won not in London over the conference table but at Agbani, where a confrontation between the new rulers and the ruled took place and, over palm wine and snuff, the rulers were given a mandate to carry on.

PART III

The Consequences
of Educational Expansion

CHAPTER 8

Education and Political Capacity: Setting Goals

In the first and second parts of this study we have analyzed the causes of educational expansion in Southern Nigeria by focusing on the major actors in the drama: Christian missionaries, the African populace, the colonial rulers, and an educated Nigerian elite that was able, on attaining regional power in the early 1950's, to carry out an unprecedented expansion of enrollment through the universal primary education schemes just described. A subsidiary concern has been the process of expansion—the techniques employed and the problems faced by those in the private sector, and later in the government itself, who pressed for higher primary and secondary school enrollment. Having asked why and how Southern Nigeria's "education explosion" occurred, we are now ready in Part III to confront the question posed in the Introduction: what are the consequences of such an explosion for the area's political development?

Attempting to answer such a question is a hazardous undertaking. A little more than a decade stands between the initiation of the programs whose impact we want to assess and the present; our limited historical perspective not only renders it impossible to speak with confidence of the long-run consequences of these programs but also quite possibly distorts our view of what is important in the short run. Moreover, it is easier to demonstrate that a number of factors—psychological, social, economic, and political—affect an educational system than to reverse the argument and show how the educational system affects an environment subject to many other influences having little or nothing to do with education. Additional problems arise when one tries to give operational meaning to such abstract terms as capacity, equality, and integration, linking them to specific events and trends. For all these reasons, subjective evaluation figures more prominently in Part III than in previous chapters. But even a tentative and admittedly subjective discussion of the short-run consequences of educational expansion can be a valuable exercise. Large sums of money were spent in the 1950's by Southern Nigerian leaders who had quite explicit notions of the benefits of popular education. If educational expenditure is not achieving its stated aims, or if unforeseen consequences outweigh the intended ones in importance, these findings should be of interest both to the academic who seeks to understand the development process and to the policy maker who seeks to accelerate it.

This chapter and the following one deal with the relationship between education and political capacity. Capacity is increased when government is able to move closer toward the realization of its major goals. But who sets the goals—political leaders and bureaucrats, or the mass of the population? Public officials in most states would agree on certain minimal goals, such as protecting citizens from civil strife and invasion, providing a modest level of individual and collective welfare, and creating opportunities for mass involvement in political life. Goals beyond these basic ones are set by the persons within the political system who participate in decision making. Thus in a nondemocratic system the views of only a few persons need be considered in estimating goals, whereas in a democratic system the views of many must be taken into account.* Modernization usually brings an increase in the functions of government and in the number of people directly affected by government decisions; in Southern Nigeria, a relatively open society, increasing government activity has been a response to pressures from the populace as well as from political and administrative elites. In this chapter we shall consider two questions: whether the expansion of education has raised popular and elite demands on government in Southern Nigeria, and whether the regional and federal governments have formally committed themselves to meeting these demands. The degree to which government agencies actually achieved their goals is considered in Chapter 9.

---

* This formulation avoids building a democratic bias into the definition of political development. In our view both democratic and nondemocratic, even totalitarian, systems may be politically developed.

TABLE 5. Students' Estimates of Their Future Monthly Earnings

Monthly earnings	Primary	Secondary modern	Secondary grammar	Sixth Form
Under £15	21.1%	8.9%	.8%	0%
£15–20	11.1	13.2	4.8	0
£21–30	12.8	12.1	11.0	3.3
£31–50	15.4	16.4	17.3	10.0
£51–100	14.6	17.5	29.2	26.7
£101–150	2.4	5.0	9.6	28.3
Above £150	3.0	5.4	6.9	18.3
Don't know	11.3	12.5	11.5	5.0
No answer; unclear; other	8.3	8.9	8.9	8.3

SOURCE: Survey made by the author in 1964 of Southern Nigerian schoolchildren; see Appendix B. This table is based on responses to the question "How much money do you think you will earn per month 10 years from now?"

THE GROWTH OF DEMANDS AMONG THE PEOPLE

The education explosion in Southern Nigeria has without question had a profoundly liberating effect on the younger generation, giving it an awareness of people, places, physical objects, and comforts that are beyond its immediate experience, and providing through literacy the means to enlarge this awareness.* Young people's income and vocational aspirations have been especially affected. Table 5 shows mid-1964 estimates by 1,360 students from randomly chosen schools throughout Southern Nigeria of what their monthly earnings would be ten years hence. Per capita monthly income was under £3 for the area as a whole at the time and could not be expected to rise in a decade to over £5. Yet the median estimated income for the primary school students was between £31 and £50, for the secondary modern school students about £50, for the grammar school students between £51 and £100, and for the Sixth Form students between £101 and £150. In other words, the income aspirations of primary school leavers were roughly ten times greater than the average for Southern Nigeria, and each increase in educational level brought a substantial increase in expected income.†

* One young school leaver in Onitsha used an appropriate Biblical image in describing his illiterate relatives to the author: "They have eyes but do not see."

† Education is not, strictly speaking, the only variable measured here, since a rise in level of education is also a rise in age level, and older students may expect, other things being equal, to earn more than younger ones by a specified date. Since the sample did not include nonpupils of different ages, educational and age variables cannot be separated. However, since virtually all high-paying positions

TABLE 6. Students' Sources of Information about Politics

Source	Primary	Secondary modern	Secondary grammar	Sixth Form
Newspapers	72.8%	85.4%	93.1%	100.0%
Radio	73.3	72.1	74.0	75.0
Rediffusion boxes	37.8	43.2	23.8	33.3
Teachers	41.9	39.3	29.2	6.7
Parents	27.6	15.0	14.2	3.3
Other adults	5.9	6.4	27.3	18.3
Friends of their own age	7.6	11.4	21.7	55.0
Other	1.5	3.6	6.3	8.3
No answer; incomplete	9.3	7.9	3.3	1.7

SOURCE: Survey made by the author in 1964 of Southern Nigerian schoolchildren; see Appendix B. This table is based on responses to the question "Which are the three most important ways in which you learn about politics?" Because of the multiple answer requested, percentages total more than 100% for each column.

In Southern Nigeria the demands of the young for a better life have almost inevitably been channeled into the political arena. Schools have been influential in this respect by conveying information about political personalities and the functions of government, both in the classroom and in the informal aspects of school life. The Southern Nigerian schoolchildren surveyed in 1964 displayed a considerable knowledge of major regional and national leaders.[1] Table 6 shows the responses of students when asked to identify their three most important sources of information about politics. Newspapers, which, of course, require literacy, are clearly most important; rediffusion boxes (large radios often placed in schools for teaching purposes) are also influential; and teachers rank above parents, other adults, and peers at all levels save the Sixth Form.[2] Of course, unschooled Nigerians have their own ways of learning about politics, particularly by radio and by word of mouth. But with educational expansion the amount of political information absorbed by the populace is bound to increase. Thus education has had the dual effect of raising personal ambitions and furthering an awareness of politics; it is not surprising that Nigerians who have been to school expect political leaders to help them realize their aspirations. In a more general sense, as Karl Deutsch has observed, "social mobiliza-

---

are in the modern sector and require extended post-primary training, we can presume that the substantial differences in aspiration between pupils at different educational levels can be explained mainly with reference to schooling.

tion brings with it an expansion of the politically relevant strata of the population."[3]

Universal primary education had another important political effect: its message to the average citizen was that regional and local governments had now assumed tasks previously performed by private agencies. Once people grew accustomed to the notion that the government was responsible for public welfare, their demands on politicians rose sharply. Two of these demands were particularly significant: the demand for more post-primary education and the demand for more employment opportunities for the educated.

THE DEMAND FOR POST-PRIMARY EDUCATION

By the early 1960's the popular demand for primary education had been largely satisfied by the programs of the previous decade. By the 1960's, too, the social and economic value of the First School-Leaving Certificate had rapidly declined, so that obtaining this certificate was no longer considered a worthwhile end in itself. Public enthusiasm for education thus shifted to the post-primary level, which became increasingly the key to respectable employment and upward mobility. So-called secondary modern schools, patterned after those in Britain, were first established on a significant scale in the Western Region in 1955. They offered a three-year post-primary course with less exacting academic standards and, hopefully, a more practical curriculum than the grammar schools.[4] Since they charged fees of £10 to £15 a year, their success depended on people's ability and willingness to pay for this new kind of education. By 1957 secondary modern education had obviously caught the public fancy: more than 30,000 Westerners were enrolled in 254 such schools administered by local authorities, voluntary agencies, and private individuals. At this point the Ministry of Education made an attempt to control the quality of secondary modern education by announcing the consolidation of the existing schools into ninety-four large institutions, each with some public funds for libraries, craft rooms, and other facilities. A few school administrators regarded this move with open hostility; many others reacted to it with utter indifference, kept their schools open, and conveniently forgot to inform the Ministry of new ones being opened. Enrollment soared to 75,000 (533 schools) in 1960 and to 111,000 (699 schools) in 1963—a phenomenal growth for a form of schooling introduced just eight years previously.

Although the rise of the secondary modern school did not make a significant demand on the financial resources of the Western regional government, it taxed the government's scarce administrative resources, and the efficiency of the publicly financed primary school system declined as many teachers trained for the primary schools chose to teach at the secondary modern level instead. Public enthusiasm for these schools, moreover, led the Western government to liberalize its initial policy of "guaranteeing" places in secondary modern schools to one-fourth of the region's primary school leavers; by the late 1950's the guaranteed figure was one-half, a goal that was virtually attained in 1960. Although this guarantee had no legal status, it is significant that regional officials felt constrained both to make such a promise in the first place and later to revise it upward.

Enthusiasm for secondary modern education was not to last, however, because the value of secondary modern certificates for obtaining employment rapidly declined during the 1960's. By 1965 enrollment in the new Western Region* was 40 per cent below the 1963 peak, and a similar drop probably occurred in the Mid-West. More lasting, and far more of a drain on government resources, has been the popular drive for secondary grammar education. Southern Nigeria's grammar school enrollments doubled from 24,000 in 1955 to 48,000 in 1960, and more than doubled again to 116,000 by 1965.[5] The number of grammar schools in Southern Nigeria also rose spectacularly, from 84 in 1952 to 176 in 1957, 296 in 1961, and 417 in 1963. This increase clearly demonstrates the strength of popular sentiment, for usually the capital and recurrent costs of a new grammar school had to be borne by its sponsors for a few years until it became eligible for grants from the regional authorities.† The government was then called upon to supplement what had been done through local initiative.

THE DEMAND FOR EMPLOYMENT

Educational expansion has not only increased popular demands for certain types of schooling; it has also led to a demand that school

---

* Because the size of the Western Region was reduced in 1963 by the formation of the Mid-West Region, it is necessary to distinguish between the "old" and the "new" West.

† Often grammar schools opened with precious little going for them except local faith that they would succeed. One English missionary in the Mid-West wrote in 1964: "The craze for opening new Grammar Schools still persists in spite of the fact that there are not enough boys and girls of the required standard to fill our present ones and that the parents of many who do begin have the greatest difficulty in finding their fees." Letter to the author from Rev. George P. Barnard, April 11, 1964.

leavers be put usefully to work. As we have seen, Southern Nigerians quickly came to realize the value of a school certificate as a passport to salaried employment in the modern sector of the economy; the prospect of such employment was perhaps the major incentive for attending school. But the very success of the regional governments in satisfying the popular demand for education during the 1950's created the almost intractable—and largely unforeseen—problem of finding employment for those educated in the new schools. The rapid increase in the number of school leavers, at a time when employment opportunities within the modern sector were increasing very slowly, lowered the economic value of primary and secondary modern school certificates and led to large-scale unemployment among school leavers. We shall briefly describe the causes and dimensions of this unemployment, called by one economist "perhaps the most serious long-run socio-political problem facing African countries,"[6] and then discuss the extent to which it has become a political issue as popular concern has been transformed into a demand for government action.

Approximately 625,000 Southern Nigerians reached the age of fifteen in 1965. Table 7, which provides a rough estimate of the educational qualifications of these young people, shows, among other things, that 94 per cent had had at least one year of primary education and 32 per cent had completed the primary course, with or without receiving the First School-Leaving Certificate. A decade earlier these figures were perhaps 60 per cent and 20 per cent respectively. The rapid upward shift in the educational qualifications of young people was naturally most pronounced when the first universal primary education classes passed out of primary school. This occurred in 1960 in the Western Region, when 150,000 passed through Standard Six (compared with 63,000 the previous year), and in 1963 in the Eastern Region, when 166,000 completed their final year (compared with 76,000 in 1962).[7] Output declined somewhat from the high points of 1960 and 1963, but by 1965 a plateau had been reached: some 200,000 Southern Nigerians a year completed their primary education, of whom 60,000, or 30 per cent, went on to post-primary institutions.

These young people, from the primary level upward, have definite employment preferences. They are eager to leave the traditional farm behind them, with its exhausting labor, low income, and low status; they want modern sector jobs, which education has put within their grasp and which make more immediate use of their formal training. The rejection of traditional occupations is especially notable

TABLE 7. Educational Composition of the Fifteen-Year-Old Age Group
and of Entries to the Labor Force in Southern Nigeria, 1965

Age and educational level	Entries to labor force	Non-entries to labor force	Total
Age 15:[a]			
No schooling	26,000[b]	13,000	39,000
Some primary school	255,000[b]	130,000	385,000
Completed primary school:			
No primary certificate	55,000	22,000	78,000
Primary certificate	64,000	59,000[c]	123,000
TOTAL	400,000	224,000	625,000
Over age 15:			
Some post primary school	52,000		
GRAND TOTAL	452,000		

SOURCE: Figures computed from Education and World Affairs, Nigeria Project Task Force, Committee on Education and Human Resource Development, *Nigerian Human Resource Development and Utilization* (New York, 1967), pp. 144–55.

[a] Based on the assumptions that Southern Nigeria's 1965 population was 25 million and that 2.5 per cent of the population turns age fifteen each year.

[b] Based on the assumption that about two-thirds of those with no schooling, or with only a few years of primary schooling, enter the labor force. Almost all of the boys and one-third of the girls in these categories enter the labor force.

[c] These go on to post-primary education.

among girls who have some education. Instead of marrying at an early age and becoming directly involved in child-rearing, farm work, or petty trading, many girls now wish to earn an independent income as nurses, teachers, or the like before they marry. An educated girl, moreover, can command a much higher dowry or bride-price than an illiterate one.[8] As more girls enter school the pressures on young men to leave traditional occupations are increased, for they must earn higher wages in order to marry girls in proper style and within a reasonable period of time.

Occupations in the intermediate or transitional sector—crafts and various small-scale construction, transport, service, and trading enterprises—are regarded by school leavers with somewhat greater favor. But here, too, the prospect of low income and low status acts as a deterrent. Educated people feel that if such jobs can be performed by illiterates, persons with schooling are not needed. Nor does the kind of education offered in Southern Nigeria encourage young people to start their own small enterprises.[9]

School leavers' preferences for employment within the modern sector are by no means restricted to clerical and administrative positions in the government hierarchy—positions that were attractive during the colonial period because of the high income, prestige, and relative security of tenure they offered. Also favored are occupations requiring technical and scientific expertise, from auto mechanic, factory worker, surveyor, and nurse to engineer, architect, and doctor. All available evidence from Nigeria and other parts of Africa indicates that school leavers do not fit the stereotype of them as petty bureaucrats who refuse to get their hands dirty. If an occupation has the ring of modernity about it, offers decent wages and security, and puts formal training to work in some visible way, it will be desired by young people even though it may entail manual labor or does not involve direct employment by the government.[10] This attitude emerges clearly from the employment preferences of schoolchildren shown in Table 8.*

In addition to raising the vocational aspirations of the young, education has increased their desire to live in the city. The elements of this desire are well known: the excitement and variety of the city, the opportunity for more interesting and higher-paying work, the freedom from parental and small-community pressures, the possibility of further education. Even though, as one economist has pointed out, the marginal productivity of unskilled labor is probably greater in Nigeria's rural areas than in its cities,[11] the farm offers the certain prospect of penury, the city at least the hope of wealth.[12]

Because of the high concentration of school leavers in such cities as Lagos, Port Harcourt, Ibadan, Onitsha, Aba, Sapele, Benin, and Enugu, their problems are highly visible. By the very act of migrating many of these persons, formerly the underemployed of traditional agriculture, have become the unemployed of the modern city.

---

* Even agriculture was given serious consideration when the school leaver associated it with the use of modern equipment on sufficient amounts of good land. Males in the survey were asked whether they would like to work in a Farm Settlement, a project to encourage progressive agriculture. Positive responses came from 55 per cent of the males in primary school, 60 per cent of those in secondary modern school, 74 per cent of those in grammar school, and 48 per cent of those at the Sixth Form level. (The numbers of males responding at each level were 311, 159, 376, and 58, respectively.) One interesting feature of the author's survey was the more favorable response of Easterners to skilled manual work and farming. This may be a function of the widely noted Ibo willingness to enter fields regarded by others as menial and dirty; it may also reflect the intensive efforts of the Eastern Region government at the time to promote interest in technology and agriculture as the keys to sustained economic growth.

TABLE 8. Students' Employment Preferences

Occupation	Primary	Secondary modern	Secondary grammar	Sixth Form
Farming or fishing	2.0%	1.4%	5.6%	1.7%
Business	4.6	1.8	1.3	3.3
Unskilled worker or artisan	6.5	1.1	.2	0
Factory worker or technician	6.5	4.3	5.8	8.3
Clerical	4.4	20.0	14.6	5.0
Civil service	1.9	1.1	8.8	13.3
Teacher	24.6	31.1	14.0	20.0
Minor medical	20.6	21.8	15.6	1.7
Professional, technical	11.7	2.9	19.6	33.3
Professional, arts	2.4	3.9	6.9	10.0
Other	5.4	7.1	5.4	1.7
No answer; unclear; don't know	9.4	3.6	2.3	1.7

SOURCE: Survey made by the author in 1964 of Southern Nigerian schoolchildren; see Appendix B. This table is based on responses to the question "When you finish your education, what job would you *like* to get?"

The problem is aggravated by the desire of young migrants to remain more or less permanently in the cities, rather than, as in previous years, to stay there for a limited period only. Since it is in the cities—particularly the regional and federal capitals—that politicians and top administrators reside and work, the urban migration of school leavers represents in a sense the physical reunion of government leaders with the "progeny of their own populist agitation."[13] Leaders cannot easily avoid a problem whose consequences, in the form of idle young men, greet their eyes every morning as they drive from home to office.

EMPLOYMENT PROSPECTS IN THE MODERN SECTOR

Table 7 shows that an estimated 171,000 of those who entered the Southern Nigerian labor force in 1965 had completed their primary education and that 52,000 of them had had some post-primary schooling as well. On the basis of our sample, about 150,000 (85–90 per cent of those entering the labor force) wanted to work in the modern sector of the economy. But how many jobs were actually available in this sector? Employment statistics must not be taken too literally, but a reasonable estimate is that 600,000 Southern Nigerians were em-

ployed in the modern or high-productivity sector in 1965; total wage
employment, which includes many positions in the intermediate sector, was probably 750,000.[14] The modern sector employment figure
represents only 6–7 per cent, and total wage employment only 8–9
per cent, of the total Southern Nigerian labor force, estimated at just
under nine million. These percentages are higher than the West
African average but considerably below those in other parts of the
continent, where manufacturing, mining, and plantation agriculture
absorb relatively more Africans in wage employment. Given this
small base, even spectacular percentage increases in employment opportunities would yield relatively few new jobs each year. Assuming,
for example, a 6 per cent growth rate in the modern sector and a
three-to-one ratio of new output to new employment, only 12,000 new
jobs would become available annually in Southern Nigeria. If the
jobs made available through death, retirement, and disability are
added (at 3 per cent of the 1965 employment level), the figure rises
to 30,000.[15] On the same assumptions, one can estimate an annual
rise of 37,500 in total wage employment.

At this point the magnitude of Southern Nigeria's employment
problem should become obvious. Even if the new modern sector jobs
in 1965 had been reserved for 1965 school leavers alone, 150,000
young Southern Nigerians would have been competing in that year
for 30,000 jobs. In fact, school leavers from previous years were also
competing for these positions—to say nothing of a substantial portion of the 255,000 young people who entered the labor force in 1965
with one to five years of primary schooling to their credit. Clearly,
the demand of Southern Nigeria's economy for wage employees could
scarcely begin to match the supply of aspirants being turned out by its
schools.[16]

The situation is made more disturbing by the prospect that wage
employment, far from increasing rapidly in the post-Independence
period, may stagnate and even decline. A survey of employment in
eleven African countries notes that in almost all of them the proportion of the African labor force in wage-earning occupations declined
over the 1948–62 period, and in many countries employment actually
fell even when capital formation was high and output was rapidly
rising.[17] This happens for several reasons. One is an increased demand for imported consumer and capital goods, which generates employment in the exporting country, not the importing one. Another
is that foreign investment in developing countries tends to be
capital-intensive, with the result that large increases in output can be

registered while employment remains virtually unaffected.[18] The government of a developing country may concur with a capital-intensive policy for its own reasons: the desire, for example, to ensure quality control on products manufactured for export, or to establish modern automated plants for prestige purposes. Whatever the causes, although manufacturing output rose fivefold in Nigeria from 1950 to 1962, employment in this sector rose only marginally. And in the most spectacular growth industry of the 1960's—petroleum—direct employment effects have been minimal.[19] Unfortunately, the introduction of modern technology in the Nigerian setting may have the effect of shifting labor from its traditionally underemployed state to the unemployment of a modern automated economy, the work force never having experienced an intervening period of full employment.

But will not employment in the services—notably government and teaching—rise rapidly as the economy grows and as the government assumes greater responsibility for stimulating growth? In developing countries the public service sector is relatively large and tends to expand more rapidly than other sectors.[20] In Nigeria expansion has occurred within the regional and federal bureaucracies, but by the mid-1960's their growth rates were declining because of the financial difficulties experienced by these governments. Employment by Nigerian local authorities and by public corporations actually declined between 1957 and 1961.[21] The teaching profession's period of greatest expansion in Southern Nigeria was during the mid-1950's, as primary and then secondary modern schools were opened with unprecedented speed. A peak was reached in 1962, when almost 88,000 primary school teachers were employed in the Southern regions and Lagos. By 1965, however, the figure had declined to 72,000—well below the 1957 level—as the East reduced its course from eight to six years and as small schools were consolidated or phased out.[22] Teachers in secondary modern schools were even more drastically affected, for this kind of school was scheduled to be phased out by 1968. By 1965 teaching, which had been widely regarded by poor rural children as an important avenue of upward mobility and by others as a convenient "fall-back" occupation if other jobs were temporarily unavailable, was no longer providing new openings for primary and secondary modern school leavers.* On the contrary, the un-

---

* With the phasing out, beginning in 1964, of Grade Three teacher training colleges throughout Southern Nigeria, primary and secondary modern school leavers lost their "traditional" opportunity to enter teaching directly without attending grammar school. Entry to Grade Two colleges normally requires a West

trained teachers who had been hastily recruited to staff new schools under the universal primary education programs in the mid-1950's frequently found themselves jobless a decade later, competing for employment with their former pupils.

The educational requirements for many of the new jobs are so high that even grammar school leavers cannot realistically hope to qualify. Shortages of high-level manpower—persons with a Sixth Form or university education—still afflict Southern Nigeria, particularly in technical fields. A sample marketing survey in 1961 estimated there were at least 10,000 high-level vacancies in the public and private sectors.[23] In 1965 there were over 3,700 senior- and intermediate-level vacancies in the ministries of the federal and the Southern regional governments, and at least 750 expatriates working for these ministries who presumably could not yet be replaced by Nigerians.[24] Thus at the upper levels of the modern sector there is a dearth of qualified Nigerian manpower, which means that at the lower levels the excess is even greater than might be imagined. This situation stems in good part from the heavy emphasis on primary education during the 1950's. The publicity given to the shortage of highly trained persons doubtless spurs young people to remain in school, but most of them will only swell the already overcrowded ranks of those with at best a year or two of post-primary education.

UNEMPLOYMENT: A POLITICAL ISSUE?

To what extent has the unemployment problem assumed political dimensions? Before we turn to this question, it is useful to note a number of factors that make unemployment more tolerable in Nigeria than it might be elsewhere. First of all, large-scale unemployment is perhaps not so serious a threat to social peace in an underdeveloped area as in a highly developed one. Because Nigerian living standards are low, the income gap between the unemployed and the rest of the population is not likely to be substantial. An unemployed young man in a Nigerian city can live on as little as £2 a month,[25] and if he fails there he can always return home. From an economist's perspective, full employment can stimulate growth in a developed country by keeping the level of demand for goods and services high; in an underdeveloped country the lack of effective demand may not be the most serious impediment to growth, and the urban unemployed may

African School Certificate. Thus, quite apart from the rate of expansion of the teaching force, access to a teaching post has become almost impossible for children who do not enter grammar school.

in any event spend more than full-time farmers. Second, the African extended family lessens the effects of unemployment by diverting family income to the support of unemployed relatives while they look for jobs. The extended family is in effect a social security system; it reduces the pressures on the state to provide unemployment compensation or to sponsor other welfare measures that a more modern society, with its nuclear family pattern, considers indispensable.

Third, both traditional and modern Nigerian cities have ways of helping the unemployed. In cities with pre-colonial roots and strong links to the countryside, such as Ibadan, Ijebu-Ode, Abeokuta, and Ogbomosho, the absorption of newcomers is a pattern of long standing, and urban life is sufficiently traditional to limit the disruptive effect of immigration from the countryside.* In modern cities, such as Onitsha and Aba, whose principal function is commerce, school leavers and other young people quickly find ways to support themselves by hawking cigarettes, candy, newspapers, or other articles in the streets.† These cities also provide opportunities for self-improvement—for example, through libraries and typing schools. Hence young people can find many things to do in the city even though they may be jobless.

A fourth factor is the ability of school leavers, despite their high vocational aspirations, to adjust to the actual employment situation. Even before they left school, the pupils surveyed by the author distinguished clearly between their preferred and their expected jobs: at least 28 per cent of those in primary school, 43 per cent in secondary modern school, 38 per cent in grammar school, and 28 per cent at the Sixth Form level thought they would not actually obtain the jobs they wanted. The jobs pupils expect, however, are usually still within the modern sector; teaching and clerical work were most often

---

* See A. L. Mabogunje, *Yoruba Towns* (Ibadan, 1962). "The old Yoruba cities were heterogeneous in both the economic and the social spheres, containing specialists in various crafts and lineage groups of varying status in the community. This background has made the intrusion of European concepts of urbanization less unsettling, and the Yorubas have absorbed new forces (resulting in large part from western influence) without having been uprooted. Thus they have been able to continue traditional family locations and ties in a familiar community, with the advantages of security and stability accompanying the new ways developing in the old cities." Hugh H. Smythe and Mabel M. Smythe, *The New Nigerian Elite* (Stanford, Calif., 1960), pp. 56–57.

† Prior to the opening of the Niger bridge in 1965, the approach to the ferry at Onitsha was crowded with school leavers selling, among other things, the success-story pamphlets for which Onitsha is well known. One enterprising young man was even trying to sell copies of Paul Samuelson's *Economics: An Introductory Analysis* and Charles Kindleberger's *Economic Development!*

named as expected occupations by those who did not anticipate getting their preferred job. Significantly, those who showed a preference for middle-level and skilled technical work within the modern sector were more pessimistic than the average pupil about their chances.[26]

Once young people leave school they are likely to lower their sights still further. Faced with long-term unemployment as a realistic possibility, many who may previously have disdained the traditional apprenticeship system* come to regard apprenticeship to a master more favorably, if they can afford to pay the initial fees. The masters often prefer to take on school leavers, particularly in such fields as printing and sign-painting, where literacy is a valuable asset.[27] The employment potential of the apprenticeship system is probably quite high, since the system is geared to the needs of the people, is far more labor-intensive than modern industry, and is more closely tied to African than to European rates of remuneration. As job aspirations decline, more and more school leavers may be expected to turn to this sector for employment.

Fifth, unemployed school leavers may express their frustrations in nonpolitical ways. Some turn to delinquency. Social workers in several Southern Nigerian cities have expressed particular concern over the increase in juvenile prostitution, owing in large part to the inability of female school leavers to earn through other means the income they feel is due them. Petty thievery and the use of drugs are other social problems accentuated by the presence of many young people in the cities. Yet delinquency, by serving as a nonpolitical outlet for youthful frustration, helps keep unemployment from becoming a political issue.

Finally, there are certain factors that tend to inhibit unemployed school leavers from expressing themselves as a group. Most consider their plight a temporary one and regard other unemployed persons not as fellow sufferers but as competitors for scarce positions. Many spend all their energy staying alive; they have none left over for political protest. Others are rendered despondent or apathetic by their prolonged inability to find a job, and give up all hope of influencing public policy by their own actions.[28] Still others feel they are too young to have a voice in matters so momentous.

But if unemployment among school leavers is not so serious a

* Through this system, which includes about two million young Nigerians at any given time, in-service training is given in traditional crafts (weaving, dyeing, carpentry, iron-working, etc.) and in more modern occupations such as auto mechanics, photography, sewing, radio repair, and sign-painting.

political problem as its dimensions might imply, by the early 1960's considerable popular pressures were already being exerted on the government to provide jobs, and these pressures are bound to increase over time. For one thing, the school leaver is not the only one frustrated by his inability to find a job; his parents and other relatives, who have financed his education and expect some return on their investment, are also upset. Older relatives, particularly those living in rural areas, are not as aware as the school leaver himself of the rapidly changing composition of the labor force, and this lag in perceptions adds to the older generation's sense of frustration. Politicians with whom the author spoke in 1964 noted an increase in requests from parents for assistance in locating jobs for young people; the appeals of adults cannot be as easily dismissed as those of young people not yet able to vote.

Second, the sheer magnitude of unemployment may in time overburden the structures that currently absorb so many of the school leavers. The extended family cannot be expected to support a young applicant indefinitely, and there are limits to the number of persons a family can support at any one time. Likewise, the Nigerian city may have a limited capacity to accommodate the jobless. Urban unemployment is difficult to estimate, but as of 1963–64 it probably averaged 15 per cent of Southern Nigeria's urban labor force; school leavers with at least six years of education probably constituted over half the total.[29] If a city lacks traditional roots, like Port Harcourt and Sapele, or if it has only limited links with the countryside, like Lagos, the problem of assimilating unemployed newcomers may be especially acute. Unfortunately, efforts at urban development may simply accelerate rural immigration, further crowding the city with "strap hangers on the developing economy."[30] The possibility of political manipulation of the unemployed under these circumstances is obvious.

Third, as the educational level of the unemployed rises it is likely that they themselves will exert increasing pressure on the government to provide jobs. In the author's survey, students were asked what they considered Nigeria's greatest problem. Unemployment was named by 6.5 per cent of those in primary school, 13.2 per cent in secondary modern school, 43.1 per cent in grammar school, and 56.7 per cent in the Sixth Form. Awareness of the unemployment problem apparently increases greatly with education, even though students with more schooling presumably stand a better chance of find-

TABLE 9. Students' Explanations for Unemployment

Explanation	Primary	Secondary modern	Secondary grammar	Sixth Form
Increase in output of schools	8.1%	12.9%	14.0%	16.7%
Too few qualified people for available jobs	10.9	12.1	6.5	1.7
Insufficient industries, Farm Settlements, etc.	3.7	14.3	39.6	26.7
Government wastes money or otherwise blamed	1.1	9.6	8.1	16.7
Inefficiency, corruption, bribery	2.4	3.2	5.0	3.3
No money	13.9	5.7	2.9	0
Nigeria underdeveloped, uncivilized, etc.	.2	.4	2.9	6.7
Overpopulation	11.7	9.3	6.7	3.3
Other[a]	15.0	15.0	10.4	20.0
Don't know; no answer; unclear	32.9	17.5	4.0	5.0

SOURCE: Survey made by the author in 1964 of Southern Nigerian schoolchildren; see Appendix B. This table is based on responses to the question "Many people say that there are more people looking for jobs in Nigeria than there are vacancies. What is the reason for this?"

[a] Includes restatement of question, unwillingness of young Nigerians to work on farm.

ing jobs for themselves.[31] The responses to a question about the causes of unemployment are presented in Table 9. Positively correlated with a rise in educational level are explanations in terms of the increased output of schools, the absence of industries and Farm Settlements, the poor performance of government, and the generally underdeveloped condition of the country; negatively correlated are explanations stressing the insufficient number of people for available jobs, the absence of money in the country, and overpopulation. Significantly enough, the more educated young Nigerians show a greater tendency both to blame the government for unemployment and to expect the government to provide a solution. The widespread expectation is that regional and federal authorities should do this indirectly, by encouraging private domestic and foreign interests to establish new industries, and directly, by expanding the bureaucracy, setting up Farm Settlements, engaging in new public works projects, and the like. With increased unemployment among grammar school leavers, the pressures for such action should greatly increase.

By 1964 there were already signs of a changed atmosphere. So-called unions of the unemployed—a new interest group in Nigerian politics—had sprung up in Ibadan and Aba. In June 1964 a General Strike was called by the country's major unions to protest the refusal of the federal and regional governments to grant wage increases recommended by an official commission. Although workers were formally the only ones involved in the strike, in many cities the unemployed joined them in condemning the actions of the government instead of using the occasion to seek jobs with strikebound employers. Participation by the jobless in these protests doubtless contributed to the success of the two-week strike.[32] Ironically, the wage increases to which the government finally agreed further reduced the employment potential of the modern sector by raising the cost of labor relative to capital.

Thus popular demands that in the pre-Independence period were concentrated on the educational system had broadened by the mid-1960's to include the larger issue of economic development itself. The very success of the regional governments in responding to earlier, quite specific demands for new schools now confronted them with a far more complex and diffuse challenge, namely, how to stimulate rapid growth and how to give those who anticipated the benefits of modern life the opportunity to participate in a modernizing economy. Failure to meet this challenge would mean that hundreds of thousands of young people had been mobilized, at great public expense, to engage in little more than parasitic inactivity.

ELITE OBJECTIVES

How far have the objectives of key decision makers in politics and the civil service coincided with the demands of the populace? In analyzing elite goals during the 1960–65 period we cannot confine ourselves to regional policies, as was possible in discussing the universal primary education programs of the 1950's. After Independence the federal government, with its expanding financial resources, access to foreign aid, and constitutional responsibilities for higher education and economic development, came to exert great influence in its own right. The centralizing trend was perhaps best symbolized in the decision of both Azikiwe and Awolowo to leave their regional premierships in 1959 for key positions in Lagos. Subsequent events confirmed that the federal government could significantly affect the political process in the regions themselves.* We must therefore consider federal as well as regional government goals.

In the areas of post-primary education and employment creation, formal government commitments were generally similar to the demands of the populace. In part, this simply indicated elite sensitivity to constituent sentiment in a competitive party situation.[33] In part, too, it derived from the elite's vision of modernity, its conception of what the leaders of an independent country should be doing. The notion of planning, with its stress on shaping the future, setting quantifiable targets, rationally linking means to ends, and minimizing uncertainty, was central to the elite's view of modernity. In this respect an analysis of key government plans can help us understand elite thinking.

In the educational field, the most significant document of 1960–65 was the *Report of the Commission on Post-School Certificate and Higher Education in Nigeria*, widely known as the Ashby Report. The commission, which presented its findings in 1960, was composed of three members each from Nigeria, the United Kingdom, and the

---

* The major personnel and power shifts in the 1960–65 period may be briefly enumerated. Following the 1959 federal elections Azikiwe went to Lagos, eventually to become President of the Federal Republic of Nigeria, and Awolowo became Leader of the Opposition to a Northern People's Congress–NCNC coalition federal government. Michael Okpara succeeded Azikiwe as Eastern Premier and President of the NCNC; S. L. Akintola succeeded Awolowo as Western Premier, although Awolowo retained national leadership of the Action Group. This personnel change did not impair the stability of NCNC rule in the East, if only because Azikiwe's retirement from party politics left Okpara a relatively free hand, and because NCNC participation in the coalition government gave the Eastern Region ready access to power at the center. The effect of the change on the Western Region, however, was disastrous. Conflicts soon arose between Awolowo and Akintola over control of the regional party apparatus and over tactics for attaining power at the center, with Akintola adopting a more conciliatory approach toward the Lagos coalition. When factions led by the two men openly broke with each other in May 1962, the federal government intervened—first to administer the region directly and later to affirm Akintola as regional premier. Awolowo was eventually imprisoned on a charge of attempting to overthrow the federal government. The Lagos coalition also encouraged non-Yoruba elements in the Western Region to form the Mid-West Region in 1963, under NCNC leadership. By 1964 serious strains appeared in the coalition, and in the election at the end of the year the NCNC formed an alliance with its old rival, the Action Group, to fight an alliance between the Northern People's Congress and Akintola's followers in the West. The election reaffirmed the predominant role of the North in Nigerian politics, though it also seriously alienated NCNC–Action Group leaders from the system; they charged electoral irregularities in the North and West, and urged a boycott of the election. The dubious legitimacy of the new federal regime, coupled with a breakdown of civil order in the West as the unpopular Akintola sought to maintain himself by force and electoral fraud, helped create the conditions for the first military coup of January 1966.

United States.* The report was noteworthy for the boldness of its vision: it discussed in broad outlines Nigeria's educational needs over the 1960–80 period, and an influential chapter by Frederick Harbison of Princeton estimated in quite specific detail the country's high-level manpower and educational needs up to 1970. Harbison estimated that the number of persons with at least a Sixth Form education or the equivalent should rise from 30,000 in 1960 (of whom 20,000 were Nigerians) to 90,000 by 1970. Allowing for replacements, this meant that about 85,000 high-level personnel would have to be educated in ten years, which in turn would require a fourfold increase in secondary school enrollment over the 1960 figure and a fivefold increase at the university level.[34] Assuming that expenditure on post-primary education was a highly productive investment (hence the report's title, *Investment in Education*), the commission tended to discount the importance of financial constraints:

We believe it would be a grave disservice to Nigeria to make modest, cautious proposals, likely to fall within her budget, for such proposals would be totally inadequate to maintain even the present rate of economic growth in the country. Accordingly we reject this approach. Our recommendations are massive, unconventional, and expensive; they will be practicable only if Nigerian education seeks outside aid and if the Nigerian people themselves are prepared to accord education first priority and to make sacrifices for it.[35]

The federal and regional governments accepted the report's "massive, unconventional, and expensive" recommendations but felt that if anything they were too conservative. Thus secondary school intake for 1961–70 was to be 50 per cent higher than proposed, and the country was to have five rather than four universities.[36] Clearly, politicians and top administrators concurred with the general public in giving high priority to post-primary educational expansion.

Within this broad setting of agreement, however, there were certain differences between the goals of the populace and those of their political leaders. Popular demands in 1960 were concentrated on expansion at the immediate post-primary level (modern and grammar schools), whereas the Ashby Report called for the most rapid expansion at the Sixth Form level. Different types of reasoning were also at work. The people were responding to the effects of universal primary education on the job prospects of individual school leavers,

---

* That foreign experts helped draw up the plans discussed here does not detract from the value of the documents as evidence of Nigerian elite thinking, since Nigerian officials were responsible for initiating the planning process and approving or amending the documents in their final form.

while government officials based their conclusions on the estimated manpower needs of the economy as a whole. And whereas the people persisted in their "traditional" preference for literary academic education,* the government emphasized the necessity of more and better science courses. Harbison had noted that although Nigeria might soon have a surplus of persons seeking administrative posts in the civil service, scientists, engineers, technologists, and doctors were in extremely short supply and were desperately needed for development purposes.[37]

There is no document comparable to the Ashby Report that indicates elite attitudes toward unemployment. However, the National Development Plan, a composite of federal and regional plans for the 1962–68 period, shows a significant shift of official opinion. None of the plans prepared during the 1950's spoke of employment creation as an objective; large-scale unemployment was not yet a problem, and political leaders did not anticipate that it would be. By contrast, a discussion of the Eastern Region's goals for 1962–68 begins by estimating the output of school leavers over the plan period and then states: "The provision of expanded opportunities of paid employment must be one of the corner-stones of the new Development Programme."[38] The Western Region's plan notes: "The Education Programme of the Government has created its own problems. There is now in the Region a growing number of primary school leavers for whom employment has to be found. Both from the economic and social viewpoints, expansion of employment opportunities is an objective which claims high priority."[39] Western Region officials even included a special chapter on the employment potential of the development program, expressing the hope that 300,000 new jobs would open up in the private sector in addition to about 225,000 in agricultural schemes sponsored by the government.[40] In both regions it was stressed that the key to providing

---

* Instructive in this regard is the difficulty the Western Region's government faced in designing a secondary modern school curriculum that would include hygiene, domestic science, agriculture, carpentry, and the like. In theory the curriculum was to be eminently practical; in practice it turned out to be as theoretical as any other. Its shortcomings were due not simply to the shortage of qualified teachers for practical subjects, but also to popular insistence that the modern school serve as a low-grade copy of the grammar school. Instances of similar pressures on comparable institutions—the Ghanaian middle schools and the Ivory Coast's *cours complémentaires*—are given in Philip Foster, *Education and Social Change in Ghana* (London, 1965), pp. 199–201; and in Remi Clignet and Philip Foster, *The Fortunate Few: A Study of Secondary Schools and Students in the Ivory Coast* (Evanston, Ill., 1966), pp. 44–45.

employment was a rapid and diversified growth of the economy, and their programs called for a significant rise in the proportion of capital expenditure devoted to agriculture and industry. In this respect the regional governments, and the federal government as well, reflected a growing realization among African planners that without productive investment to stimulate growth few of their other objectives could be financed even in the short run.[41] The national plan also projected an increasing governmental responsibility for economic growth. Government recurrent expenditure on goods and services was 3.4 per cent of Gross Domestic Product in 1950 and 7.5 per cent in 1960; the plan estimated a further rise to 12.1 per cent by 1967–68.[42] The official policy has been to stimulate the private sector, but in the very act of encouraging private investment—particularly from abroad—officials were using the powers of government and could expect to assume some of the credit or blame for the actions of private entrepreneurs.

Generally speaking, then, the demands of the populace for education and employment have been paralleled by the stated objectives of the Southern Nigerian elites. More Nigerians at all levels wanted more things from the government, and wanted them provided more quickly than ever before—a trend due in large measure to the education explosion of the 1950's. Whether the federal, regional, and local governments possessed the resources to satisfy all these new demands is the question to which we now turn.

CHAPTER 9

Education and Political Capacity: Realizing Goals

How did educational expansion affect the capacity of Southern Nigeria's governments to carry out their plans? Capacity clearly depends on a government's resources. Three kinds of resources are particularly important: the level of popular support for persons in authority, the institutions and procedures of government, and the political community; the availability of funds and the freedom to allocate them according to the government's priorities; and the competence of a country's public institutions.[1] In this chapter we shall first examine the impact of educational expansion on Southern Nigeria's resources in these three areas in 1960–65, and then consider the appropriateness of federal, regional, and local government policies in the light of official commitments to foster development.

POPULAR SUPPORT

As we have seen, Southern Nigeria's political leaders sought during the 1950's to gain legitimacy chiefly by promising and then providing more of the good things of life for their constituents. One of these good things was universal primary education, and the program's initial effect, in spite of the controversies it generated, was probably to increase popular support for the regional governments. But this support was to be only transitory. By the early 1960's people were proving less willing to help finance ongoing educational programs, and students were showing signs of increased disaffection from the ruling authorities with each advance in educational level. The overall effect of rapid educational expansion may thus have been to lower support for regional and federal elites and to raise widespread doubts about the Nigerian political process itself—trends that make the first Nigerian coup d'etat of January 1966 more readily understandable.

Gratitude is a scarce commodity in politics everywhere, and a highly perishable one as well. In Southern Nigeria, where all sorts of amenities are in great demand, people readily take for granted the benefits already provided by the government, such as free education, and concentrate on other wants that are not yet satisfied. A related problem for a government that would establish legitimacy through performance is the public's tendency to associate a program with the leader who initiated it and not with his successors. This tendency can work two ways, and did so in Southern Nigeria. In the Eastern Region, religious controversy and the 1958 reintroduction of fees seriously diminished the support Azikiwe hoped to gain from universal primary education, but precisely because Azikiwe assumed much of the blame for unpopular decisions his successor as Premier, Okpara, could begin office with a relatively clean slate. In the Western Region, on the other hand, people associated the success of universal primary education with the Awolowo regime and tended to criticize Premier Akintola for not providing new amenities as liberally as his predecessor. That the region had been brought to the edge of bankruptcy by the end of Awolowo's premiership made him no less popular; that Akintola continued the earlier policy of free primary education made him no better liked. Ironically, the transfer of legitimacy from one leader to another was hindered by the very success of a scheme designed to enhance support for the regional elite as a whole.*

Nor could Southern Nigerian leaders depend on continued popular willingness to pay for government programs. To be sure, the enormous increase in the demand for secondary education during the 1960's was accompanied by the same spirit of self-help that had characterized the expansion of primary schooling in the 1930's and 1940's. The proceeds from communal palm harvests, special education levies, and the contributions of progress unions now went to the local grammar school building fund or to university scholarships. In this respect the effect of universal primary education in generating new demands was offset by the increased sums people were willing to pay to satisfy

* His inability to provide additional amenities on a large scale was not the only reason for Premier Akintola's unpopularity. He was also disliked for his efforts at alliance with the Northern People's Congress, his alleged betrayal of Awolowo, and his rough treatment of local elites loyal to Awolowo's wing of the Action Group.

them. But precisely because Southern Nigerians were willing to make great sacrifices for the sake of this new goal, they failed to maintain their support for existing educational programs. In both regions parents and local authorities were expected to contribute to the costs of running the primary schools; the introduction of universal primary education reduced expected contributions but did not eliminate them.* In practice, these contributions became extremely difficult to collect. For one thing, funds and enthusiasm had already begun to shift to secondary and higher education. For another, the politicians' claim that the government would henceforth provide free primary education was taken more literally by the populace than the politicians themselves might have wished. Why should people help themselves when the government promised to do the job for them?[2] Largely as a result of this attitude, parents and local authorities began to shirk even the responsibilities that had been specifically assigned to them. By 1964 many schools lacked such bare essentials as books, pencils, and paper; in many others children went without lunch, and school buildings deteriorated for lack of routine maintenance. In rural areas of the Eastern Region where the Assumed Local Contribution could not be raised, teachers often worked several months without pay, or the voluntary agencies went deeply into debt to reimburse them.

Unfortunately, this decline in local financial support occurred just as the regional governments began to search anxiously for ways to reduce expenditures for primary education, which amounted to some 25 per cent of their recurrent budgets. Clearly the only hope was to increase the share paid by local authorities and parents, but just as clearly any leader who proposed such a move was risking his political career.[3] Who, then, would pay for a service that all now took for granted and that, by itself, was insufficient to provide salaried employment? This became an extremely sensitive political question, and no politician was prepared to give it an unequivocal public answer.

Another source of support or nonsupport for the government was the young people themselves, the products of the new schooling. A

---

* In the Western Region parents were encouraged to finance school meals and keep school buildings and teachers' quarters in good repair. Local authorities were expected to provide their schools with an Other Expenses Grant to pay for blackboards, chalk, paper, benches, library books, and the like. In the East, of course, communities were responsible for raising the Assumed Local Contribution, which was reimposed in 1958. The Assumed Local Contribution varied over time, but as of 1964 it was about £8 per student for the top class and about £5 per student for the two preceding classes. No fees were charged for the first three classes.

major purpose of educational expansion, after all, was to train a new generation committed both to the emerging Nigerian political process and to the elite that had made expansion possible. Considered as a "political investment," did funds spent on education earn the intended rate of return in the production of loyal citizens? Any effort to answer this question must rely heavily on the attitudes of students at the secondary level, from whose ranks the political and administrative leaders of the future will presumably be drawn.*

Students surveyed by the author in 1964 evidenced a high level of political awareness, for example in identifying leading Nigerian politicians.[4] As it happened, the political environment in which these young people were growing up was a turbulent one. One grammar school student wrote, "Nigeria is a very large country which makes political struggle her business." The Action Group crisis, the imprisonment of Chief Awolowo, a heated controversy over the census, the General Strike of June 1964—these were some of the events that thrust themselves on the consciousness of the new generation. Even greater turbulence was soon to follow: the disputed federal election of December 1964, the dissolution of the civilian regime in early 1966, a second coup accompanied by the massacre of 30,000 Ibos in the Northern Region, and the civil war started in 1967 by the secession of the Eastern Region. So intense was the internal struggle to control Nigeria's destiny that the younger generation found small cause for gratification in the mere fact of independence. If anything, they felt the sense of disillusionment that almost inevitably follows the attainment of independence, when the shouting dies down and people turn to the prosaic task of making freedom work. In such troubled and rapidly changing circumstances, one must be cautious about drawing conclusions from any study of political orientations. Still, it is worth noting that the author's survey, conducted before the first Nigerian Republic had begun visibly to collapse, revealed signs of a quite mixed attitude toward the country's political life.

Table 10 shows students' attitudes toward politicians as revealed in their answers to the question "What do politicians do?" Of the

* The effects of education on political awareness would best be determined by comparing children who had attended school with those who had not, as well as by studying changes in student attitudes over time. In the absence of such data we shall rely on the author's 1964 questionnaire, paying particular attention to changes occurring as children advanced from primary through secondary school. Because the sources of the students' information about politics were so closely connected to the education process (as shown in Table 6), we shall assume that differences between various educational levels are not simply a function of age but reflect the impact of schooling as well.

TABLE 10. Students' Attitudes Toward Politicians

Attitude	Primary	Secondary modern	Secondary grammar	Sixth Form
Positive	14.8%	12.9%	14.4%	16.7%
Neutral	26.3	46.1	50.6	46.7
Negative	5.4	8.6	25.2	35.0
Other or unclear	7.8	3.2	.8	0
Don't know	10.4	2.5	1.7	1.7
No answer	35.4	26.8	7.1	0

SOURCE: Survey made by the author in 1964 of Southern Nigerian schoolchildren; see Appendix B.

primary sample, over half did not answer in a way that could be coded as positive, neutral, or negative, and the positive responses outnumbered the negative by almost three to one. Among Sixth Form students the politician's image was more distinct. The percentage with positive views was virtually the same, but the percentage with neutral views had nearly doubled and the percentage with negative views was nearly seven times larger. More than twice as many Sixth Form students held negative views as held positive views. To be sure, negative orientations did not predominate even at the Sixth Form level, but at all levels they were more prominent than among American schoolchildren who have been asked comparable questions.[5] Several of the Nigerian students' unfavorable remarks about politicians deserve quotation: "They promise heaven upon earth but after elections they make earth worse than hell." "First they yearn for money for themselves, secondly they are tribalistic, thirdly they are the greatest liars during the Election Campaigns." "They plan a welter of intrigue against one another, behave like weathercocks." "Shout much and do nothing." "The pillars of our country are turning to be caterpillars of it." Greater education seems also to breed an unwillingness on the part of Nigerian students to enter politics themselves. Some 45 per cent of the primary sample hoped to become politicians one day, whereas 40 per cent did not; at the grammar school and Sixth Form levels negative answers outnumbered positive by more than two to one.

Thus support for political authorities apparently decreased with educational level. In certain other respects, however, the survey data bear out the expectations of those who initiated the educational schemes of the 1950's. As of 1964 the students accepted Nigeria as a single political community; in essays on what the country would be like in ten years' time, only 4 per cent of the post-primary sample envisaged a breakup of the federation or a civil war, and only 5 per cent spoke of a possible revolution or coup d'etat. In general, their prognosis for Nigeria was favorable; of 755 essays that could be coded on an optimism-pessimism scale, 49 per cent were optimistic, 15 per cent were hopeful provided certain changes occurred, and only 11 per cent were pessimistic. The students' disaffection with their political leaders had evidently not affected their loyalty to the political community itself, though by 1967 doubts about the viability of Nigeria must have grown to enormous proportions among Southern Nigerians, particularly in the East.

Nor would it be fair to say that increased education brought greater unwillingness to tackle Nigeria's problems. Although the proportion of students considering a career in politics declined with education, the proportion willing to enter politics for idealistic reasons increased from 5 per cent for the primary sample to 30 per cent for the Sixth Form.* Finally, education correlated positively with a belief that the individual could help solve Nigeria's problems. Table 11 confirms hypotheses about political competence that have been proposed elsewhere.[6] Its findings only superficially conflict with those on political aspirations; obviously some secondary school students felt that politics would not be the only useful career.

The students' disaffection with political leaders seemed linked to a rather positive sentiment about Nigeria through a belief that members of their own generation would provide more talented and more dedicated national leadership than their predecessors. One-third of the 285 post-primary students who discussed future leadership in their essays mentioned the shift of power to a younger generation. One student optimistically wrote: "I think in ten years to come when some of our youths will join the politics there will be a great change and we will love ourselves whichever tribe we are. Morning shows the day." Such sentiments among Nigerian students probably reflected a faith in the beneficial effects of their own formal training.

In terms of our discussion of support, the students' reaction against the older generation's leadership may have mixed consequences. It indicates a high commitment to political institutions and to the political community, but at the same time a low level of support for the

---

* It is possible, of course, that as children became better educated and more sophisticated, they perceived idealistic motivations as more acceptable, whether to society or to an interviewer; and one can readily imagine other possible influences of the same sort on the answers to questions about personal motivation. These percentages must accordingly be approached with caution.

TABLE 11. Students' Beliefs about Their Ability to Help
Solve Nigeria's Problems

Belief	Secondary modern	Secondary grammar	Sixth Form
Can help	28.6%	61.5%	61.7%
Cannot help now, but can help later	5.0	5.0	13.3
Cannot help	39.7	25.2	20.0
Don't know; no answer	28.6	8.3	5.0

SOURCE: Survey made by the author in 1964 of Southern Nigerian schoolchildren; see Appendix B. This table is based on responses to the question "Is there anything you can do about Nigeria's greatest problem?"

existing authorities. To the extent that Nigeria's authorities were in fact misusing their power, disaffection with them was a healthy sign in the long run. But student responses were also based on the expectation that the new generation would be uncorrupted by power—an expectation that is seldom ever borne out in practice. One suspects that many a young Nigerian was frustrated in 1964 not so much because his elders misused power as because they possessed it, and that in realizing his own ambitions he would use the same tactics he claimed to despise in others.* In such a case a society continues to be politically unstable, for leaders are replaced over time but the style of leadership that alienates the young remains much the same.

It is also of interest to examine the distribution of student support among the local, regional, and federal governments. The author's post-primary sample was asked to chose which government did the most good, and which the least, for the common people of Nigeria. Responses varied considerably between the Western and Eastern Regions,† but overall the regional government was regarded most favorably. Positive descriptions of the regional governments increased markedly, moreover, with education.[7] This suggests that the grievances of the more educated students were directed primarily against

---

* Of the forty students who named bribery and corruption as Nigeria's greatest problem, twenty wrote that their most serious difficulty in finding a job was the lack of money or influential friends. These students seemed likely to engage in the same practices to obtain a job that they had deplored in their countrymen.

† Most Westerners ranked the federal government highest and local government lowest; most Easterners ranked regional government highest and the federal government lowest. These differences clearly reflect the political situation of the time: the West's regional and local governments were in turmoil, and Easterners increasingly resented the federal goverment, which was controlled by Northerners.

local and federal structures. That the regional governments were directly responsible for educational programs may help explain their relative popularity. In this respect the return on their educational investments was probably considerable.

In general, however, it would seem that education had a mixed effect on young Nigerians' support for political authorities, government institutions, and the Nigerian community. It would be going too far to speak of our post-primary sample as politically alienated, but it is clear that in some ways their support declined with education. A high level of political awareness in a situation of great turmoil can lead to frustration and disillusionment that cause further turmoil; in this sense the socialization process promotes instability in Nigeria. Certainly the beneficiaries of an educational program do not automatically become supporters of the regime responsible for instituting it. The consequences of education are too complex, and the political life of a country too important an independent socializing agent, to make such a result at all likely, however greatly it may have been desired by the men who launched the educational programs of the 1950's.

FINANCIAL RESOURCES

A government's financial resources depend in part on the condition of the economy; in part on the government's ability to obtain funds for its own use, both domestically and in the form of foreign aid; and in part on its freedom to allocate funds in accordance with its own changing priorities. Following a brief discussion of trends in Nigeria's regional and federal budgets, we shall examine the effects of heavy educational expenditure on the ability of the regional and federal governments to meet their objectives in the 1960's.

Current government revenue at the federal and regional levels combined rose approximately 10 per cent a year from 1955–56 to 1966–67. This increase was made possible by a relatively rapid growth rate of over 4 per cent for the economy as a whole, and particularly by a remarkable rise in the production and export of petroleum, which by the mid-1960's enabled the Eastern Region to reverse its former economic inferiority to the West. However, during the same period recurrent expenditure slightly exceeded revenue. This meant that instead of providing extra capital as had been hoped, current revenue was insufficient to meet regular government expenses. The inability of Nigeria's governments to marshal domestic savings for development was all the more serious in light of the disappointing inflow of foreign loans and grants, which financed only 12 per cent of public capital expenditure during 1962–64 instead of an anticipated 50 per cent. The scarcity of funds for productive investment was an important reason for the failure of the Six-Year Plan, at its halfway point in 1965, to meet many of its output targets.[8]

It cannot be doubted that educational expenditure was an important cause of the 1955–65 deficit. During this period outlays for education rose over 15 per cent annually—considerably faster than overall expenditure for the federal and regional governments combined.[9] Taking private as well as public contributions into account, education absorbed 1.6 per cent of the Gross Domestic Product in 1952, 3.5 per cent in 1962, and close to 4 per cent by 1967.[10] Education was the major charge on the regional government budgets, averaging just over 40 per cent of recurrent expenditure in the Southern regions for the post-1955 decade.[11]

Three factors account for the rapid rise in Nigeria's educational expenditure. First of all, enrollments rapidly expanded at all levels. Second, the regional governments were committed to financing a larger portion of school costs than in the past by bringing almost all primary schools into the grant-in-aid system, increasing the size of the grants as fees were eliminated or reduced, and bearing a high proportion of costs in the primary sector, which was the most expensive. At the same time the federal government assumed the major responsibility for higher education. The regional and federal governments contributed an estimated 64 per cent of Nigeria's total education expenditure in 1952, and 75 per cent ten years later.[12] Third, unit costs rose at all levels, principally because teaching qualifications were upgraded after 1960 and because all teachers' salaries were increased substantially in 1955–57, 1959–60, and 1964.[13] At the post-primary level the introduction of new science courses requiring special imported laboratory equipment further raised unit costs.

The prospect that the rising cost of education would continue to push overall expenditure higher than revenues confronted Southern Nigerian leaders with an allocation crisis of the first order. Was 40 per cent of a region's budget too much to spend for education in view of the region's overall economic commitments? The anwser to this question ultimately depends on the role of education in fostering economic development. There is wide agreement that under certain conditions education ought to be considered productive investment rather than consumption. But this argument is most convincing when applied to already developed countries, which require an extensive research and development apparatus to sustain economic growth. It is less convincing in underdeveloped countries, where the effect of education may be to increase consumption at the expense of capital investment, and where expenditure on education may seriously drain the supply of funds for areas such as agriculture, industry, and transportation that are just as critical as education in laying the foundations for sustained growth. As the formal title of the Ashby Report indicates, an explicit effort has been made in Nigeria to give education top priority by labeling it an investment,[14] yet the history of Southern Nigeria suggests that if anything it was economic growth that made educational expansion possible, not the reverse. Economic growth occurred when largely illiterate peasants expanded their cocoa, palm oil, and rubber holdings in response to favorable prices. Many of these peasants then proved willing to finance the education of their own children, and eventually they were able to finance, via the marketing boards, the education of an entire region's young people. Whether the educational explosion will in turn stimulate the economy is quite another question. The more a region spends on education, the less will be available for agriculture, industry and commerce, and community development. And the more educated people the schools turn out, the more productive jobs the economy must generate if educational expenditure is not to be wasted. In 1966 the chief architect of the Nigerian Six-Year Plan, Wolfgang Stolper, expressed the fear that too much was being spent on education and too little on the directly productive sectors of the economy.[15]

But even if high expenditures on education could be justified, there remains a serious question of the allocation of funds within the educational system itself. In 1955–65 the Western and Eastern regions spent more than 60 per cent of their education budgets on primary schools. From an economic standpoint, however, the most important function of primary education is to give a child a "personal infrastructure" of literacy and numerical skills that may then be utilized in further specialized training;[16] if the child does not continue in school, his first few years have in this sense been wasted. Moreover, to the extent that heavy expenditure at the primary level reduces the funds available for higher levels, the imbalance between primary school output and post-primary intake capacity is maintained and even increased. High primary costs also limit the resources available for adult education, which offers a more immediate and perhaps greater economic return than primary education.*

Theoretically, education is both an economic investment and a

---

* Adult education has received little attention in Southern Nigeria, since school has been considered strictly for children. The mid-1960's, when disillusionment

consumption item, but in practice the kind of education provided in Southern Nigeria encourages demands for consumption without concurrently providing the skills necessary for production. Even if universal primary education were ultimately to have a positive effect on output and productivity, this effect would not be immediately felt, for it normally takes many years before a primary school pupil becomes a useful member of the labor force. Southern Nigeria opted, in effect, for one aspect of a welfare state at a time when it was unable to finance a welfare state. A conference of "leading personalities" of the Eastern Region in 1962 concluded: "It is not prudent to continue to provide social services and amenities at the expense of directly productive activities. Such a policy would destroy the foundations of orderly economic growth."[17]

The diagnosis, however, was easier than the cure. It proved very difficult to shift funds from education to other sectors, and from primary to secondary education. The public had come to expect certain services from the government, and interests had inevitably arisen within the ministries of education and the voluntary agencies that favored maintenance of the status quo. Cost-cutting measures, particularly at the primary level, proved politically unpopular: efforts made in the East in 1962 and 1963 to stabilize recurrent regional expenditure on primary education by raising the Assumed Local Contribution created a great furor, particularly in the backward rural areas, and in 1964 the scheme had to be abandoned.[18] The regional governments were more successful in reducing the size of the teaching force and in closing down or merging marginal schools. Even these gains, however, were offset economically by a substantial rise in teachers' salaries and politically by the disaffection of the thousands of dismissed teachers and their dependents.

Given the commitments of the 1950's, the popular expectation that these commitments would henceforth be honored, and the limited resources available to the regional governments, there was little opportunity in the early 1960's to reallocate resources in line with changing needs. In this respect Southern Nigeria followed the trend of West Africa as a whole, where expenditure for the social and administra-

---

with primary education was setting in, might have been a good time to increase literacy classes and other extension work among adults. But the funds available for such work were pitifully small, and the prior commitment to primary and secondary formal education seemed to preclude rapid expansion in a less formal educational field. P. G. H. Hopkins persuasively argues the virtues of adult education in "The Role of Adult Education in Economic Development," in E. F. Jackson, ed., *Economic Development in Africa* (Oxford, 1965), pp. 51–70.

tive sectors has generally exceeded planned targets while expenditure for the directly productive sectors has lagged.[19] Government plans, in short, have adapted to new challenges, but the political and administrative apparatus charged with implementing the plans has not.*

INSTITUTIONAL CAPACITY

In addition to popular support and financial resources, political leaders need institutions to carry out their policies and to keep them in touch with the populace. Institutions vary greatly in their capacity to perform these tasks; among other things their performance depends on the qualifications of their personnel and the manner in which tasks are assigned and coordinated. Here we shall discuss the impact of rapid educational expansion on these aspects of institutional capacity, giving special attention to the administrative structures of the regional governments.

To what extent did the educational expansion of the 1950's improve the qualifications of the regional civil service? As we have already noted, universal primary education can be regarded as a formative learning experience for the Nigerians who carried out the scheme. These officials gained valuable administrative experience prior to national independence, an advantage that was not shared in many parts of Africa where qualified indigenous civil servants were simply not available in the 1950's and where the major decisions were made by Europeans up to, and frequently after, the moment of independence.[20] By its very nature, universal primary education required the coordination of efforts between several ministries, between governmental and private bodies, and between regional and local authorities. Its success, moreover, hinged on the ability of civil servants to use new methods—working with people in the bush rather than merely passing out directives, and pressing for rapid changes in the environment rather than merely maintaining law and order. Nigerians involved with the program were made keenly aware of the developmental approach required of bureaucrats in an independent country, and of their potential to accomplish tasks that had previously been considered too difficult. At the same time they gained a sense of the limitations imposed on them by deadlines, by influences from their environment, and by the strains of working under continual pressure. It is hardly surprising that many Nigerians who were

* In a sense Southern Nigeria was less flexible in allocating its resources than Northern Nigeria, which in the absence of a universal primary education drive in the 1950's had a more balanced allocation pattern between education and other sectors and within the educational system itself.

local education officers in the mid-1950's had moved a decade later to key positions not only in the ministries of education but in other ministries as well. Just as the teaching profession served as a recruiting ground for Southern Nigeria's politicians, so did the regional ministries of education serve as a supplier of skilled administrators to the rest of the civil service.

It is too early, of course, to tell whether universal primary education was able to produce a class of well-qualified civil servants, for the first primary school leavers under the program have only recently entered the labor force or are still in secondary school. The signs were not encouraging, however. Almost inevitably the rapid expansion of the educational system in the 1950's precluded simultaneous reform of the system; administrative energies were spent duplicating existing buildings and materials rather than encouraging innovation, and thousands of untrained teachers could hardly be expected to handle an ambitious new curriculum, even had one been devised. Thus the scheme offered children the same kind of education that Nigeria's political and educational leaders had decried as alien and impractical. Not until the first universal primary education class had completed primary school did curricular reform begin to make even a slight impact on the school system.[21] Primary and secondary modern schools might be expected, at the very least, to produce competent clerks. Yet in 1960 only eleven out of 220 secondary modern students were able to pass a civil service examination for such minor positions as Clerical Assistant and Field Overseer.[22] Elementary science, an obviously useful subject in training a technically oriented civil service, was ignored in many primary schools for want of properly trained teachers.

Even if it employs highly qualified people, an institution cannot be effective unless their work is properly assigned and coordinated. Bureaucracies in Southern Nigeria, as elsewhere in the developing world, are characterized by a very uneven division of labor: a few top officials are overburdened with responsibility for making minor as well as major decisions, while at the bottom of the hierarchy is a large number of poorly trained clerks whose productivity is low if not, at times, negative. In particularly short supply is the competent middle-level official, with at least a secondary education, who can screen demands coming from below, make minor decisions himself, and see to the execution of policy. In the wake of secondary school expansion the number of qualified middle-level administrators rapidly increased. In 1966, moreover, some 4,500 Nigerians graduated from Nigerian or foreign universities,[23] and a substantial number of them applied for intermediate positions in the civil service. In theory, the influx of these young people should have led to a more rational allocation of tasks and greater efficiency at all levels of the bureaucracy. But in practice it produced internal tensions that frequently lowered the bureaucracy's overall performance. To understand why, we should examine recent recruitment patterns into the civil service.

The years of most rapid upward mobility were those just prior to and after Independence, when British officials left in large numbers and new positions were created in line with the government's expanding responsibilities. The men who filled these positions were mostly young and could therefore expect to hold them for years to come. The university graduate of the mid-1960's, whose ambitions were whetted by the success of Nigerians not much older than he, now found his own advancement blocked by these very Nigerians. As a result of increasing educational opportunity, moreover, the graduate was usually better educated than his superiors and felt that he was more qualified than they for high-level posts. To compound his frustration, the salary scales inherited from the colonial era were disproportionately high at the top levels of the hierarchy. The result was intense generational conflict.* The young graduate, preoccupied with the politics of personal advancement, often did his best to make his superiors look incompetent; the latter responded by giving him few chances to demonstrate his ability.[24] The graduate also resisted assignment outside the capital city, where decisions regarding his promotion were made. This resistance to transfer helped perpetuate the excessive centralization of the bureaucracy.[25] So much time and energy were consumed by generational conflict that officials at all levels failed to perform as effectively as their academic qualifications would have led one to expect.

FEDERAL GOVERNMENT PERFORMANCE

Having considered the impact of educational expansion on government resources, we turn to the actual performance of federal, regional, and local authorities. How effectively did policy makers

* The term "generational" may not seem appropriate, but in societies that are changing rapidly conflicts may occur between age groups separated by only a few years. David Apter has noted of Ghana: "It must be remembered that a political generation . . . is very short. One finds new cadres appear in roughly five-year intervals." *Ghana in Transition* (New York, 1963), p. 363. Clearly, more research is needed on the conflicts between age groups at all stages of the development process—a phenomenon that may be fully as important as the far more familiar cleavages along ethnic, racial, religious, sex, and class lines.

act to meet the education, employment, and general development goals outlined in their plans and policy statements? In evaluating performance we must remember that maintaining and consolidating power was in itself a full-time occupation for Nigeria's beleaguered politicians and that they did not spend more than a fraction of their time dealing with the policy issues discussed here. This helps explain certain decisions that were made, though it does not necessarily justify them.

The federal government proved unable to meet many of its formal commitments. It did take the initiative in educational and economic planning, as the Ashby Report and the Six-Year Plan attest, but no effort was made to integrate the two documents into a single strategy for growth. The plan, for example, did not share the Ashby Report's optimism about investment in education, and its project proposals were not closely linked to the report's estimate of available manpower. Moreover, federal officials seemed generally indifferent to the problems of the populace and excessively concerned with their own well-being. Popular resentment reached a peak in the General Strike of 1964, called when the government, invoking the need for austerity, refused to grant the full salary increases proposed by an official commission while at the same time making no serious move to reduce the salaries and perquisites of top government officials. Elite insensitivity was perhaps best illustrated when the Minister of Labour appeared at a negotiating session with strike leaders in a gold brocaded robe. Such incidents may help to account for the relief with which many Southern Nigerians greeted the overthrow of the federal government in January 1966.

REGIONAL GOVERNMENT PERFORMANCE

At the regional level, where demands generated by educational expansion were concentrated, one tactic employed by officials was to meet goals by deflecting demands elsewhere—upward to the federal government and downward to the local authorities and the populace. But scant relief was forthcoming from the federal government because it was dominated by Northerners anxious not to increase the enormous educational imbalance already obtaining between the North and the South. Local authorities proved incapable of handling many of the responsibilities assigned them by the regions, and the people of the East and the Mid-West strongly resisted the prospect of an increase in the Assumed Local Contribution. Efforts to deflect demands were therefore generally unsuccessful.[26]

The capacity of the regional governments to make use of the

voluntary agencies for official purposes is of interest in this connection. As shown in Part II, leaders in both regions saw in universal primary education an opportunity to assume greater control over an educational system that was predominantly in private—and foreign—hands. In the West the distribution of grants-in-aid was assigned to local education authorities, and in the East limits were set on the expansion of voluntary agencies at the primary level. Yet the voluntary agencies remained essential to the program's success, for it was impossible to expand the educational system rapidly without help from those who knew the system best and actually made it operate. Universal primary education in effect legitimized the position of the voluntary agencies as no previous policy had done. By 1965 local authorities still controlled only one-fourth of Southern Nigeria's primary schools, enrolling one-fifth of its primary school students; in the vital area of secondary grammar education the voluntary agencies slightly increased their share of the schools after Independence. Education ministries in both regions attempted during the early 1960's to control voluntary agency schools more closely, but the idea of directly taking them over was never seriously considered.

To be sure, conflicts arose between the government and the voluntary agencies. Agency administrators in both regions complained that policy decisions were made hastily and without consultation outside government circles.[27] In the East the Catholic hierarchy remained opposed to any limits on new Catholic schools; several hundred Catholic women of Port Harcourt marched on the Provincial Commissioner's office in 1964 in an unsuccessful attempt to open more Catholic primary schools for their rapidly growing city.[28] Many Catholics were suspicious of the top officials in the Ministry of Education, who were almost all Protestant. Yet these tensions, far from causing a breakdown in communications or in effective administration, were kept under control by conciliatory moves on both sides. The government appointed a Catholic to be Minister of Education from November 1957 to the end of 1962; the Catholics for their part, in response to the charge that they represented a white foreign interest, Africanized many top posts in the religious hierarchy. Indeed, as all voluntary agencies Africanized they increasingly came to be regarded as indigenous rather than foreign interest groups, and the political problem diminished accordingly.

On balance, the ability of the regional governments to meet the goals of the 1960's was probably increased, rather than reduced, by their indirect control of primary and secondary education. Voluntary agencies operated their own "parallel taxation system," raising funds through church fairs, bazaars, and Annual Mission Contributions. These extra funds enabled the agencies to provide better education than grants-in-aid alone could ensure and kept government tax rates from becoming unacceptably high. One expert on Nigerian education has estimated that if the voluntary agency schools were taken over by regional or local authorities, recurrent costs to the government might rise by one-third.[29] The voluntary agencies also supplied the school system with skilled and experienced administrators. In both the financial and administrative spheres, then, the capacity of private bodies to perform public functions has enabled public funds and personnel to be used for other tasks; in this respect the devolution of authority has increased rather than decreased the power of regional officials. In fact, many voluntary agencies have come to feel exploited by the government. The Anglican Bishop of Ibadan, Rev. Simeon Odutola, complained in 1964: "When it is becoming clearer that education must primarily be the duty of the State it seems that the State is trying, at least in Western Nigeria, to ask the Church to bear the costs to an extent which its revenue and the nature of its administration as a charitable and voluntary organization cannot afford."[30]

Finally, the voluntary agencies served to deflect some popular demands and grievances from the regional governments. When a mission teacher lost his job, he looked to the mission for a new one as well as to the government. When Assumed Local Contributions in the East or Other Expenses Grants in the West were not paid by a community or local authority, voluntary agencies frequently went into debt to pay their teachers and buy essential school supplies. Since efforts to pay off such debts pitted the agencies against the populace, regional officials were spared the thankless task of collecting money for services already rendered. In these and other ways, private interests helped relieve the public sector of the burdens imposed on the nation by its educational policy.*

In their development plans the Eastern and Western regions gave

---

* If a government is to take the credit for successful development, it should be prepared to take the blame for failure to develop—or at least for the difficulties encountered in initiating sustained growth. This is a point not often appreciated by advocates of socialism for newly developed countries. One reason for involving the private sector in the development process might be to protect the government from popular wrath should this effort go astray, thereby strengthening the long-run capabilities of the public sector.

top priority to agriculture, industry, and technical education —
choices that seemed appropriate for increasing income and employment.[31] A serious effort was made to shift resources into agriculture,
and several directly productive enterprises were begun. In general,
however, regional leaders favored grandiose projects that symbolized
modernity rather than simpler, capital-saving projects that might
have more effectively modernized the economy. The Western government, for example, launched in 1959 an ambitious Farm Settlement scheme designed to attract school leavers into modern farming. But costs per settler were so high that at best only a few thousand
families could be accommodated, and the planners had the same
misplaced faith in heavily mechanized farming that has caused innumerable African settlement schemes to fail.[32] Industries established in Nigeria generally used the latest capital equipment and
hence had minimal effects on employment. The £12 million Port
Harcourt oil refinery provided less than 400 jobs, a £4 million cement
factory only 300, and government-sponsored ceramics, textile, beer,
and cigarette factories had very high capital-labor ratios. Although
creating new jobs was an explicit goal of the plan, "Nigerian industry, faced with the familiar conflict between employment and output
objectives, to date has opted clearly for the latter, leaving employment to be taken up, if at all, in small industry and the services."[33]
In technical education, expensive equipment was imported to train
individuals who were unlikely to use it once they had left school. In
each of these fields, the emphasis was on projects that absorbed a few
people into the modern sector rather than on those with "backward
linkages" to the traditional and transitional sectors. Largely ignored
were efforts to upgrade the typical peasant farm, small indigenous
business, and the apprenticeship system through various kinds of extension services. Unfortunately, the Nigerian elite's preference for
highly visible symbols of modernity was reinforced by foreign governments and private investors from abroad, whose interests lay in
exporting the most up-to-date products and techniques whether or
not these were relevant at Nigeria's stage of development.*

* It could be argued, in fact, that countries rich enough to offer foreign aid
have reached a stage of development at which the aid is likely to be extravagant
and irrelevant for the recipient, whereas the countries that have undertaken the
most interesting recent experiments in modernization—like India, China, Mexico,
Cuba, Chile, Yugoslavia, Tunisia, and Tanzania—are too poor to share their
experiences widely with others. Israel is often cited as a particularly relevant
example for Afro-Asian countries; the Western Region's Farm Settlements were
actually patterned after the *moshavim*. But the success of communal agriculture

LOCAL GOVERNMENT PERFORMANCE

If the federal government exhibited an insufficient response to the challenges of the 1960's and the regional governments a vigorous but often inappropriate response, the performance of local authorities in Southern Nigeria clearly illustrates the "overload" problems that arise when a public institution is asked to do far more than can reasonably be expected of it. The high expectations in this case did not come from the populace, but from the regional governments, which hoped to expand local authority functions as a means of limiting the influence of voluntary agencies and of decentralizing the financial and administrative responsibilities imposed by universal primary education. In the mid-1950's, as a result of policy decisions made in Ibadan, district and divisional councils in the Western Region were designated "local education authorities." These authorities were made responsible for paying 15 per cent of teachers' salaries, providing Other Expenses Grants for all primary schools within their territory, disbursing grants-in-aid to all such schools, and managing such local authority schools as were set up. In the East voluntary agency pressures prevented the actual formation of local education authorities, but local councils were charged with the monumental task of staffing and managing the new schools, and later (after 1958) of collecting the Assumed Local Contribution.

As it happened, the resources available to the local authorities were insufficient for them to perform these tasks properly. In the first place, their popular support was limited. The democratization of local councils had not been a response to mass pressure for local self-government but a reform imposed from above. The councils lacked the legitimacy and the tradition of community service that characterized many of their counterparts in the Northern Region, and elected local officials frequently misused their position. Over time the quality

---

in Israel is surely due in part to the belief that Israel is quite literally a holy land, and to the attraction of farming for Jewish immigrants previously confined to the urban ghettos of Europe. In a country like Nigeria it is the desire to escape from the land, not to it, that is overwhelming. Then, too, land settlement has a militarily strategic significance in Israel that is lacking in Nigeria. Insofar as special motivational factors explain the Israeli growth rate, the export of Israeli institutions to underdeveloped countries will not necessarily prove equally successful. More generally, as Cyril Black has warned, "The influence of foreign models is likely to divert [the leaders of new societies] from empirical experimentation and to interfere with a more discriminating consideration of the adaptability to modern functions of native traditional heritage and institutions." *The Dynamics of Modernization* (New York, 1966), p. 98.

of local authority schools greatly improved, but the belief that they were inferior to voluntary agency schools remained widespread.

In the second place, the tax base of most councils was limited by the poverty of the people, and the actual collection of taxes came increasingly under the control of regional authorities, who did not sufficiently compensate the councils for revenue previously collected locally. Chief Akintola, in a bid for popularity prior to the 1960 regional election, abolished local general and education rates and empowered local councils to collect the regional income tax for their area instead; since the new arrangement would bring in about £1 million less than the old, he promised a tax equalization subsidy to make up the difference. However, the promise was not kept, and the councils never recovered the million pounds. The financial crisis was less acute in the East, but there, too, the local authorities became increasingly dependent on grants-in-aid from the regional government. In both regions the problem was compounded by parochial conflicts, which frequently caused the fragmentation of existing local government units. By the early 1960's most local councils, whatever their political standing with their constituents, were too limited in size to be economically viable.[34] In the West their 15 per cent contribution toward teachers' salaries was reduced to 13 per cent in 1957 and then abolished altogether in 1959. In 1962 local authorities paid only 12.1 per cent of the recurrent costs of primary schooling in the East, and only 5.4 per cent in the West;[35] even so, education absorbed about one-third of all expenditures by local authorities in Southern Nigeria —by far the largest single item in their budgets. By 1964 arrears on Other Expenses Grants in the West, and on Assumed Local Contributions in the East, had reached alarming proportions.

Finally, local authorities had little to work with in the way of institutional resources. Local councillors themselves were rarely competent and frequently untrustworthy; for obvious reasons able administrators preferred to work for the regional governments. In the East the hope that county council proprietorship of schools would eliminate religious controversy proved premature, for the councils themselves became new arenas for perpetuating old conflicts. Protestant and Catholic councillors divided sharply over the choice of a headmaster or a religious syllabus, and majorities of one faith felt free to ignore the claims of minorities of the other. The resulting tension and bad feeling further reduced the capacity of many local governments to meet their educational responsibilities.

To sum up, local government in Southern Nigeria tended to be unpopular, inadequately financed, and strife-ridden. Given this state of affairs, we can understand the Western Region's 1959 decision to bypass the local councils and transfer grants-in-aid for voluntary agencies directly to these bodies, and the Dike Report's recommendation that many educational tasks performed by the local councils be assumed by new education committees at the provincial level. Eventually local authorities will have to assume much of the burden of financing and administering the primary school system in order to free the higher levels of government for more complex operations. But as of 1965 there were no signs of a trend in this direction.

POPULAR EDUCATION AND POLITICAL CAPACITY

We are now in a position to assess the effect of educational expansion on political capacity in Southern Nigeria. As we argued in the previous chapter, universal primary education and related programs at the secondary level increased the scope, volume, intensity, and explicitly political content of popular and elite demands. The same programs also in some respects increased the resources available for meeting these demands: for example, the populace proved eager to pay for post-primary education, students (as of 1964) considered themselves members of a national political community, the financial and administrative resources of voluntary agencies were used to good effect, Nigerian officials gained valuable administrative experience, and the basis was laid for a suitably educated labor force.

But the effect of educational expansion in limiting and even reducing available resources was probably even more pronounced. Government initiatives undermined the spirit of local self-help in primary education that had been so noticeable prior to the 1950's. Popular education did not produce a generation loyal to regional elites; in fact, the more students learned in school, the more disenchanted they became with politicians. The high and steadily rising cost of education, moreover, deprived the regions of resources to meet the employment and development crises of the 1960's. An examination of the performance of federal, regional, and local authorities from 1960 to 1965 suggests that many government goals were ignored, could not be met, or were met in inappropriate ways. The prime reason for this was the unprecedented opportunity for power and wealth available to politicians and bureaucrats, combined with a pervasive sense of insecurity about their continued hold on power. But this insecurity was only heightened by the knowledge that an entire younger generation, armed with the skills and ambitions of literates, would soon be contending with its elders for power.[36]

If we define political capacity in terms of the relationship of goals to resources, then it may be argued that universal primary education and related programs, by raising goals and in certain respects lowering resource levels, in fact contributed to a decline in Southern Nigeria's political capacity in the 1960–65 period. This conclusion appears to be supported by Nigeria's subsequent history of military coups and civil war. One must be cautious about linking universal primary education directly to these events, if only because many other important factors were operative in the "political decay" of the country. However, one must be even more cautious about crediting educational expansion with achieving a net gain in political capacity in a country where the spread of schooling was accompanied by the decline, in many respects, of effective government. The fact is that one can infer very little about the political culture or structure of a country from a reading of its educational statistics. The point is made in general terms by Eisenstadt:

In many cases . . . a negative correlation has developed at certain levels between a high degree of development of various socio-demographic indices, such as the degree of literacy and the spread of mass media, of formal education, or of urbanization, and the institutional ability to sustain growth. . . . [These indices] do not in themselves indicate the extent to which a new, viable, modern society capable of such continuous growth may develop, or exactly what kind of society will develop, what its exact institutional contours will be.[37]

The Southern Nigerian experience should help us to understand why this unexciting, inconclusive, and somewhat depressing observation comes closer to the truth than the optimistic pronouncements of educational missionaries.

CHAPTER 10

Education and Equality

Equality is a norm that pervades modern political life, however limited and imperfect the efforts of men to attain it in any particular society. Clearly, a major theme in the history of many Western and non-Western countries during the past century has been the struggle for equality of participation in the political realm. The issues have included the right to join organizations representing one's interests, the right to vote, and the right to be governed by laws applying with the same force to all citizens. With the growth of governmental power, individual citizens have become equal in the sense that they all deal directly with the same central bureaucracy. Moreover, strong political pressures have been exerted by both rulers and ruled to realize that "equality of conditions" of which Tocqueville wrote so percipiently. Most governments attempt by progressive taxation to reduce the income gap between rich and poor, and by other measures to provide a minimal level of welfare for all citizens. Indeed, the very concept of citizenship has broadened over time to include socioeconomic as well as political rights.[1] Equality is not easily established in modern societies, because of the high degree of stratification that inevitably develops in complex, dynamic institutions. In accepting stratification as necessary and desirable, however, a modern government normally tries to ensure its citizens equal opportunity for upward mobility—an equal chance, in short, to become unequal.

A country's educational system is linked to the drive for equality in several ways. Education may be considered an egalitarian end in itself: that is, a certain amount of schooling may be regarded as the right of each citizen and part of the minimal package of welfare services a government ought to provide. Since primary education can be dispensed so widely and easily, it has not surprisingly become "the most universally approximated implementation of national citizenship."[2] And schooling at any level provides a set of experiences which students of widely different backgrounds hold in common.

Education may also be considered a means to the realization of equality. Widespread schooling qualifies large numbers of people for participation in politics and enables the authorities to instill an egalitarian ethic in the younger generation through civics courses and other means. Since a school system is one of the chief agents of stratification in any society, the amount of schooling available to the average citizen and the degree to which recruitment to specialized roles is based on academic achievement will determine in large measure the extent to which equality of opportunity is actually realized in that society. This last point is particularly important (1) in an ex-colonial country whose official language is different from its indigenous languages and hence can best be taught in school; (2) in a country with a powerful and prestigious bureaucracy, whose members are recruited on the basis of their performance in examinations; (3) in a country that starts to modernize relatively late, and thus needs technical and scientific skills that can best be acquired through formal or informal training programs. Nigeria, it need hardly be added, meets all three of these conditions.

To assess education's role in bringing about equality we will use rather different criteria for the primary and post-primary levels. For primary education the central question is whether it is made available to an entire age-group, regardless of parents' capacity to pay and regardless of a child's sex, religion, or even academic ability. The availability of primary schooling is determined by the total number of school places, the distribution of enrollment with respect to population, and the cost to parents. Thus the more school places there are, the more equitably different categories of the population are represented in the classroom, and the lower the school fees are, the more egalitarian the primary school system is. At the post-primary level it is unrealistic, at least in poor countries, to enroll an entire age-group, and in any event the training at this level becomes more germane to the stratifying than to the leveling function of education. Here the central question, apart from the number of available school places, is whether students are selected according to their academic achievement and intellectual potential. If all students have an equal opportunity to advance to secondary school or beyond on the basis of merit, we may speak of equality in post-primary education. Since the criteria differ for the two levels, developments in primary and post-primary education will be discussed separately.

EQUALITY IN PRIMARY EDUCATION

If universal primary education was anything, it was an effort to attain equality by making primary education available to all. Schools were opened in areas that did not have them so that no child who desired an education would be turned away for lack of school space, supplies, or teachers. Fees were eliminated in the West, and none were imposed for the initial classes in the East even after that region's financial crisis of 1957–58, so that as far as possible no child would be denied an education because his parents were too poor to afford it. The best way to see whether these egalitarian aims were in fact realized is to examine the record of five often overlapping groups of young people who did not have an equal chance to attend school prior to universal primary education: poor children, girls, Muslims, children in educationally backward areas, and members of minority groups.

We may indirectly estimate the effect of school fees on primary enrollments by comparing dropout rates for classes that completed a six-year course in 1965. In the West and Mid-West, where no fees were charged, 55 per cent and 58 per cent, respectively, of those initially enrolled did not enter the sixth year; in the East, where fees were charged, the figure was 74 per cent. That the £5 enrollment fee for the East's Primary Four class deterred a significant number of pupils is indicated by the dropout figures from Primary Three to Four in the different regions: 33 per cent in the East as against 8 per cent in the West and Mid-West.[3] The point here is not that the children of poor parents were penalized in the East relative to those in the old Western Region; rather, the effort in both regions to reduce the cost of primary education for all parents undoubtedly benefited the poorer ones in particular. Had fees of £2 or £3 been set for Primary One classes, overall dropout rates throughout the South would have been much lower, since impoverished farmers would not have sent their children to school at all. Thanks to universal primary education these children experienced at least a year of schooling, and perhaps more.

Universal primary education also gave a fillip to the education of young girls, who have traditionally been regarded by Nigerian parents as less suited for academic pursuits than boys. In the West, female enrollment in Primary One rose by 374 per cent from 1954 to 1955 as compared with a 184 per cent rise among the males; for the primary course as a whole girls accounted for 25 per cent of total enrollment in 1954 and 34 per cent the following year. That proportion rose steadily, if less spectacularly, after the introduction of universal primary education, reaching 41 per cent by 1965. The proportion in the East rose from 34 per cent in 1956 to 39 per cent in 1965.[4] That an educated girl could command a higher bride-price than an illiterate one probably influenced the decision of many parents to let their daughters attend school. Whether the trend toward sexual equality in education would continue in view of massive unemployment among school leavers, however, remained an open question.

The Muslim population of the Western Region constituted another disadvantaged group prior to universal primary education, largely because of the dominant position held by Christian missions in the school system. Accommodating Muslim children thus entailed not simply expanding the number of school places in Muslim areas but altering the pattern of school proprietorship in favor of local authorities and, to a lesser extent, Muslim voluntary agencies. There is indirect evidence that Muslims took particular advantage of the new facilities offered by universal primary education. Whereas the overall increase in primary enrollment from 1954 to 1955 was 78 per cent, the figure rose by over 110 per cent in Abeokuta, Ibadan, and Oyo, the three divisions with the highest proportion of Muslims.[5] The steeper rise in female enrollments in the West as compared to the East suggests a significant shift in the attitude of Muslim parents toward sending their daughters to school. In the author's questionnaire survey, 32.3 per cent of the primary sample west of the Niger River were children of Muslim parents; this figure corresponds almost exactly with the proportion of Muslims in the old West. The survey also suggests that the policy of expanding local authority and Muslim schools had an important impact on Muslim enrollments. Of the 84 Muslim children in the primary school sample, 43 per cent were attending Muslim and 24 per cent local authority schools as against 17 per cent in Church Missionary Society schools and 8 per cent in all other denominational schools combined. (The remaining 8 per cent were attending private schools.) By reducing Muslims' fears that education would result in the conversion of their children to Christianity, universal primary education made a valuable contribution toward equality of opportunity among the various religious groups in the Western Region.*

The consequences of the program were more mixed with regard to parts of Southern Nigeria that were educationally backward prior to the 1950's. The favorable response of Muslim areas in the West has just been noted; enrollment in the non-Yoruba Benin and Delta provinces, which had been somewhat neglected by the missionaries, rose from 29 per cent of the total in 1954 to 32 per cent the following year, which corresponded well with their proportion of the total population.[6] In the East, on the other hand, there was a tendency for the areas that had the highest enrollment rates prior to 1957 to expand more rapidly as a result of universal primary education than the areas that were already far behind. Thus the program did not have an automatic leveling effect; indeed, where the motivation of backward areas to catch up was low, the provision of schooling on a mass basis may have simply accentuated existing enrollment differences between various areas. On the whole, however, universal primary education served as an equalizer by bringing education—and with it jobs for teachers and contractors—to the less progressive rural areas. As one Eastern legislator said in 1958: "U.P.E. is a necessity. It is the only social service which meets the needs of every community in the Eastern Region. Take all social services one by one and you would find that many of them do not go to rural areas. Big roads do not pass through all villages but every village has a school."[7] Since the rural areas in effect subsidized the development programs of the regions through the marketing board system, they would seem amply entitled to their own primary schools.

Minority groups in each region tended to benefit more than Yorubas and Ibos from the free education schemes. The non-Yoruba groups of the Western Region increased their proportion of the total enrollment; charges of educational discrimination did figure in the drive for a Mid-West Region, but they focused on the allocation of grammar schools and scholarships to non-Yorubas rather than on primary education. In the East, Calabar Province minorities increased their enrollment 66 per cent over the 1956–61 period. The record for non-Ibos in Ogoja and Rivers provinces was quite uneven,

* Ten primary school children with Muslim parents claimed to be Christian themselves; of these, seven were attending Christian schools. Although the sample is small, the figures indicate that Muslim fears about conversion were fairly well justified.

but in at least a few divisions, like Brass and Ogoni, expansion was well above the regional average.

Thus the statistics indicate that a pronounced leveling-*up* process was set in motion by universal primary education. Previously disadvantaged groups benefited disproportionately from the scheme; in this sense educational expansion at the primary level has had a significant egalitarian effect.

EQUALITY IN SECONDARY EDUCATION

Equality of opportunity at the post-primary level depends partly on the number of places available to students, but even more on the criterion of selection to what is inevitably an elite-producing brand of education. If selection is based on merit, determined by native ability and academic performance, and if other factors such as ability to pay do not seriously affect the selection process, we may say that an educational system maintains equality of opportunity no matter how small the number of students. Equality is increased if the caliber of primary education is the same for all students, if entrance examinations provide a proper index of merit, and if the cost to an individual student of post-primary education is kept to a minimum. As shown in Chapter 8, one consequence of universal primary education was a remarkable expansion of enrollment in secondary modern and grammar schools; because of this the chances that a Primary Six pupil would continue his education have risen over time. There is also evidence that the modern school experiment increased the mobility of able Westerners who happened to be otherwise disadvantaged.[8] We shall concentrate here, however, on selection criteria, paying particular attention to the level of secondary school fees—a matter of obvious importance in any poor country. These fees were already high by 1960 and have risen rapidly since, directly raising the possibility that secondary, not to mention university, education would be available only to the children of the rich.

School fees are affected by several factors. One is the colonial legacy. The British believed that fees were not only a useful device for financing secondary education but also a good way of building character: one appreciates what one receives if one has to pay for it. Thanks to the British practice of collecting fees from the public, there were more secondary school places in Nigeria than in any of the neighboring French territories, but the principle of selection was not egalitarian because it depended on a student's financial resources. The French, by contrast, operated a secondary system that was small in size but egalitarian in selection procedures; the able student, from whatever background, had the cost of his education underwritten by the state. As a former British colony, Nigeria accepted more or less by default the notion that fees should cover a substantial portion of educational expenses.[9]

A second factor affecting school fees is the high recurrent cost of secondary education. Boarding facilities, the salaries of graduate and expatriate teachers, imported laboratory equipment, the heavy administrative burden borne by small schools—these help to account for 1965 per capita costs of about £100 in grammar school and £200 in the Sixth Form.[10] As the quality of secondary education improved and the general cost of living rose sharply, school proprietors turned both to the government and to the public for funds to defray their rapidly rising expenses. But government grants per student were increasing very slowly, and contributions from voluntary agencies, progress unions, and local authorities were irregular and uncertain. School fees, on the other hand, could be easily raised in view of the demand for secondary education, and until quite recently the government did not set upper limits on what might be charged. Consequently, the increased cost of secondary education was financed principally by charging higher fees.[11]

A third factor affecting fees is that in an underdeveloped country owning and managing a school is one of the few ways enterprising persons or groups have of making money. Government regulations prohibited the operation of schools for profit, and most proprietors operated well within the official limits. It was only natural, however, that persons who in more advanced economies would have become prosperous business magnates were strongly tempted to become educators in Nigeria.[12] The demand for secondary education was high, alternative means of profit-making were limited, especially in the rural areas, and Ministry of Education officials were too busy with other administrative tasks to keep a close check on the finances of each school. The way was therefore open for "educational entrepreneurs" to charge what the traffic would bear. In addition to the usual tuition and boarding fees, many proprietors levied additional charges for laundry, games, library services, uniforms, medical care, and the like. In some cases principals or proprietors used school funds to supplement their regular salary and received generous compensation on resigning from the Board of Managers.[13]

The confluence of these three factors—the colonial legacy, rising costs of education, and the profit motive—made for high and rapidly increasing fees. The amount varied greatly from one grammar school to the next, but tuition and boarding fees probably averaged £40 throughout the South in 1957; by 1962 the Western average was about £50, and by 1964 the Eastern average was just under £60. In addition, up to £20 might be charged for real or imagined services. If we assume that the actual annual cost of educating a grammar school student was £100, then the average Southern Nigerian student had to defray only about two-thirds of this expense. At the same time, if we assume that per capita income in the South was £35, then fees for each grammar school place were equivalent to the total annual income of two Southern Nigerians. Such a burden was of course intolerable for the average Nigerian parent.

How could equality of opportunity be attained under these circumstances? Lest one conclude too hastily that it quite obviously could not, certain qualifying remarks are in order. It must not be forgotten that the social structures and values of most traditional African societies tend to be highly egalitarian. The extended family is an important mechanism for distributing resources evenly among its many members, and to a lesser extent the lineage and clan serve the same redistributive function. School fees for a promising student were therefore likely to be shared among many persons. When asked who was paying for their education, 60 per cent of the author's grammar school sample named parents, 14 per cent brothers and sisters, 5 per cent uncles and aunts, 1.5 per cent other relatives, and 7.5 per cent a combination of parents and one of the above sets of relatives.[14] Most wealthy Southern Nigerians contributed as a matter of course to the education of several relatives, near and distant, whose parents' means were limited.[15] Local progress unions relied heavily on their wealthy members to provide scholarships for the most capable "sons of the soil." These mechanisms for equalizing resources were reinforced by the conviction among Nigerians that a good education should be available to anyone who can qualify academically, regardless of socioeconomic background.[16] This conviction, which reflects the lack of class distinctions in traditional African society, is more modern than the attitudes still prevailing in the more class-conscious countries of Europe.

THE EMERGENCE OF A SOUTHERN NIGERIAN ELITE

But if the egalitarian spirit of traditional African society was reflected by Southern Nigerians in modern times, it is also true that the far-reaching economic and political changes introduced by colonial-

ism created powerful forces leading away from egalitarianism. For a
variety of reasons outlined earlier, certain persons took greater advantage than others of the opportunities for mobility offered by British rule and Western education, and as the economy developed, the
social structure of Southern Nigeria became more highly stratified.
Stratification along income, educational, and status lines appears to
be an inevitable part of early modernization in any society, but the
gap between haves and have-nots tends to be especially pronounced
in a country with a recent colonial legacy, where a few people enjoy
living standards similar to those of former colonial rulers while the
mass of the population remains at subsistence or near-subsistence
levels. Since the salaries and perquisites of the colonial rulers were
set high to attract Europeans to serve in the colonies, and since the
emerging elite in Southern Nigeria, as elsewhere, was able for the
most part to retain these salary scales for itself on acceding to power,
the new elite possessed enormous financial resources relative to other
members of the society. In 1964 the average farmer earned under
£35 a year; a young civil servant fresh from the university started at
£750, often lived in heavily subsidized government housing, and
could obtain a low-interest loan on a new car. A permanent secretary
in a ministry or a university professor earned about £3,000 and enjoyed even more substantial perquisites.[17] Taxes on income above
£500 were more regressive in Southern Nigeria than in England,[18] it
was relatively easy to avoid paying taxes on nonsalaried income (of
women traders, for example), and of course persons in positions of
power had greater opportunities than others to make extra money by
dishonest means. Thus the Biblical saying "Unto him that hath it
shall be given" came close to fulfillment for those who benefited most
from the transition to independence.

What exactly are the defining features of the new elite, and is it a
class in the conventional sense of the word? To avoid a prolonged
discussion, we shall accept Peter Lloyd's view that a Western education—normally at the secondary or post-secondary level—and an annual income of at least £250 are the signs of elite status in Africa.[19]
Lloyd further argues that it may be premature to term the new elite
a class, since it lacks direct control of the means of production, distribution, and exchange, is often internally fragmented along ethnic
lines, is linked through traditional social structures to poorer members of the society, and is not intensely aware of its common economic
interests.[20] In what follows we shall regard the new elite as an incipient class, in the sense that its members might be expected to recog-

nize their common interests as the economy developed and eventually, barring outside interference, to control the economic levers of society. At the same time we recognize that the elite is not a class in the conventional Western sense of the word, for its position in Nigerian society is in some respects the opposite of the position of the elites that arose in the West after the Industrial Revolution. If one accepts the Marxist analysis, the bourgeoisie in Europe gained wealth and influence from its control of the private sector of the economy and then employed the state as an instrument to protect its privileges. In Africa the elite gained its initial influence from its control of the political or administrative apparatus of the state and then employed its public power to entrench itself more firmly in the private sector. It therefore makes sense to speak of a "political class" or of "an administrative bourgeoisie," as some scholars have done in recent years.[21] This class might be defined as the group that *controls the means of controlling the means* of production, distribution and exchange.

If in the early 1960's Southern Nigeria was witnessing the emergence of a ruling class, and if access to secondary education was the key to elite status for the younger generation, then the crucial question becomes whether the children of this new class monopolized the available grammar school places. One would on *a priori* grounds expect them to do so. Since the elite was by definition enormously wealthy in relation to the average Southern Nigerian, elite parents could afford more easily than anyone else to send their children to grammar school. And since the elite was by definition well-educated, its members were particularly aware of the role of a good education in improving their children's economic and social position. Finally, since elite members exercised political power and administrative influence, they were able to bring considerable pressure to bear on secondary school principals to admit certain favored children. Many principals staunchly resisted this pressure, but principals who were themselves politicians found it extremely difficult to deny their colleagues' requests. Under the circumstances admission to secondary school often became a form of political patronage, a favor conferred on a current or potential political ally in the expectation of an equivalent favor later on.

According to the author's 1964 questionnaire data, the children of the new elite did in fact occupy a disproportionate number of grammar school places, though they were far from monopolizing enrollment at this level. Of the grammar school sample of 480, 14 per cent

TABLE 12. Occupational Distribution among the Fathers of Grammar
School Students and among Southern Nigerian Men

Occupation	Fathers of sample	Southern Nigerian men over 15	Selectivity index
Farmer, fisherman	35.8%	70.0%	.51
Craftsman (skilled or unskilled)	8.5	6.7	1.27
Trader, clerk	25.7	9.6	2.68
Administrative, professional or technical	19.2	3.5	5.49
Other	10.9	10.2	1.07

SOURCES: Nigeria, Department of Statistics, *Population Census of Lagos, 1950* (Kaduna, 1951), pp. 73–74; Western Region, *Population Census of the Western Region of Nigeria, 1952* (Lagos, 1953), pp. 2, 8; Eastern Region, *Population Census of the Eastern Region of Nigeria, 1953* (Enugu, 1954), pp. 2, 6.

listed their father's annual income as under £50 and 26 per cent as over £200. Since almost a third of the sample did not, for various reasons, answer this question, we may assume that the percentages at both ends of the scale are in fact higher. Probably a third of the sample came from elite homes, using the income criterion. As for education, 32 per cent said that their fathers had had no education, 18 per cent that their fathers had had at least some secondary education. Allowing once more for those who did not answer, we may estimate on the basis of the education criterion that 20 per cent of the sample came from elite homes. Another criterion of elite status is occupation. As Table 12 shows, 36 per cent of the grammar school sample's fathers were farmers or fishermen, as against about 70 per cent of Southern Nigerian men. At the other end of the scale, 19 per cent of the sample's fathers were in administrative, professional, and technical work, as against 3 to 4 per cent of Southern Nigerian men.[22] Clearly, the children of wealthy, educated, and high-status parents constituted a significant proportion of those students who would in turn become the future elite—though the data also suggest a good deal of upward mobility from within the more disadvantaged sectors of the population. The results of this survey correspond very closely with Foster's findings in Ghanaian grammar schools in 1961.[23]

The data do not indicate, however, what the trend in secondary school recruitment has been over time, and this is an important question in assessing the impact of educational expansion on equality of opportunity in Southern Nigeria. If it is true that universal primary education benefited various disadvantaged groups, does it not follow that it increased the opportunity of these groups to enter secondary school relative to groups that had already taken advantage of education prior to the abolition of primary school fees? There are grounds for a negative answer to this question, apart from the obvious fact that disadvantaged families lacked the funds to pay for a grammar school education and the power to influence admissions.

The populace had the impression that since the start of universal primary education the quality of primary education had seriously declined. This view was correct in the limited sense that standards probably fell for the first five or six years, as the ratio of trained to untrained teachers fell below previous levels and as school inspectors proved unable to maintain close contact with a vastly inflated teaching force. But the belief that standards continued to decline persisted into the mid-1960's, when trained primary teachers outnumbered the untrained for the first time, and when the percentage of those who passed the First School-Leaving Certificate Examination was not significantly lower than it was in the late 1950's. Popular sentiment on this score may have reflected the initial hope that universal primary education would both expand the school system and reform the curriculum; when reform proved impossible owing to the government's commitment to expansion, disillusionment may have set in. Another factor was doubtless the decline in the employment value of a primary education; people blamed the school system for producing unemployable young people when in fact the trouble came from the very success of the school system in bringing about a sharp rise in the supply of literate labor. However irrational it may have been, the belief that educational standards were declining was widespread; certainly it was a favorite theme of correspondents to Southern Nigerian newspapers.[24]

This belief, together with the increased ability of elite families (relative to average-income families) to pay for secondary education, led members of the elite to establish and subsidize a totally private school system offering high-quality primary and even pre-primary education to their children with a view to giving them an advantage over others in the competition for admission to secondary grammar school. After 1960 several nursery schools were opened in the major cities; some even offered boarding facilities and charged up to £50 a year. These schools concentrated on improving the English-language competence of young children, which was already relatively high since the mother in an elite family was likely to be literate and to speak English in the home.[25] Expensive primary schools were established that engaged expatriates as teachers and frequently enrolled the children of English and American businessmen, government officials, and academics; in these multiracial schools the elite Nigerian child was in an excellent position to improve his English and learn the niceties of "civilized" Western behavior. Increasingly, too, wealthy parents sent their children to "cram schools" for the last year or two of the primary cycle; here English, arithmetic, and fragments of arcane knowledge were endlessly drilled into the heads of youngsters desperately anxious to pass the grammar school entrance examination.[26] One such school, located in Ibadan, was illegally offering cram courses to 340 children when it was closed down by the Ministry of Education. Thus the very egalitarian tendencies encouraged by universal primary education, and the lowering of standards for which it was blamed, prompted the emergence of a separate elite system of primary education based on ability to pay. Obviously, the products of this parallel system tended to perform better on grammar school entrance examinations than others, because such tests reflect prior training more surely than they do the innate ability of candidates. The elite child therefore enjoyed an unequal opportunity to attend secondary school in terms not only of finance but also of academic performance.

At the secondary level itself certain schools catered to the new elite, whether by setting fees very high or by biased admissions policies. A school that charged between £18 and £24 for such items as "golden corsair" shirts, white piqué dresses, woolen cardigans, blazers with the college badge, and preshrunk gabardine raincoats[27] was making the elite pay for the trappings of social status and indirectly advertising that its services were unavailable to the children of the poor. By far the most expensive secondary school in Nigeria was the International Secondary School of the University of Ibadan. Opened in 1963 as a "demonstration school" for teachers at the Institute of Education and as a high-quality institution for the growing number of expatriate children residing in Nigeria, the International School charged it its inception about £200 for day students and £450 for boarders. Three-quarters of the sixty Nigerians attending the school in its first year were receiving scholarship aid, but at most this aid reduced fees for some day students to £50. As might be expected, the children of some of the country's most prominent men were enrolled.[28] Another option available to elite families was to send their children to English schools. Considerable publicity attended the news in 1964 that

Chief Akintola's son had become the first African admitted to that preserve of the English aristocracy, Eton.

ELITE FORMATION AND EDUCATIONAL POLICY: THE POPULAR RESPONSE

As we have seen, the emerging Southern Nigerian elite established a separate fee-charging primary school system as a means of ensuring that elite children entered good secondary schools. In addition, the high and rising cost of secondary education—which is not a function of educational expansion as such but is related to the drive for curriculum improvement—inevitably discriminated against the children of the poor. Insofar as grants-in-aid subsidized grammar school students by limiting school fees to 50–70 per cent of the actual cost of this kind of education, the regional governments were in effect subsidizing the rich.[29] And insofar as scholarships were based on academic performance—leaving aside for argument's sake the possibility of a corrupt awarding system—children who had attended elite schools were likely to win a disproportionate share of these funds. Thus the egalitarian impact of universal primary education at the primary level was countered by an increasing inequality of opportunity at the secondary level.

Prior to the 1950's the grammar school was a mechanism for selecting able young Nigerians, most of whom had illiterate parents, and giving them the opportunity for rapid upward mobility based on their own achievements. These persons used their education to gain power at the regional and later the national level, and then used their power and the wealth that accompanied it to obtain the best secondary and university education for their own children. At first a secondary school diploma was a good index of personal achievement; after Independence it was more likely to be considered a sign of ascriptive status, an indication of the wealth and influence of one's parents. The sharp increase in post-primary enrollment after about 1960 changed the situation only marginally; the issue was not the number of places available, but the criteria for selection to those places.

In a society that regards inequality as a fact of life and post-primary education as a preserve of the elite, the trends outlined above might have little political effect. But in a traditionally egalitarian society like Southern Nigeria, the shift from achievement to ascription in the educational system—reversing, in short, the Parsonian order of things—could well prove politically disruptive. The Ajayi Commission, which was appointed by the Western Region government to examine secondary school fees, made the point concisely:

The standard of living of Nigerians is becoming increasingly differentiated. But the average Nigerian at the moment apparently does not worry too much about this because with good secondary education his child could rise to the top and he will at once become associated with the higher standards. If increasingly the average person begins to find this passport beyond his means, the class structure will fossilise and discontent will grow.[30]

And discontent based on the *manner* in which upward mobility is restricted is likely to be linked to discontent based on the slow *pace* of upward mobility at all levels following Independence. In the first case it is the poor who complain, in the second the young—and many Nigerians are both poor and young.

There were signs by the mid-1960's that literate Southern Nigerians were becoming aware of the process of class formation in their midst and of the role education played in that process. Journalists frequently wrote about the topic; Tai Solarin, an indefatigable foe of privilege in all its forms, made it perhaps the major theme of his widely read weekly column in the *Daily Times*.[31] Politicians excluded from power and seeking support among the young, like Chike Obi of the Dynamic Party and Tunji Otegbeye of the Socialist Workers and Farmers Party, charged that the educational policy of the regions was simply perpetuating the power of those currently in office. Letters published in various newspapers often echoed this charge; an Easterner wrote in 1960, "One cannot help getting the impression that the policy in awarding scholarships is to make the rich even richer and poor people even poorer, thus enabling the former to continue to lord it over the latter."[32] Newspaper reaction to young Akintola's admission to Eton was ambivalent; pride that an African could prove his intellectual ability when matched against privileged Englishmen was mingled with apprehension that a dynasty of privileged Akintolas might be in the making. And of course the General Strike of 1964 reflected widespread dissatisfaction over the unequal distribution of economic benefits since Independence.

Ironically enough, the public's increased awareness that the educational system was contributing to class formation was itself a byproduct of rapid educational expansion. An entire generation of Southern Nigerians who benefited from the egalitarian thrust of universal primary education were at the same time made sensitive to the trends within the educational system and outside it that were moving Southern Nigerian society toward greater inequality.

ELITE FORMATION AND EDUCATIONAL POLICY:
THE GOVERNMENT RESPONSE

How did government officials respond to these trends? The officials, it seems fair to say, were quite ambivalent on the relationship between equality and educational policy. On the one hand, the regional and federal governments were committed to equal opportunity and to greater equality in standards of living. The Six-Year Plan explicitly aimed "to develop as rapidly as possible opportunities in education, health, and employment, and to improve access for all citizens to these opportunities"; it also envisaged "a more equitable distribution of income both among people and among regions."[33] As popular sentiment against the privileged elite became more intense, many leaders felt the need to reaffirm these egalitarian goals publicly. On the other hand, Nigeria's political and administrative leaders tended privately to regard the emergence of an affluent elite as an inevitable part of modernization, believing that the concentration of wealth in a few hands was a useful means of accumulating and investing capital—scarcely a surprising view, since they constituted the incipient ruling class. The government had committed itself to bring about greater equality, yet it was the government officials themselves who were far above the masses in education, income, social status, and political power; hence the officials would be the first to suffer losses from any leveling reforms they might institute. This conflict of interest proved difficult, if not impossible, to resolve.

In several ways the regional and federal governments might have done more to promote greater equality. To begin with, the salaries of civil servants and politicians might have been reduced to bring remuneration in a large part of the modern sector more in line with the income of the peasant farmer, and the substantial salary gap between top government officials and low-level workers in the public and private sectors might have been closed somewhat. In October 1963, in response to pressure from an increasingly restive trade union movement, the federal government appointed a commission headed by Justice Adeyinka Morgan to examine the need for a national minimum wage and for an upward revision of the wages and salaries of junior employees in the public and private sectors. The Morgan Commission, whose report was made public in May 1964, proposed a considerable increase in minimum wage scales, salary increases of over 10 per cent for junior employees earning up to £318 a year, much smaller increases for those earning between £318 and £588, and no increase for employees earning more than £588. In minority reports, some members of the commission went further and proposed drastic cuts in the perquisites granted to top civil servants and politicians—the automobile allowance, heavily subsidized government housing, and other legacies of the colonial era.[34] The net effect of the commission's recommendations was to lessen income disparities within the modern sector, although it may have unintentionally increased the gap between salaried employees and wage earners on the one hand and peasant farmers and the unemployed on the other.

The federal and regional governments did not accept these modest recommendations, on the grounds that the country could not afford substantial increases at the lower income levels; instead, much smaller increases were proposed.[35] The fact that the public share of the Morgan Commission's proposals could have been financed by abolishing the automobile allowance was conveniently overlooked. The government's refusal to carry out the commission's proposals led directly to the General Strike, through which the workers forced the government to satisfy many of their demands. Thus some equalization of income, at least in the modern sector, took place during the first five years of independence, but only after the new elite was pushed from below. And even the successful strike only slightly modified the inequalities built into the salary structure of an ex-colonial economy.

In the field of educational policy, public officials interested in equality might have tried to curb the growth of a separate school system for the wealthy, to increase the number of post-primary scholarships, and to limit secondary school fees. The first of these moves was a difficult one to make—and not simply because the ministries of education lacked the staff even to supervise the grant-in-aid system properly. In order to attract foreign capital, high-quality schools had to be provided for the children of expatriates; and since it was politically impossible to segregate these schools by refusing to admit Nigerian children, officials were in effect forced to allow some Nigerian enrollment in private primary schools. Moreover, these officials commonly sent their own children to private schools, whose fees they could afford and whose advantages they perceived only too well. In general, primary schools that charged fees were permitted to expand without hindrance, though Premier Okpara made a vague commitment to close so-called multiracial schools by the mid-1970's.

The regional governments might have increased their outlay for scholarships, perhaps restricting awards to poor children who had attended grant-aided schools. In fact, only about 3 per cent of recurrent educational expenditure for the Southern regions in 1964–65 was devoted to scholarships of any sort,[36] though local authorities also contributed substantially from their own limited resources. At most, about 15 per cent of the grammar school students in the South received scholarships from one or more sources; in the author's survey only 7 per cent of the grammar school students and 18 per cent of the Sixth Form students were on full or partial scholarship. Officially, at least, financial assistance was to be awarded on the basis of academic performance, with some preference to children from educationally backward and minority areas. Since parental income was normally not considered, it is probable that many scholarships actually subsidized the children of the elite.*

Both Ibadan and Enugu took some action following Independence to limit the steady rise in secondary school fees. But unfortunately the regional governments did not take the next logical step of increasing grants-in-aid so that grammar schools could remain solvent. Bureaucrats in both regions suspected that the profit motive accounted for most of the rise in school fees. They were unwilling, moreover, to raise their subsidy for each secondary school when the number of these schools was increasing so rapidly.

The government's unwillingness to spend more on secondary education brings us to the heart of the matter. In order to achieve equality at the primary school level the regions established a system of free primary education that proved enormously expensive. There were consequently only limited resources available for achieving equality of opportunity at the secondary level, whether by an expanded scholarship program or by a substantial reduction of grammar school fees. The very commitment of the regions to equality at one level made it more difficult to realize equality at the next level; and the more rapidly expansion occurred in the primary schools, the less significant for social mobility became the equality realized there. By the mid-1960's the key to individual mobility in Southern Nigeria was admission to a grammar school, and in a very real sense the process by which admission was determined had a crucial bearing on the area's political stability. As the inequalities built into that process became more apparent to Southern Nigerians, they tended to ignore the egalitarian impact of universal primary education and to concentrate instead on the ways in which the educational system was stratifying a traditionally classless society.

* In a revealing episode, the Port Harcourt Municipal Council once rejected eighteen secondary and post-secondary scholarships proposed by its Education Committee on the grounds that the recipients came from families who could already afford to educate their children. *Eastern Outlook*, Jan. 5, 1961.

CHAPTER 11

Education and Integration

Conflict is the very stuff of politics; in every age men have competed more or less violently with each other for power to shape their own destiny and the destiny of society as a whole. Conflict is particularly evident in the early stages of modernization, when traditional ways of life and thought are upset, new patterns of dominance and dependence are forged, and politics may become a matter literally of life and death. This being so, it would be unrealistic to define an integrated society as one in which political conflict has been eliminated; there is no such society outside Utopia. Rather, we should recognize that the integrative forces in a particular society are closely bound up with the conflicts affecting it. Three questions arise in this connection. First, are there cultural and structural mechanisms for transcending conflict—that is, for focusing attention on those things that unite the members of a political unit in spite of their differences? Second, are there mechanisms for limiting conflict, so that it may be channeled through existing political institutions with a minimum of disruptive violence? Third, is it possible to manage conflict creatively, so that in the very process of competing with each other people contribute, almost by accident, to holding their society together? According to our usage, a polity is integrated to the extent that it is able to transcend domestic conflict, limits conflict to a certain level of intensity while providing political channels for its expression, and has cleavages that cut across rather than reinforce each other.

Before considering the integrative and disintegrative consequences of rapid educational expansion in Southern Nigeria, we must choose a suitable unit of analysis. Should we discuss the individual region, the South, or the whole of Nigeria? The choice is important, since what is integrative for one part of a country may well be disintegrative for the country as a whole, and vice versa. The region might at first seem best, for in the 1960–65 period each region had recognizable institutions of government, and the elites in Ibadan and Enugu who had initiated universal primary education were eager to unify and strengthen their respective regions in response to the mounting influence of the federal and Northern regional governments. But precisely because each region was part of a larger federation that in 1960 became an "emerging nation," and because events in the federation as a whole increasingly affected political life within its constituent parts, Nigeria might be a more appropriate unit of analysis. That the educational system in the South supposedly emphasized loyalty to Nigeria as a nation reinforces this point. As for Southern Nigeria, it has the obvious drawback of being not a distinct political entity but simply a geographical designation referring to Nigeria minus its Northern Region. During the 1950's it was possible to consider the South one political system, in the sense that NCNC and Action Group leaders were principally competing with each other over the distribution of power in the Eastern and Western regions. But by the 1960's the North was far more visibly involved in Nigerian politics, and the differences between North and South overshadowed those between East and West. The ability of Nigeria to handle North–South conflict and to remain a single political system became the crucial issue following Independence. For these reasons Nigeria has been selected as the unit of analysis, even though this study deals in depth with the educational history of the Southern regions only.

It is rarely easy for scholars to determine whether integrative tendencies in a given country have outweighed disintegrative ones over a short period of time. In Nigeria, however, there is no room for doubt; the evidence for disintegration, even in the short run, is all too compelling. The military coup of January 1966 marked the first use of extralegal violence to overthrow existing political elites in the federal and regional governments; partly by accident and partly by design, the coup also marked the end of Northern dominance and an increase in the power of Southern military men and civilians. The massacre of Ibos living in the North, which began in May 1966 and continued intermittently throughout the year, demonstrated the extent of ethnic tension in the country and convinced many Ibos that their only hope was to break away from Nigeria entirely. The counter-coup of July 1966 marked another resort to violence, this time by

Northern elements in the army; one result was the virtual disintegration along regional lines of the Nigerian army, the one institution that had held the country together following the events of January. With Northerners in control of Lagos, it was only a matter of months before the Eastern Region seceded, declaring itself the independent Republic of Biafra in May 1967. There followed a costly and bloody civil war, which was still taking its toll of both sides two years after Biafra's secession. Given this tragic series of events, one must necessarily emphasize those factors that have led to the disintegration of Nigeria, rather than those that kept the country together for the first five years of independence.

Many factors were at work in transforming what appeared to outsiders as the "bright hope of Africa" into one of the continent's most intractable problem areas. A federal structure in which one region was more populous than all the others combined, different rates of regional economic development, religious tensions, personality conflicts among leaders, the assassination of some leaders and not others —all these played an important part. Not least was the attainment of independence itself, for as Clifford Geertz has noted, "It is the very process of the formation of a sovereign civil state that . . . stimulates sentiments of parochialism, communism, racialism, and so on, because it introduces into society a valuable new prize over which to fight and a frightening new force with which to contend."[1] In what follows, however, we shall concentrate on the role played by rapid educational expansion in the Southern regions, while freely granting that only for analytical purposes may education be separated from other aspects of Nigerian life.

NATIONAL INTEGRATION

One criterion for integration is whether the citizens of a country possess certain things in common and believe these common possessions to be important. If people feel that they belong to a "terminal community"[2] whose values and institutions are worth preserving, they are unlikely to permit conflicts among them to reach the point where they threaten the continued existence of the community. The view that unity can exist in spite of diversity is well expressed in the American motto, "E Pluribus Unum," and in the Nigerian national anthem:

> Though tribe and tongue may differ,
> In Brotherhood we stand,
> Nigerians all, and proud to serve
> Our sovereign Motherland.

A successful emphasis on unity that transcends conflict—without necessarily eliminating it—will be termed national integration.[3]

One of the major contributions to national integration made by educational expansion in the South has been the introduction of a common language, English, to an entire younger generation. As a result of their schooling, Ibos and Yorubas can talk with each other and with Northerners who have attended European-type schools. English is not only a common language among the educated but also the official language of the country. In this respect Nigeria, along with virtually all sub-Saharan African countries, is fortunate in not possessing indigenous written languages of long standing, whose claim to official status might pit various linguistic groups against each other. The language controversy that has bedeviled the politics of India, Ceylon, Malaysia, and other Asian countries has been averted in Africa precisely because African vernaculars were not vehicles for the written transmission of culture before the coming of the European. Where, as in India or Ceylon, educational expansion has strengthened various vernaculars, it has failed to break down the communication barriers of pre-modern times; in Nigeria, by contrast, universal primary education and related programs have made possible communication among all moderately educated persons.[4]

In addition to teaching a common language, the schools have provided a common cultural experience for millions of young Nigerians. One dilemma faced by African nation builders is that the culture of their people either is rooted in a subnational entity, like a tribe, or shares with all African cultures those features attributed to "negritude" or "the African personality"; there is little in the cultural realm that is the common—and at the same time exclusive— property of the citizens of a given state. When young Nigerians attending school learn to reach the classroom on time, to stand up when reciting their lessons, to tend the school grounds, and so forth, they are building up a common store of experiences. And to the extent that the Nigerian educational system differs from that of neighboring countries—in the language used, and in the content and quality of instruction—the common educational experiences of Nigerians are also exclusive ones. From the point of view of integration, it matters little that the education is often of dubious quality, for even if, as some educators contend, the next generation of Nigerians will be intelligible only to each other, the atrocious English taught in primary schools could be the foundation for a distinctly Nigerian dialect!

If educational expansion in the South has been integrative in these respects, in other ways it has probably had the opposite effect. One important task for curriculum reformers in a new state is to write history texts emphasizing the unity of their country and minimizing its internal conflicts.[5] In fact, little has been done to revise Nigerian history texts, and British authors continue to dominate the history and civics fields.[6] But even if new texts are written by Nigerians, a serious question remains: how much can one truthfully write about Nigerian unity? When school books discuss the enormous ethnic and linguistic diversity of the country, the separate administration of North and South in the formative early years of the twentieth century, and the predominantly Southern origins of nationalism, they cannot but make explicit how few past experiences have affected all Nigerians equally. And since education has made young Nigerians acutely aware of their country's troubles following Independence, increased knowledge of their fellow countrymen cannot be expected, by itself, to create good feelings among the educated members of contending groups. When students in the author's survey did express a commitment to national unity, their views were based less on knowledge than on the hope that an unhappy state of affairs would one day right itself.

A school can, however, provide more than academic knowledge about a country. Through its recruitment policies it can bring together members of many different groups, and the school can become a miniature nation by instilling cooperative habits among a diverse student body. This integrative function is particularly important when one considers that grammar school and university graduates constitute a substantial portion of the elite whose decisions will affect a country's destiny. If leaders of competing groups have in common an "old school tie" and the memory of eccentric teachers, mutual friends, and devilish pranks that binds Old Boys everywhere together, it is more likely that their political differences can be mediated than if their educational experiences are quite dissimilar. In the early years of a country's educational history, when few schools are operating, each school tends to recruit from a wide geographical area; the best early schools may have a national or even international clientele. This was true, for example, of Achimota College in Ghana, the Ecole Ponty in Senegal, Munali Secondary School in Northern Rhodesia, and Gordon College in the Anglo-Egyptian Sudan. In Southern Nigeria, as noted in Chapter 1, St. Andrew's College, Oyo, in its first years recruited from as far away as the Niger Delta; Table 13 shows

TABLE 13. Matriculation by Ethnic Group in Boarding Section, Hope Waddell Training Institute, Calabar, 1902–63

Ethnic group and area of origin	1902 (N=59)	1910 (N=65)	1920 (N=97)	1930 (N=106)	1940 (N=86)	1945 (N=87)	1950 (N=59)	1955 (N=98)	1960 (N=79)	1963 (N=90)
Eastern Region:										
Lower Cross River groups [a]	38.9%	30.7%	40.2%	23.5%	19.7%	11.4%	13.5%	10.2%	12.6%	20.0%
Upper Cross River groups	5.0	4.6	10.3	4.7	3.4	5.7	3.3	3.0	1.2	5.5
Ibibio	5.0	26.1	15.4	18.8	24.4	34.4	13.5	30.6	16.4	22.2
Eastern Ibo	10.1	27.6	23.7	30.1	37.2	36.7	55.9	50.0	64.5	45.5
Ijaw	3.3	3.0	1.0	3.7	1.1	2.2	1.6	0	2.5	2.2
Others; unknown	1.6	0	0	6.6	0	1.1	3.3	1.0	2.5	1.1
Western Region:										
Bini	3.3	0	1.0	2.8	1.1	0	0	0	0	0
Western Ibo	3.3	1.5	0	3.7	3.4	0	3.3	1.0	0	1.1
Yoruba	15.2	1.5	3.0	2.8	2.3	3.4	3.3	2.0	0	1.1
Other West African countries [b]	13.5	4.6	5.1	2.8	6.9	4.5	1.6	2.0	0	1.1

SOURCE: Principal's Roll Book, 1900–1963.

[a] The Lower Cross River category includes Efiks, Quas, Efuts, and Efik-speakers up to Ikorofiong, a town about twenty miles north-west of Calabar. The Upper Cross River category includes non-Ibos north of Ikorofiong.

[b] Includes British Cameroons, Gold Coast, Togo, Sierra Leone, and Liberia (Kru).

TABLE 14. Recruitment Radius of Secondary Schools, 1964

Parental residence	Schools founded before 1950 (Enrollment: 140)	Schools founded 1956–64 (Enrollment: 400)
Within 10 miles of school	31%	37%
10–50 miles from school	27	32
Over 50 miles from school	42	31

SOURCE: Survey made by the author in 1964 of Southern Nigerian schoolchildren.

that in 1902 Hope Waddell Training Institute drew more than one-third of its students from areas outside the Eastern Region, including several West African countries.

With educational expansion the recruitment radius for the older schools tends to contract, since new schools enroll local young people who in earlier days would have traveled much greater distances to obtain a good education. At Hope Waddell, for example, fewer students from outside the Eastern Region were enrolled as the twentieth century advanced, although within the region itself a certain leveling process occurred; by the 1930's the numerically dominant Ibos and Ibibios had surpassed the Efiks and other Lower Cross River peoples living in the immediate vicinity of Calabar. As for the new schools, their initial recruitment radius is limited not only by their lack of reputation but also by the need to enroll "sons of the soil" to attract local financial support. Table 14, based on the author's survey, shows that secondary schools founded before 1950 recruited from a wider area than schools founded between 1956 and 1964; a similar phenomenon has been noted in Ghana, Indonesia, and India.[7] One consequence of educational expansion, therefore, is that schools become progressively less capable of giving their students the kind of personal contact with different groups that can give rise to truly national sentiments. What little instruction there was in the early 1960's concerning Nigeria was not reinforced outside the classroom by inter-ethnic contacts, which were much more frequent thirty years earlier, when the elite that brought Nigeria to independence was attending grammar school.[8] Hence the nationalism of the post-Independence generation of secondary students, such as it was, remained an abstract sentiment that could not readily be translated into concrete action.

Government secondary schools can recruit their students from many different parts of Nigeria as a matter of policy. With the regionalization of education, however, pressures were exerted on such schools to admit only children born in their own region. Edo College, Benin, for example, admitted more Eastern Ibos than Binis in 1949–51; in 1952 its examination center east of the Niger was closed down and a verbal arrangement was made with the Western Region Director of Education to exclude Eastern Ibos except those whose parents were working in the West. Within the West, moreover, government schools during the 1950's tended to recruit locally: Edo College concentrated on Benin Province, Government College Ughelli on Delta Province, and Government College Ibadan on the Yoruba-speaking areas.[9] With Independence the federal government proposed a large National High School for each region that would draw students from all the regions. The idea found its way into the Six-Year Plan but was never implemented. In general, political pressures prevented government schools from realizing their integrative potential.

Thus far we have considered the mixed effects of educational expansion on young Southern Nigerians attending school. We consider next its effect on the central institutions that should be the most effective expressions of Nigerian unity. It should be said at the outset that the federal government has always lacked those features one associates with an actively centralizing regime: a powerful single party, a centralized civil service, charismatic leadership, and a coherent ideology. Of all the world's countries Nigeria is perhaps second only to India in the diversity of its peoples, and the kind of regime best able to accommodate this diversity has been not a mobilization system but a reconciliation system, to use David Apter's terms.* When Southern Nigerians looked to Lagos, therefore, they found little to elicit their active loyalty. It may be argued—although this is difficult to document—that rapid educational expansion has further reduced the integrative capacity of the federal government in two respects. First, the educational programs of the Southern regions, which initially reflected the decentralization taking place in the early 1950's, in turn strengthened the influence of the regional governments; the ministries of education responsible to Ibadan and Enugu were enlarged, and it was to the politicians in the regional capitals that people attributed both the successes and failures of universal

---

* See Apter's *Politics of Modernization* (Chicago, 1965), pp. 397–402. "The role of government in a reconciliation system is not organizational; rather, it works to reconcile diverse interests; it mediates, integrates, and above all coordinates, rather than organizes and mobilizes. In contrast to the mobilization system, which 'fights' society, the reconciliation system is often a prisoner of society." *Ibid.*, pp. 398–99.

primary education. When in the 1960's the Southern regions looked to the federal government for assistance in meeting their educational obligations, the unwillingness of federal officials to help out probably increased tensions between the two levels of government. Many Southern Nigerians felt that at least in the educational field the federal government had done little for them in the past and had no interest in improving its record.

Second, the fact of an increasingly educated populace in the South may have encouraged Southern politicians to enflame ethnic and regional tensions. The security dilemma confronting federal politicians in the 1960's was if anything more acute than that confronting regional leaders a decade earlier: how could each leader maintain influence within his own party and within a federal coalition of parties that threatened at any moment to collapse? The power base of each politician lay within his own region and ethnic group, and it was tempting for him to protect his position by posing as the champion of his constituents against real or imagined threats from other groups. This temptation increased as the politician realized that his words and deeds were being given careful attention by increasing numbers of voters. Politicians typically responded to this interest by phrasing their ideas simply, directly, and dramatically, and more often than not in the language of what is commonly termed tribalism. For their purposes it was irrelevant that tribal tensions were not an important feature of traditional Nigerian life and still mattered little in the daily life of the average farmer. As we have argued in Part I, seeing the world in terms of Ibo, Yoruba, Hausa, and so forth requires a fundamental break with a traditional outlook based on face-to-face and kinship relationships. Mass education enabled large numbers of people to expand their horizons from the parochial to the ethnic level, and federal politicians intuitively realized that the language of tribalism would strike a responsive chord among such people, who probably felt more comfortable with an ethnic identity than with any alternative identity open to them. In a word, politicians said what the voters wanted to hear, until a time came when neither leaders nor followers could prevent the tensions within Nigeria from shattering the fragile institutions of unity.

HORIZONTAL INTEGRATION: NORTH VERSUS SOUTH

If a polity lacks a sense of unity-in-diversity, it may still be considered integrated if its domestic conflicts do not become so intense that extralegal methods must be used to resolve them. A polity may also be considered integrated if the lines of conflict cut across rather than reinforce each other, and if this cross-cutting pattern leads not to a stalemate of hostile forces but to a dynamic process of mutual interaction that strengthens the institutions through which contending groups struggle for power.[10] Many of the new states are beset by conflict among ethnic, racial, religious, and linguistic groups that may be equal or unequal to each other in power, wealth, or status (the vertical dimension of society) but are different from each other in certain other objective respects (the horizontal dimension). Conflict among these groups is particularly threatening when, as often happens, each one occupies a fairly well-defined piece of land and can use this territory as a base for launching a civil war or establishing an independent government. The most serious horizontal cleavage in Nigeria, one that eventually took on aspects of vertical cleavage as the parties contended for political dominance, was between the Northern Region and the rest of the country. By the early 1960's it was clear to Nigerians that the North–South conflict overshadowed the conflict between Ibos and Yorubas and the conflict between dominant ethnic groups and minorities, although to be sure ethnic rivalries remained an important part of Nigerian politics following Independence. We shall now consider whether educational expansion in the South contributed to the "horizontal integration" of Nigeria by moderating North–South conflict and by fostering new cleavages that cut across North–South lines.

Differences between Southern Nigeria and the North—particularly the far North with its powerful emirates—may be discussed from several points of view: traditional factors, the British impact, response to the forces of change, and the drive for independence. The people of the South are primarily forest dwellers growing root and tree crops, whereas Northerners live in the drier Sudanic belt and have a grain-oriented subsistence economy. Traditional political structures are less centralized in the South than in the far North, and prior to this century most Southerners were pagan whereas the Northern emirates were officially, and aggressively, Islamic. With the coming of the British, the impact of modernization in its many forms—education, health facilities, a cash economy, roads, ports, and so on—was more direct and persistent along the coast than in the Northern hinterland. British efforts at indirect rule proved fruitless in the East and only moderately successful in the West; in the North, on the other hand, the British strengthened in many respects the existing native authority system. The North was separately administered by the British from 1900 to 1914, and not until 1946 were Northerners

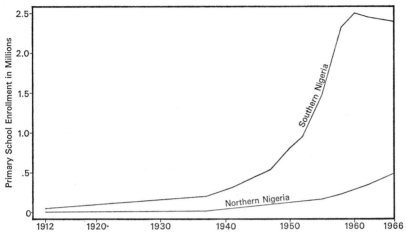

Fig. 1. Primary School Enrollment, 1912–65 (from annual reports of the education departments of the federal and regional Nigerian governments).

and Southerners permitted to meet together in the Legislative Council. In general, Southerners responded quickly to the forces of change in their midst; moreover, as we have seen, their acceptance of Christian missionaries meant that educational opportunities were widely diffused. Northerners, on the other hand, responded more cautiously and selectively to change;[11] in at least the Muslim areas Christian missionaries were discouraged from operating schools, and officially sponsored schools like Katsina Training College tended to reinforce the existing indigenous power structure by recruiting heavily from leading families within the emirates. The significant Southern lead in primary education from the early years of the twentieth century is shown in Figure 1.

The drive for independence helped to call attention to these traditional differences between North and South, and also created new grounds for conflict. The nationalist movement was led predominantly by Southerners, but the very success of Southerners in pressing for Nigerian self-determination and democracy meant that the real holders of political power after Independence would be Northerners, whose region contained 55 per cent of the country's population. Thus, the North stood to gain many of the benefits of an independence that its leaders had not particularly sought. Indeed, the man who subsequently became Nigeria's first Prime Minister, Alhaji Abubakar Tafawa Balewa, earned his reputation as an orator by stressing the artificiality of Nigeria and the North's unreadiness for self-government.[12] Most articulate Southerners deeply resented the dominant role of the Northern People's Congress in national life; to them the very name of the party betrayed an unseemly preoccupation with its own region that was confirmed when the Sardauna of Sokoto, party president and "éminence noire" behind Prime Minister Balewa, chose to remain Premier of the North rather than assume national office.

But if the North had sufficient voting strength to dominate Nigerian political life, why should its leaders have been reticent about attaining independence and generally defensive toward Southerners? The answer lies in Northern fears that administrative power would be monopolized by the Southerners because of their long-standing educational lead. The Sardauna made this point quite explicit in his autobiography:

As things were at that time [the early 1950's], if the gates to the departments were to be opened, the Southern Regions had a huge pool from which they could find suitable people, while we had hardly anyone. In the resulting scramble it would, we were convinced, be inevitable that the Southern applicants would get almost all the posts available. Once you get a Government post you are hard indeed to shift. . . . [This] was a matter of life and death to us. . . . If the British Administration had failed to give us the even development that we deserved and for which we craved so much—and they were on the whole a very fair administration—what had we to hope from an African Administration, probably in the hands of a hostile party. The answer to our minds was, quite simply, just nothing, beyond a little window dressing.[13]

Were a Southerner to reply that administrators simply carry out the orders of political leaders, the Sardauna might well have asked why, if that were so, Southern politicians were so concerned about the reliability of their British civil servants.

Perhaps even more disturbing to Northerners were the possible effects of independence on their own region. For to a greater degree than any other political party in Africa, the Northern People's Congress recruited its leadership from and based its political power on a powerful administrative apparatus, the native authority system.[14] If educated Southerners were to replace the British in key positions in the Northern civil service, they might not only sabotage their ministers' programs but undermine the very structure of traditional authority on which the ministers relied for their political power. For understandable reasons, therefore, an explicit policy of Northernization was followed when the Nigerian civil service was regionalized in 1954: British civil servants would remain in office until they could be

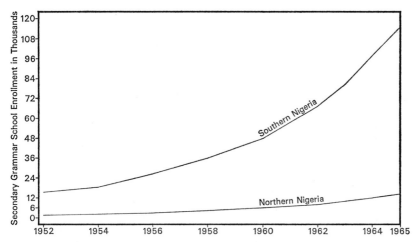

Fig. 2. Secondary Grammar School Enrollment, 1952–65 (Archibald Callaway and A. Musone, *Financing of Education in Nigeria* [Paris, 1968], Table 8, p. 115; Education and World Affairs, *Nigerian Human Resource Development and Utilization* [New York, 1967], p. 43.

replaced by Northerners with the proper qualifications. As might be expected, Southerners, especially those qualified in administration, interpreted the Northernization policy as a calculated insult, a denial of the common nationality of Nigerians, and further evidence that "feudal" Northern leaders were closely collaborating with the colonial regime.

Thus the different rate of educational expansion between South and North, dating back over a century, contributed significantly to tension between these two areas of Nigeria. The events of the 1950's described in Part II simply widened the educational gap: the South concentrated its energies on a crash program in primary education, whereas the North worked on a more balanced and less spectacular program of regional development. As Figure 1 shows, the absolute gap in primary enrollment levels was far greater in 1960 than ten years earlier; in fact, the Northern figure as a proportion of the Southern fell during the decade from 20 per cent to slightly above 10 per cent. Following Independence the North's position rapidly improved, its growth curve approaching that of the South during the 1940's while enrollment levels in the South declined somewhat. But even if these enrollment trends were to continue, the North would not approach parity with the less populous Southern regions until about 1980. At the highly important grammar school level, Figure 2 suggests that the North's chances of catching up to the South following Independence were slim, and were, in fact, growing slimmer with every passing year. Thus the drive for equality in the South, expressed in the rapid expansion of primary and secondary school enrollments, accentuated educational inequalities in Nigeria as a whole.

Of course, the education explosion in the South doubtless stimulated expansion in the North,[15] much as the initial Yoruba lead acted as an incentive for Ibos from the 1930's onward. But the North–South gap was too large to be rapidly closed, and its effects were far more damaging politically after Independence than when Ibos and Yorubas were both under British control. On the one hand, educated Southerners in the 1960's, faced with unemployment in their own regions, grew increasingly bitter at being denied jobs in the North. On the other hand, Northerners grew increasingly worried over the prospect of being "swamped" by educated Southerners, in private business if not in the civil service. Northern resentment of Ibos was particularly intense, for educated Ibos were quick to move North in search of commercial opportunities.[16] The very ethnic group whose traditional way of life Northerners respected least—the Ibos were not Muslim and lacked hierarchical patterns of government— seemed to be benefiting disproportionately from the modernization of the North. The stage was set for the pogroms of 1966.

Although this study does not extend to the events of 1966, a word may be in order on their relationship to educational expansion in the South. For the first few years of independence, Southerners were willing to permit Northern domination of politics in the hope that eventually the South would come into its own: a new census might shift the balance of power, for example, or the Northern populace might rise up against the feudal system on which the Northern People's Congress was built. But the results of two national censuses (1962 and 1963), of the federal election of 1964, and of an obviously rigged Western Region election of 1965 that retained the NPC's ally, Chief Akintola, as Premier, made it clear that the North would continue to dominate Nigerian politics, perhaps even more openly and ruthlessly than in the past. The only tactic open to those who found this situation unacceptable was to overthrow the democratic process itself; this the military coup of January 1966 accomplished by eliminating key political leaders and outlawing all political parties.

In certain respects the January coup represented a triumph not simply for the South, but for Nigerian nationalism. Both Colonel Nzeogwu, who initiated the assassination plot, and General J. T. U. Aguiyi Ironsi, who became first Head of the Military Government, were genuinely bent on saving the nation as a whole from civil disorder. But the tragedy was that nationalist policies, in a situation where conventional politics had been suspended, inevitably favored the South. The old political class, dominated at the federal level by Northerners, was gone; in its place, elevated to unprecedented power and status as advisers to the military rulers, were the nation's higher civil servants, who because of the country's educational history happened to be predominantly Southern. General Ironsi probably believed that delegating greater authority to the civil servants was an eminently nonpolitical act, and his May 1966 announcement of the unification of the country's regional civil services seems to have been an honest expression of nationalist sentiment. Influential Northerners, however, saw the first move as highly political, given the number of Southerners in administrative positions, and the second as a thinly disguised plot to flood the North with Southern civil servants. Significantly, it was the unification announcement that triggered protests by leading Northern emirs, as well as the first large-scale massacres of Ibos living in the North.[17] General Ironsi's well-meaning efforts to change the status and organization of the civil service probably contributed more than any other factor to his demise. The counter-coup of July 1966 replaced him with a Northerner, Lieutenant Colonel Yakubu Gowan, and put an end to all talk of a unified civil service. This counter-coup in turn led to the secession of the Eastern Region, whose predominantly Ibo population was more directly affected than Westerners by events in the North.

The effect of rapid educational expansion in the South, therefore, was to increase the South's already substantial lead over the North at a time when educational inequalities had become a source of bitter political conflict. This conflict was merely intensified by the attempt to replace democratic politics with the rule of "neutral" civil servants, for the close link between the educational system and civil service recruitment meant that any upgrading of the administrative apparatus was also an upgrading of the most educationally advanced groups in the country.*

To what extent did educational expansion foster cleavages that cut

---

* There is an interesting parallel between recent developments in Nigeria and the Muslim-Hindu tensions that eventually led to the partition of India. As Bruce McCully noted in 1940, "English education failed to bridge the gap permanently between the two great communities. Indeed, by qualifying disproportionate numbers of Hindus for Government service and professional employment, it probably accentuated inter-communal rivalry." *English Education and the Origins of Indian Nationalism* (New York, 1940), p. 395.

across North–South lines? The question is not easily answered, but certainly there were conflicts within Southern Nigeria prior to 1966 that diverted attention from the basic division in the country at large, conflicts in which education played a part. For one thing, tension between Yoruba and Ibo members of the elite remained high following Independence. Matters were hardly helped by a public dispute between the Yoruba Federal Minister of Communications and the Ibo Chairman of the Nigerian Railways Corporation in which each charged the other's agency with tribal favoritism, or by the unexplained replacement of an Ibo by a Yoruba educator as Vice-Chancellor of the University of Lagos.[18] A prominent Yoruba once known for his nationalist sentiments told the author in 1964 of his bitterness at the Ibos' aggressiveness and duplicity, and concluded, "My heart is filled with tribalism." This cleavage, which as we have seen is based in part on patterns of educational expansion dating back several decades, helps to explain the Yorubas' cool response to the news that Ibos had been massacred in the North and the isolation of Ibo military leaders in the delicate negotiations following the July coup—an isolation that led eventually to the East's secession.

A second set of cleavages was between minority and dominant ethnic groups within each Southern region. Resentment of Yoruba hegemony over the people of Benin and Delta provinces was the prime motive behind the creation of the Mid-West State in 1963; here the accidents of missionary history played a rather ironic part, for non-Yorubas ascribed the small number of secondary grammar schools in their area to Yoruba discrimination rather than to missionary settlement patterns.[19]

Third, the denominational tensions that were so important an aspect of educational expansion in the South may have served a useful cross-cutting function. Loyalty to particular voluntary agencies created conflicts within a given ethnic group or region—the 1961 Eastern Region election was if anything more openly a Protestant-Catholic struggle than the election of 1957—while at the same time it fostered links across ethnic and regional lines.[20] The very fact that denominational tensions were imported from abroad and hence had little in common with other cleavages in Nigerian society may be a compelling argument not for their divisiveness but for their integrative potential. Unfortunately, however, none of the cleavages within Southern Nigeria was sufficient in magnitude to offset the major cleavage between the North and the South.

VERTICAL INTEGRATION: THE ROLE OF TEACHERS

In Chapter 10 we saw how the elite-mass gap became a politically explosive issue in Nigeria. Here we are concerned with ways of bridging this gap, of getting rulers and ruled to see themselves as belonging to the same society. Vertical integration, as we shall use the term, is a two-way communications process by which elite attitudes and values are transmitted to the populace and popular demands and grievances are transmitted to the elite. Successful vertical integration does not necessarily mean that the elite loses power relative to the populace; it means only that each listens to the other and gains some comprehension of what the other is trying to say. Meaningful communication will not automatically lead to a sense of community, but it is almost a prerequisite.[21]

In practice top politicians and administrators have little occasion to meet any of the poor farmers who constitute most of Southern Nigeria's population. Direct contact is made possible by the mass media, but the integrative potential of radios and newspapers is limited by their unavailability in many rural areas, their impersonality, and the one-sided nature of the announcements they carry. In Nigeria, at least, a steady two-way flow of ideas depends heavily on the existence of intermediaries who can serve as brokers and even, quite literally, as translators between the elite and the masses. As we have seen, teachers were ideally suited for this role in Southern Nigeria; it was for precisely this reason that so many of them were elected to federal and regional office in the early 1950's, when the British were still the ruling elite. As the politicians themselves became an elite, teachers continued to perform an intermediary role; indeed, in some ways the teacher's potential as a vertical integrator increased. Teachers were responsible for disseminating the language of the elite—English—to an entire generation, and for conveying, through their own behavior as well as through classroom instruction, the rudiments of good citizenship. They were also in a good position to transmit messages from students and their parents upward to the new elite, particularly in rural areas, where there were few educated adults. Furthermore, as the size of the teaching force grew, teachers were increasingly able to command the respectful attention of the government by well-organized pressure tactics.

The realization of a teacher's potential as an intermediary depended in large measure on his status in the community; generally speaking, the higher and more secure his status, the more likely he was to play a constructive role as an interpreter of ideas. The net effect of rapid educational expansion, however, was to erode the teacher's standing seriously, and to give at least the primary teacher a general feeling of insecurity. For as he taught children to read and write, the teacher was imparting to others the very knowledge that had formerly raised him above the illiterate populace. Recruitment standards inevitably declined with the onset of universal primary education, and as thousands of untrained teachers were hired to staff the new classes of the mid-1950's, the public image of the profession suffered. Indeed, the early years of universal primary education made a mockery of the idea that teaching was a profession requiring prolonged and rigorous training; the proliferation of untrained teachers had a greater effect on the public than the continued presence of grammar school principals and other educators who were professionals in every sense of the word. The teacher's status was further lowered by the public's tendency to attribute rising unemployment among school leavers to a decline in educational standards—that is, to the failure of the teacher to get his material across to the students. Finally, his status was probably lowered by the shift in primary school proprietorship toward the local authorities. Voluntary agency teachers enjoyed a certain reputation for probity and benevolence by virtue of their links to the missionary past; local authority teachers had no such legacy to protect them, and were widely regarded as little more than the hired men of the local council.

Untrained and poorly trained primary teachers faced an additional problem: the very real prospect that they would soon be in the same position as the students they were preparing for the "unemployment market." Teacher training colleges, enlarged in the late 1950's in a belated effort to improve the quality of the primary school teaching force, were by the mid-1960's producing a large number of well-trained teachers. Enrollment in Southern Nigerian Grade II colleges, many of whose students had earned the West African School Certificate, was over 18,000 in 1965;[22] of these, about one-third were in their final year and ready to assume classroom duties. It was assumed by the government that trained teachers would replace the untrained, and this process occurred so rapidly that by 1965 some 75 per cent of the primary teachers in the East and 55 per cent in the old West had at least Grade III qualifications. Many untrained or uncertificated teachers enrolled in a teacher training college, thus temporarily securing their positions against the claims of the better-qualified.

But thousands of others—the very ones without whom universal primary education would have been impossible—found themselves jobless, or about to become so. They had been drafted in an emergency, and once the emergency was over they found they were no longer needed. Like the Nigerian ex-serviceman of the 1940's returning to civilian life, the untrained teacher of the 1960's returned to his home and small farm, the embittered veteran of years of thankless service.

The declining status of the teacher, combined with insecurity of tenure at the lower end of the scale, had a profoundly demoralizing effect on Southern Nigeria's teaching force at the secondary as well as the primary level. Morale has deteriorated further in recent years because thousands of primary school teachers, particularly in the East, have had to wait months before their salaries were paid. Under the circumstances, far from continuing to serve as a vertical integrator of his society, the teacher became preoccupied with his own problems; in search of his own scapegoat, he tended to blame the government for his plight. Discouraged over their prospects, many teachers left the classroom to seek more lucrative and secure jobs elsewhere. But those who remained inevitably communicated their discontent to those around them—their students, neighbors, and employers, as well as the regional and federal governments.

The institution through which Nigeria's teachers have normally channeled their demands for better salaries and service conditions is the Nigeria Union of Teachers. The educational expansion of the 1950's vastly increased the union's membership—from 22,000 in 1950 to 57,000 in 1962—but this very increase brought problems. Among the new members were thousands of young, poorly educated teachers who increasingly came to favor union action—including strikes—as a way of protecting their jobs and of increasing the income and prestige of their profession. The union's leaders, however, remained essentially unchanged from the 1940's, and the philosophy of close collaboration with the British that had won them the gratitude of the colonial regime* continued to guide their relationships with the federal, the Western, and to a lesser extent the Eastern government. Many teachers resented this collaboration, which they saw as a preference for mediating between the teachers and the government rather than for presenting the teachers' case as forcefully as

---

* The key leaders of the union possessed British "titles" as of 1964: E. E. Esua (C.B.E.), Alvan Ikoku (O.B.E.), Bishop Seth Kale (M.B.E.), and Canon E. O. Alayande (M.B.E.).

possible. Indeed, it was widely believed that the N.U.T., by virtually refusing to strike against the regional and federal governments, had confined itself to presenting humble petitions that could be ignored with impunity.

Teachers with little or no training were further disturbed by the union's apparent lack of concern for their welfare. The N.U.T. carefully nurtured an image of itself as a professional organization with high recruitment standards that had been only temporarily lowered. Thus although the union did sponsor some quite successful vacation courses for its untrained members to improve their qualifications, its annual conferences did little more than express regret when thousands of teachers, including many who had served long before universal primary education, were sacked to make way for a new, more academically qualified generation. The resulting bitterness felt by dismissed teachers against the N.U.T. as well as the regional governments is well expressed in this poignant letter from the president of a breakaway group, the Nigerian Association of C/S [uncertificated] Teachers, to the N.U.T. Executive Working Committee:

We C/S teachers view it with great concern that we are the pioneers and the stepping stone and the runnersup of civil, political, religious and educational advancement of this growing National.

Now that we should reap the fruits of our strenuous labour, now that we should be raised shoulder high, now that we should be proud because we have moulded you up as useful Nigerians: — the Graduates, Premiers, Prime Ministers, Ministers with or without Port-folios, other Parliamentarians, Professors, Lecturers, doctors and Magistrates, judges, and Lawyers, engineers, all certified teachers, School Certificate holders and all educated elements of varying educational outlook, you form the vile brooms by which we are swept away because of non-certification which is not an evidence of inefficiency or old age.[23]

To disaffection among the lower ranks of the teaching force should be added restlessness among recent university graduates teaching in the secondary schools. These graduates felt that the N.U.T. represented the interests of an older group of men who had not obtained university degrees and who were in fact threatened by the new intelligentsia. A Graduate Teachers Association was formed in the late 1950's with the aim of bypassing the N.U.T. and negotiating directly with the government for better salaries and working conditions. Thus as the teaching force became more differentiated, cleavages developed within its ranks, and the N.U.T. found it increasingly difficult to speak convincingly for all members of the profession.

A turning point in the history of the union came in May 1964 with E. E. Esua's retirement from the post of General Secretary, which he had held since 1941. He was thereupon appointed Chairman of the Federal Electoral Commission, a move that merely confirmed the widespread suspicion that he was more a member of the ruling elite than a representative of the "sub-elite"[24] of teachers. With Esua's departure from the union, pressures for more radical tactics built up. This change in the internal dynamics of the N.U.T. coincided with a general increase in labor-government tension that finally resulted in the General Strike. Teachers in Lagos and a few other parts of the country joined in the strike, but it was not supported by the N.U.T. National Executive, which at that time placed its hopes on the Morgan Commission's proposal (in line with a long-standing union demand) of a National Joint Negotiating Council for Teachers that would set salaries and working conditions on a national rather than a regional basis. It soon became clear, however, that the regional and federal governments were not going to participate voluntarily in such a body. The regional governments were particularly uneasy because the establishment of national scales would reduce their policy-making power in the educational field. In the Western and Eastern regions, where salary scales were below those in Lagos and the North, authorities feared the financial implications of revising their scales upward. The authorities in Kaduna for their part feared the implications of a unified teaching service, which might bring Southern teachers to the North.

Faced with stalling tactics by the bureaucrats, the N.U.T. National Executive took the unprecedented step of calling a nationwide teacher strike beginning on the fourth anniversary of Independence, October 1, 1964. The selection of this date was quite significant, for on previous Independence Day celebrations teachers had shown their commitment to the nation-building effort by organizing public parades of their students, raising the Nigerian flag in ceremonies on the school grounds, and the like. The strike went ahead as planned, and for a week virtually the entire Nigerian teaching force of 100,000 failed to show up in school. The teachers did finally win their point, and a National Joint Negotiating Council was established. But the victory was a Pyrrhic one, for the council turned out to be another stalling device, and the various governments refused to regard its recommendations as anything more than advisory. Threats of strike action again grew loud in late 1965, and only the military coup halted what would probably have been an even more decisive confrontation between the country's teachers and its rulers.

The teacher's changing role illustrates the rather complex effect of rapid educational expansion on vertical integration at both the regional and the federal level. As the teaching force grew, so did its potential for bridging the elite-mass gap by transmitting messages between the elite and the populace. But the very increase in the size and competence of the teaching force lowered the teacher's effectiveness as a vertical integrator, for in the face of greater job competition he became increasingly preoccupied with defending his status and security and began to give top priority to expressing his own viewpoint. Since, as we have seen, this viewpoint was likely to be in conflict with the government's, and since the teacher was the most important live source of political information for his students, his expressions of discontent were likely to play a significant part in alienating the younger generation from political authority.

INTEGRATIVE BEHAVIOR

A fourth and for our purposes final aspect of integration is "the readiness of individuals to work together in an organized fashion for common purposes and to behave in a fashion conducive to the achievement of these common purposes."[25] Integrative behavior, in this broad sense, depends on a minimal level of interpersonal trust and a belief that cooperation with others is both possible and worthwhile for all concerned.[26] The importance of what Lucian Pye calls "associational sentiments"[27] lies in their effect not only on a society's capacity to get things done but also on the way things get done; a society is in our view more truly integrated if people cooperate willingly than if they do so out of suspicion or fear. In this sense, integrative behavior is relevant in all kinds of organizations, nonpolitical as well as political, small as well as large and complex.

Spokesmen for the new states, anxious to attribute to their societies virtues believed to be lacking in the West, often describe their people as skilled in the arts of cooperation. Certainly this is the dominant theme of the doctrine of African socialism. Sekou Touré insists that solidarity is the richest resource of the black race; Julius Nyerere that *ujamaa*, or familyhood, is a traditional resource that can be used in nation-building; Léopold Senghor that the African is not an individual so much as a member of a collectivity.[28] However correctly these views apply to traditional society—and there is an almost irresistible temptation for intellectuals in the new states to idealize the pre-colonial era—there is some reason to believe that in the early transition to modernity the willingness of people to cooperate with each other actually decreases. Modernization creates value conflicts within and between individuals, puts them in unfamiliar situations, whets the appetites of the ambitious, and produces a general atmosphere of uncertainty about the future that increases the risk of trusting others. To be sure, new and often quite powerful organizations are formed in the modernization process, but it is by no means certain that the rise of a powerful single party, for example, automatically increases the total organizational capacity of a society.

One of the striking features of Southern Nigerian life in 1960–65 was the extent to which people complained about the absence of trust. Another was the large number of organizations—from tribal unions to divisional councils to political parties—that appeared to the outside observer less effective after Independence than in earlier years. Remarks on this score are necessarily impressionistic, but it is surely significant that Nigerians themselves made so much of the decline in associational sentiments. One primary school student described the situation succinctly on the author's questionnaire: "The Nigeria greatest problem is that we don't like ourselfs."

Difficult as it is to measure changes in integrative behavior over time, let alone to isolate the effect of particular events on these changes, we may speculate on the role played in Nigeria by educational expansion. It seems reasonable to assert that universal primary education and related schemes at the post-primary level increased the cooperative capacity of Southern Nigerians, in the sense that a common language and the tools of literacy widened the possibilities for communication. At the same time, however, educational expansion may have had a negative effect on people's incentive to cooperate with each other. We have already noted the decline in the spirit of voluntarism that occurred when the regional governments took over educational responsibilities formerly borne by tribal unions, progress associations, and voluntary agencies; an increase in governmental capacity was offset to some extent by the decreased capacity of the private sector. Moreover, rapid educational expansion produced generational tensions between young literates and older illiterates that weakened many different kinds of organizations. For example, the Ibibio and Ibo national high schools were both plagued in the 1950's and 1960's by conflict between well-educated principals—normally young men who had received scholarship aid from their tribal union —and the older, more traditional members of the school's Board of Managers. A third factor conductive to mistrust, at least between the people and their rulers, was the increasing awareness of educated people that resources were being wasted by those rulers, often on luxuries for themselves and their families.* When government officials invoked the need for austerity as a reason for rejecting the salary scales recommended by the Morgan Commission, they sounded insincere. Why should people cooperate with the government when the government was not cooperating with them?

Charges of corruption in awarding jobs and contracts assumed the proportions of a favorite national pastime in post-Independence Nigeria. As some political scientists have recently pointed out, corruption can have an important integrative effect on a society in that the expectation of money or other favors binds people to each other and facilitates action that might never occur in a society that relied solely on legal procedures and formal institutions; certainly the overall impact of corrupt practices need not be as harmful to political development as moralists might imagine.[29] In Nigeria, however, the widespread belief that other people were making money and getting ahead by corrupt means probably had an important disintegrative effect, for it reduced public trust in the integrity of officials at all organizational levels and caused deep resentment among those who lacked "long leg," the West African term for influence or "pull." As one secondary student wrote in response to a question about his problems in finding a job, "My parents are illiterates, and if no 'long leg' no work in Nigeria."

It may be that rapid educational expansion contributed to the belief that corruption was widespread—leaving aside the imponderable question of the actual incidence of bribery and nepotism. Prior to the education explosion, when a primary or secondary school certificate was an automatic passport to salaried employment, it could be reasonably argued that a person obtained a particular job by his academic achievements; the certificate, as a kind of personal merit badge, legitimated the officeholder in the eyes of the public. Once the link between certificate and job was broken, the lucky recipient of a job could no longer credibly explain his good fortune solely in terms of educational achievement, since large numbers of school leavers with similar or even better qualifications were going jobless. An inevitable result was the charge of corruption, which seriously affected the performance and morale of the civil service when directed

---

* Archibald Callaway observed of unemployed school leavers he met in the Enugu slums that in 1960 they complained in a vague way about the wealth of politicians, whereas in 1963 they frequently knew government officials' precise incomes, car allowances, and so on. Interview, Dec. 15, 1963.

against its members. It would be a mistake to take all allegations of corruption in a developing country at face value; one should appreciate the function such allegations perform for those who fail in the competition for scarce resources, as well as the function corruption itself may serve for those who succeed.

SUMMARY

It must be concluded that the educational developments of the 1950's and early 1960's in Southern Nigeria had, on balance, a disintegrative effect on the country as a whole. Their most important consequence was to widen the already substantial educational disparity between North and South, thus intensifying the potential conflict between the two areas. Since any effort to reduce political tension by strengthening and unifying the civil service was bound to arouse Northern opposition, the Nigerian political system had no way of transcending or reducing the North–South conflict, or of coming to grips with it in a creative manner.

But apart from the North–South cleavage, even if we take the South alone as our unit of analysis, the disintegrative effects of educational expansion seem to outweigh the integrative ones. To be sure, a general consequence of universal primary education was to raise the integrative potential of the Nigerian political system by spreading literacy in a common language and increasing the size of the teaching force—by widening and deepening, in short, the communications network. But far more important for integration than the sheer amount of communication within a system is the content of that communication,[30] and here the signs were not favorable. Teachers ceased to be effective vertical integrators and concentrated on venting their own grievances against the government; charges of tribalism and corruption filled the communications channels. These things happened in part because of the very spread of literacy among the populace. That educational expansion increased Nigeria's potential for integration is theoretically interesting; that it also contributed despite itself to the underutilization and distortion of that potential is of greater practical relevance.

Conclusion: Confronting the Dilemma

This study has examined the causes and consequences of rapid educational expansion in Southern Nigeria; as such, any conclusions drawn from it properly apply only to this area of 75,000 square miles and 25 million people. But Southern Nigeria is significant because in many ways it typifies the underdeveloped areas of the world, and the belief that popular education should be given high priority as a means toward political and economic development is shared by leaders throughout the new states of Africa and Asia. The conclusions and policy proposals that emerge from this case study may therefore be relevant elsewhere.

We have seen how varied—and how powerful in combination—have been the forces pressing for educational expansion. The missionaries' concern for religious conversion; the perception by individuals and groups that Western schooling was the key to upward mobility; the increased involvement of the colonial government through the grant-in-aid system; competition among villages, ethnic groups, voluntary agencies, political parties, and regions; the new political elite's need for a dramatic, far-reaching welfare scheme to win popular support—all of these factors were at work, and all of them were mutually reinforcing. As a result, Southern Nigerian politicians came close to providing a few years of free primary education for all young people a little more than a century after Western education was introduced to the area and less than sixty years after the consolidation of British rule there. One marvels at the magnitude of the accomplishment; at the same time one senses, with the benefit of hindsight, the almost irresistible nature of the drive for popular education.

The enrollment increases of the 1950's were intended as decisive moves toward regional and national political development. For the new elite it was obvious that a literate younger generation would strengthen the government's capacity to meet the goals of rapid economic growth, Africanization of key positions in the civil service and the private sector, and Nigerian independence. A crash program to satisfy existing popular demands would harness the precious resources of hope and enthusiasm that the colonial regime had conspicuously failed to utilize and would give the new elite the legitimacy it needed to carry out other aspects of its modernization program. A second objective in expanding school enrollments was greater equality. Southern Nigerian leaders had strong populist leanings, and they wanted all the people to have the benefits of an educational experience that had enabled a few Nigerians to challenge colonial rule successfully. To be sure, the rivalries springing from inequalities in access to schooling had contributed to educational expansion prior to the 1950's. But there were certain groups—the very poor, girls, Muslims—who were unlikely ever to gain equal educational opportunity unless the regional government itself undertook to abolish primary school fees, increase the teaching force, and secularize to some extent the ownership and management of the educational system. A less prominent but still important objective was to encourage integration by spreading knowledge of English and by using the schools for nation-building purposes. As shown in Part III, these objectives were partly realized. It may be that the education explosion we have witnessed was a necessary condition for the political development of Southern Nigeria and of Nigeria as a whole.

But as Part III has also shown, the educational policies of the 1950's contributed significantly to political decay. Large numbers of young people were mobilized for participation in a modern economy and polity at a time when the economy could neither employ them nor afford what was in effect a costly social welfare scheme, and the political system lacked the resources to adapt to new demands. The very success with which Southern Nigerian leaders in the 1950's met their educational commitments hindered the reallocation of resources in the 1960's to meet new employment and output goals. The drive for equality in access to primary schools made inequality at the secondary school level more difficult to eradicate and more visible to a frustrated populace. The growth of enrollment in the Southern regions, by increasing the education gap between North and South, had a disintegrative impact on Nigeria as a whole, and the schools failed to realize their integrative potential, owing largely to changes in recruitment patterns and in the status and motivations of teachers. Just as the introduction of education in Southern Nigeria had as its unforeseen consequence the overthrow of the British colonial elite, so the expansion of enrollments in recent years has contributed to the overthrow of the Nigerian elite that introduced universal primary education, and to the serious problems any ruling group must face in the future. Herein lies the dilemma of popular education: it is both a necessary condition for political development and quite possibly a sufficient condition for political decay.

The two sides of this dilemma were well expressed in the conflict between Southern Nigerian politicians and British civil servants in the early 1950's over the wisdom of introducing universal primary education. The African leaders dwelt almost exclusively on the program's benefits, the British on its costs. At first there was no way of reconciling the two viewpoints; each side mistrusted the other and took its own partial hold on truth for the whole truth. Once in power, however, the Nigerian elite began to modify its optimistic views, for with power went responsibility for the unforeseen as well as the intended consequences of policy, and the very magnitude of universal primary education brought the new elite quickly to grips with the financial, employment, and other problems of which the British had warned. There was no substitute for self-government in bringing about this more balanced perspective; certainly no amount of lecturing by expatriate civil servants, however well-intentioned, would change a nationalist's mind. One of the major accomplishments of self-government was to permit a synthesis of views that were in fact complementary rather than contradictory, giving the new elite an insight into both the opportunities and the dangers of rapid educational expansion.

But if this synthesis leads to a more realistic assessment of the situation, does it provide any guide to public policy? To state the dilemma of popular education in developing countries is one thing; to confront and try to resolve the dilemma is quite another. Indeed, recognizing the complex and unexpected consequences of an action can make it more difficult for a policy maker to decide what action to take. It would be tempting to assure him that the dilemma is only temporary, and that in the long run educational expansion and political development are fully compatible. But no one can guarantee that in one or two decades the positive effects of expansion will clearly outweigh the negative; administrative capacity will have increased, for example, but so will the rate of unemployment among school leavers. Moreover, policy makers cannot be expected to act on the basis of long-range forecasts, however optimistic these may be; the far-sighted statesman who thinks he can ignore short-run considerations is likely to find himself thrown out of office. The essential task of men in power is to maximize the creative potential of their environment and minimize its destructive potential, and to do this within the limits of what is politically and administratively feasible in the readily foreseeable future.

THE CREATIVE POTENTIAL OF CRISIS

The problems caused by educational expansion in Southern Nigeria would seem at first glance to deprive its leaders of the opportunity to act creatively. Yet such a view overlooks the dual nature of crisis. In certain respects a crisis severely limits freedom of choice, but in other respects it may open up a range of choices that under normal circumstances would not have been seriously considered. Furthermore, the effort to surmount a crisis can mobilize and give direction to the energies of an entire population. Leaders of developing countries who face serious educational problems therefore should not avoid these problems but rather confront them directly, trying to transform them from liabilities into assets for political development. The outlines of such a strategy of "creative transformation" for Southern Nigeria will now be sketched.

As long as Southern Nigerians regarded education as the key to individual and social progress, they gave little serious attention to the kinds of environmental changes, apart from an expansion of the school system, that would be needed to ensure modernization. As it became clear, however, that popular education had mixed consequences, and that the link between primary education and modern sector employment had been broken, a certain disillusionment about education's role set in. But this disillusionment can stimulate fresh thinking about noneducational obstacles to modernization and about the government's overall priorities.

In the author's opinion four main kinds of change are needed. First, priorities should shift from social services to directly productive activities and economic infrastructure, so that future welfare measures can be financed and school leavers usefully employed. Second, resources from the modern urban sector must be applied to the immensely difficult but necessary task of developing the traditional rural sector. Rural schools unintentionally accelerate the flight of the countryside's most talented young people to the cities, thus increasing urban-rural inequalities while at the same time creating serious problems in the overcrowded cities. What is needed is more emphasis on agricultural extension work, more mobile libraries and public health clinics, more cooperative credit and marketing facilities, more rural public works—in short, more of everything that will cause living standards in the country to rise, making more attractive the return to the land that will be necessary for most school leavers.

Third, changes are required in the nation's inequitable salary structure, one of the most pernicious legacies of colonialism. So long as the rewards for white-collar work far exceed those for technical work and farming, and so long as salaries at the top of the political-administrative hierarchy are a hundred times the nation's per capita income, no sensible allocation of manpower can take place. Fourth, there should be an active policy of creating opportunities for productive employment, with emphasis on labor-intensive rural public works—dams, irrigation ditches, feeder roads, afforestation projects, storage facilities, covered markets—and on small industry using capital-saving technology.

These changes will not be easy to carry out, for they will be opposed by many entrenched interests. But they become more feasible politically if the public, in undergoing its crisis of confidence in education, can be reoriented to consider broader environmental changes needed for political and economic development.*

How can the educational system facilitate these broader changes? In the past education has been popularly equated with formal training for young people in institutions closely linked to the modern sector of the economy. The crisis produced by the weakening of this link could prompt new thinking about informal education, adult education, and programs specifically directed at the transitional sector, where prospects for increased output and employment are in fact quite favorable. More correspondence courses, night schools, and in-service training programs could sensitize educators to the needs of people outside the classroom and thus lead to an environment-oriented curriculum. Parents who are discouraged by the low value of primary education for their children might be persuaded for the first

---

* The effect of educational expansion in raising basic questions about the environment is well illustrated by the 1966 Kericho conference in Kenya. See James Sheffield, ed., *Education, Employment, and Rural Development* (Nairobi, 1967).

time to attend adult literacy classes that directly benefit them and their communities. Programs to teach accounting methods to small businessmen or basic science to masters in the apprenticeship system could increase the transitional sector's capacity to absorb school leavers productively. Many of the school leavers might in fact be trained as agricultural, small business, or technical extension agents to provide services and information to the traditional and transitional sectors. Where to find the teachers for expanded informal educational programs may not be an insuperable problem, thanks to the large numbers of untrained primary school teachers. These persons, who are being thrust into the "unemployment market" by the graduates of teacher training colleges, are literate and have pedagogical experience, relatively low income aspirations, and—perhaps most important—rural roots. If given short courses in agriculture or public health and employed as community development workers, untrained teachers could be as important in fostering balanced rural development as their predecessors were in bringing literacy to the countryside.

A new emphasis on noneducational expenditure and on informal education means, in effect, a smaller share of the budget for primary and secondary education. Government leaders thus face the unenviable task of asking the people to pay more for their schools, most likely through fees imposed on all primary school classes. If properly planned, however, this measure need not produce the explosive reaction that the Eastern Region's government experienced in 1958. For one thing, the financial crisis caused by burgeoning educational expenditures can be a powerful weapon in convincing some segments of the populace, at least, of the necessity of fees. For another thing, official encouragement of informal and adult education programs can help blunt the charge that the government is reneging on its educational commitments. Finally, reduced government expenditure on primary education could release funds for secondary education, either by subsidies to reduce grammar school fees or by a greatly expanded scholarship program, with scholarships reserved for poor children who have attended grant-aided primary schools. The inegalitarian effects of imposing primary school fees would thus be counteracted, and made more politically feasible, by greater equality of opportunity at the post-primary level.

The priority given to educational expansion in earlier years has prevented serious work on curriculum reform. With an increasingly trained teaching force it should be possible to introduce new course content more easily. The effect of curriculum changes on cognitions, skills, and motivations can be exaggerated, but it might be useful to acquaint students with their own job prospects, for example, by basing mathematics questions on Nigeria's education and employment statistics. An important change would be to regard the school as an agency not only for dispensing information but also for gathering it—on local history and crafts, community structure, patterns of farm management, family budgets, and so forth. Even primary schools can conduct interesting research projects, the findings from which can be incorporated into the following year's syllabus. An information-gathering approach could relate schools more closely to their communities and even provide government officials with relevant data for national planning.

In many respects, then, the crises caused by educational expansion can point to new ways of fostering economic development, political capacity, and equality. But whether the creative potential of these crises can be realized depends on the outcome of a bitter struggle over the integration, or disintegration, of Nigeria. East of the Niger, hundreds of thousands have died; for the survivors, securing a decent education is among the least of their immediate goals. The war lends an air of unreality to the foregoing discussion, for it has diverted scarce resources to military ends, destroyed the patient work of generations, and pitted young people, educated at great public expense, against each other on the battlefield. Yet once the integration issue is settled, and however it is settled, government officials must confront the recurring dilemma posed by the drive for popular education. Many of the options presented here may still be open to them. Their ability to resolve the dilemma creatively will be a supreme test of leadership.

Appendixes

Southern Nigeria: A Sketch

The area referred to in this study as Southern Nigeria forms a rough rectangle of about 75,000 square miles bounded to the south by the bights of Benin and Biafra, to the west by the Republic of Dahomey, to the east by the Cameroun Republic (part of which, formerly known as the British Cameroons, was administered under the British along with Southern Nigeria), and to the north by Nigeria's Northern Region. The area is bifurcated by the Niger River, which flows into the sea through a large, marshy delta. A coastal strip between ten and sixty miles wide is covered with mangrove swamps, sand bars, and innumerable coves and rivulets. North of this is an area of tropical rain forest fifty to a hundred miles wide, succeeded by open woodland and grass savannah the farther north one travels.

The traditional African economy was based on subsistence agriculture, with some fishing along the coast and in major rivers. The last century has seen the rise of cash cropping primarily for export, the major items being cocoa and rubber in the Western Region and palm products in the Eastern. Prior to Independence the West, with its cocoa revenues, was considerably wealthier than the East. But with the recent commercial production of oil in the East, and a decline in cocoa prices, the regions' financial fortunes were reversed in the 1960–65 period.

Population figures are available, but their accuracy is open to doubt since census counts under the British were probably too low (owing to the popular association of a census with tax collection) and the official Nigerian count of 1963 is probably too high (owing to pressures within each region to inflate its own figure, thereby increasing its influence within the federal system). Estimates for Southern Nigeria totaled 8.07 million in 1921, 13.56 million in 1952–53, and 25.87 million in 1963. The 1952–53 census indicated a population of 6.08 million in the Western Region, 267,000 in Lagos Township, and 7.21 million in the Eastern Region. The tragic events since 1966—including massacres, the large-scale emigration of Easterners from the North, and the appalling losses from starvation as a war of attrition was waged east of the Niger—make it an exercise in futility to estimate how many are now living in what was once a peaceful and relatively prosperous area of West Africa.

Among the Yoruba people of the West there is a tradition, almost unique to Africa, of living in large towns. In 1952–53 some 46 per cent of the West's population lived in towns of 5,000 or more and 29 per cent lived in cities of over 20,000; comparable figures for the East were 14 per cent and 6.3 per cent. Yet the East has a considerably greater population density than the West (245 compared to 134 persons per square mile), and its Owerri Province, with 537 persons to the square mile, has been one of the most densely populated rural areas of Africa.

The Yorubas in the West and the Ibos in the East constitute about two-thirds of the population in their respective regions. The remaining third consists of a number of different groups, among them the Edo-speakers (Binis, Urhobos, Isokos, and others), Ibos, Ijaws, and Itsekiris in the West, and the Ibibios, Ijaws, Efiks, and a multitude of small groups speaking semi-Bantu languages in the East. Since the Yorubas and Ibos are the predominant peoples of Southern Nigeria, it is of interest that their political and social structures are quite dissimilar. The Yorubas tend to have well-organized, hierarchical forms of government, ranging from the *bale* (oldest male member) of an extended family compound up to the *oba* (king) of a town and the surrounding countryside. The Ibos, on the other hand, never developed institutions for handling disputes beyond the level of the village group—a cluster of villages with a common marketplace—nor have they traditionally tried to formalize and centralize power within the village. The Ibos have tended to pay more attention to achieved status and to have a more egalitarian outlook than the Yorubas.

The Student Questionnaire Project

Some of the data used in this study are based on a questionnaire administered by the author in June and July 1964 to 1,360 schoolchildren in 68 Southern Nigerian schools. Sampling procedures were as follows: Southern Nigeria was divided into nine geographical zones of roughly equal numbers of secondary grammar schools. Three grammar schools for each of the nine zones were then randomly selected from an official list of such schools; the school principals were notified of the project in advance and their cooperation was solicited. The interview team consisted of eight second-year students at the University of Ibadan, each of whom was able to speak the major vernacular in the area to which he was assigned. The interviewers visited the grammar schools selected and with the principal's approval distributed the questionnaire forms to twenty students in the top class of the school (since there were usually more than twenty students in this class, the interviewers selected twenty from the assembled group with an eye to maintaining the male–female ratio in the smaller sample). Breakdowns by top class were as follows: Sixth Form, three schools; Fifth Form, thirteen; Fourth Form, four; Third Form, seven. Students in the Third and Fourth forms were asked to respond to questions about their immediate educational and employment prospects as if they were in the Fifth Form—that is, as if they were at the next terminal point in the school system. The questionnaires were self-administered and usually took 50–60 minutes of classroom time; interviewers were present to answer questions and to pick up the completed forms. In addition, short interviews were held with the principal concerning the school's history, size, and composition, the qualifications of the teaching force, and so on.

In order to collect data quickly at lower educational levels, each interviewer was instructed to repeat the operation with twenty students in each of the top classes of the primary and secondary modern schools nearest the grammar school already selected. All primary schools covered in this way were of Standard Six level, and all secondary modern schools except one, which offered a four-year commercial course, stopped at the Modern Three level. Certain features of the project as it related to the primary and secondary modern schools should be noted. First, if the nearest lower-level school was owned by the proprietor of the selected gramar school and was obviously a "feeder" to it, then the next-nearest school was chosen. Second, only the Western and Mid-Western regions—not the Eastern Region or Lagos—had secondary modern schools in substantial numbers. Hence not 27 but only 14 such schools were covered in the sample. Third, since it was obvious that primary school students would have great difficulty comprehending many of the questions and answering them in English, a short version of the regular questionnaire was prepared for children at this level, and the interviewer (or the teacher, when necessary) read each question slowly in the vernacular to the students. Of course, allowance had to be made for the "don't know" and "no answer or unclear" categories, which figured prominently in returns from the primary schools.

Before handing out the questionnaire forms, the interviewer stressed that the questionnaire was not a test with right or wrong answers and that no student would be marked or graded on his responses (indeed, no one was asked to write his name on the form). Thus no student had to fear that the questionnaires would be shown to anyone in the school or in the government.

Unless otherwise indicated in the text, the number of students who completed questionnaires at each educational level is as follows:

Educational level	Western Region	Eastern Region	Total
Primary	300	240	540
Secondary modern	280	0	280
Secondary grammar	260	220	480
Sixth Form	40	20	60
Total	880	480	1,360

Here "Western Region" includes Lagos and the Mid-Western Region. The secondary grammar category covers students in the Third, Fourth, and Fifth forms.

Notes

Notes

Full authors' names, titles, and publication data for works cited in the Notes will be found in the Bibliography, pp. 331–46. Government publications are identified in the Notes and Bibliography by bracketed numbers and are listed in the Bibliography under Eastern Region, Great Britain, Nigeria, and Western Region.

INTRODUCTION

1. For recent discussions of modernization, particularly its political aspects, see Geertz; Shils; Pye, *Aspects of Political Development*; Kautsky; Bendix; Apter, *Politics of Modernization*; and Black.

2. Harbison and Myers, *Education, Manpower, and Economic Growth*, p. 181.

3. Speech at Sadiqi College, Tunis, June 25, 1958, quoted in Coleman, *Education and Political Development*, p. 157.

4. In India, for instance, 30% of the elementary-age population was attending school at the time of Independence in 1947; by 1960 this figure had reached 61%, and the Third Five-Year Plan projected a goal of 76% for 1966; figures cited in Weiner, *Politics of Scarcity*, p. 179. Indonesia has witnessed a spectacular educational expansion since the end of Dutch rule in 1949: secondary enrollment rose from 140,000 in 1950 to 730,000 a decade later, and by 1961 the university population had tripled to 46,000. Guinea's primary enrollments increased from 47,000 at the time of Independence in 1958 to 160,000 by 1962; figures cited in Harbison and Myers, *Manpower and Education*, pp. 177, 187, 240.

5. In 1961, 3% of the secondary school age group was enrolled in school; the conferees pledged to increase facilities to accommodate 23% by 1980. They further pledged to raise the percentage of national income devoted to education from 3% to 6%. See UNESCO and United Nations Economic Commission for Africa, especially "Outline of a Plan for African Educational Development," p. 19.

6. Vaizey; Theodore W. Schultz, *The Economic Value of Education* (New York, 1963).

7. See Harbison and Myers, *Education, Manpower, and Economic Growth* and *Manpower and Education*.

8. Stages in American thinking on foreign aid since World War II are discussed in Piper and Cole, pp. 136–40.

9. Daniel Lerner, "Toward a Communication Theory of Modernization," in Pye, *Communications and Political Development*, p. 341. For links between literacy, urbanization, and the mass media, see Lerner's *Passing of Traditional Society*, chaps. 2, 3. For the effect of literacy on the individual's perceptions, motivations, and behavior, see Everett M. Rogers and William Herzog, "Functional Literacy among Colombian Peasants," *Economic Development and Cultural Change*, XIV, 2 (Jan. 1966), 190–203. See also Jack Goody and Ian Watt, "The Consequences of Literacy," *Comparative Studies in Society and History*, V, 3 (April 1963), 304–45.

10. Some writers consider these psychological factors indispensable for initiating growth. See David McClelland, *The Achieving Society* (Princeton, N.J., 1961), and Hagen.

11. Bowman and Anderson's data on ninety countries revealed that in none of the thirty-two with literacy below 40% was 1955 per capita income up to $300. They state, "It is tempting to conclude that a literacy rate of 30 to 40 per cent is a prerequisite to incomes exceeding $200 in most cases and $300 in all." Mary Jean Bowman and C. Arnold Anderson, "Concerning the Role of Education in Development," in Geertz, pp. 251–52. For another detailed study using a similar comparative approach, see Adam Curle, "Education, Politics, and Development," *Comparative Education Review*, VII, 3 (Feb. 1964), 226–45.

12. David McClelland, "Does Education Accelerate Economic Growth?" *Economic Development and Cultural Change*, XIV, 3 (April 1966), 257–78. "Tropical countries" are omitted from McClelland's sample, though India and Pakistan are included.

13. In *Aspects of Political Development* (pp. 31–45), Pye lists ten uses of the term in the recent literature, almost all of which has been written by Americans.

14. Capacity and equality are treated along with differentiation as elements of a "development syndrome" by Pye in *ibid.*, pp. 45–48, and by Coleman in *Education and Political Development*, pp. 15–18. For a discussion of integration, see Weiner, "Political Integration," and Coleman and Rosberg, pp. 8–12.

15. As Pye has pointed out in *Politics, Personality, and Nation-Building*, fear of being incompetent frequently prevents administrators and politicians in underdeveloped countries from performing up to their potential. Obtaining academic distinction in Western-type schools has enabled many non-Westerners to outgrow an inferiority complex, though of course education of a type considered inferior might have served only to deepen self-doubt.

16. See Huntington, especially pp. 393–405.

17. For the expanding implications of equality in the English setting, see Marshall. Equality as a value for modernizers is discussed by Shils and by

Lloyd Fallers, "Equality, Modernity, and Democracy in the New States," in Geertz, pp. 158–219.

18. Almond and Verba's recent five-nation study, *The Civic Culture*, showed striking cross-country uniformities in finding that the greater a person's education the more aware he is of the activities of his government and the more likely he is to have opinions on a wide range of political topics, to engage in political discussions, to consider himself capable of influencing his government, and to join voluntary organizations. "This set of orientations," the authors conclude, "constitutes what one might consider the minimum requirements for political participation.... It is just this basic set of orientations that those of limited education tend not to have." Almond and Verba, p. 382.

19. "In almost every aspect of their social structures, the societies on which the new states must be based are characterized by a 'gap.' It is the gap between the few very rich and the mass of the poor, between the educated and the uneducated, between the townsman and the villager, between the cosmopolitan or national and the local, between the modern and the traditional, between the rulers and the ruled. It is the gap between a small group of active, aspiring, relatively well-off, educated, and influential persons in the big towns and an inert or indifferent, impoverished, uneducated, and relatively powerless peasantry." Shils, p. 30.

20. For an excellent discussion with numerous examples from Asia and Africa, see Clifford Geertz, "The Integrative Revolution: Primordial Sentiments and Civil Politics in the New States," in Geertz, pp. 105–57.

21. Educational achievement may, in fact, be a more important criterion for determining elite status in former Western colonies than in the West itself. Smythe and Smythe (p. 167) write of Nigeria: "The new elite ... can be defined as a variable group of people consisting at least potentially of all who have completed upper secondary school." Tardits, discussing the problem of defining the *évolué*, states that "the fact of having attended school is the sole criterion one can retain for distinguishing in a fairly rigorous way the traditionalist portion of the population from that which most clearly departs from ancient ways of life and values. In the opinion of people generally, the new elite is identified with the literate portion of society." Tardits, p. 11; translation supplied.

22. For recent interpretations of the role of missions, see Scanlon, and Joseph Mullin, *The Catholic Church in Modern Africa* (London, 1965).

23. This theme recurs throughout Coleman, *Education and Political Development*; see also Cowan *et al.*, pp. 14–20. Relevant comments by Touré, Nyerere, Nkrumah, and Houphouët-Boigny may be found in *ibid.*, pp. 125–39, 309–21.

24. This language may have indigenous roots—as with bahasa Indonesia, Tagalog in the Philippines, and Swahili in Tanzania—or it may be that of a colonial ruler. McCully points out the crucial role of the English language in early Indian nationalism: English united the educated class across vernacular lines, enabled this class to communicate directly with colonial authorities, and facilitated the spread of knowledge about events in Great Britain. For a discussion of language problems in the new states, with special reference to India and Malaysia, see LePage.

25. The integrative role of early elite schools has been particularly noted by scholars. See the descriptions of Ecole Ponty in Morgenthau, pp. 12–20, and of Sadiqi College in Leon Carl Brown, "Tunisia," in Coleman, *Education and Political Development*, pp. 145–46, 149.

26. Nuffield Foundation and Colonial Office, p. 8.

27. Huntington; Eisenstadt, "Breakdowns of Modernization."

28. Foster, *Education and Social Change*, pp. 89–91, 133–37.

29. Elliot Berg, "Senegal, Guinea, Ivory Coast," in Harbison and Myers, *Manpower and Education*, p. 264.

30. On the problems of over-expanded educational systems, see Joseph Fischer, "The University Student in South and South-East Asia," *Minerva*, II, 1 (Autumn 1963), 39–53; J. Van Der Kroef, "Asian Education and Unemployment: The Continuing Crisis," *Comparative Education Review*, VII, 2 (Oct. 1963), 173–80; Guy Hunter, "Issues in Manpower Policy: Some Contrasts from East Africa and Southeast Asia," in Harbison and Myers, *Manpower and Education*, pp. 325–43; and Malcolm H. Kerr, "Egypt," in Coleman, *Education and Political Development*, pp. 169–94.

31. "It is clear that investment in formal schooling has less short-run economic pay-off in underdeveloped than in developed economies, so long as complementary and on-the-job training opportunities lag behind school expansion." C. Arnold Anderson, "Economic Development and Post-Primary Education," in Piper and Cole, p. 7. In Adam Curle's view, "Schools constitute only one method—though the most important in the long run— of producing a sufficient volume of educated persons for development." Curle, p. 157.

32. W. Arthur Lewis estimates that eight years of primary education for all would cost .8% of national income in the United States, 1.7% in Jamaica, 2.8% in Ghana, and 4% in Nigeria. He notes that primary school teachers' salaries are 1.5 times greater than per capita income in the U.S., three times greater in Jamaica, five in Ghana, and seven in Nigeria. "Education and Economic Development," p. 116.

33. In the words of a Nigerian economist, "The currently underdeveloped countries have learned the taste of the fruits of development before learning to plant its trees." Adebayo Adedeji, "Economic Planning in Theory and Practice," *Nigerian Journal of Economics and Social Studies*, IV (March 1962), 9.

34. Of fifty-one countries for which 1938 income data were available, 1938 income correlated 0.712 with 1955 primary enrollments while 1930 enrollments correlated 0.591 with 1955 incomes. If countries with 90% literacy or over are excluded, the first set of correlations becomes 0.568, and the second set becomes 0.205. Mary Jean Bowman and C. Arnold Anderson, "Concerning the Role of Education in Development," in Geertz, pp. 263–64.

35. The notions of multivariate causation and of a "syndrome of conditions" affecting change are elaborated by Lipset, pp. 45–76, and by Lerner in *Passing of Traditional Society*, chaps. 2, 3. Karl Deutsch employs the term "social mobilization" to refer to a cluster of changes occurring in the modernization process, such as increased exposure to the mass media, urbanization, the shift from agriculture to secondary and tertiary occupations,

an increase in literacy, higher per capita income, and so forth. See Deutsch, "Social Mobilization."

36. See, for example, Bendix; Black; and Moore.

37. Mary Jean Bowman and C. Arnold Anderson, "Concerning the Role of Education in Development," in Geertz, p. 253.

38. In 1835 Charles Trevelyan defended English education for the Indian elite thus: "Educated in the same way, interested in the same objects, engaged in the same pursuits with ourselves, they become more English than Hindus, just as the Roman provincials became more Roman than Gauls or Italians." Quoted in McCully, p. 72.

39. McCully (pp. 99–100) quotes a resolution on education by the Lieutenant-Governor of India in 1853–54: "It is a remarkable circumstance, and one much to be regretted, that so few of the higher classes, or of the superior native officers in the different branches of administration, have as yet seen sufficient prospect of benefit, to induce them to send their children into the Anglo-vernacular colleges under the Government." The British hoped that university education, established in 1857, would attract the scions of the Indian aristocracy. But in Bengal, "far from possessing wealth, the majority of the student class . . . belonged to families of moderate and less than moderate means. . . . Many of them actually lived from hand to mouth." *Ibid.*, p. 188. Foster notes in *Education and Social Change* that in southern Ghana the British dutifully recruited the sons of chiefs into the early government schools, not realizing that under the matrilineal system of the Akan the sons of chiefs were not eligible for high traditional office!

40. Kautsky, p. 45.

41. Geertz, pp. 125–26. For specific illustrations see LePage; Selig Harrison, *India: The Most Dangerous Decades* (Princeton, N.J., 1960), pp. 55–95, 278–84; W. Howard Wriggins, "Impediments to Unity in a New Nation: The Case of Ceylon," *American Political Science Review*, LV, 2 (June 1961), 313–20; Joseph Oduho and William Deng, *The Problem of the Southern Sudan* (London, 1963); articles on Tunisia and Egypt in Coleman, *Education and Political Development*; and Philip Foster, "Ethnicity and the Schools in Ghana," *Comparative Education Review*, VI, 2 (Oct. 1962), 127–35.

42. For example, Edmund King's introduction to L. John Lewis, *Society, Schools, and Progress* (p. xi) fails to take into account the restrictions imposed by environment on educational development: "The less settled educational patterns of 'developing countries' . . . make it easier for them to be radical. They can bypass the institutions, methods and curricula of older-established school systems in their eager pursuit of unprecedented but valid objectives." The approach of Harbison and Myers in *Education, Manpower, and Economic Growth* is far more sophisticated and openly admits that "the range of realistic choices in developing formal education is narrowly limited by economic, political, and social imperatives" (p. 17 and *passim*). Yet their general tendency is to base "strategies of human resource development" on the stocks and flows of manpower obtaining in a given country, rather than on other variables that might seriously affect the impact of existing manpower on the environment.

43. L. John Lewis, *Education and Political Independence*, p. 99.

44. Coleman, *Education and Political Development*, p. 8. See *ibid.*, pp. 6–13, for an interesting discussion of the reasons for this neglect. Recent attempts to remedy the situation have been made by Coleman; Piper and Cole; and Almond and Verba. Almond and Verba's *Civic Culture* was inspired by Charles E. Merriam's earlier work, *The Making of Citizens: A Comparative Study of Methods of Civic Training* (Chicago, 1931).

45. A number of recent books provide detailed accounts of the geography, history, anthropology, and political evolution of Southern Nigeria: Buchanan and Pugh; Hodgkin, *Nigerian Perspectives*; Crowder; Forde; Forde and Jones; Bradbury; Coleman, *Nigeria*; Ezera; and Schwarz.

CHAPTER 1

Epigraph: Isaac Watts, "Praise to God for Learning to Read," in *Divine and Moral Songs for Children* (New York, 1866), p. 34.

1. The most important discussion of missionary activity in Nigeria is Ajayi's *Christian Missions*. Other general discussions include Coleman, *Nigeria*, pp. 91–112; Solaru; and David B. Abernethy, "Nigeria," in Scanlon, pp. 197–244. For descriptions of Methodist missionary work, see Methodist Church, *Foundation Conference*, and Fox. For the Anglicans, see Dike, *Origins of the Niger Mission*, and Epelle. The Southern Baptists are discussed in Florin, and the Church of Scotland (Presbyterian) Mission, in McFarlan. For the Roman Catholic Mission, see Bane; Jordan; Walsh; and Sanni.

2. McFarlan, p. 72.

3. Minute, Dec. 21, 1840, quoted in Ronald Robinson and John Gallagher, with Alice Denny, *Africa and the Victorians: The Official Mind of Imperialism* (London, 1961), p. 16.

4. See, for example, A. F. C. Ryder, "Missionary Activity in the Kingdom of Warri to the Early Nineteenth Century," *Journal of the Historical Society of Nigeria*, II (Dec. 1960), 1–26. In both Benin and Warri these early efforts lapsed.

5. This theme is by no means confined to nineteenth-century missionaries. In 1946, McFarlan (p. 34) wrote of an early school established by the Church of Scotland in Calabar: "The children had almost everything to learn but evil."

6. This consideration figured in the choice of Dahomey during the 1850's by the founder of the Société des Missions Africaines de Lyon, who "had the courageous thought of devoting himself to the most abandoned people of Africa." Abbé E. Desribes, *L'Evangile au Dahomey et à la Côte des Esclaves (ou Histoire des missions africaines de Lyon)* (Clermont-Ferrand, 1877), p. 42; translation supplied. Through the writings of Sir Richard Burton, F. E. Forbes, and others, nineteenth-century Europeans came to identify the Kingdom of Dahomey with arbitrary, despotic rule. Similar reasoning figured in the decision by the Church of Scotland to establish a mission in Arochuku, site of the famous "long juju" that had played a prominent part in the Cross River slave trade. See MacFarlan, pp. 105–10.

7. For Buxton's and Venn's ideas, see J. F. Ade Ajayi, "Henry Venn and the Policy of Development," *Journal of the Historical Society of Nigeria*, I (Dec. 1959), 331–42, and Webster, "Bible and Plough."

8. Quoted in McFarlan, p. 9.

9. Dike, *Origins of the Niger Mission*, pp. 6–10.

10. For a description of this penetration and of African reactions, see Dike, *Trade and Politics*.

11. Biobaku, p. 58.

12. Ajayi, *Christian Missions*, p. 52. Kopytoff discusses in detail the role of these emigrants in the evolution of Nigeria.

13. Kopytoff, p. 51.

14. Webster, "Bible and Plough."

15. Rev. Henry Townsend, quoted in Biobaku, p. 37.

16. See the brief biography of Crowther in Dike *et al.*, *Eminent Nigerians*, pp. 49–58. Also, see Dike, *Origins of the Niger Mission*.

17. Quoted in Dike *et al.*, *Eminent Nigerians*, p. 54. Rev. J. C. Taylor, an Ibo ex-slave from Sierra Leone, staffed the 1857 station at Onitsha. Epelle (p. 25) mentions several other Africans trained in Sierra Leone who were active in Eastern Nigeria during the late nineteenth and early twentieth centuries.

18. Dike, *Origins of the Niger Mission*, p. 18.

19. Quoted in *ibid.*, p. 13.

20. Quoted in Webster, *African Churches*, p. 128.

21. Coleman, *Nigeria*, p. 98

22. See Ajayi and Smith; Biobaku; and Newbury.

23. See Dike, *Trade and Politics*; G. I. Jones.

24. Macrae.

25. See Great Britain [6], *Commission Report on Fears of Minorities*, pp. 18–19. The Commission (on p. 19) counters the accusation as applied to secondary schools with a reference to mission history: "That there should be a greater number of secondary schools provided by voluntary agencies in the Yoruba areas is due to the fact that missionary bodies started to build schools a century ago and that their efforts were mainly in Yoruba country; this was because with limited funds and staff they could not cover the whole country at once."

26. For the distinction between these two approaches, see Wise, pp. 15–17.

27. A description of such activities among the Isoko of Delta Province is given by Alfred Lion Odhogbi, "A Study of the History of the C.M.S. Mission Schools in Isokoland" (B.A. thesis, Harden College of Education, Univ. of Nigeria, Nsukka, 1964), pp. 6–7.

28. Letter from M. Wauters to C. Sanni, May 26, 1961, quoted in Sanni, p. 143.

29. Sanni, p. 193.

30. Bishop Shanahan, quoted in Jordan, p. 32.

31. Bishop Shanahan to Cardinal Gotti in a 1912 report, quoted in *ibid.*, p. 90.

32. Bishop Shanahan, quoted in *ibid.*, p. 94.

33. Jordan, pp. 194–95.

34. Ojike's autobiography, *My Africa*, graphically illustrates the phenomenon of upward mobility and its relation to mission education.

35. Henry Venn, quoted in Ajayi, *Christian Missions*, p. 176.

36. For a discussion of these developments, see Solaru.

37. These figures include a few hundred Europeans. Talbot, p. 134; Awani-Alele, p. 118.

38. "Memorial to General Secretaries and Committee of the Wesleyan Missionary Society, January 27, 1874," quoted in Wesleyan Boys' High School, *Jubilee Souvenir* (Lagos, 1928), pp. 9–10.

39. The results of the first, and most important, conference are summarized in a letter from Rev. J. K. Macgregor at Hope Waddell to the Provincial Secretary, Calabar, Nov. 9, 1910 (National Archives, Enugu, E. Ref. 3231/10, Rivers Province 2/4/108).

40. Examples from interviews with Canon Hawkins of the Anglican Cathedral, Onitsha, Aug. 26, 1964, and with Father Woulfe, Catholic Education Secretary, Onitsha, Aug. 27, 1964.

41. Talbot, p. 108.

42. In 1919 the ratio of Christians to Muslims was one to three west of the Lagos-to-Kano railroad, where most missionary work had been carried out, whereas it was one to one in Yoruba country east of the railroad. Webster, *African Churches*, p. 98.

43. *Ibid.*, p. 43; Kopytoff, pp. 236–43.

44. The independent religious movements among the Yorubas are described in great detail by Webster in *African Churches*.

45. Hodgkin, *Nationalism*, p. 23. For the political dimensions of separatism, see *ibid.*, pp. 93–114, and Bengt Sundkler, *Bantu Prophets in South Africa*, 2d ed. (London, 1962).

46. Ajayi, "Nineteenth Century Origins," p. 197.

47. Bretton, p. 163.

48. Information from interviews with D. O. Opoko, Principal, Elementary Training Centre, and O. Onokala, Principal, Secondary School, Uzuakoli, July 21, 1964.

49. Epelle.

50. Jordan, p. 246.

51. Quoted in *ibid.*, p. 156.

CHAPTER 2

Epigraph: Phillipson, p. 67.

1. Arnold Toynbee has developed the notion of cultural "strands," with varying capacities to penetrate other cultures, in *The World and the West* (London, 1953), pp. 67–70.

2. Read, pp. 105–11.

3. *Ibid.*, p. 110.

4. Adogbeji Salubi, "The Origins of Sapele Township," *Journal of the Historical Society of Nigeria*, II (Dec. 1960), 127.

5. "Half-Yearly Report on Aba District, June, 1911" (National Archives, Enugu, E. Ref. 227/11, Rivers Province 2/5/76).

6. Letter from Crowther to Venn, Dec. 2, 1858, quoted in Ajayi, *Christian Missions*, pp. 135–36.

7. Nigeria [5], *Annual Report, 1931*, p. 10.

8. Read, p. 100.

9. For discussions of the bush school as it operated in West Africa, see Mark Hanna Watkins, "The West African 'Bush' School," in George D. Spindler, ed., *Education and Culture: Anthropological Approaches* (New York, 1963), pp. 426–43.

10. Ojike, pp. 10, 13, 17.

11. Such an instance is given in Lloyd, *Yoruba Land Law*, pp. 104–5.

12. Talbot, pp. 9–10, 132–34.

13. European missionary work among the Yorubas has been concentrated along or to the west of the railway line between Lagos and Ogbomosho. In 1921 this area contained about 90,000 Christians. East of the railway, where the serious conversion efforts of African religious leaders did not begin until the 1890's, the Christian population in 1921 numbered 105,000. Webster, *African Churches*, p. 97.

14. McFarlan, p. 133. Cf. Roland Oliver's remarkably similar description of the Baganda in *The Missionary Factor in East Africa* (London, 1952), pp. 184–87.

15. McFarlan, p. 132.

16. Jordan.

17. Talbot, p. 131.

18. The 1910 official report for Bonny District noted: "The Bonny chiefs do not send as many boys to the [government] school as they might easily do, making the excuse that on the completion of their education they lose control over the members of their houses who usually enter the Government Service and pay no tax to the Head of the house as they would be compelled to do if they were employed as traders." "Annual Report for Bonny District, 1910" (National Archives, Enugu, E. Ref. 2072/10, Rivers Province 2/4/62).

19. Murray, p. 83.

20. A. K. Ajisafe, *History of Abeokuta* (Bungay, Suffolk, 1924), p. 92, quoted in Awani-Alele.

21. McFarlan, p. 110.

22. See Foster's study of education in Ghana, *Education and Social Change*, pp. 38–70 and *passim*.

23. The role of village pride, and of fear that a village will be shamed if its new school is moved elsewhere, is mentioned in Green (p. 29). An instance of rivalry on a wider scale is discussed by Lloyd, who feels that early mass conversions among the Ijebu "seem to have stemmed principally from the fear of the Ijebu that they were falling behind other Yoruba." Lloyd, *Yoruba Land Law*, p. 141.

24. McFarlan, p. 117.

25. *Ibid.*, p. 135.

26. Michael Obafemi Olomolaiye, "A Study of the Historical Development of Primary Education in Ilesha" (B.A. thesis, Harden College of Education, Univ. of Nigeria, Nsukka, 1964).

27. Sanni.

28. By 1921 the African Church movement had developed into five major denominations claiming the adherence of one-third of the Yoruba Christians and one-fifth of the total Christian population of Southern Nigeria. Webster, *African Churches*, pp. 42, 47.

29. See Webster, *African Churches* and "Bible and Plough."

30. Forde and Jones, *The Ibo*, p. 83. For a discussion of Egbado and Ibibio efforts to catch up to their neighbors, see Chapter 4, pp. 109–11 below.

31. Uchendu (p. 38) stresses the importance of village loyalty, and of

rivalry with neighboring villages, as a key element in the progressive orientation of the Ibos: "For the [Ibos], helping the town 'to get up' is nothing short of an obsession."

32. Simon Ottenberg, "Ibo Receptivity to Change," in Bascom and Herskovits, pp. 130–43; Eyo B. E. Ndem, *Ibos in Contemporary Nigerian Politics: A Study in Group Conflict* (Onitsha, 1961); Levine.

33. Apter, *Politics of Modernization*, pp. 83–106 *passim*. Apter cites both Ashanti and the traditional kingdom of Dahomey as societies with consummatory values. Dahomeans, however, proved remarkably receptive to change; they quickly perceived the advantages of schooling and since the beginning of this century have occupied many civil service and minor clerical posts throughout French West Africa. Whether even the Ashantis' values are consummatory is a debatable question, when one considers their willingness to take up cocoa farming while simultaneously preserving other aspects of their traditional culture.

34. Apter has stated that instrumental values and hierarchical structures tend to be found together, as do consummatory values and pyramidal structures. Thus, he argues, differences in Baganda and Ashanti responses are due to a particular mixture of values and structures. Apter, "Role of Traditionalism," pp. 45–68. In *The Politics of Modernization* he presents a wider discussion of the combinations of value systems and authority structures that are possible. For other suggestive hypotheses, see Ethel Albert, "Socio-Political Organization and Receptivity to Change: Some Differences between Ruanda and Burundi," *Southwestern Journal of Anthropology* (Spring 1960), pp. 46–74.

35. Foster, *Education and Social Change*, p. 247.

36. Williams; McCully.

37. J. S. Trimingham, *Islam in West Africa* (Oxford, 1959), p. 222, quoted in Sklar, p. 247.

38. The strong early-twentieth-century trend toward Christianity east of the railroad has already been noted. Yet as Lloyd observes, "East of Ibadan the commerical revolution, at its present intensity, had . . . scarcely begun before the [Second World] War and only since 1945 had the new wealth begun to change the economy of these towns." Lloyd, "Local Government," p. 51.

39. See Helleiner.

40. See Walsh for a discussion of the phenomenon in Nigeria, and Foster for Ghana. Of the early efforts of Fanti traders to open and maintain schools, Foster notes (p. 100): "There is not one instance of African funds actually being utilized for the support of industrial or agricultural institutions." By 1900, however, four academic secondary schools totally staffed and financed by Africans were operating in the Gold Coast.

41. Undocumented criticisms of this sort are scattered liberally throughout Ikejiani.

42. Shils, p. 18.

CHAPTER 3

1. J. C. Anene, "The Protectorate Government of Southern Nigeria and the Aros, 1900–1902," *Journal of the Historical Society of Nigeria*, I (Dec. 1956), 23.

2. Commenting on the official census of 1921, P. A. Talbot notes (p. 3) that "one great disadvantage under which the census laboured was the scarcity of educated and trustworthy clerks." A Nigerian historian, Chief T. A. Salubi, observed in writing about early administration in Urhobo country that the "scarcity of court clerks was one of the difficulties that faced the working of the native court system in the early stages." Adogbeji Salubi, "The Establishment of British Administration in the Urhobo Country (1891–1913)," *Journal of the Historical Society of Nigeria*, I (Dec. 1956), 23.

3. Lugard, p. 61. In 1905 Lugard even imported ten clerks from India for distribution among various departments. Walsh, p. 290.

4. Foster, *Education and Social Change*, p. 108, n. 40.

5. The best sources here are Walsh; Wise; and Awani-Alele.

6. National Archives, Enugu, E. Ref. 3369/09, Rivers Province 2/3/117.

7. Governor Carter of Lagos wrote in 1892: "It will take a long time before the Moslem population will take any initiative in this matter [education]. If anything is to be accomplished it must be by direct government intervention—a proper school must be established with proper teachers who would be Moslems." Letter from Governor Carter to Lord Knutsford, 16/8/92, quoted in Walsh, p. 172.

8. Phillipson, in *Grants in Aid of Education in Nigeria*, dates the commencement of grants-in-aid at 1877, but Walsh (p. 26) insists on 1872.

9. Phillipson, p. 15.

10. There were about 400 unassisted schools operating in 1913, as compared to 80 mission schools benefiting from grants-in-aid and only about 40 schools directly administered by the government. Great Britain, *Colonial Annual Report for Southern Nigeria, 1913*, p. 17, cited in Awani-Alele.

11. The French administrators' fear of Catholic influence was expressed in the official report on Dahomean education for 1911: "Most of the native functionaries now working for us are fully devoted to the [Catholic] Fathers whose pupils they once were. This is a stranglehold on the administration which could pose some danger." Dahomey, *Rapport annuel sur le service de l'enseignement pendant l'année 1911* (Porto Novo, 1912), p. 1; translation supplied. The Lieutenant-Governor of Dahomey wrote in 1910 of "the financial sacrifices that would have to be made ... to replace mission by lay instruction" and spoke of a future day when "provided with teaching personnel better prepared for the struggle we may be able to oppose school against school in those centers where mission education is most strongly organized." Letter from Lieutenant-Governor of Dahomey to Governor-General, French West Africa, Nov. 24, 1910 (Archives Nationales, Dakar), Vol. J-26, pp. 8–10; translation supplied. Replacement of the mission effort was estimated at 500 million c.f.a. francs, which was admittedly an impossible sum to spend in view of Dahomey's financial situation. In French Equatorial Africa relations with the Catholic Church were more cordial.

12. In the classic words of French West Africa's Governor-General Brévié in 1930, the French desired "the evolution of a real elite, marked by outstanding personality and impeccable dependability, and bound to us by the realization of the friendly nature of the motives by which we are actuated." Quoted in Mumford and Orde-Brown, p. 95.

13. For descriptions of the Yoruba rebellions and the Aba Women's Riots, see Perham, *Native Administration*, pp. 77–78, 201–20. For the troubles in

Sapele and Warri, and a general account of tax policy in Western Nigeria, see Orewa, *Taxation*.

14. Lugard, p. 60.

15. Quoted in Perham, *Lugard*, p. 489.

16. See *ibid.*, pp. 581–606. Fearful that the Lagos elite would use the advisory Legislative Council as a forum for spreading dissension, Lugard in 1914 reduced the council's zone of responsibility from Southern Nigeria to Lagos and Colony. Governor Clifford, operating under some pressure, restored the position of the council in 1923 and permitted Nigerians to elect four of its African members—three from Lagos, one from Calabar.

17. Lugard, p. 19.

18. *Ibid.*, p. 59.

19. Clifford, pp. 199–200.

20. Lugard's 1916 education code, which had as its "primary object... the formation of character and habits of discipline," viewed the Christian religion in strictly utilitarian terms as "an agent for this purpose." Lugard, p. 62.

21. Nigeria [5], *Annual Report, 1929*, p. 44.

22. A. Victor Murray was dubious, to say the least, about the value in Africa of such books as Samuel Smiles's *Self-Help and My Duties*. Smiles, he commented sardonically, "fails to co-ordinate the ideal British shopkeeping qualities with the divine government of the universe." Murray, p. 180.

23. Thomas Jesse Jones, *Education in Africa* and *Education in East Africa*. For an abridged version see L. John Lewis, *Phelps-Stokes Reports*.

24. Great Britain [3], *Education Policy* (1925), p. 4.

25. *Ibid.*, p. 7.

26. *Ibid.*, p. 4.

27. See Clarke for a description of an experiment among the Yorubas of Northern Nigeria.

28. Philip Foster comments extensively in *Education and Social Change* on the unintended consequences of the transfer of educational institutions from one culture to another; see especially pp. 6–10.

29. Murray, p. 309. Murray also criticized the reports for assuming that what was appropriate for the American Negro, a member of a permanent minority group, was equally appropriate for the African in his own country. For other critiques see Wilson, pp. 40–50, and Foster, *Education and Social Change*, pp. 155–66.

30. The *Gold Coast Leader* accused the Chairman of the Phelps-Stokes Commission of trying "to make the African fit in with the European's scheme of exploitation and control." Quoted in David Kimble, *A Political History of Ghana* (London, 1963), p. 114.

CHAPTER 4

1. See the general discussion in Coleman, *Nigeria*, pp. 230–67.

2. Hussey's proposals are found in Nigeria [10], *Educational Policy* (1930).

3. E. R. J. Hussey, quoted in Wise, p. 57.

4. Nigeria [10], *Educational Policy* (1930), p. 15. The pages of the semi-official quarterly *Oversea Education* were filled during the 1930's and early 1940's with curricular proposals that would presumably develop Africans

"along their own lines." For an example, see M. J. Field, "Toward Tribalized Literacy: A Suggestion," *Oversea Education*, XII (Oct. 1940), 1–4.

5. Clarke, p. 135.

6. The Education Department's expenditures, which had reached £281,000 in 1930–31, fell to £225,000 four years later, and with one year's exception did not exceed the earlier level until 1941–42. Grants-in-aid to the voluntary agencies stabilized at about £80,000 yearly from 1930–31 to 1935–36, rising somewhat to a new plateau of £100,000 by the end of the decade. These figures have been rounded off from those given in Phillipson (p. 108).

7. Official expenditure for education reached £2,400,000 by 1950–51. Whereas during the 1929–39 period, education had never absorbed over 5.5% of government expenditure, by 1949–50 it accounted for about 10%.

8. The 1945 Colonial Development and Welfare Act pledged £120,000,000 to the colonies over a ten-year period.

9. Examples were Nigeria [28], *Ten-Year Educational Plan* (1944); Nigeria [29], *Ten-Year Plan of Development* (1946), and its revision, Nigeria [27], *Revised Plan of Development, 1951–56*.

10. Nigeria [28], *Ten-Year Educational Plan* (1944), p. 29.

11. For a description and evaluation that compares the British to other colonial powers, see Niculescu.

12. These general trends are lucidly described in Emerson.

13. Great Britain [2], *Mass Education* (1944); Great Britain [1], *Education for Citizenship* (1948); Great Britain [8], *Higher Education in the Colonies* (1945); Great Britain [9], *Higher Education in West Africa* (1945).

14. Prior to 1941 only certificated teachers in assisted schools run by government-approved voluntary agencies were eligible for grants-in-aid. By 1947 funds were available to uncertificated teachers in assisted schools and to all certificated teachers, even in unapproved voluntary agencies (a category that included many Nigerian private proprietors). The government further agreed to subsidize part of the salary bill of uncertificated and probationary teachers in unassisted schools. See Phillipson, pp. 43–45, and Nigeria [5], *Annual Report, 1947*, for a longer treatment of this complicated subject.

15. Phillipson.

16. Accounts by the University's first two principals are given in Kenneth Mellanby, *The Birth of Nigeria's University* (London, 1958) and J. T. Saunders, *University College, Ibadan* (Cambridge, Eng., 1960).

17. By 1944 only 40 government scholars were studying abroad; by 1950 there were 207, and 111 scholarships were awarded in that year alone. Awani-Alele, pp. 186–87.

18. Chadwick, p. 636; see also Chadwick, "Mass Education in Udi Division," *African Affairs*, XLVII (Jan. 1948), 31–41. A film, "Daybreak at Udi," documented changes in this part of Eastern Nigeria. For a general discussion of the effect of literacy on other aspects of change, see Everett M. Rogers and William Herzog, "Functional Literacy among Colombian Peasants," *Economic Development and Cultural Change*, XIV, 2 (Jan. 1966), 190–203.

19. See the discussions in Coleman, *Nigeria*, pp. 271–95; Ezera, pp. 64–81.

20. The education estimates of the Nigerian government accordingly fell from 11.5% of its total estimated expenditure in 1948–49 to 2.1% the following year; in the same years the proportion of regional expenditure de-

voted to education rose from 8.4% to 35.2% in the West, 7.1% to 31.1% in the East, and 7.1% to 20.5% in the North. The education sector for all of these budgets combined remained at about 10% for the two years. Nigeria [5], *Annual Report, 1948*, p. 14, and *Annual Report, 1949*, p. 39.

21. See Sir Bernard Bourdillon, "The Future of Native Authorities," *Africa*, XV (April 1945), 123–28. Bourdillon was Governor of Nigeria at the time.

22. These committees were most active in the Western Region; see Western Region [3], *Local Education Committees*. Although a few similar groups were established east of the Niger—for example, in Aba, Port Harcourt, and Abakaliki—they were never very successful, perhaps because Protestant-Catholic rivalry in the East precluded effective cooperation and planning at the local level.

23. W. T. Mackell, Deputy Director of Education, in addressing the 1947 conference of the Nigeria Union of Teachers, dismissed the widespread belief among Nigerians that a tax of one shilling per head could finance universal compulsory education. He estimated the cost of four years of universal education at eight shillings per capita (N.U.T. File No. 2, Vol. 10).

24. Nigeria [5], *Annual Report, 1946*, p. 9, quoted in Awani-Alele, p. 272.

25. Phillipson, p. 67.

26. During the late 1940's the enrollment drop was estimated as 50% to 60% between the first and second years alone and as over 90% between the first and eighth years. Estimates made in a speech by S. Milburn, Deputy Director of Education, Western Provinces, to the 1949 Benin Conference of the Nigeria Union of Teachers (N.U.T. File No. 2, Vol. 11).

27. Letter from Chief Inspector of Education, Western Provinces, Sept. 27, 1947, "Primary Schools and Expansion" (mimeo., N.U.T. File No. 2, Vol. 10).

28. See Nigeria [5], *Annual Report, 1949*, pp. 18–19. Tuition and boarding expenses in voluntary agency secondary schools ranged from £16 to £38 a year.

29. Interview with Father James O'Connell, May 23, 1964.

30. Federal Association of Catholic Teachers memorandum, June 29, 1945 (Files of J. F. Odunjo).

31. Phillipson, p. 112.

32. Five Catholic secondary schools were established during the war, in Benin, Onitsha, and Calabar provinces; a postwar drive by Owerri Ibos to catch up to Ibos elsewhere led to the opening of at least six Catholic secondary schools in Owerri Province alone between 1947 and 1951.

33. Ojike, p. 74. Margery Perham records meeting a woman in Aba who spent most of her time walking with a petrol tin of palm oil from her village to one nearer the railway, where the price was slightly higher. The money thus earned went for the education of her children, for as she explained, "They [the villagers] all knew their children had no hope unless they could learn to understand the white man's ways." Perham, *Native Administration*, p. 252.

34. Chief Ekwulo Idu, Regent of Onitsha-Ugbo, Benin Province, quoted in *West African Pilot*, April 3, 1943.

35. Jackson, p. 55. *Oversea Education* and *Community Development Bulletin* contain numerous references to self-help schemes during the 1940's.

36. Coleman, *Nigeria*, p. 214. Numerous illustrations are provided in Little.

37. Jackson (pp. 97–98) discusses the advantages of the informal clan union tax system as compared with local government rating.

38. A specific instance is cited in Uzoma.

39. See Karl Deutsch, "Social Mobilization." Coleman's study, *Nigeria*, amply demonstrates the connection between social mobilization and nationalism in Nigeria.

40. There is a growing literature on this topic. See in particular Wallerstein, "Ethnicity and National Integration"; Paul Mercier, "Remarques sur la signification du 'tribalisme' actuel en Afrique noire," *Cahiers Internationaux de Sociologie*, XXXI (1961), 61–80; Jean Rouch, "Migrations au Ghana," *Journal de la Société des Africanistes*, XXVI, 19 (1956), 163–64; Epstein; J. Clyde Mitchell, *The Kalela Dance* (Manchester, 1956); Young, pp. 232–72; Little; and Leonard Plotnicov, *Strangers to the City: Urban Man in Jos, Nigeria* (Pittsburgh, Pa., 1967). Related literature for other parts of the world includes Oscar Handlin, *The Uprooted* (Boston, 1951); Ruth Trouton, *Peasant Renaissance in Yugoslavia, 1900–1950* (London, 1952); Harrison; and G. W. Skinner, *Local, Ethnic, and National Loyalties in Village Indonesia*, Yale University Cultural Report Series, No. 8 (New Haven, Conn., 1959).

41. The complementary aspects are stressed in Wallerstein, "Ethnicity and National Integration," and Azikiwe, *Tribalism*. The history of post-Independence Nigeria amply illustrates the conflicts.

42. On Azikiwe's role as a journalist, see Coleman, *Nigeria*, pp. 220–23, and Jones-Quartey, pp. 144–51.

43. Zolberg, p. 69.

44. "Efik" actually means "tyrant" or "he who oppresses," a reference to the group's role in the slave trade. Forde and Jones, p. 90. Forde and Jones classify the Efiks as Ibibio-speaking, but socially the two groups consider themselves quite distinct. For many years the Ibibios enjoyed the dubious reputation of being "more artistic, less industrious, more backward, and perhaps even more excitable than their neighbors." Perham, *Native Administration*, p. 233.

45. Biobaku, p. 20.

46. The list of the Egbado Union's early leaders is quite typical: Dudley T. Coker (contractor; grandson of a Saro), Chief S. A. Adesina (United Africa Company salesman), Isaac B. Joda (Railway Department), J. F. Odunjo (Headmaster, Catholic School, Ebute Metta; later Headmaster in Abeokuta), D. A. Fafunmi (teacher, Methodist School, Tinubu, Lagos), T. J. Adewale (native authority visiting teacher), Canon S. E. O. Soyemi (Anglican Church, Ilaro), Chief B. F. Adesola (Accountant-General's Office; ex-serviceman), and E. A. A. Fadayiro (Public Relations Office).

47. This was the first objective of the Urhobo Progress Union, quoted in Salubi, *Revolutions of Our Time*, p. 10.

48. The initial ambitions of the Ibo and Ibibio state unions were much grander: thirty and six secondary schools, respectively. But financial difficulties, coupled with power struggles among union leaders, resulted in a drastic cutback of plans.

49. The Ibibio State College Principal, I. U. Akpabio, was one of six

young men sent abroad by his union in 1938. Each person was to study a different subject—education, law, agriculture, medicine, and the like—and then return to help his people. As it turned out, only the prospective educators, Akpabio and J. L. Nsima, were able to carry out their part of the original plan, through their association with the Ibibio State College.

50. The foregoing discussion is based on interviews, personal files, school histories, and log books. I am particularly grateful to T. J. Adewale, Colin Humphrey, M. G. Ejaife, I. U. Akpabio, and B. O. N. Eluwa, and to Chiefs J. F. Odunjo, J. A. O. Odebiyi, and J. U. Eka for their cooperation.

51. Nigeria [5], *Annual Report, 1932,* pp. 31, 34, and *Annual Report, 1950,* pp. 13, 19. More than 98% of the African teachers were employed in primary schools.

52. Mbonu Ojike notes in his autobiography that schoolteachers were the first in many areas to wear trousers, a robe, and sandals. Teachers in turn insisted on a certain "civilized" standard among their charges, as the following letter from an Uzuakoli Old Boy makes clear: "We were not pleased from the beginning, to see our boys wearing native towels with ragged cloths round their necks. . . . We told them that each must possess a white singlet and a khaki drill shorts. . . . As soon as this order was carried out, there was a smiling face in the school. One of the natives who saw us at drill said, 'Our teachers make their boys neat and clean.'" "Uzuakoli Institute Old Boys' Letter," Dec. 1928, quoted in Nwosu, pp. 219–20.

53. A Church Missionary Society newsletter, *In Leisure Hours* (Vol. XXVII, No. 315, 1936), tells of two young men of the same age and ability who had left primary school ten years earlier. One started as a mission teacher at £24 a year and was earning about £73 by 1936, whereas the other entered the government teaching service at £48 and was earning close to £104 a decade later.

54. Significantly, teachers were also the first to form a union in French West Africa, in 1937. See Morgenthau, pp. 21–22.

55. Information drawn from N.U.T. File No. 2, Vols. 7–11 (1931–64). I am indebted to E. E. Esua for permission to look through this file. Invaluable assistance in reconstructing the history of the union, and in analyzing the general role of teachers in Nigerian society, was provided by Mr. Esua; Alvan Ikoku, President of the union since 1955; Oke Osanyintolu, Assistant General Secretary in 1964; Chief J. F. Odunjo; Bishop Seth Kale; and Canon E. O. Alayande.

56. Twenty-two branches were operating in the North as of 1947. When a separate body, the Northern Teachers' Association, was formed in 1948, the Nigeria Union of Teachers invited an association representative to attend its annual conference at the union's expense, with a view to cooperation and a possible merger of the two organizations.

57. Letter from E. E. Esua to E. I. Oli, Hon. Secretary, C.M.S. Niger Mission Teachers' Conference, Dec. 12, 1934 (N.U.T. File No. 2, Vol. 7).

58. A union memorandum submitted in 1934 to C. C. Adeniyi-Jones of the Nigerian Legislative Council concludes that "so long as [mission] teachers are treated as belonging to a class which must not only suffer but also suffer to any extent, reasonable or unreasonable, it will be absolutely impossible to attract the best brains in the country into the profession" (N.U.T. File No. 2, Vol. 7).

59. Nigeria Union of Teachers Presidential Address, quoted in *Nigerian Daily Times*, Jan. 11, 1936.

60. The Department of Education estimated in 1936 that paying mission teachers at the same rate as government teachers would cost £ 100,000, which would almost double that year's grant-in-aid bill. Nigeria [5], *Annual Report, 1936*, p. 16.

61. Coleman, *Nigeria*, pp. 153–54.

62. This fascinating episode is recorded in N.U.T. File No. 8, Vol. 1.

63. Interview with Alvan Ikoku, July 22, 1964.

64. Lucian Pye has characterized the "non-Western political process" as having "relatively few explicitly organized interest groups with functionally specific roles" and as operating "largely without benefit of political 'brokers.'" Pye, "The Non-Western Political Process," in Eckstein and Apter, pp. 662, 664; see also Weiner, *Politics of Scarcity*.

65. Quoted in Sampson, pp. 89–90.

66. Nnamdi Azikiwe to Dr. T. J. Jones, Director, Phelps-Stokes Fund, June 16, 1928, quoted in Jones-Quartey, p. 249.

67. Coleman, *Nigeria*, p. 218.

68. This episode is described in some detail in Sklar, pp. 56–57.

69. These men included Rev. L. R. Potts-Johnson (Enitonna High School, Port Harcourt, 1932), Alvan Ikoku (Aggrey Memorial College, Arochuku, 1933), Eyo Ita (Ogbomosho People's Institute, Ogbomosho, 1938; National Institute, Calabar, 1938), and O. L. Oyesina (Ibadan Boys' High School, 1938).

70. Quoted in Awolowo, *Awo*, p. 123.

71. N.U.T. File No. 2, Vol. 8.

72. *Legislative Council Debates* (Lagos, 1949), March 1949, pp. 673–84.

CHAPTER 5

1. For a discussion of the Macpherson constitution, see Ezera, pp. 105–75. Coleman summarizes the principal features of the constitutions of 1951, 1954, and 1957 in *Nigeria*, p. 372.

2. See Sklar, pp. 101–7, for a discussion of the formation of the Action Group.

3. *Ibid.*, p. 35. The Western Region figures changed somewhat over time as elected members changed their party affiliation. By the first meeting of the House of Assembly, in January 1952, forty-nine members had declared for the Action Group. *Ibid.*, p. 116.

4. Quoted in Awolowo, *Awo*, p. 263. The region's development plan for 1955–60 adhered to the policy of giving first priority to social welfare measures: "The primary function of a Government is the provision of those public services without which individual effort and initiative would be futile—education and health services, water, electrical energy, and that network of communications without which private enterprise could not flourish.... That is why the present Government of the Western Region makes the expansion of the education and health services its first object of policy." Western Region [2], *Development, 1955–60*, pp. 8–9. Expenditure projections for 1955–60 called for an outlay of £ 104.8 million, of which £ 34 million—by far the largest single amount—was for education. *Ibid.*, p. 17.

5. Western Region [13], *Proposals for an Education Policy* (1952), p. 5.

6. *Ibid.*, p. 22.

7. For Awokoya's speech, see Western Region [5], *Debates*, July 30, 1952, pp. 463–70.

8. Eastern Region [13], *Policy for Education* (1953); Eastern Region [14], *Policy for Introduction of U.P.E.* (1953).

9. Eastern Region [13], *Policy for Education* (1953), pp. 3, 4.

10. Western Region [12], *U.P.E.* (1955), p. 2.

11. Western Region [5], *Debates*, Dec. 20, 1954, pp. 97–98.

12. Western Region [7], *Education Statistics, 1953–58*, pp. 15, 30; Western Region [17], *Triennial Report on Education, 1955–58*, p. 41. The 5–14 age group is estimated at 20% of the census figure, with allowance for a 3% growth rate.

13. On grants-in-aid, see Western Region [10], *Annual Report, 1954–55*, p. 22.

14. Western Region [10], *Annual Report, 1954–55*, p. 24; Western Region, Ministry of Information, *Western Nigeria Quiz*, 3d ed. (Ibadan, n.d.), p. 38.

15. Eastern Region [10], *Education and U.P.E.* (1957), p. 1.

16. Michael Ogon, in Eastern Region [4], *Debates*, March 22, 1957, pp. 42–43.

17. Eastern Region [6], *Annual Report, 1957*, p. 10, and *Annual Report, 1956*, p. 28; Dike Report, p. 11.

18. Eastern Region [6], *Annual Report, 1956*, p. 33, and *Annual Report, 1957*, p. 32. These figures are not based on the fiscal year, hence the proportion they constitute of the total regional expenditure can be only roughly calculated. That figure was £6.7 million for 1955–56 and £12.6 million for 1956–57.

19. O. A. Akitoye, "The Need for Self-Government," *Daily Service*, July 13, 1950.

20. Western Region [5], *Debates*, July 14–15, 1952, pp. 21–65.

21. Western Region [13], *Proposals for an Education Policy* (1952), p. 10.

22. Awokoya, p. 5.

23. Western Region [13], *Proposals for an Education Policy* (1952), p. 6.

24. These themes were sounded insistently by Eyo Ita in pamphlets written during the 1930's and 1940's; see, for example, *Two Vital Fronts* and *Decade of National Education Movement.*

25. Awolowo, *Awo*, p. 268. See also Awolowo's speech "Education for Citizenship," reported in the *Daily Service*, April 16, 1952, and Awokoya's remarks in Western Region [13], *Proposals for an Education Policy* (1952), p. 26.

26. Edward Shils has written extensively about the populism of elites in the new states. See Shils, *Political Development in the New States*, and "The Intellectuals in the Political Development of the New States," in Kautsky, pp. 195–234. A perceptive essay on the ambivalent attitude of elites about their own people is Mary Matossian's "Ideologies of Delayed Industrialization: Some Tensions and Ambiguities," in Kautsky, pp. 252–64.

27. Eastern Region [17], *Self-Government* (1957), p. 6.

28. Western Region [14], *Educational System Review, 1960–61*, p. 30.

29. These observations are in accord with a recent tendency among politi-

cal scientists to emphasize the weakness of African political parties, even those parties of a supposedly "mass" or "revolutionary-centralizing" nature. See Zolberg; Bienen.

30. Awolowo, *Path to Nigerian Freedom*, p. 32.

31. Philip Whitaker, "The Western Region of Nigeria, May 1956," in Mackenzie and Robinson, p. 22.

32. Sklar, p. 465.

33. Victor Uchendu (p. 38) has observed of the Ibos: "For the mass of the people, good government is synonymous with good roads, schools, maternity homes, and post offices. It is around these that local and national politics revolve."

34. Philip Whitaker, "The Western Region of Nigeria, May 1956," in Mackenzie and Robinson, p. 27.

35. See Ezera, p. 135, Table 8, for the composition of the 1951 assemblies. Five of the Western and eight of the Eastern teachers were secondary school principals. The totals of eighty-seven and eighty-eight include European and nominated members. Cf. Gold Coast legislators as described in J. H. Price, *West Africa*, No. 2041 (May 26, 1956), pp. 324–25.

36. Leaders of the Nigeria Union of Teachers who were interviewed by the author in 1964 claimed that they found it no easier, and sometimes more difficult, to press their case among legislators with a teaching background than among those with other backgrounds. For further comments, see David B. Abernethy, "Teachers in Politics: The Southern Nigerian Case," in Joseph Fischer, ed., *The Social Sciences and the Comparative Study of Education* (Scranton, Pa., forthcoming).

37. Ezera, p. 146. Ezera (p. 151) aptly describes the 1951 constitution as a "curious blend of regional subordination to the centre in matters of legislation and finance with a corresponding federal dependence on the regions arising out of the relations between central Ministers and their parties and the regional character of the parties themselves."

38. Western Region [13], *Proposals for an Education Policy* (1952), p. 17; Eastern Region [6], *Annual Report, 1960*, Chart 7. Estimates of the school-age population were made prior to the 1952–53 census.

39. *Daily Service*, Jan. 26, 1953.

40. J. F. Odunjo, in Western Region [5], *Debates*, Jan. 24, 1953, p. 157. Later, when campaigning in the region for acceptance of the levy, Awolowo was asked why Azikiwe favored only 2/6 shillings rather than 10/6. "The truth is simple," he replied. "Azikiwe wants the West to be outdone in the race for education, and we must not fall victims to his retoflex [*sic*] propaganda." Quoted in the *Daily Service*, Oct. 7, 1953.

41. Sklar, pp. 396–98, n. 38, and p. 116.

42. *Ibid.*, pp. 119–24.

43. *Ibid.*, p. 268.

44. Action Group publicists estimated that the West contributed 40–45% of central government revenue during the 1945–54 period but received only 27% of that revenue during 1948–51 and 36% during 1952–54. Figures taken from the Action Group review of the Chick Report, *Daily Service*, Jan. 13, 1954.

45. Hazlewood, p. 13.

46. Carney, p. 109.

47. International Bank for Reconstruction and Development, pp. 169–70.

48. Sklar, p. 449, n. 25.

49. Eastern Region [4], *Debates*, May 16, 1955, pp. 78–79. On universal primary education in the Federal Territory, see Nigeria [25], *Educational Development in Lagos* (1957).

50. Dike Report, p. 8.

51. *Ibid.*, p. 9.

CHAPTER 6

1. The policy paper was printed in the *Daily Service*, May 12, 1951.

2. Awokoya observed in 1952: "To restrict the benefits of this great social service to only the parents of pupils in Primary One would occasion great dissatisfaction among the majority of parents who contribute directly toward educational services by way of rates." Western Region [13], *Proposals for an Education Policy* (1952), p. 19.

3. See R. A. Agbajeola, "The Farmers and Compulsory Education," *Daily Service*, April 4 and 5, 1952, for misgivings in this regard.

4. Sklar, pp. 278–79.

5. Western Region [5], *Debates*, Dec. 20, 1954, p. 98.

6. See Nigeria [5], *Annual Report, 1952*, p. 26. The view that the universal primary education program planned by the West was premature, as well as too expensive, was also held by the International Bank mission to Nigeria. See International Bank for Reconstruction and Development, p. 572.

7. Estimates of the school-age population contained in Western Region [13], *Proposals for an Education Policy* (1952), were based on admittedly unreliable tax return data; Awokoya warned that his calculations were "based on assumptions which may be totally falsified by the forthcoming census." *Ibid.*, p. 18. The 1952 census figures, in turn, probably undercounted the actual population.

8. C.M.S. Ibadan File A34-B, 1954.

9. Descriptions of the district planning committees may be found in Crookall and in Adetunji.

10. This view was reinforced by the conclusions of the 1952 Cambridge Conference on African Education, which several Nigerian politicians and civil servants attended. See Nuffield Foundation and Colonial Office, pp. 51, 143–47.

11. Y. P. O. Shodeinde, "Have Muslims Been Fairly Treated?" *Daily Service*, March 15, 1952. The Muslim Welfare Association of Nigeria, formed in April 1952, threatened to wage an "education *jihad*" against the government for its alleged grant-in-aid discrimination. See *Daily Service*, April 24, 1952. See also the bitter speech given in the House of Assembly by trade union leader Alhaji H. P. Adebola in Western Region [5], *Debates*, Feb. 3, 1953, pp. 351–60.

12. Western Region [13], *Proposals for an Education Policy* (1952), p. 15.

13. Awokoya's estimates are taken from *ibid.*, appendixes B and C. Actual figures are taken from Western Region [7], *Education Statistics, 1953–58*, p. 30.

14. Argument paraphrased in Sklar, p. 300. Sklar notes (p. 300, n. 30): "This is a perplexing argument in view of the fact that the vast majority of Ibadan people have not had the benefit of any education and object to the local rates which include an education levy."

15. Western Region [5], *Debates*, Dec. 20, 1954, p. 111.

16. *Ibid.*, Jan. 24, 1953, p. 166. Awolowo's justification of the levy is given in *ibid.*, Jan. 23, 1953, pp. 135–47.

17. Interview with Peter Lloyd, Nov. 10, 1963.

18. See Sklar, pp. 235–38, for details.

19. Awolowo, *Awo*, pp. 275–76. For the election and the anti-tax groups, see Sklar, p. 35 and p. 257, n. 67.

20. Western Region [8], *Education Statistics, 1955–60*, p. 51.

21. Western Region [13], *Proposals for an Education Policy* (1952), Appendix A.

22. *Daily Times*, April 23, 1956, quoted in Philip Whitaker, "The Western Region of Nigeria, May 1956," in Mackenzie and Robinson, p. 41.

23. Quoted in *Daily Service*, Jan. 31, 1953.

CHAPTER 7

1. Eastern Region [14], *Policy for Introduction of U.P.E.* (1953), p. 2.

2. *Ibid.*, p. 8.

3. Ezera, pp. 217–20.

4. Eastern Region [6], *Annual Report, 1956*, p. 2.

5. Ezera, p. 259.

6. *Daily Times*, Jan. 11, 1955.

7. Eastern Region [4], *Debates*, June 26, 1956, p. 75.

8. Eastern Region [3], *Education Law*, paras. 10–42.

9. Dike Report, p. 23.

10. Interview with J. C. Menakaya, July 2, 1964.

11. Percentages calculated from Ezeanya, p. 7.

12. The Roman Catholic Mission was proprietor of seventeen of the twenty-nine Grade Three and Grade Two teacher training colleges opened in 1956 and of five of the seven grammar schools opened in that year. Eastern Region [6], *Annual Report, 1956*, pp. 16, 24–25.

13. C.M.S. Niger Diocese, File 122, 1956 Report.

14. *The Leader*, May 19, 1956.

15. J. H. Price observed of the Anglicans during 1956–57: "It seemed ... that the Church Missionary Society had slipped into the position of non-conformists in England in the nineteenth century; they would sooner have secular education for all than allow the dominant church to run its own schools." Price, "The Eastern Region of Nigeria, March, 1957," in Mackenzie and Robinson, pp. 112–13.

16. Eastern Region [13], *Policy for Education* (1953), pp. 5–6.

17. See the statement by Joseph Whelan, Bishop of Owerri, in *The Leader*, Feb. 18, 1956.

18. Eastern Region [18], "U.P.E. Policy Statement" (1956).

19. Dike Report, p. 9.

20. "Statement by the Education Authorities of the Niger Diocese on Educational Policy," mimeo., Oct. 1956 (Eastern Region, U.P.E. Files, D.E.E. 10532, Vol. VII). The Education Secretary of the diocese, E. O.

Enemo, described the universal primary education program as "an altruistic measure adopted by Government ... a bold venture which must cost millions and millions of pounds. It will shake to the very roots the financial stability of the Region. But it is a wise step all the same." C.M.S. Niger Diocese, File 122, 1956 Report.

21. Bishops of the Eastern Region, "A Short Note from the Catholic Bishops on Universal Primary Education," issued May 22, 1956, printed in *The Leader*, June 9, 1956. The date of this statement suggests that the Catholic Church anticipated the government's policy well before it was announced.

22. Editorial in *The Leader*, Sept. 8, 1956.

23. P. N. Okeke in Eastern Region [4], *Debates*, April 1, 1957, p. 123.

24. Sklar, p. 188, n. 100. The Dike Report (p. 44) cites allegations that priests denounced local authority schools as godless and threatened parents with excommunication if they sent their children there.

25. Letter from Chiefs and Elders, Ndielo Nkporo, Sept. 10, 1956 (Eastern Region, U.P.E. Files, D.E.E. 10532, Vol. VI, p. 643).

26. *Daily Times*, Dec. 1, 1956.

27. Sklar, p. 188. For a discussion of the ethnic conflict, see pp. 151–57. Sklar notes (p. 189, n. 102) that the "ethnic hatchet" was buried by the end of 1958, for which "the religious controversy deserves no little credit."

28. As of the end of 1956, twenty-eight out of thirty-one district councils in Calabar Province (excluding the Calabar Urban District Council) and nineteen out of twenty-three district councils in Owerri Province had decided to manage all their schools themselves. Eastern Region, U.P.E. Files, D.E.E. 10532, Vols. V, VI.

29. Only about 5% of the teachers in local authority schools were trained in 1958, compared to more than 30% in previously aided schools. Eastern Region [6], *Annual Report, 1958*, p. 30.

30. See Azikiwe, *After Three Years of Stewardship*. The Ministry of Education's viewpoint is elaborated in Eastern Region [10], *Education and U.P.E.* (1957). Twenty thousand copies of this document were distributed to all parties concerned with education.

31. *The Leader*, March 15, 1957.

32. Sklar, p. 189.

33. Rev. M. D. Opara in Eastern Region [4], *Debates*, April 1, 1957, p. 124.

34. Dike Report, p. 9. The number of such schools rose from 46 in 1956 to 1,490 in 1957; see Eastern Region [6], *Annual Report, 1959*, p. 12.

35. B. C. Okwu in Eastern Region [4], *Debates*, Feb. 13, 1958, p. 10. The financial problem is well summed up in the Dike Report, p. 12. If educational expenditure is calculated by the school year, it rose from £3.57 million in 1956 (of which £2.1 million was recurrent primary expenditure) to £6 million in 1957 (of which £4.45 million was recurrent primary expenditure). Eastern Region [6], *Annual Report, 1956*, p. 33, and *Annual Report, 1957*, p. 32.

36. Eastern Region, U.P.E. Files, D.E.E. 10532/S.6B/2, Vol. VIII, Jan. 8, 1958. Assumed Local Contribution was estimated on the basis of thirty students for each class.

37. The Commission of Enquiry into Education Rating observed on its

tour of the East during 1950–51: "Speakers were apt to imagine that Government funds were inexhaustible." It added: "Even among the [local] leaders there is a lack of appreciation of the cost of education, particularly of the cost of universal education." Nigeria [6], *Enquiry into Local Rating Proposal*, pp. 15, 22.

38. B. C. Okwu in Eastern Region [4], *Debates*, Feb. 13, 1958, p. 10.

39. Azikiwe in *ibid.*, p. 20; excerpts from his speech are printed in Azikiwe, *Zik*, pp. 43–45.

40. S. E. Imoke in Eastern Region [4], *Debates*, Feb. 17, 1958, p. 88.

41. E. Emole in *ibid.*, Feb. 13, 1958, p. 47.

42. E. O. Eyo in *ibid.*, p. 24.

43. Primary school enrollment for 1958 was 1,221,000, but the Dike Commission estimated that it would have been 1,485,000 had there been no modification. Dike Report, p. 11.

CHAPTER 8

1. Of the Primary Six pupils surveyed by the author in 1964 (their median age was 13), 74% could correctly identify Nigeria's President, 52% the federal Prime Minister, 55% their regional premier, and 35% one regional minister; over 95% of the secondary grammar and Sixth Form pupils gave correct answers to almost all of these questions.

2. For evidence from East Africa confirming the importance of the media and of teachers as sources of political information, see David Koff and George von der Muhll, "Political Socialization in Kenya and Tanzania—A Comparative Analysis," *Journal of Modern African Studies*, V, 1 (May 1967), 22–26.

3. Deutsch, "Social Mobilization," pp. 497–98.

4. It is interesting to note that the important policy makers in the Western Region (Awolowo, Awokoya, Odebiyi, and others) were British-trained and thus tended to draw on Great Britain for educational innovations, whereas the key figures in the East (Azikiwe, Akpabio, and Ojike) were American-trained and looked to the United States for such innovations as the land-grant college—the model for the University of Nigeria at Nsukka.

5. Callaway and Musone, Appendix B, Table 8, p. 115; Education and World Affairs, p. 43.

6. Callaway, "Unemployment," p. 371.

7. Output for the Western Region in 1960 and for the East in 1963 was unusually high, since in both cases the original class in the universal primary education program left school together with remnants of the class immediately preceding it. Moreover, as noted in Part II, initial enrollment in the universal primary education programs was inflated by children above and below the legally sanctioned age limits.

8. An official commission on bride-price in the Eastern Region reported the following figures for Owerri Town: £100 for an illiterate girl, £200 for a girl who had completed primary school, and £300 for a certified teacher, nurse, or midwife. Eastern Nigeria, *Report of the Committee on Bride Price* (Enugu, 1955), p. 6. See also Phoebe V. Ottenberg, "The Changing Economic Position of Women among the Afikpo Ibo," in Bascom and Herskovits, pp. 205–23.

9. See Clignet and Foster (pp. 146–73) for a description of attitudes toward occupational structure in the Ivory Coast. The authors note that formal education can hardly be said to encourage the entrepreneurial spirit.

10. Foster, *Education and Social Change*, pp. 205–8, 275–80; Clignet and Foster, pp. 127–29; Callaway, "Unemployment"; Albert J. McQueen, "Aspirations and Problems of Nigerian School Leavers," *Bulletin, Inter-African Labour Institute*, XII, 1 (Feb. 1965), 35–42; articles by David Koff, John Anderson, and J. D. Heijnen, in Sheffield. Foster's findings from his 1961 sample of 963 Fifth Form students in Ghana correspond fairly closely to the Nigerian findings reported here. The three most favored occupational categories in Ghana were in scientific and technical fields (21.7%), medicine (16.1%), and secondary school teaching (16.3%).

11. Helleiner, p. 145.

12. This aspect of urbanization is, of course, a worldwide phenomenon, but some of the most striking statistics come from African countries. In one Ashanti village surveyed in the mid-1940's, it was found that 95% of the boys who had passed through the local school had left for urban areas. See Meyer Fortes, "The Ashanti Social Survey: A Preliminary Report," *Rhodes-Livingstone Journal* (London, 1948), p. 29, cited in Foster, *Education and Social Change*, p. 146, n. 49. Of 1,000 rural Senegalese youths who had completed primary education in 1954, 750 were found living in cities five years later; only 20 were farmers. See Père Lebret *et al.*, *Rapport général sur les perspectives de développement du Sénégal* (Dakar, 1960), I, 1–5, cited by David Hapgood, "Sub-Saharan Education and Rural Development," in William H. Lewis, ed., *French-Speaking Africa: The Search for Identity* (New York, 1965), p. 124.

13. Coleman, *Education and Political Development*, p. 30.

14. In Education and World Affairs (p. 19) high-productivity sector employment for Nigeria as a whole is estimated at 700,000. K. C. Doctor and Hans Gallis estimate Nigeria's wage employment at 900,000 in "Size and Characteristics of Wage Employment in Africa: Some Empirical Estimates," *International Labour Review*, XCIII, 2 (Feb. 1966), 167–68. We assume that Southern Nigeria accounted for about 85% of both figures.

15. Education and World Affairs (pp. 20–24) estimates that the gross annual employment intake for Nigeria as a whole is unlikely to reach 40,000 in the high-productivity sector even if one optimistically assumes a 4.9% rise in the Gross Domestic Product and an output–employment ratio of two to one.

16. Similarly, in Ghana the absolute increase in modern employment is under 30,000 a year, yet the output of the middle schools alone is about 40,000. See Foster, *Education and Social Change*, pp. 182, 205. In Tanzania projections for the 1964–69 plan period showed 116,000 new jobs available and 232,000 Standard Seven or Eight school leavers directly entering the labor market. See Hunter, *Manpower, Employment, and Education*, p. 15. Tanzania's total wage employment was actually lower in 1967 than in 1962, however, making it unlikely that more than a fraction of the 116,000 jobs expected would become available. At the same time, estimates of the number of school leavers have proved realistic.

17. See Edgren. Kenya's output rose 18% from 1957 to 1962, but employ-

ment fell by 5%; in Zambia during the same period output rose 28%, but employment fell by 16%. Among African countries the employment lag is perhaps most serious in Zambia. *Ibid.*, pp. 189–90.

18. There are quite rational reasons for the investor's apparently irrational preference for capital-intensive methods in labor-surplus economies. See *ibid.*; Gabriel Ardant, "Automation in Developing Countries," *International Labour Review*, XC, 5 (Nov. 1964), 432–71.

19. In 1964 Shell–British Petroleum directly employed 2,800 workers of all grades, in addition to about 2,000 who were on contract to clear drilling sites, while managing to export £32 million worth of petroleum. See Helleiner, p. 35. Production technology and the quasi-competitive nature of the oil industry both require highly capital-intensive methods.

20. Walter Galenson, "Economic Development and the Sectoral Expansion of Employment," *International Labour Review*, LXXXVII, 6 (June 1963), 505–19; Edgren; K. C. Doctor and Hans Gallis, "Size and Characteristics of Wage Employment in Africa: Some Empirical Estimates," *International Labour Review*, XCIII, 2 (Feb. 1966), 149–73, and "Modern Sector Employment in Asian Countries: Some Empirical Estimates," *International Labour Review*, XC, 6 (Dec. 1964), 544–68.

21. Nigeria [17], *Employment and Earnings, 1961*, p. 2, cited in Helleiner, p. 232.

22. Nigeria [13], *Educational Statistics, 1962*, pp. 17, 41; Education and World Affairs, p. 78.

23. Post, p. 153.

24. Figures from Education and World Affairs, p. 37.

25. The expenses of a single male living on his own in an urban center were estimated after conversations with unemployed school leavers in Sapele, Onitsha, and Aba.

26. Of the 35 primary school students who preferred modern technical work, 57% expected to obtain such work. Of the 33 students in the grammar school and Sixth Form sample with similar preferences, only 33% were optimistic.

27. The definitive work on the contemporary Nigerian apprenticeship system has been done by Archibald Callaway. See his "Continuing Education"; and "From Traditional Crafts to Modern Industries," in Lloyd *et al.*, *City of Ibadan*, pp. 153–72.

28. For further discussion of the importance of a sense of political competence, see Almond and Verba, esp. pp. 236–39. This point is not sufficiently stressed by Huntington. A mobilized population is in a good position to make heavy demands on its government, but for various reasons it may not realize this potential.

29. An urban unemployment survey conducted by the federal Ministry of Labour in 1963 estimated unemployment in relation to the total population as 8.8% for Lagos, 6.7% for the new Western Region, 9.8% for the Mid-West, and 10.7% for the East. The labor force may be 60% of the urban population. (Information courtesy of the Ministry of Labour, Benin office.) Archibald Callaway's sample survey of three areas of Ibadan in 1964 revealed that 15% of the female and 28% of the male labor force were unemployed; of the latter, about three-fourths had six years of education.

Callaway estimated there were about 30,000 unemployed males in Ibadan, of whom at least 20,000 had six to nine years of education. Ibadan's population at the time was probably over 700,000. See Callaway, "Education and the Rise of Youth Unemployment," in Lloyd *et al.,* pp. 191–212.

30. Archibald Callaway, "School Leavers and the Developing Economy of Nigeria," in Tilman and Cole, p. 223.

31. The perceived seriousness of unemployment can also be measured by analyzing the essays of the author's post-primary sample on the question, "What will Nigeria be like in ten years?" Of the 820 essay writers, 52% mentioned some aspect of employment—more than discussed any other topic for which responses were coded, including wealth, the provision of amenities, education, domestic or external politics, population, and the state of public and private morals. Of those who mentioned employment, slightly less than half thought the situation would improve in ten years; 28% thought it would deteriorate further. The more educated students tended to be slightly more pessimistic.

32. The unemployed apparently played a part in the overthrow of regimes in two countries—Dahomey and the Congo (Brazzaville)—where school enrollment figures are relatively high and the economy stagnant. See William Friedland, "Paradoxes of African Trade Unionism: Organizational Chaos and Political Potential," *Africa Report* (June 1965), 6–13. In Cotonou, which in 1964 had a population of 109,000, one-fourth of the people were of working age but unemployed; about half of those between fifteen and nineteen were jobless. See "Back to the Land: The Campaign Against Unemployment in Dahomey," *International Labour Review,* XCIII, 1 (Jan. 1966), 30.

33. "In the remotest parts of Western and Eastern Nigeria . . . politicians when meeting the local villagers have found it is often better to talk about 'jobs for school leavers' than about access roads. This is good politics." Archibald Callaway, "School Leavers and the Developing Economy of Nigeria," in Tilman and Cole, p. 221. Reporting on interviews with Southern Nigerian political elites, Henry Bretton wrote: "Consultations with constituents appear to center on matters related to the education of the young, including the procurement of scholarships, the settlement of domestic disputes, employment questions, procurement of loans for trade and construction, political career advice, taxes, and defense against political victimization, in that order of frequency." Bretton, "Political Influence in Southern Nigeria," in Spiro, p. 81. In Lloyd Free's Nigerian opinion survey, 33% of the federal Members of Parliament who were sampled expressed concern over the unemployment situation, as compared to only 19% of the public. See Free, p. 52.

34. Ashby Report, pp. 60–64.

35. *Ibid.,* p. 41. Ironically, the report had earlier (on p. 4) criticized "a tendency for the aspirations of those who plan education to outrun the money and teachers available."

36. Nigeria, *Educational Development, 1961–70* (Lagos, 1961). The financial implications of the Ashby Commission's recommendations were spelled out in Archer.

37. Ashby Report, pp. 57–58.

38. Nigeria [18], *National Development Plan, 1962–68*, p. 206.

39. *Ibid.*, p. 273. The provision of employment is considered fourth on the West's priority list. The region's 1960–65 development plan was even more outspoken: "The first objective is to ensure that there is useful and worthwhile employment for all—so that the human, social and financial resources invested in the Government's education programme will yield a return in productive effort and higher standards of living that will more than justify the vision of those who sponsored it." Western Region [18], *Development Plan, 1960–65*, p. 3. This plan was incorporated into the 1962–68 plan so as to be in phase with the other governments of the federation.

40. Nigeria [18], *National Development Plan, 1962–68*, pp. 327–30.

41. For Nigeria as a whole, capital expenditure on primary production was expected to rise from 3.7% of actual expenditure during 1955–61 to 13% of a much larger amount during 1962–68. *Ibid.*, p. 35. The widespread realization of the importance of directly productive investment is described in "Social Aspects of African Development Planning: Patterns and Trends," *Economic Bulletin for Africa*, IV (Jan. 1964), 64–101; and in Forrest, pp. 52–53.

42. Helleiner, p. 27; Nigeria [18], *National Development Plan, 1962–68*, p. 29.

CHAPTER 9

1. The author acknowledges diverse debts in setting up these three categories. The notion of support is drawn from David Easton; see "An Approach to the Analysis of Political Systems," *World Politics*, IX, 3 (April 1957), 383–400, and the more elaborate discussion in *A Systems Analysis of Political Life*. The section on the availability of funds has profited from the capabilities analysis found in Gabriel Almond, "A Developmental Approach to Political Systems," *World Politics*, XVII, 2 (Jan. 1965), 183–214, and in Almond and Powell's *Comparative Politics*. The importance of competent institutions is stressed in Huntington.

2. At least one local authority in the East had not quite learned the lesson of the universal primary education financial fiasco, as its 1959 memorandum to the Dike Commission shows: "School fees in all the educational institutions in the Region should be drastically reduced.... Government should then step up the grants-in-aid to say 90% of any school expenditure with a view to raising it to 100% in future when all the schools shall become state schools and the Government is financially well off." Eastern Region, Dike Commission File, Ibiono Rural District Council Memorandum, p. 3. Such views were likely to be even more widespread in the 1960's than before, if only because with the passage of time school maintenance costs rose and the limited economic value of a First School-Leaving Certificate became increasingly obvious to parents and local officials.

3. Chief Dennis Osadebay, who was to become the first premier of the Mid-West Region, said in Benin on August 17, 1963: "We must ... overhaul our present system of education." This statement was interpreted as a warning that primary school fees might be reimposed. So strong was the protest from all quarters that the Commissioner for Education had to call a

special press conference to deny that free education would be abolished. See Mid-West Region, Ministry of Information, *Daily Press Releases*, No. 36 Sept. 6, 1963) and No. 426 (Dec. 2, 1963). In the *Midwest Champion* (Benin) of Dec. 12, 1963, a renewed allegation was made, also officially denied, that Osadebay planned to reintroduce fees.

4. See note 1 of Chapter 8.

5. American children, at least until the early 1960's, have tended to take a positive, uncynical view of political leaders. See Fred I. Greenstein, "The Benevolent Leader: Children's Images of Political Authority," *American Political Science Review*, LIV, 4 (Dec. 1960), 934–43; Greenstein, *Children and Politics*, esp. pp. 37–42; Robert D. Hess and David Easton, "The Child's Changing Image of the President," *Public Opinion Quarterly*, XXIV (Winter 1960), 632–44; Easton and Hess, "The Child's Political World," *Midwest Journal of Political Science*, VI (Aug. 1962), 229–46. Although the American students sampled were younger on the average than the Nigerian students sampled by the author (Greenstein's were between nine and thirteen, Easton and Hess's between the second and eighth grades), there is sufficient overlap in age to allow a meaningful comparison.

6. See Almond and Verba, pp. 204–9; David Easton and Jack Dennis, "The Child's Acquisition of Regime Norms: Political Efficacy," *American Political Science Review*, LXI, 1 (March 1967), 25–38. For other references see *ibid.*, p. 27.

7. We may score support for each level of government by subtracting the percentage of the sample who ranked that level lowest from the percentage who ranked it highest. For the entire post-primary sample, support for local government totaled -11%, for the federal government -4%, and for regional government 15%. Regional government received $.4\%$ from the secondary modern sample, 21.5% from the grammar school sample, and 46.7% from the Sixth Form sample. Support for the federal government declined markedly with educational level—from 27% to -19% to -30%.

8. Nigeria [12], *National Development Plan, Progress Report 1964*, p. 34. Dean's article stresses other obstacles to performance as well, including administrative failures and insufficient allocation to the productive sector. More recent evaluations are found in Alan Rake and J. D. Farrell, "Nigeria's Economy: No Longer a Model," *Africa Report*, XII, 7 (Oct. 1967), 19–22, and in W. Arthur Lewis, *Reflections on Nigeria's Economic Growth*.

9. Changes in educational expenditure, as against overall expenditure, are detailed in Education and World Affairs, Table IX-4, p. 92.

10. Education and World Affairs, p. 89. Estimates for 1952 and 1962 are taken from Callaway and Musone, Table 1, p. 23.

11. Yearly breakdowns are given in Education and World Affairs, pp. 91, 177, 179, 181.

12. *Ibid.*, p. 89.

13. In the Eastern Region, for example, the percentage of Grade II and III teachers in the primary school teaching force rose from 28.6% in 1956 to 47.7% by 1962; the average Eastern primary school teacher's income rose from £120 in 1960 to £225 in 1965. The average recurrent cost per primary student for Nigeria as a whole was £3.7 in 1952, £5.7 in 1962, and almost £8 by 1966. Callaway and Musone, Table 11, p. 43; Education and World Affairs, p. 110.

14. "Of all Nigeria's resources her young people are the most valuable; expenditure upon their education should be a first charge upon the nation's finances.... In the modern world economic advance depends on skilled manpower, and the manpower must come first. Investment in Nigerian education is therefore an investment in her economic future and political stability, and as such may command international attention." Ashby Report, pp. 7, 35.

15. Stolper; see also Okigbo, pp. 169–79. Stolper goes too far in suggesting that allocations for education and health should ideally be made only on noneconomic grounds (p. 73). But he is surely right in criticizing the other extreme position, the argument that virtually all educational expenditure is to be considered investment.

16. Clifton Wharton, "Education and Agricultural Growth: The Role of Education in Early-Stage Agriculture," in Anderson and Bowman, p. 203.

17. Eastern Region, *Report on the Conference of Leading Personalities of Eastern Nigeria Origin, 2–4 March, 1962* (Enugu, 1962), p. 8.

18. A summary of the complaints is to be found in "Memorandum Submitted by the Nigeria Union of Teachers to the Minister of Education, Eastern Nigeria, on the Changes in Primary School Organization in 1963" (mimeo., Aba, 1963).

19. Forrest, p. 41.

20. See, for example, Elliott Berg, "Senegal, Guinea, Ivory Coast," in Harbison and Myers, *Manpower and Education*, pp. 232–67; Hunter, *Education for a Developing Region*; and Young, pp. 163–83, 398–437.

21. The 1954 Western Region primary school syllabus was slightly revised in 1955 and 1958, and then given a more local and practical orientation in 1962. The Eastern Region syllabus, based on the standard British syllabus of 1948, was somewhat modified in 1958 and 1960; an improved six-year version was published in 1963. Comparing the latest Eastern Region history syllabus with its predecessors, L. J. Lewis comments: "[It] reveals but a superficial adaptation and minor adjustment of content and treatment that shows little awareness of the historical studies that have been carried out in Nigeria and but a superficial understanding of what adaptation really involves." Lewis, *Society, Schools, and Progress*, p. 114.

22. Western Region [10], *Annual Report, 1960*, p. 59. Although an announced purpose of the modern school was to provide commercial training, the first group of 28 Nigerian commercial teachers was not ready for classroom work until 1960. This suggests that sizeable numbers of students were not receiving commercial training until the mid-1960's, when the entire secondary modern venture was being phased out!

23. Education and World Affairs, p. 65. Of these, we may assume that over 4,000 were of Southern Nigerian origin.

24. For similar comments pertaining to French-speaking West Africa, see Harbison and Myers, *Manpower and Education*, p. 266.

25. Of the 12,602 Western Region staff employees on duty as of the end of 1962, about 40% were stationed in Ibadan. Western Nigeria, *Report of the Public Service Commission, April 1, 1962, to March 31, 1963* (Ibadan, 1963), p. 21.

26. An exception was the cost of secondary school expansion, which was borne largely by the populace rather than by the regional governments.

Whereas the private sector contributed 10.3% of the total recurrent expenditure for primary education in Nigeria as of 1962, its share of secondary education costs was 53.3%. Regional contributions were 73.1% and 40.6%, respectively. Education and World Affairs, Diagram IX-2, p. 96.

27. Complaints were registered in the East over the 1964 announcement, made without prior consultation, that a common religious syllabus would be introduced into the primary schools. Protests from both Protestant and Catholic bodies—including the Eastern Nigeria Association of Catholic Women, which staged a noisy rally in front of the House of Assembly—forced the Minister of Education, Dr. Samuel Imoke, to withdraw his proposal. See the *Daily Express*, March 25, 1964. Board of Education members in both regions complained of the unilateral way in which ceilings on secondary school fees were set. Church-State relations in the West, normally cordial before Independence, grew more tense in the 1960's, particularly after the dual post of Permanent Secretary and Chief Inspector of Education was assumed by a man widely regarded as autocratic in his methods and hostile to mission influence. The 1962 Report of the (Anglican) Diocesan Education Secretary-General, Ibadan, notes that "the Western Region Advisory Board of Education and its Committees were not as active as in some previous years ... and we have been disappointed that there seems to have been less consultation and more direction than before" (C.M.S. Ibadan File A34-B).

28. *Daily Express*, Feb. 15, 1964. The government responded by releasing £100,000 for the construction of new local authority schools throughout the region; one-fourth of the sum was to be spent in Port Harcourt. A recent and essentially unaltered version of the Church's position is presented in Catholic Hierarchy of Eastern Nigeria, *A Catholic View of Education* (Owerri, n.d. [1964]).

29. Letter to the author from Father James O'Connell, Lecturer in Political Science, University of Ibadan. The Eastern Region Minister of Education, G. E. Okeke, made the same general point in 1961, as reported in *Nigerian Outlook*, Feb. 3, 1961; see also Dike Report, p. 47. If voluntary agency teachers had been paid on the Government Service scale, costs would have been far higher.

30. Quoted in the *Daily Times*, March 3, 1964. For a more detailed discussion of Church-State relations, see David B. Abernethy, "Nigeria," in Scanlon, pp. 197–244.

31. The employment aspect was also emphasized by a report of the FAO, which estimated that even with rapid urbanization the absolute number of Nigerians in agriculture would increase from 38.5 million in 1963 to 55 million by 1980; the percentage of the population employed in agriculture was projected as declining only 5%, from 70% to 65%. See United Nations, Food and Agriculture Organization, pp. 400–401.

32. The Farm Settlement scheme was drastically altered in 1964. For discussions of agricultural policy in the early 1960's, see J. C. Wells, "Government Investment in Nigerian Agriculture: Some Unsettled Issues," *Nigerian Journal of Economics and Social Studies*, VIII, 1 (March 1966), 37–48; Carl K. Eicher, "Transforming Traditional Agriculture in Southern Nigeria: The Contemporary Experience" (mimeo. paper presented at the Oc-

tober 1966 meeting of the African Studies Association). Baldwin documents the failure of the Mokwa scheme in Northern Nigeria, which almost precisely paralleled the failure of the Farm Settlements in many respects: improper selection of settlers, overreliance on mechanized equipment, insufficient research prior to land clearance, choice of oversized farm sites, and so on. An even more spectacular failure of "modern" agriculture in Africa is described in Alan Wood, *The Groundnut Affair* (London, 1950). For a general survey see the two-volume work by John C. deWilde *et al.*, *Experiences with Agricultural Development in Tropical Africa* (Baltimore, 1967).

33. Helleiner, p. 330. As the International Labour Office notes, in most development plans employment creation is not even considered a major objective but "has been looked on as a by-product of general economic development," even when development may not in fact lead to a substantial rise in employment. See International Labour Office, p. 33. Relevant works on Nigerian small industry, which tends to be labor-intensive, include Peter Kilby, *African Enterprise: The Nigerian Bread Industry* (Stanford, Calif., 1965); Kilby, *The Development of Small Industry in Eastern Nigeria*; and Archibald Callaway, "From Traditional Crafts to Modern Industries," in Peter C. Lloyd *et al.*, *City of Ibadan*, pp. 153–71. A more general treatment of the possibilities afforded by small industry in developing countries is to be found in Staley and Morse.

34. For an excellent survey of recent developments, see Ronald Wraith, "Local Government," in Mackintosh, pp. 200–267. Wraith's earlier work, *Local Government in West Africa*, provides a useful background.

35. Callaway and Musone, Table 8, p. 40.

36. I. U. Akpabio remarked after returning from a tour of the provinces in 1964 that it was inspiring—but also frightening—to see the long rows of schoolchildren lining the school grounds to welcome him. Interview, June 30, 1964.

37. Eisenstadt, *Modernization*, p. 146; see also Huntington.

CHAPTER 10

1. Changes in the conception of citizenship in the important case of England are discussed by Marshall in *Class, Citizenship, and Social Development*, pp. 71–134.

2. Bendix, p. 102.

3. Education and World Affairs, pp. 116f.

4. Nigerian Association of University Women, Appendix, tables 1, 2; Nigeria [15], *Statistics of Education, 1964*, p. 9; Eastern Region [6], *Annual Report, 1957*, p. 27. Data for 1965 courtesy of Education and World Affairs.

5. Western Region [7], *Education Statistics, 1953–58*, p. 16.

6. *Ibid.*

7. K. J. N. Okpokam in Eastern Region [4], *Debates*, Feb. 17, 1958, p. 172.

8. Until its demise the modern school was an important mechanism for upward mobility, particularly when in practice it afforded access to the grammar school. It is remarkable that in the author's survey there was a higher percentage of students from every disadvantaged category in secondary modern school than at any other educational level in the Western Region, including the primary:

Disadvantaged category	Primary	Secondary modern	Secondary grammar	Sixth Form
Girl	39%	43%	20%	5%
Born in rural area	47	50	35	40
Parents now living in rural area	41	44	30	33
Father a farmer or fisherman	40	49	40	33
Father's income £ 100 or under	n.a.	37	28	18
Father illiterate	31	46	35	28
Parents Muslim	32	34	19	10

9. For comments on the French system, see Clignet and Foster, pp. 83, 90. At least one former British colony, Tanzania, abolished secondary school fees in 1964 to encourage selection by merit. Knight, p. 38.

10. Education and World Affairs, Table X-1, p. 110.

11. A careful discussion of changes in the cost and financing of secondary education may be found in the Ajayi Report, pp. 3–13.

12. It is also true that several Nigerians who have become successful businessmen have become proprietors of secondary schools. This further confirms the argument that running a school can be a profitable enterprise.

13. The Ajayi Report (pp. 13–18) provides a detailed list of abuses the commission uncovered.

14. A regional breakdown of these figures indicates a greater spread of educational costs among relatives in the East than in the West. Whereas parents alone supported 69% of the grammar school students in the West, they supported only 49% in the East. Brothers and sisters contributed to the support of more students in the East (17%) than in the West (11%); the same applies for uncles and aunts (7% to 3%). These statistics suggest a wider and more cohesive net of relationships among Ibo than among Yoruba extended families.

15. Peter Lloyd has estimated that many members of the Ibadan elite contribute 20% of their incomes to this end. See "The Elite," in Lloyd et al., *City of Ibadan*, p. 144.

16. That students were willing and considered themselves intellectually able to continue their education, finances permitting, is made abundantly clear from the author's 1964 survey. Of the 1,360 students in the sample, 569 said their chances of continuing in school the following year were poor or nonexistent. When asked why they would be stopping their education, their responses were as follows:

Response	Primary (N = 195)	Secondary modern (N = 112)	Secondary grammar (N = 231)	Sixth Form (N = 31)
Do not wish to continue	7%	3%	0%	3%
Marks not good enough	10	5	.5	0
Parents unable to pay fees	73	88	87	90
Other reason; no answer	10	4	12	7

17. A senior official earning £2500 may pay £150 for a spacious, completely furnished government house, whereas a subordinate who earns under £700 is fortunate if he pays £240 a year for an unfurnished private flat. Morgan Report, p. 56.

18. Orewa, *Taxation*, p. 104.

19. Lloyd, *New Elites*, p. 4. The Smythes stress the educational component: "The new elite . . . can be defined as a variable group of people consisting at least potentially of all who have completed upper secondary school." Smythe and Smythe, p. 167.

20. Lloyd, *New Elites*, pp. 56–59. For a discussion of the defining characteristics of class in modern societies, see Ralf Dahrendorf, *Class and Class Conflict in Industrial Society* (Stanford, Calif., 1959).

21. The notion of a rising "political class" is central to Richard Sklar's analysis of Nigerian political parties; see Sklar, pp. 480–94. See also O'Connell, "Political Class." Immanuel Wallerstein discusses the role of the "administrative bourgeoisie" in "Elites in French-Speaking West Africa: The Social Basis of Ideas," *Journal of Modern African Studies*, III, 1 (May 1965), 1–33. Martin Kilson describes the elite in Sierra Leone as a "politically conscious group which enters politics to advance its over-all position in society and ultimately to become a ruling or governing class." Kilson, *Political Change in a West African State: A Study of the Modernization Process in Sierra Leone* (Cambridge, Mass., 1966), p. 69.

22. The population data used are from the early 1950's. Since then the percentage of farmers has probably fallen and that of white-collar workers has probably risen; if so, the gap as measured in selectivity indices is overstated. But it must still be very great indeed. The selectivity indices in Table 12 should be treated with some caution, since the occupational categories used in the census and in the questionnaire do not completely coincide.

23. In Philip Foster's 1961 survey of 963 Ghanaian Fifth Form students, 28% had fathers who had not attended school, and 26% had fathers with at least some secondary school or teacher training experience. The selectivity index for children of farmers it was .5; for the children of professional, higher technical, administrative, and clerical workers it was 5.8. See *Education and Social Change*, Table 22, p. 241, and Table 23, p. 243. Data indicating a more egalitarian recruitment pattern for the Ivory Coast may be found in Clignet and Foster, pp. 56–59.

24. See, for example, P. A. O. Mozia, "The Falling Standard of Education in Nigeria," *Daily Express*, May 4, 1964, and "We Must Save This Nation," *Daily Express*, May 8, 1964; E. A. Anijekwu, "Standard of Education Is Falling," *West African Pilot*, July 9, 1964; editorial, *Daily Times*, May 4, 1964.

25. An excellent discussion of the impact of family life on language and achievement motivation is to be found in Barbara B. Lloyd, "Education and Family Life in the Development of Class Identification among the Yoruba," in Peter C. Lloyd, *New Elites*, pp. 163–81.

26. I am grateful to Mrs. Bolanle Awe of the Department of History, University of Ibadan, a member of the Ajayi Commission, for information on elite nursery and primary schools given to me in an interview, Nov. 15, 1963.

27. Examples quoted in the Ajayi Report, pp. 17–18.

28. Interview with D. S. Snell, Headmaster, International Secondary School, Ibadan, Dec. 1, 1963.

29. Ajayi Report, pp. 22–23.

30. *Ibid.*, p. 23. Peter Lloyd corroborates the point: "In Africa at present, the elite is characterized by the number of its members who have come from humble homes. . . . [But] the well-educated and wealthy elite is tending to become a predominantly hereditary group." *New Elites*, p. 57.

31. A collection of Solarin's delightful but biting essays has been published in his booklet entitled *Towards Nigeria's Moral Self-Government.* See also Tony Onyeisi, "Should We Have Segregated Schools?" *Sunday Express* (Lagos), Dec. 1, 1963; and editorials in the *Daily Express*, Nov. 13, 1963, and in the *Daily Times*, Nov. 22, 1963.

32. *Eastern Outlook*, Nov. 19, 1960.

33. Nigeria [18], *National Development Plan, 1962–68*, p. 23.

34. Minority reports are found on pages 49–69 of the Morgan Report.

35. Nigeria [3], *Conclusions on Morgan Report.*

36. Estimate derived from Education and World Affairs, Appendix Two, tables 2D–2F, pp. 177–82.

CHAPTER 11

1. Clifford Geertz, "The Integrative Revolution," in Geertz, p. 120.

2. Emerson, p. 96.

3. "National integration . . . refers specifically to the problem of creating a sense of territorial nationality which overshadows—or eliminates—subordinate parochial loyalties." Weiner, "Political Integration," p. 53. Rupert Emerson (pp. 95–96) makes a similar point when he defines a nation as "the largest community which, when the chips are down, effectively commands men's loyalties, overriding the claims both of lesser communities within it and those which cut across or potentially enfold it." Other relevant literature on integration includes Jacob and Toscano; Deutsch, *Nationalism*; Ake; and Coleman and Rosberg.

4. See John Spencer, ed., *Language in Africa* (Cambridge, Eng., 1963). Relevant sources on Asia include LePage; Harrison, pp. 55–95; and Wriggins, pp. 241–70. As Dankwart Rustow (p. 56) has observed, "In a country where only a small elite can read and write, it makes little difference in what language the vast majority are illiterate. Concerted drives for literacy and mass education, by contrast, emphasize the importance of the linguistic alternatives."

5. McKim Marriott, "Cultural Policy in the New States," in Geertz, pp. 27–56; Wallerstein, *Social Change*, pp. 592–674. For a revisionist effort in the field of African history, see Cheick Anta Diop, *L'Unité culturelle de l'Afrique noire* (Paris, 1959).

6. Timidity in curriculum reform is not confined to "moderate" states like Nigeria. As Philip Foster notes of Ghanaian education, "The startling thing . . . is not the radical break with the colonial past but the persistence of neo-colonial values and practices among a political elite which ostensibly rejects them." *Education and Social Change*, p. 299. See also Coleman, *Education and Political Development*, pp. 43–48.

7. Joseph Fischer, "Indonesia," in Coleman, *Education and Political De-*

velopment, pp. 102–7; Joseph DiBona, "Indiscipline and Student Leadership in an Indian University," *Comparative Education Review*, X, 2 (June 1966), 309; Foster, *Education and Social Change*, pp. 238–39.

8. It would be most unlikely for a young Ibo in the 1950's or 1960's to have matched the educational mobility, in a geographical sense, of Nnamdi Azikiwe: birth and early childhood in the North; primary education in Onitsha and Lagos; secondary education in Calabar (Hope Waddell) and Lagos (Methodist Boys High School); higher education in the United States. Jones-Quartey, p. 49.

9. Interview with the Principal of Edo College, Jan. 28, 1964. The rolls of the Benin and Ughelli schools confirm these statements. In both schools roughly 70% of the students from 1950 on were recruited from the province where the school was located.

10. An integrated polity, in this formulation, is similar to David Easton's "political community," in which people may or may not be culturally unified but in which they at least agree to struggle with each other through common institutions. Easton, esp. p. 177. The functions of cross-cutting cleavages are discussed in Georg Simmel, *Conflict* and *The Web of Group-Affiliations* (Glencoe, Ill., 1955); in Lewis A. Coser, *The Functions of Social Conflict* (Glencoe, Ill., 1956); and in Lipset, pp. 88–90.

11. C. S. Whitaker, "A Dysrhythmic Process of Political Change," *World Politics*, XIX, 2 (Jan. 1967), 190–217.

12. Coleman, *Nigeria*, p. 361.

13. Bello, pp. 110–11. Similar remarks are to be found in Coleman, *Nigeria*, p. 362.

14. "The party acts in defense of traditional authority, and traditional authority sustains the party." Richard L. Sklar and C. S. Whitaker, "Nigeria," in Coleman and Rosberg, p. 625. Detailed confirmation is given in Sklar, pp. 323–38, 365–71.

15. Recent educational developments in the North are described by Thornley.

16. Levine (pp. 69–71) gives striking evidence that achievement motivation among the Ibos is far higher than among the Hausa-Fulani.

17. *West Africa*, May 28, June 4 and 11, 1966.

18. *West African Pilot*, April 6 and 8, 1964; "The Chronicle," *Minerva*, III, 3 (Spring 1965), 415, and III, 4 (Summer 1965), 592.

19. Great Britain [6], *Commission Report on Fears of Minorities*, p. 19.

20. The leadership of the First Conference of the Methodist Church of Nigeria, which met in Lagos in 1962, reflected the inter-ethnic appeal of many religious bodies. The President-Designate was Rev. J. O. B. Soremekun, a Yoruba; the Vice-President Designate was E. Eyo Moma, an Efik; and the Secretary-Designate was Rev. George Egemba Igwe, an Ibo. See Methodist Church, pp. 72–74.

21. The concept used here is similar to Weiner's "elite-mass integration" and to Coleman and Rosberg's "political integration." See Weiner, "Political Integration," pp. 60–62; and Coleman and Rosberg, p. 9. The importance of communications in all aspects of integration is stressed in the writings of Karl Deutsch; see *Nationalism* and his contributions to Jacob and Toscano, pp. 46–97.

22. Education and World Affairs, p. 80.

23. Letter from F. M. Obasi to N.U.T. Executive Working Committee, Oct. 16, 1964. I am indebted to Dr. Dennis Storer, who has conducted a detailed study of the N.U.T., for making available a copy of Mr. Obasi's letter.

24. Lloyd, *New Elites*, p. 13.

25. Weiner, "Political Integration," p. 62.

26. The importance of trust for effective political action is emphasized in Pye, *Politics, Personality, and Nation-Building*; and in Edward C. and L. F. Banfield, *The Moral Basis of a Backward Society* (Glencoe, Ill., 1958). The related notion of empathy is discussed in Lerner, pp. 49–50.

27. Pye, *Aspects of Political Development*, p. 100.

28. For exposition and analysis of the African socialist doctrine, see Friedland and Rosberg; and "Special Issue on African Socialism," *Africa Report*, May 1963.

29. J. S. Nye, Jr., "Corruption and Political Development: A Cost-Benefit Analysis," *American Political Science Review*, LXI, 2 (June 1967), 417–27; Colin Leys, "What Is the Problem about Corruption?" *Journal of Modern African Studies*, III, 2 (Aug. 1965), 215–30. Both Nye and Leys attack the moralism of Ronald Wraith and Edgar Simkins' *Corruption in Developing Countries* (London, 1963).

30. Even the volume of domestic communications can be a misleading index of transactions within a country. Karl Deutsch infers from increases in the domestic flow of Nigerian mail from 1929 to 1948 that conditions grew more favorable over time for independence demands; see Jacob and Toscano, pp. 76–77. Given the different literacy rates of the North and South, it is probable that greater mail flow over this period simply reflected the increasing solidarity of the South rather than of Nigeria as a whole. For a discussion of the dangers of using national statistics without breaking them down by regions, see Myers, *Education and National Development in Mexico*.

Bibliography

This Bibliography, divided into two parts, lists files and works consulted. Government publications are grouped in the second list under Eastern Region, Great Britain, Nigeria, and Western Region, and are identified by bracketed numbers for convenience in citation.

Journals and newspapers useful in this study were *Africa* (London), 1952–61; *Daily Express* (Lagos), 1963–64; *Daily Service* (Lagos), 1950–55; *Daily Times* (Lagos), 1954–55; *Eastern Outlook* (Enugu), 1953, 1960–61; *Journal of the Historical Society of Nigeria* (Ibadan), 1956–64; *The Leader* (Owerri), 1956–57; *The Nigerian Journal of Economics and Social Studies* (Ibadan), 1959–67; *Oversea Education* (London), 1940–62; and *West African Pilot* (Lagos), 1963–64.

FILES

C.M.S. (Church Missionary Society), Niger Diocese. Supervisors' Reports and Education Secretary's Reports. File 122, 1927–33 and 1955–63. Onitsha.

C.M.S. (Church Missionary Society), Synod of Ibadan. Diocesan Education Secretary-General's Reports, File A34-B. 1947–64. Ibadan.

Eastern Region, Commission to Review the Educational System in Eastern Nigeria (Dike Commission). Research Papers and Memoranda. Ibadan.

Eastern Region, Ministry of Education. Universal Primary Education Files. File D.E.E. 10532, Vols. V–VIII. 1956–58. Enugu.

National Archives, Enugu. District Reports, 1909–12. Enugu.

N.U.T. (Nigeria Union of Teachers). File No. 2, Vols. 1–12; File No. 8, Vol. 1. 1931–64. Yaba.

Odunjo, J. F. Personal Files. Ibadan.

Port Harcourt Municipal Council. Universal Primary Education File, Admission of Children, File No. 953, Vols. 1–3, 1956–64. Port Harcourt.

Smith, W. T. Annual Reports to Director of Education and Methodist Synod. 1936–61 *passim.* Port Harcourt.

WORKS CONSULTED

Action Group. For the Welfare of Us All. Manifesto of the Action Group for the Eastern Region General Election, March, 1957. Ibadan, 1957.

Adetunji, Ezekiel Oyelami. "The Organization and Administration of Primary Education in Western Nigeria since the Middle Nineteenth Century, with Special Reference to the Free Primary Education Scheme Launched in 1955." M.Ed. thesis, Birmingham Univ., 1964.

Ajayi, J. F. Ade. Christian Missions in Nigeria, 1841–1891: The Making of a New Elite. Evanston, Ill.: Northwestern Univ. Press, 1965.

———. "Nineteenth Century Origins of Nigerian Nationalism," *Journal of the Historical Society of Nigeria,* II, 2 (Dec. 1961), 196–210.

———, and Robert Smith. Yoruba Warfare in the Nineteenth Century. Cambridge, Eng.: Cambridge Univ. Press in association with Inst. of African Studies, Univ. of Ibadan, 1964.

Ajayi Report. Short form for: Report of the Commission of Inquiry into the Rise of Fees Charged by Public Secondary Grammar Schools and Teacher Training Colleges in Western Nigeria. Western Region. Ibadan: Government Printer, 1963.

Ake, Claude. A Theory of Political Integration. Homewood, Ill.: Dorsey Press, 1967.

Almond, Gabriel, and G. Bingham Powell. Comparative Politics: A Developmental Approach. Boston: Little, Brown, 1966.

———, and Sidney Verba. The Civic Culture. Princeton, N.J.: Princeton Univ. Press, 1963.

Anderson, C. Arnold, and Mary Jean Bowman, eds. Education and Economic Development. Chicago: Aldine, 1965.

Apter, David. Ghana in Transition. New York: Atheneum, 1963.

———. The Politics of Modernization. Chicago: Univ. of Chicago Press, 1965.

———. "The Role of Traditionalism in the Political Modernization of Ghana and Uganda," *World Politics,* XII, 1 (Oct. 1960), 45–68.

Archer, J. N. Educational Development in Nigeria, 1961–70. Lagos: Government Printer, 1961.

Ashby Report. Short form for: Investment in Education: The Report of the Commission on Post-School Certificate and Higher Education in Nigeria. Nigeria, Ministry of Education. Lagos: Government Printer, 1960.

Awani-Alele, Grace. "Dynamics of Education in the Birth of a New Nation: Case Study of Nigeria." Ph.D. diss., Univ. of Chicago, Dept. of Education, March 1963.

Awokoya, S. O. England as I Saw Her. Ibadan: Advent Press, n.d.

Awolowo, Obafemi. Awo: The Autobiography of Chief Obafemi Awolowo. Cambridge, Eng.: Cambridge Univ. Press, 1960.

———. Path to Nigerian Freedom. London: Faber and Faber, 1947.

Azikiwe, Nnamdi. After Three Years of Stewardship. Enugu, 1957.

———. "How Shall We Educate the African?" *Journal of the African Society*, XXXIII (April 1934), 143–50.

———. Political Blueprint of Nigeria. Lagos: African Book Company, 1943.

———. Tribalism: A Pragmatic Instrument for National Unity. Enugu: Eastern Nigeria Printing Corporation, 1964.

———. Zik—A Selection from the Speeches of Nnamdi Azikiwe. Cambridge, Eng.: Cambridge Univ. Press, 1960.

Baldwin, K. D. S. The Niger Agricultural Project: An Experiment in African Development. Oxford: Basil Blackwell, 1957.

Bane, Martin J. Catholic Pioneers in West Africa. Dublin: Clonmore and Reynolds, 1956.

Bascom, William R., and Melville J. Herskovits, eds. Continuity and Change in African Cultures. Chicago: Univ. of Chicago Press, 1959.

Bello, Alhaji Sir Ahmadu. My Life. Cambridge, Eng.: Cambridge Univ. Press, 1962.

Bendix, Reinhard. Nation-Building and Citizenship. New York: Wiley, 1964.

Bienen, Henry. Tanzania: Party Transformation and Economic Development. Princeton, N.J.: Princeton Univ. Press, 1967.

Biobaku, Saburi O. The Egba and Their Neighbours, 1842–1872. Oxford: Oxford Univ. Press, 1957.

Bishops' Joint Circular on Education—Education Circular from Catholic Bishops of Nigeria to All Their Adherents. Onitsha: J. Etukokwu and Sons, n.d.

Black, C. E. The Dynamics of Modernization. New York: Harper Torchbooks, 1966.

Bradbury, R. E., with P. C. Lloyd. The Benin Kingdom and the Edo-Speaking Peoples of South-Western Nigeria. London: International African Inst., 1957.

Bretton, Henry L. Power and Stability in Nigeria: The Politics of Decolonization. New York: Praeger, 1962.

Brown, G. N. "British Educational Policy in West and Central Africa," *Journal of Modern African Studies*, II, 3 (Nov. 1964), 365–77.

Buchanan, K. M., and J. C. Pugh. Land and People in Nigeria. London: Univ. of London Press, 1955.

Buell, Raymond Leslie. The Native Problem in Africa. Vol. I. New York: Macmillan, 1928.

Busia, K. A. "Educational Policy in West Africa: A Rejoinder," *Oversea Education*, XVII, 2 (July 1946), 343–46.

Callaway, Archibald. "Continuing Education for Africa's School Leavers: The Indigenous Apprentice System," *Bulletin, Inter-African Labour Institute*, XVII, 1 (Feb. 1965), 61–73.

————. "Unemployment among African School Leavers," *Journal of Modern African Studies*, I, 3 (Sept. 1963), 351–71.

————, and A. Musone. Financing of Education in Nigeria. Paris: UNESCO, International Inst. for Educational Planning, 1968. African Research Monographs, No. 15.

Carney, David E. Government and Economy in British West Africa: A Study of the Role of Public Agencies in the Economic Development of British West Africa. New York: Bookman Associates, 1961.

Catholic Hierarchy of Eastern Nigeria. A Catholic View of Education. Owerri: Assumpta Press, n.d. [1964].

Catholic Proprietors, Eastern Region. The Catholic Case in Eastern Education. Owerri: Assumpta Press, n.d. [Oct. 1956].

Chadwick, E. R. "Communal Development in Udi Division," *Oversea Education*, XIX, 2 (Jan. 1948), 627–44.

Clarke, J. D. Omu: An African Experiment in Education. London: Longmans, Green, 1937.

Clifford, Sir Hugh. An Address to the Nigerian Council on 29 December, 1920. Lagos: Government Printer, 1920.

Clignet, Remi, and Philip Foster. The Fortunate Few: A Study of Secondary Schools and Students in the Ivory Coast. Evanston, Ill.: Northwestern Univ. Press, 1966.

Coleman, James S., ed. Education and Political Development. Princeton, N.J.: Princeton Univ. Press, 1965.

————. Nigeria: Background to Nationalism. Berkeley: Univ. of California Press, 1958.

————, and Carl G. Rosberg, Jr., eds. Political Parties and National Integration in Tropical Africa. Berkeley: Univ. of California Press, 1964.

Cowan, L. Gray, James O'Connell, and David G. Scanlon, eds. Education and Nation-Building in Africa. New York: Praeger, 1965.

Crookall, R. E. "Universal Education in Western Nigeria," *Oversea Education*, XXX, 1 (April 1958), 3–11.

Crowder, Michael. A Short History of Nigeria. New York: Praeger, 1962.

Curle, Adam. Educational Strategy for Developing Societies: A Study of Educational and Social Factors in Relation to Economic Growth. London: Tavistock Publications, 1963.

Dean, E. R. "Factors Impeding the Implementation of Nigeria's Six-Year Plan," *Nigerian Journal of Economics and Social Studies*, VIII, 1 (March 1966), 113–28.

Deniga, Adeoye. The Nigerian Who's Who for 1934. Lagos: Awoboh Press, 1934.

Deutsch, Karl. Nationalism and Social Communication. Cambridge, Mass.: M.I.T. Press, 1966.

————. The Nerves of Government. New York: Free Press, 1966.

————. "Social Mobilization and Political Development," *American Political Science Review*, LV, 3 (Sept. 1961), 493–514.

Diejomaoh, Victor P. Economic Development in Nigeria: Its Problems, Challenges, and Prospects. Princeton, N.J.: Princeton Univ., Industrial Relations Section, 1965. Research Report Series, No. 107.

Dike, K. Onwuka. Origins of the Niger Mission, 1841–1891. 2d impression. Ibadan: Ibadan Univ. Press, 1962.

———. Trade and Politics in the Niger Delta, 1830–1885. Oxford: Clarendon Press, 1956.

——— et al. Eminent Nigerians of the Nineteenth Century. Cambridge, Eng.: Cambridge Univ. Press, 1960.

Dike Report. Short form for: Report on the Review of the Educational System in Eastern Nigeria. Official Document No. 19 of 1962. Eastern Region, Ministry of Education. Enugu: Government Printer, 1962.

Eastern Region, government publications. Printed in Enugu by the Government Printer unless otherwise noted.

[1] Distribution of Amenities in Eastern Nigeria, Data and Statistics. Official Document No. 20 of 1963.

[2] Eastern Nigeria Information Service. Legislators of Eastern Nigeria, Regional and Federal, 1958.

[3] Education Law. Law No. 28 of 1956.

[4] House of Assembly. Debates. 1955–58.

[5] Mba, M. K. The First Three Years: A Report of the Eastern Nigerian Six-Year Development Plan. N.d. [1966].

[6] Ministry of Education. Annual Reports. 1956–63.

[7] ———. Directory of Teachers' Colleges, Secondary Schools, Commercial Schools, Trade and Technical Schools, 1962. Official Document No. 1 of 1963.

[8] ———. Education Graphs and Statistics, from Annual Report, 1961.

[9] ———. Education Handbook 1964. Official Document No. 26 of 1964.

[10] ———. Education in the Eastern Region with Special Reference to Universal Primary Education. 1957.

[11] ———. Report on the Review of the Educational System in Eastern Nigeria. Official Document No. 19 of 1962. Cited in the Notes as Dike Report.

[12] Ministry of Information, Publicity Division. Eastern Nigeria: The System of Education. Vol. I, No. 2. Enugu: Eastern Nigeria Printing Corporation. Sept. 1963.

[13] Policy for Education. Sessional Paper No. 6 of 1953.

[14] Policy for Introduction of Universal Primary Education. Sessional Paper No. 9 of 1953.

[15] Report on Investigation of Vocational Education in Eastern Nigeria. 1962.

[16] Report on the General Election to the Eastern House of Assembly, 1957, including Recommendations for Consideration in Connection

with the Drafting of New Electoral Regulations. Sessional Paper No. 1 of 1957.

[17] Self-Government in the Eastern Region—Part I: Policy Statements. Sessional Paper No. 2 of 1957.

[18] "Universal Primary Education: Statement of Policy and Procedure for the Guidance of Education Officers, Local Government Councils, and Voluntary Agencies." Aug. 17, 1956. Mimeo.

Easton, David. A Systems Analysis of Political Life. New York: Wiley, 1965.

Eckstein, Harry, and David E. Apter, eds. Comparative Politics: A Reader. New York: Free Press, 1963.

Edgren, Gus. "The Employment Problem in Tropical Africa," *Bulletin, Inter-African Labour Institute*, XII, 2 (May 1965), 174–90.

Education and World Affairs, Nigeria Project Task Force, Committee on Education and Human Resource Development. Nigerian Human Resource Development and Utilization. New York: Education and World Affairs, Dec. 1967.

Eisenstadt, S. N. "Breakdowns of Modernization," *Economic Development and Cultural Change*, XII, 4 (July 1964), 345–67.

———. Modernization: Protest and Change. Englewood Cliffs, N.J.: Prentice-Hall, 1966.

Ekwensi, Cordelia O. "A Study of the Universal Primary Education in Eastern Nigeria (1957–1963)." B.A. thesis, Univ. of Nigeria, Harden College of Education, Nsukka, 1964.

Emerson, Rupert. From Empire to Nation. Cambridge, Mass.: Harvard Univ. Press, 1960.

Epelle, E. M. T. The Church in the Niger Delta. Port Harcourt: C.M.S. Niger Press, 1955.

Epstein, A. L. Politics in an Urban African Community. Manchester: Manchester Univ. Press, 1958.

Equali, Vincent Egbe. "The Catholic Mission and the Evolution of Education in the Former Ogoja Province, 1937–1962 (A Historical and Critical Approach)." B.A. thesis, Univ. of Nigeria, Harden College of Education, Nsukka, 1964.

Ezeanya, Stephen Nweke. "The Method of Adaptation in the Evangelization of the Igbo-Speaking Peoples of Southern Nigeria." Diss., Pontifical Urban Univ., "De Propaganda Fide," Rome, 1956.

Ezera, Kalu. Constitutional Developments in Nigeria. Cambridge, Eng.: Cambridge Univ. Press, 1960.

Florin, Hans Wilhelm. "The Southern Baptist Foreign Mission Enterprise in Western Nigeria: An Analysis." Ph.D. diss., Boston Univ., 1960.

Forde, Daryll. The Yoruba-Speaking Peoples of South-Western Nigeria. London: International African Inst., 1951. Reprinted 1962.

———, and G. I. Jones. The Ibo and Ibibio-Speaking Peoples of South-

Eastern Nigeria. London: International African Inst., 1950. Reprinted 1962.

Forrest, Ona. Financing Development Plans in West Africa. Cambridge, Mass.: M.I.T. Center for International Studies, 1965.

Foster, Philip. "Comparative Methodology and the Study of African Education," *Comparative Education Review*, IV, 2 (Oct. 1960), 110–17.

———. Education and Social Change in Ghana. London: Routledge & Kegan Paul, 1965.

Fox, A. J. Uzuakoli. London: Oxford Univ. Press, 1964.

Free, Lloyd A. The Attitudes, Hopes and Fears of Nigerians. Princeton, N.J.: Inst. for International Social Research, 1964.

Friedland, William H., and Carl G. Rosberg, Jr., eds. African Socialism. Stanford, Calif.: Stanford Univ. Press, 1964.

Geertz, Clifford, ed. Old Societies and New States: The Quest for Modernity in Asia and Africa. New York: Free Press, 1963.

Great Britain, Colonial Office publications. All printed in London by HMSO.

[1] Advisory Committee on Education in the Colonies. Education for Citizenship in Africa. Colonial No. 216. 1948.
[2] ———. Mass Education in African Society. Colonial No. 186. 1944.
[3] Advisory Committee on Native Education in British Tropical African Dependencies. Education Policy in British Tropical Africa. Cmnd. 2374. 1925.
[4] Lugard, Sir F. D. Report by Sir F. D. Lugard on the Amalgamation of Northern and Southern Nigeria, and Administration, 1912–1919. Cmnd. 468. 1920.
[5] Memorandum on the Education of African Communities. Colonial No. 103. 1935.
[6] Nigeria: Report of the Commission Appointed to Enquire into the Fears of Minorities and the Means of Allaying Them. Cmnd. 505. July 1958.
[7] Nigeria: Report of the Fiscal Commissioner on the Financial Effects of the Proposed New Constitutional Arrangements. Cmnd. 9026. 1953.
[8] Report of the Commission on Higher Education in the Colonies. Cmnd. 6647. 1945.
[9] Report of the Commission on Higher Education in West Africa. Cmnd. 6655. 1945.

Green, M. M. Ibo Village Affairs. London: Sidgwick and Jackson, 1947. 2d ed. published by Frank Cass, 1964.

Greenstein, Fred I. Children and Politics. New Haven, Conn.: Yale Univ. Press, 1965.

Hagen, Everett. On the Theory of Social Change. Homewood, Ill.: Dorsey Press, 1962.

Hailey, Lord. An African Survey. London: Oxford Univ. Press, 1938.

————. An African Survey, Revised 1956. London: Oxford Univ. Press, 1957.

Harbison, Frederick, and Charles A. Myers, eds. Education, Manpower, and Economic Growth: Strategies of Human Resource Development. New York: McGraw-Hill, 1964.

————. Manpower and Education: Country Studies in Economic Development. New York: McGraw-Hill, 1965.

Hardy, Georges. Une Conquête Morale: L'Enseignement en Afrique Occidentale Française. Paris: Librairie Armand Colin, 1917.

Harrison, Selig. India: The Most Dangerous Decades. Princeton, N.J.: Princeton Univ. Press, 1960.

Hazlewood, Arthur. The Finances of Nigerian Federation. London: Oxford Univ. Inst. of Colonial Studies. Reprint Series No. 14 (from *West Africa*, Aug. 27, 1955).

Helleiner, Gerald K. Peasant Agriculture, Government, and Economic Growth in Nigeria. Homewood, Ill.: Irwin, 1966.

Hilliard, F. H. A Short History of Education in British West Africa. London: Thomas Nelson, 1957.

Hirschman, Albert. The Strategy of Economic Development. New Haven, Conn.: Yale Univ. Press, 1958.

Hodgkin, Thomas. Nationalism in Colonial Africa. London: Frederick Muller, 1956.

————. Nigerian Perspectives. London: Oxford Univ. Press, 1960.

Hunter, Guy. Education for a Developing Region: A Study in East Africa. London: Allen and Unwin, 1963.

————. Manpower, Employment, and Education in the Rural Economy of Tanzania. Paris: UNESCO, International Inst. for Educational Planning, 1966.

————. The New Societies of Tropical Africa: A Selective Study. London: Oxford Univ. Press, 1962.

Huntington, Samuel. "Political Development and Political Decay," *World Politics*, XVII, 3 (April 1965), 386–430.

Huq, Muhammad Shamsul. Education and Development Strategy in South and South-East Asia. Honolulu: East-West Center Press, 1965.

Hyman, Herbert H. Political Socialization. Glencoe, Ill.: Free Press, 1959.

Igboko, Pius Mbonu. "Adult Education in Nigeria." M.Ed. thesis, Univ. of Birmingham, April 1964.

Ikejiani, Okechukwu, ed. Nigerian Education. Ikeja: Longmans of Nigeria, 1964.

International Bank for Reconstruction and Development. The Economic Development of Nigeria. Baltimore: Johns Hopkins Press, 1955.

International Labour Office. Employment Objectives in Economic Development. Geneva, 1961.

Ita, Eyo. Crusade for Freedom. Calabar: W.A.P.I. Press, n.d.

———. A Decade of National Education Movement. Calabar: W.A.P.I. Press, n.d. [1949].

———, ed. National Youth Renaissance. Calabar: W.A.P.I. Press, n.d.

———. The Nigeria Union of Teachers Faces the Problems of Adult Education. Lagos, n.d. Nigeria Union of Teachers' Series.

———. The Revolt of the Liberal Spirit. Calabar: W.A.P.I. Press, n.d. [1949].

———. Sterile Truths and Fertile Lies. Calabar: W.A.P.I. Press, n.d. [1949].

———. Two Vital Fronts in Nigeria's Advancement. Calabar: W.A.P.I. Press, n.d. [1949].

Jackson, I. C. Advance in Africa: A Study of Community Development in Eastern Nigeria. London: Oxford Univ. Press, 1956.

Jacob, Philip E., and James V. Toscano, eds. The Integration of Political Communities. Philadelphia: Lippincott, 1964.

Jones, G. I. The Trading States of the Oil Rivers: A Study of Political Development in Eastern Nigeria. London: Oxford Univ. Press, 1963.

Jones, Thomas Jesse. Education in Africa: A Study of West, South, and Equatorial Africa by the African Education Commission. New York: Phelps-Stokes Fund, 1922.

———. Education in East Africa: A Study of East, Central, and South Africa by the Second African Education Commission. New York: Phelps-Stokes Fund, 1925.

Jones-Quartey, K. A. B. A Life of Azikiwe. Baltimore: Penguin, 1965.

Jordan, John P. Bishop Shanahan of Southern Nigeria. Dublin: Clonmore and Reynolds, 1949.

Kautsky, John H., ed. Political Change in Underdeveloped Countries: Nationalism and Communism. New York: Wiley, 1962.

Kilby, Peter. The Development of Small Industry in Eastern Nigeria. Enugu: Ministry of Commerce, USAID, 1962.

Kopytoff, Jean Herskovitz. A Preface to Modern Nigeria: The "Sierra Leoneans" in Yoruba, 1830–1890. Madison: Univ. of Wisconsin Press, 1965.

LePage, R. B. The National Language Question. London: Inst. of Race Relations, Oxford Univ. Press, 1964.

Lerner, Daniel. The Passing of Traditional Society: Modernizing the Middle East. New York: Free Press, 1958.

Levine, Robert A. Dreams and Deeds. Chicago: Univ. of Chicago Press, 1966.

Lewis, L. John. Education and Political Independence in Africa and Other Essays. Edinburgh: Thomas Nelson, 1962.

———. Phelps-Stokes Reports on Education in Africa. London: Oxford Univ. Press, 1962.

————. Society, Schools, and Progress in Nigeria. Oxford: Pergamon Press, 1965.

Lewis, W. Arthur. "Education and Economic Development," *Social and Economic Studies*, X, 2 (June 1961), 113–27.

————. Politics in West Africa. Toronto: Oxford Univ. Press, 1965.

————. Reflections on Nigeria's Economic Growth. Paris: Organization for Economic Co-operation and Development, Development Centre, 1967.

Lipset, S. M. Political Man. Garden City, N.Y.: Doubleday, 1959.

Little, Kenneth. West African Urbanization. Cambridge, Eng.: Cambridge Univ. Press, 1965.

Lloyd, Peter C. "Local Government in Yoruba Towns: An Analysis of the Roles of the Obas, Chiefs, and the Elected Councillors." Ph.D. diss., New College, Oxford, 1958.

————, ed. The New Elites of Tropical Africa. London: Oxford Univ. Press, 1966.

————. Yoruba Land Law. London: Oxford Univ. Press, 1962.

————, A. L. Mabogunje, and B. Awe, eds. The City of Ibadan. Cambridge, Eng.: Cambridge Univ. Press, 1967.

Lugard, Sir F. D. Report by Sir F. D. Lugard on the Amalgamation of Northern and Southern Nigeria, and Administration, 1912–1919. Cmnd. 468. London: HMSO, 1920.

Mabogunje, A. L. Yoruba Towns. Ibadan: Ibadan Univ. Press, 1962.

McCully, Bruce. English Education and the Origins of Indian Nationalism. New York: Columbia Univ. Press, 1940.

McFarlan, Donald M. Calabar: The Church of Scotland Mission, Founded 1846. Rev. ed. London: Thomas Nelson, 1957.

Mackenzie, W. J. M., and Kenneth E. Robinson, eds. Five Elections in Africa. Oxford: Clarendon Press, 1960.

Mackintosh, John P. Nigerian Government and Politics. Evanston, Ill.: Northwestern Univ. Press, 1966.

Macrae, Norman C. The Book of the First Sixty Years, 1895–1955: Hope Waddell Training Institute, Calabar. Calabar: Hope Waddell Press, 1956.

McWilliam, H. O. A. The Development of Education in Ghana: An Outline. London: Longmans, Green, 1959.

Marshall, T. H. Class, Citizenship, and Social Development. Garden City, N.Y.: Doubleday, 1964.

Mba, M. K. The First Three Years: A Report of the Eastern Nigerian Six-Year Development Plan. Enugu: Government Printer, n.d. [1966].

Methodist Church, Nigeria. Foundation Conference, Lagos: 28-9-62. Yaba: Pacific Printers, 1962.

Moore, Barrington, Jr. Social Origins of Dictatorship and Democracy: Lord and Peasant in the Making of the Modern World. Boston: Beacon Press, 1966.

Morgan Report. Short form for: Report of the Commission on the Review of Wages, Salary and Conditions of Service of the Junior Employees of the Federation and in Private Establishments, 1963–64. Nigeria. Lagos: Government Printer, 1964.

Morgenthau, Ruth Schachter. Political Parties in French-Speaking West Africa. Oxford: Clarendon Press, 1964.

Mumford, William Bryant, and G. St. J. Orde-Brown. Africans Learn to Be French. London: Evans Brothers, 1937.

Murray, A. Victor. The School in the Bush. London: Longmans, Green, 1929.

Myers, Charles Nash. Education and National Development in Mexico. Princeton, N.J.: Princeton Univ., Industrial Relations Section, 1965.

Nduka, Otonti. Western Education and the Nigerian Cultural Background. London: Oxford Univ. Press, 1964.

Newbury, Colin W. The Western Slave Coast and Its Rulers. Oxford: Oxford Univ. Press, 1961.

Niculescu, Barbu. Colonial Planning: A Comparative Study. London: Allen and Unwin, 1958.

Nigeria, government publications. Printed in Lagos by the Government Printer unless otherwise noted.

[1] Archer, J. N. Educational Development in Nigeria, 1961–70. 1961.

[2] Clifford, Sir Hugh. An Address to the Nigerian Council on 29 December, 1920. 1920.

[3] Conclusions of the Federal Government on the Report of the Morgan Commission. 1964.

[4] Department of Statistics. Population Census of Nigeria, 1952–53. 1953.

[5] Education Department. Annual Reports, 1929–53.

[6] An Enquiry into the Proposal to Introduce Local Rating in Aid of Primary Education in the Eastern Region. Enugu: Government Printer, 1952.

[7] Federal Office of Statistics. Annual Abstract of Statistics. 1960–63.

[8] ———. Digest of Statistics, XIII, 2 (April 1964).

[9] Local Government in the Western Provinces of Nigeria, 1951. Ibadan: Government Printer, 1951.

[10] Memorandum on Educational Policy in Nigeria. Sessional Paper No. 31 of 1930.

[11] Memorandum on Educational Policy in Nigeria. Sessional Paper No. 20 of 1947.

[12] Ministry of Economic Development. National Development Plan, Progress Report 1964. 1965.

[13] Ministry of Education. Annual Digest of Educational Statistics. Series No. 1, Vol. II, 1962.

[14] ———. Investment in Education: The Report of the Commission on Post-School Certificate and Higher Education in Nigeria. 1960. Cited in the Notes as Ashby Report.

[15] ——. Statistics of Education in Nigeria, 1964, 1965. Series No. 1, Vols. IV, V. 1966, 1967.

[16] Ministry of Information. Guide to the Parliament of the Federation. 1961.

[17] Ministry of Labour. Report on Employment and Earnings Enquiry, December 1961. 1962.

[18] National Development Plan, 1962–68. 1962.

[19] National Economic Council. Economic Survey of Nigeria, 1959. 1959.

[20] Phillipson, Sidney. Grants in Aid of Education in Nigeria: A Review, with Recommendations. 1948.

[21] Proceedings of the General Conference on Review of the Constitution, January, 1950. 1950.

[22] Report of the Coker Commission of Inquiry into the Affairs of Certain Statutory Corporations in Western Nigeria, 1962. 4 vols. 1962.

[23] Report of the Commission on the Public Services of the Governments in the Federation of Nigeria, 1954–55. 1955.

[24] Report of the Commission on the Review of Wages, Salary, and Conditions of Service of the Junior Employees of the Federation and in Private Establishments, 1963–64. 1964. Cited in the Notes as Morgan Report.

[25] Report on Educational Development in Lagos. 1957.

[26] Review of the Constitution: Regional Recommendations. 1949.

[27] A Revised Plan of Development and Welfare for Nigeria, 1951–56. Sessional Paper No. 6 of 1951.

[28] Ten-Year Educational Plan. Sessional Paper No. 6 of 1944.

[29] A Ten-Year Plan of Development and Welfare for Nigeria. Sessional Paper No. 24 of 1945 as amended by the Select Committee of the Council and approved by the Legislative Council. Feb. 7, 1946.

[30] White Paper on Education. March 1955.

Nigerian Association of University Women, Ibadan Branch. Survey of Women's Education in Western Nigeria. Ibadan, 1963. Mimeo.

Nuffield Foundation and the Colonial Office. African Education: A Study of Educational Policy and Practice in British Tropical Africa. London: Oxford Univ. Press, 1953.

Nwosu, Sunday Nnanta. "The Development of Western Education in Eastern Nigeria: 1846–1939." Ed.D. diss., Harvard Univ., 1965.

Obi, Chike. Our Struggle, Part II. Enugu, 1962.

O'Connell, James. "The Changing Role of the State in West Africa," *Nigerian Journal of Economics and Social Studies*, III, 1 (Nov. 1961), 1–12.

——. "The Political Class and Economic Growth," *Nigerian Journal of Economics and Social Studies*, VIII, 1 (March 1966), 129–40.

Ojike, Mazi Mbonu. My Africa. New York: John Day, 1946.

Okigbo, Pius. Nigerian Public Finance. Evanston, Ill.: Northwestern Univ. Press, 1965.

Orewa, G. Oka. Report on the Problems of Local Government Finance in

Western Nigeria. Ibadan: Administrative Research Group, Western Nigeria, ARGA 19, May 1963.

———. Taxation in Western Nigeria. London: Oxford Univ. Press, 1962.

Oron Boys' High School. Fifty Years, 1905–55. London: Lawrence Bros., n.d.

Parker, Franklin. African Development and Education in Southern Rhodesia. Columbus: Ohio State Univ. Press, 1960.

Perham, Margery. Lugard: The Years of Authority, 1898–1945. London: Collins, 1960.

———. Native Administration in Nigeria. London: Oxford Univ. Press, 1937. Reprinted 1962.

Phillipson, Sidney. Grants in Aid of Education in Nigeria: A Review, with Recommendations. Lagos: Government Printer, 1948.

Piper, Don C., and Taylor Cole, eds. Post-Primary Education and Political and Economic Development. Durham, N.C.: Duke Univ. Press, 1964.

Post, Ken. The New States of West Africa. Rev. ed. Baltimore: Penguin, 1968.

Prest, A. R., and I. G. Stewart. The National Income of Nigeria, 1950–51. London: HMSO, 1953. Colonial Research Studies, No. 11.

Pye, Lucian. Aspects of Political Development. Boston: Little, Brown, 1966.

———, ed. Communications and Political Development. Princeton, N.J.: Princeton Univ. Press, 1963.

———. Politics, Personality, and Nation-Building: Burma's Search for Identity. New Haven, Conn.: Yale Univ. Press, 1962.

Read, Margaret. Education and Social Change in Tropical Areas. London: Thomas Nelson, 1955.

Rustow, Dankwart. A World of Nations. Washington, D.C.: Brookings Inst., 1967.

Salubi, T. E. A. National Day Message to Urhobo People, 3rd November, 1963. Ibadan: Government Printer, 1963.

———. Patriotism on Trial. Presidential Address, December 1963. Ibadan: Government Printer, 1963.

———. Revolutions of Our Time. A National Day Message, November 1962. Ibadan: Government Printer, 1962.

———. This Is Our Heritage. Presidential Address, December 1962. Ibadan: Government Printer, 1962.

Sampson, Magnus J. West African Leadership. Bristol, Eng.: Burleigh Press, 1949.

Sanni, Charles J. "The Role of Mission Schools in the Establishment of the Church, with Special Reference to Ondo Diocese in Nigeria." Diss., Pontifical Urban Univ., "De Propaganda Fide," Faculty of Canon Law, Rome, 1962.

Scanlon, David, ed. Church, State, and Education in Africa. New York: Teachers College Press, Columbia Univ., 1966.

Schwarz, Frederick A. O., Jr. Nigeria: The Tribes, the Nation, or the Race. Cambridge, Mass.: M.I.T. Press, 1965.

Shattock, B. A. "A Criticism of Educational Policy in West Africa," *Oversea Education*, XVII, 3 (April 1946), 292–95.

Sheffield, James R., ed. Education, Employment, and Rural Development. Nairobi: East African Publishing House, 1967.

Shils, Edward. Political Development in the New States. The Hague: Mouton, 1962.

Sklar, Richard L. Nigerian Political Parties: Power in an Emergent African Nation. Princeton, N.J.: Princeton Univ. Press, 1963.

Smythe, Hugh H., and Mabel M. Smythe. The New Nigerian Elite. Stanford, Calif.: Stanford Univ. Press, 1960.

Sokolski, Alan. The Establishment of Manufacturing in Nigeria. New York: Praeger, 1965.

Solarin, Tai. Our Grammar School Must Go. Ibadan: Ibadan Univ. Press, 1963.

———. Towards Nigeria's Moral Self-Government. Published by the author in Ikenne, 1959.

Solaru, T. T. Teacher Training in Nigeria. Ian Espie, ed. Ibadan: Ibadan Univ. Press, 1964.

Spiro, Herbert J., ed. Africa: The Primacy of Politics. New York: Random House, 1966.

Staley, Eugene, and Richard Morse. Modern Small Industry for Developing Countries. New York: McGraw-Hill, 1965.

Stolper, Wolfgang. Planning without Facts: Lessons in Resource Allocation from Nigeria's Development. Cambridge, Mass.: Harvard Univ. Press, 1966.

Talbot, P. Amaury. The Peoples of Southern Nigeria, Vol. IV: Linguistics and Statistics. London: Oxford Univ. Press, 1926.

Tardits, Claude. Porto-Novo: Les Nouvelles Générations africaines entre leur traditions et l'Occident. The Hague: Mouton, 1958.

Thornley, J. F. The Planning of Primary Education in Northern Nigeria. Paris: UNESCO, International Inst. of Educational Planning, 1966.

Tilman, Robert O., and Taylor Cole, eds. The Nigerian Political Scene. Durham, N.C.: Duke Univ. Press, 1962.

Uchendu, Victor. The Igbo of Southeast Nigeria. New York: Holt, Rinehart and Winston, 1965.

UNESCO and United Nations Economic Commission for Africa. Final Report, Conference of African States on the Development of Education in Africa, Addis Ababa, 15–23 May, 1961. New York: UNESCO, 1961.

United Nations, Food and Agriculture Organization. Agricultural Development in Nigeria, 1964–1980. Rome, 1965.

Uzoma, R. I. "Universal Schooling in Ngwa Clan of Aba Division, Nigeria," *Oversea Education*, XXIII, 2 (Jan. 1952), 234–36.

Vaizey, John. The Economics of Education. New York: Free Press, 1962.

Wallerstein, Immanuel, ed. Social Change: The Colonial Situation. New York: Wiley, 1966.

———. "Ethnicity and National Integration in West Africa," *Cahiers d'Etudes Africaines*, No. 3 (Oct. 1960), pp. 129–38.

Walsh, M. L. "The Catholic Contribution to Education in Western Nigeria, 1861–1926." M.A. thesis, Univ. of London, Inst. of Education, 1951.

Ward, W. E. F. "A New Attitude to Education," *Oversea Education*, XX, 4 (July 1949), 912–17.

Webster, James Bertin. The African Churches among the Yoruba, 1888–1922. Oxford: Clarendon Press, 1964.

———. "The Bible and the Plough," *Journal of the Historical Society of Nigeria*, II, 4 (Dec. 1963), 418–34.

Weiler, Hans N., ed. Education and Politics in Nigeria. Freiberg im Breisgau: Verlag Rombach, 1964.

Weiner, Myron. "Political Integration and Political Development," *Annals of the American Academy of Political and Social Science*, CCCLVIII (March 1965), 52–64.

———. The Politics of Scarcity. Chicago: Univ. of Chicago Press, 1962.

Western Region, government publications. Printed in Ibadan by the Government Printer unless otherwise noted.

[1] An Appraisal of the Development of Western Nigeria, 1955–60. Sessional Paper No. 8 of 1961.

[2] Development of the Western Region of Nigeria, 1955–60. Sessional Paper No. 4 of 1955.

[3] Education Department. Local Education Committees: A Review, 1943–48. Ibadan: Union Printing Press, 1948.

[4] Education Law, 1954. Law No. 6 of 1955.

[5] House of Assembly. Debates. 1948–56.

[6] Legislation of the Western Region of Nigeria. 1952–56.

[7] Ministry of Economic Planning, Statistics Division. Annual Abstract of Education Statistics, 1953–58. June 1959.

[8] Ministry of Economic Planning and Community Development, Statistics Division. Annual Abstract of Education Statistics, 1955–60. Sessional Paper No. 7 of 1962.

[9] ———. Annual Abstract of Education Statistics 1962 and 1963 combined. January 1964.

[10] Ministry of Education. Annual Reports. 1953–59.

[11] ———, General Publications Section. Primary School Syllabus, Parts I and II. 6th ed. 1962.

[12] Ministry of Information. Universal Primary Education in the Western Region of Nigeria: Commemorative Brochure. London, 1955.

[13] Proposals for an Education Policy for the Western Region, Nigeria, by the Minister for Education, Western Region. July 1952.

[14] Report of the Commission Appointed to Review the Educational System of Western Nigeria. 1961.

[15] Report of the Commission of Inquiry into the Rise of Fees Charged by Public Secondary Grammar Schools and Teacher Training Colleges in Western Nigeria. 1963. Cited in the Notes as Ajayi Report.

[16] Secondary Modern School Syllabus. Oshogbo: Kebo and Sons, 1958.

[17] Triennial Report on Education, 1st April, 1955, to 31st March, 1958. Sessional Paper No. 11 of 1959.

[18] Western Nigeria Development Plan, 1960–65. Sessional Paper No. 17 of 1959.

[19] Western Nigeria Development Plan, 1962–68. Sessional Paper No. 8 of 1962.

Wheare, Joan. Studies in Colonial Legislatures, Vol. IV: The Nigerian Legislative Council. London: Faber and Faber, 1950.

Williams, D. H. A Short History of Education in Northern Nigeria. Kaduna: Northern Nigeria Ministry of Education, 1959.

Wilson, John. Education and Changing West African Culture. New York: Teachers College Press, Columbia Univ., 1963.

Wise, Colin G. A History of Education in British West Africa. London: Longmans, Green, 1956.

World Confederation of Organizations of the Teaching Profession, Commission on Educational Policy for Africa. Survey of the Status of the Teaching Profession in Africa. Washington, D.C., n.d. [1962].

Wraith, Ronald. Local Government in West Africa. London: Allen and Unwin, 1964.

Wriggins, W. Howard. Ceylon: Dilemmas of a New Nation. Princeton, N.J.: Princeton Univ. Press, 1960.

Young, Crawford. Politics in the Congo. Princeton, N.J.: Princeton Univ. Press, 1965.

Zolberg, Aristide. Creating Political Order: The Party-States of West Africa. Chicago: Rand McNally, 1966.

Index